Handbook of Operant Behavioral Economics

Handbook of Operant Behavioral Economics

Demand, Discounting, Methods, and Applications

Edited by

Derek D. Reed
Institutes for Behavior Resources, Inc., Baltimore, MD, United States

Brent A. Kaplan
Codedbx, United States; Innovation Department, Advocates for Human Potential, Inc., Sudbury, MA, United States

Shawn P. Gilroy
Louisiana State University, Baton Rouge, LA, United States

ACADEMIC PRESS
An imprint of Elsevier

Academic Press is an imprint of Elsevier
125 London Wall, London EC2Y 5AS, United Kingdom
50 Hampshire Street, 5th Floor, Cambridge, MA 02139, United States

Copyright © 2025 Elsevier Inc. All rights are reserved, including those for text and data mining, AI training, and similar technologies.

For accessibility purposes, images in electronic versions of this book are accompanied by alt text descriptions provided by Elsevier. For more information, see https://www.elsevier.com/about/accessibility.

Books and Journals published by Elsevier comply with applicable product safety requirements. For any product safety concerns or queries, please contact our authorised representative, Elsevier B.V., at productsafety@elsevier.com.

Publisher's note: Elsevier takes a neutral position with respect to territorial disputes or jurisdictional claims in its published content, including in maps and institutional affiliations.

No part of this publication may be reproduced or transmitted in any form or by any means, electronic or mechanical, including photocopying, recording, or any information storage and retrieval system, without permission in writing from the publisher. Details on how to seek permission, further information about the Publisher's permissions policies and our arrangements with organizations such as the Copyright Clearance Center and the Copyright Licensing Agency, can be found at our website: www.elsevier.com/permissions.

This book and the individual contributions contained in it are protected under copyright by the Publisher (other than as may be noted herein).

Notices
Knowledge and best practice in this field are constantly changing. As new research and experience broaden our understanding, changes in research methods, professional practices, or medical treatment may become necessary.

Practitioners and researchers must always rely on their own experience and knowledge in evaluating and using any information, methods, compounds, or experiments described herein. In using such information or methods they should be mindful of their own safety and the safety of others, including parties for whom they have a professional responsibility.

To the fullest extent of the law, neither the Publisher nor the authors, contributors, or editors, assume any liability for any injury and/or damage to persons or property as a matter of products liability, negligence or otherwise, or from any use or operation of any methods, products, instructions, or ideas contained in the material herein.

ISBN: 978-0-323-95745-8

For information on all Academic Press publications visit our website at https://www.elsevier.com/books-and-journals

Publisher: Stacy Masucci
Acquisitions Editor: Simonetta Harrison
Editorial Project Manager: Deepak Vohra
Production Project Manager: Omer Mukthar
Cover Designer: Greg Harris

Typeset by TNQ Technologies

Contents

Contributors   xi

1 The birth and evolution of operant behavioral economics   1
Steven R. Hursh and Madison E. Graham
Introduction   1
Applications of economic concepts for the analysis of behavior   2
Normalized demand   10
Exponential demand and essential value   12
Human demand analysis and hypothetical purchase tasks   18
Behavioral economics and empirical public policy   19
Retrospective and prospective views of behavioral economics   20
References   25

2 Introduction to operant demand   33
Derek D. Reed, Madison E. Graham and Samuel F. Acuff
Introduction to operant demand   33
Origins of operant demand   34
Capturing "demand"   36
Validity of demand analyses   41
Conclusion   44
References   45

3 Nonhuman research methods and procedures for studying operant demand   51
Cassandra D. Gipson, Christa L. Corley, Ashley Craig, Mikhail N. Koffarnus and Joshua S. Beckmann
Introduction   51
Schedules of reinforcement   51
Preclinical models of demand using natural reinforcers:
A historical perspective   53
Utilizing preclinical demand models for drugs of dependence   56
Neurobiological mechanisms of operant demand: Implications
for drugs of dependence   61
Conclusions   64
References   64

4	**Human research methods for studying operant demand**	**71**
	Sarah Weinsztok, Brandon Miller, Elizabeth Aston and Michael Amlung	
	Introduction	71
	Historical perspectives on measuring behavior under constraint	72
	Purchase task methodology as a novel alternative to operant choice tasks	75
	Progression of purchase task methodology: Verification and applications	76
	Purchase Task Toolkit	79
	Further refinements and applications of purchase tasks: Utilization of qualitative methods to improve assessment of behavioral economic substance demand	81
	References	85
5	**Quantitative models of operant demand**	**91**
	Brent A. Kaplan	
	Quantitative models of operant demand	91
	Regression approaches to demand	94
	Brief overview of models of demand	95
	Tools for demand analysis	97
	General steps for demand analysis	98
	Issues and considerations for demand curve analyses	121
	Conclusion	123
	Appendix	124
	Biography	127
	References	128
6	**Practical applications of the Operant Demand Framework**	**131**
	Shawn P. Gilroy	
	Economics and behavior analysis	131
	Defining the Operant Demand Framework	134
	Applications of demand to preference assessment	138
	Applications of demand to reinforcer evaluations	139
	Applications of demand to token economies	142
	Challenges associated with applications of demand	143
	Future directions in research	144
	References	144
7	**An introduction to discounting**	**149**
	Mariah E. Willis-Moore, Kiernan T. Callister, David N. Legaspi, Daniel S. Da Silva and Amy L. Odum	
	An introduction to discounting	149
	A brief history of discounting	149
	How do we measure discounting?	151
	How do we analyze discounting data?	155

	Robust findings in delay and probability discounting	158
	Is two better than one? Comparing delay and probability discounting	162
	Future applications of discounting research	165
	Conclusion	168
	References	168
8	**Nonhuman research methods and procedures for studying delay discounting**	**181**
	Robert S. LeComte and Erin B. Rasmussen	
	Nonhuman delay discounting procedures	182
	Identifying neural substrates in delay discounting	191
	Conclusions	196
	References	196
	Further reading	203
9	**Human research methods for studying discounting**	**205**
	Mikhail N. Koffarnus, Mark J. Rzeszutek,	
	Haily K. Traxler and Sarah E. Iglehart	
	Examples of discounting studied in humans	205
	Delay discounting	205
	Probability discounting	206
	Effort discounting	206
	Social discounting	207
	Multiple dimensions	207
	Discounting of monetary versus nonmonetary commodities	208
	Hypothetical outcomes versus real outcomes	209
	Methods of obtaining indifference points	210
	Fixed ascending/descending procedure	210
	Adjusting amount	212
	Adjusting delay	214
	Single-question indifference procedures	215
	The Kirby Monetary Choice Questionnaire	215
	Single-question discount rates procedures	216
	Three-choice discount rate	216
	Multiple dimensions	217
	Experiential discounting	218
	Discounting tasks for neuroscience research	219
	General recommendations	219
	Choosing task parameters	220
	Choosing task reward	221
	Handling nonsystematic responding	221
	Conclusions	222
	References	222
	Further reading	226

10	**Quantitative models of discounting**	**229**
	Christopher T. Franck	
	Overview of the chapter	229
	How to use this chapter	230
	R and RStudio	230
	Use R to import and examine data	232
	Comparing discounting between males and females	257
	Comparing discounting between smokers and nonsmokers	259
	The role of planning in scientific investigation	265
	References	275
11	**Practical applications of discounting**	**279**
	Maribel Rodriguez Perez, Shahar Almog,	
	Andrea Vásquez Ferreiro and Meredith S. Berry	
	Practical applications of discounting	279
	The utility of delay discounting across diverse applications:	
	Select examples	279
	Delay discounting as a transdiagnostic tool	280
	Clinically relevant applications of sexual discounting and	
	implications for individual risk behavior	281
	Clinically relevant applications of food discounting	
	and implications for individual eating behavior	284
	Environmentally relevant discounting applications	286
	The utility of discounting applications: Implications and conclusions	291
	Conclusions	294
	References	295
	Further reading	301
12	**Policy implications of applied behavioral economics**	**303**
	Brett W. Gelino and Justin C. Strickland	
	Policy implications for applied behavioral economics	303
	What is public policy?	304
	On the importance of timing	305
	Behavioral economic compatibility with empirical public policy	305
	Policy-relevant choice procedures	307
	Policy targets for applied behavioral economists	309
	Describing molar patterns of behavior	310
	Measuring reinforcer valuation	311
	Evaluating intervention effects	311
	Finding and filling the gap	312
	Examples of policy-relevant choice data	312
	Nonhuman and human laboratory studies	313
	Incentivized and simulated studies	314
	Next steps for continued policy success	314
	Advancing conceptual approaches	315

	Incorporating new intervention frameworks	**315**
	Establishing methodological consistency	**316**
	Conclusion	**316**
	References	**316**
13	**Consumer behavior analysis as a foundation of operant behavioral economics**	**323**
	Gordon R. Foxall, Jorge M. Oliveira-Castro and Rafael Barreiros Porto	
	Operant behavioral economics	**323**
	The Generic Behavioral Perspective Model	**325**
	Establishing a market value	**328**
	Empirical evidence	**330**
	The marketing firm	**336**
	Conclusion	**339**
	References	**339**

Index   **347**

Contributors

Samuel F. Acuff Recovery Research Institute, Center for Addiction Medicine, Massachusetts General Hospital and Harvard Medical School, Boston, MA, United States

Shahar Almog Department of Health Education and Behavior and Center for Behavioral Economic Health Research (CBEHR), University of Florida, Gainesville, FL, United States

Michael Amlung University of Kansas, Lawrence, KS, United States

Elizabeth Aston Brown University, Providence, RI, United States

Joshua S. Beckmann Department of Psychology, University of Kentucky, Lexington, KY, United States

Meredith S. Berry Department of Health Education and Behavior and Center for Behavioral Economic Health Research (CBEHR), University of Florida, Gainesville, FL, United States; Department of Psychology, University of Florida, Gainesville, FL, United States

Kiernan T. Callister Utah State University, Logan, UT, United States

Christa L. Corley Department of Pharmacology and Nutritional Sciences, University of Kentucky, Lexington, KY, United States

Ashley Craig Department of Pharmacology and Nutritional Sciences, University of Kentucky, Lexington, KY, United States

Daniel S. Da Silva Utah State University, Logan, UT, United States

Andrea Vásquez Ferreiro Department of Health Education and Behavior and Center for Behavioral Economic Health Research (CBEHR), University of Florida, Gainesville, FL, United States

Gordon R. Foxall Cardiff University, Cardiff, United Kingdom; Reykjavik University, Reykjavik, Iceland

Christopher T. Franck Department of Statistics, Virginia Tech, Blacksburg, VA, United States

Brett W. Gelino Department of Psychiatry and Behavioral Sciences, Johns Hopkins University School of Medicine, Baltimore, MD, United States

Shawn P. Gilroy Louisiana State University, Baton Rouge, LA, United States

Cassandra D. Gipson Department of Pharmacology and Nutritional Sciences, University of Kentucky, Lexington, KY, United States

Madison E. Graham University of Kansas, Department of Applied Behavioral Science, Lawrence, KS, United States

Steven R. Hursh Institutes for Behavior Resources, Inc., Baltimore, MD, United States

Sarah E. Iglehart Department of Family and Community Medicine, University of Kentucky, Lexington, KY, United States

Brent A. Kaplan Codedbx, United States; Innovation Department, Advocates for Human Potential, Inc., Sudbury, MA, United States

Mikhail N. Koffarnus Department of Family and Community Medicine, University of Kentucky, Lexington, KY, United States

Robert S. LeComte Department of Psychiatry & Behavioral Sciences, Behavioral Pharmacology Research Unit, Johns Hopkins University School of Medicine, Baltimore, MD, United States

David N. Legaspi Utah State University, Logan, UT, United States

Brandon Miller University of Kansas, Lawrence, KS, United States

Amy L. Odum Utah State University, Logan, UT, United States

Jorge M. Oliveira-Castro University of Brasilia, Brasilia, Brazil

Maribel Rodriguez Perez Department of Health Education and Behavior and Center for Behavioral Economic Health Research (CBEHR), University of Florida, Gainesville, FL, United States

Rafael Barreiros Porto University of Brasilia, Brasilia, Brazil

Erin B. Rasmussen Department of Psychology, Idaho State University, Pocatello, ID, United States

Derek D. Reed Institutes for Behavior Resources, Inc., Baltimore, MD, United States

Mark J. Rzeszutek Department of Family and Community Medicine, University of Kentucky, Lexington, KY, United States

Justin C. Strickland Department of Psychiatry and Behavioral Sciences, Johns Hopkins University School of Medicine, Baltimore, MD, United States

Haily K. Traxler Department of Behavioral Science, University of Kentucky, Lexington, KY, United States

Sarah Weinsztok University of Kansas, Lawrence, KS, United States; Rutgers, The State University of New Jersey, New Brunswick, NJ, United States

Mariah E. Willis-Moore Utah State University, Logan, UT, United States

The birth and evolution of operant behavioral economics

Steven R. Hursh[1] and Madison E. Graham[2]
[1]Institutes for Behavior Resources, Inc., Baltimore, MD, United States; [2]University of Kansas, Department of Applied Behavioral Science, Lawrence, KS, United States

Introduction

This is my personal story of discovering the principles we now refer to as operant behavioral economics, or just simply "behavioral economics," as I called it in 1984 (Hursh, 1984). That name, as it turns out, unbeknownst to me at the time, was beginning to be used by economists interested in the cognitive properties of choice, especially choice outcomes that appeared to violate standard economic models of rational decision-making. This story will not cover that territory. To avoid confusion with that literature, we have adopted the term "operant behavioral economics" to differentiate this behavior-analytic framework from the like-named cognitive economic framework. Although the two fields of study are distinct, their trajectory of interest is parallel, as shown in Fig. 1.1. The graph below depicts the cumulative rate of publications in all of behavioral economics (left y-axis) and the cumulative rate of my behavioral economic citations, starting in 1980 (right y-axis). Note that activity in the entire field accelerated around 1991, nearly a decade after interest in operant behavioral economics began in the early 1980s.

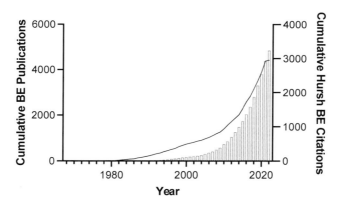

Figure 1.1 The cumulative rate of publications identified as behavioral economics (left y-axis) and the cumulative rate of citations by Hursh (related to behavioral economics) (right y-axis) from 1967 to 2022 based on the *Web of Science* database.

It is important to acknowledge that the field of operant behavioral economics is roughly divided into two subfields. One that has been very fertile is focused on inter-temporal choice and delay discounting (Killeen, 2009, 2015; Koffarnus & Bickel, 2014; Myerson & Green, 1995; Rachlin, 2006; Rachlin & Burkhard, 1978; Rachlin et al., 1976), while my work has largely focused on concepts having to do with what we call demand for reinforcers or commodities. Delay discounting is thoroughly discussed in Chapters 7−11. This chapter is a story of the origins of operant behavioral economics associated with demand analysis from my personal perspective. The story starts with my graduate training in operant conditioning in the laboratory of Edmund Fantino between 1968 and 1972. Part of our training was on the determinants of response rate and choice, and the dominant theory at the time was the "law of effect" (Herrnstein, 1970). To summarize:

- Absolute rate of responding is directly proportional to the relative rate of reinforcement (Catania & Reynolds, 1968; Chung & Herrnstein, 1967; Herrnstein, 1961).
- Relative rates of responding tend to match relative rates of reinforcement (Catania, 1963; Guilkey et al., 1975; Herrnstein, 1961; Pliskoff & Brown, 1976).

Numerous experiments supported these notions, and they were largely regarded as "laws" of behavior. At that time, I shared an office with another graduate student, James Norborg, who had transferred to the doctoral program in psychology after having a career in business and schooling in classical economics. Our discussions led us to challenge some of these assumed "laws," not because the results were suspect but because the conditions arranged to conduct the experiments may have constrained the observations and limited their generality to the economic world. For the most part, research animals used in studies of choice were nearly always offered a choice between two identical reinforcers: Grain for pigeons or food pellets or sugar solution for rodents. However, microeconomics was more broadly applied to choices between diverse and heterogeneous commodities. In those contexts, economists pointed out a range of interactions, such as substitution, in which one commodity replaces another more expensive one, and complementarity, when two commodities vary in value together because they are mutually interdependent, such as tires for the car, or independence, in which two commodities are unaffected by the price of the other. We imagined that under such diverse conditions, matching was highly unlikely in all cases, and we mapped a series of experiments to explore those possibilities in an operant choice situation. As it turned out, time and money did not permit us to conduct that line of research, and it was not for another 6 years that the crucial experiments were performed.

Applications of economic concepts for the analysis of behavior

Even then, the idea that economics and behavior analysis should be related was not a new concept. Others have pointed to the possible connections, such as Allison et al.

(1979), Lea (1978), and Rachlin et al. (1976). However, none of these experiments directly explored the implications of economics for principles of operant behavior analysis. The opportunity to test those ideas came during my first work assignment at the Walter Reed Army Institute of Research (WRAIR) in 1972. At that time, Congress tasked the Army to undertake experiments to understand the biology of heroin addiction and the general problem of "drug abuse." WRAIR established a laboratory to use a relatively new methodology of drug self-administration in primates to study behavior reinforced by drugs. The laboratory setup was ambitious, with 10 enclosures for baboons, each given concurrent access to food, water, and heroin delivered by an indwelling catheter available 23 hours a day by pressing pushbuttons. This was the perfect opportunity to begin looking at heterogeneous choices in a traditional operant environment with three powerful reinforcers, solely available by pressing buttons in the chambers. The schedules of reinforcement were fixed-ratio (FR) schedules for each alternative. However, this was not the ideal preparation for testing the matching law because FR schedules guarantee matching by their very nature. Yet, there was suggestive evidence that the law of effect had its limits. For example, when we observed low rates of responding on one of the alternatives, the finding was that INCREASING the FR size increased responding, not decreased, as you might expect from the law of effect. As the FR increased, rates of reinforcement declined, yet rates of responding increased. This relationship was true of all three reinforcers. However, this specific finding with the baboons was never published.

Nevertheless, the one publication that arose from the baboon laboratory pointed to an economic framework for understanding the choice between heterogeneous reinforcers, entitled "Reduction of heroin intake in baboons by an economic constraint" (Elsmore et al., 1980), referring to the economic concepts I had presented earlier (Hursh, 1978, 1980). That experiment arranged periodic choices between either heroin or food on an FR5 schedule in a long session from 0800 to 2400 hours daily. As the time between trials increased, the number of opportunities for either reinforcer or heroin decreased. The results showed that when forced to choose between heroin or food under conditions of decreasing opportunities ("income," in economic terms), heroin consumption decreased more than food consumption. In economic terms, surprisingly, heroin consumption was more "elastic" than food consumption.

I recognized that the baboon preparation with concurrent FR schedules was not ideal for testing the matching law with heterogeneous reinforcers. In a separate laboratory using rhesus monkeys, I set up a more traditional experiment involving concurrent variable-interval (VI) schedules of reinforcement that controlled rates of reinforcement (Hursh, 1978). It was a three-choice experiment with two alternatives for food pellets, one under a constant VI 60 seconds and the other at a varying VI x sec. The third alternative was a water schedule, also a constant VI 60 seconds schedule. That arrangement would explore the choice between heterogeneous reinforcers as the rate of reinforcement for the one food alternative was varied. But there was another dimension of interest. I observed that the baboon experiment was not only unique in offering heterogeneous reinforcers, but it was also unique in setting up a situation in which the subjects worked under the prevailing schedules for 23 hours a day with no supplemental food, water, or drug to artificially hold intakes constant. To explore the importance of this arrangement in the monkey experiment, I arranged two phases. In experiment 1, sessions ended based on a fixed amount of time. Hence, the amount of food or water consumed could vary with rates of responding, a situation we later came to call a "Closed Economy" (Hursh, 1980). In experiment 2, sessions were terminated after a fixed number of food pellets were delivered (150). Post-session access to water was arranged to ensure a constant amount of water intake (140 squirts). Under these conditions, the total daily consumption of food and water was disconnected from the rates of responding, a situation called an "Open Economy" (Hursh, 1980).

The results of this experiment were fundamental in establishing the importance of the economic context for determining the outcome of operant experiments. To briefly summarize the findings, in the second experiment (open economy), which mimicked the usual operant experiment with constant levels of deprivation, as the size of the VI schedule for one food alternative was decreased, and the rate of reinforcement increased, responding for that alternative increased and responding for food from the constant alternative decreased, confirming in this situation the matching law. However, the story was not entirely positive for matching because responding to water remained constant despite a decreasing *relative* rate of reinforcement compared to the food alternatives. Hence, matching was found between the two qualitative equal reinforcers but not between the qualitatively different reinforcers. What seemed to control responding for water was the total amount of food consumed, which was held constant.

The results of the second experiment (closed economy) were even more divergent from matching. First, consider the food alternatives. As the constraint on food decreased and rates of reinforcement *increased*, responding for food overall and for food from the constant alternative, both *decreased*, which was the opposite of what might be expected from the law of effect. Furthermore, as the rates of food reinforcement and overall food consumption increased, and relative rates of reinforcement from water *decreased*, rates of responding for water *increased*, which is "countermatching." So, in summary, this one experiment established the economic importance of the nature of the commodities in a choice and the importance of the economic context, be it an open or closed economy.

Over the next 6 years, from 1978 to 1984, I sought to formalize the concepts illustrated in that experiment and confirmed and extended those concepts in subsequent experiments. The first task was to relate conceptually operant experiments and behavior analysis principles to principles from microeconomics. Fundamental to that discussion was the concept of a demand curve, which relates the levels of consumption of a commodity to the price of a commodity. To perform this translation, we had to define terms. Consumption was the number of reinforcers earned per day, and price was the number of responses required for each reinforcer. The translation of microeconomics to terms compatible with behavior analysis took more than a definition of terms, however. Most expositions of demand curves in textbooks at that time (Samuelson, 1976; Watson, 1977) plotted demand curves with price on the y-axis as the dependent variable and consumption on the x-axis as the independent variable. That may seem odd today, but reasonable if we examine the purpose of those charts. For the economist, the question was what forces determine the market price of a commodity. The conceptualization offered was the intersection of a demand function that represented the price someone would pay for various amounts of a good and a supply function that represented how much would be produced by the supplier given different prices, where those two competing functions crossed was the point of equilibrium price.

To translate this diagram into operational terms that relate to an operant experiment, the axes are reversed, as described in Hursh (1980). One function describes the feedback function or supply function created by the schedule of reinforcement, and the second function is the level of consumption that would be supported by responding under that schedule of reinforcement. I diagrammed that process for both interval and ratio schedules in Fig. 1.2. With FR schedules, the supply function is a vertical line with the price fixed independent of consumption. For interval schedules, the rate of consumption is an increasing function of responding with a limit set by the average interval of the schedule. In both cases, the resulting level of reinforcement per day is comparable to an economic demand curve, the level of consumption across a range of prices. When studied in a closed economy without other sources of food, that function tends to slope downward at a rate lower than the rate of increase in price and is said to be inelastic (up to a point). Accompanying this inelastic decrease in consumption,

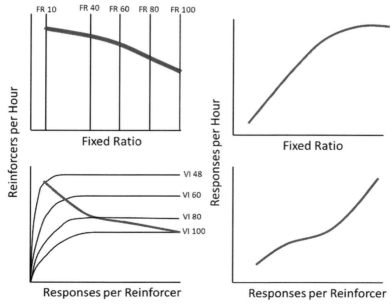

Figure 1.2 (Left panel) The supply curves of reinforcers arranged by FR schedules (top left) and VI schedules (bottom left) with the resulting levels of daily consumption (heavy line), which defines the demand curve. (Right panel) The increasing output of responses supports inelastic demand under these supply schedules in a closed economy.

we would expect to see increasing responding (up to a point) to minimize decreases in daily consumption of the necessary food commodity (Right panel, Fig. 1.2).

One critical ingredient for plotting a demand curve is a definition of "price." As early as 1980, I realized that a specification of price as "responses per reinforcer" was not adequate if the size of the reinforcers varied. In that paper, I demonstrated with a replot of data (Hill & Collier, 1978) from an experiment that arranged a series of FR schedules in combination with three sizes of reinforcers when plotted as a function of responses per gram of food (unit price), the data converged to a single demand curve. Several years later, we conducted an experiment to explore demand as responsive to price, defined as a cost-benefit ratio. In that experiment, we varied the size of reinforcers, the probability of reinforcement, and the response lever weight across a range of six FR schedules (Hursh et al., 1988). The results were a dramatic demonstration that all those combinations converged to a single underlying demand relationship for food; food consumption across eight permutations of size, probability, and effort was controlled by price specified as grams of effort per grams of food or "unit price."

Experimental Demand Curves. Methodologically, the standard paradigm had shifted more toward closed economies in which rates of reinforcement are not arbitrarily held constant. Schedules of reinforcement shifted away from using interval schedules that limit rates of reinforcement toward using FR schedules to set prices and externalize the subjects' self-selected levels of consumption or demand. Many experiments that varied the ratio value systematically to reveal the demand curve were conducted (Hursh et al., 1989). Hursh et al. (2005) summarized a series of experiments with monkeys in closed economies between 1984 and 1990. In retrospect, that paper not only summarized the key principles of operant behavioral economics but also provided key laboratory evidence to illustrate those principles. Fig. 1.3 illustrates a typical experiment that became the paradigm for closed economy experiments (Hursh, 1991); the subjects lived in their research environments, and the only food and water were from the apparatus available 23 hours a day. In a typical experiment, monkeys had access to either food (the only food source) or non-nutritive saccharin, without water deprivation. Over about 21 days, the FR schedule required for food and saccharin was increased each day from 10 to 372. The result was a remarkably systematic and repeatable pattern of results obtained in less than a month of study. This was in contrast to prior studies in open economies that normally required 20—30 days of study at each schedule condition. This new style of studying behavior greatly increased the throughput of research and was a small revolution for behavior analysis with animals. The pattern of results in Fig. 1.3 introduced a fundamental characteristic of demand, demand elasticity. The demand curve for food decreased at a slow rate relative to increases in price, with a slope in log-log units less negative than -1. This is defined as inelastic demand. Beyond that point, consumption declined more rapidly. Looking at the response output associated with food demand, we see that response output increased up to the point of unit elasticity (-1), after which responding decreased. Response output is maximal at that point and is called P_{max}, and the level of responding at P_{max} is called O_{max} or maximum output. The demand curve for saccharin is distinctly different, and the point of elasticity occurs at a much lower price; consequently, responding increases over a limited range and decreases at prices greater

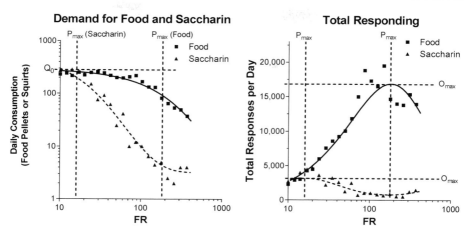

Figure 1.3 (Left panel) Consumption of food or saccharin under increasing FR schedules, called demand curves. The horizontal line is Q_0, or the highest level of consumption at a minimal price. The vertical dashed lines are at the prices associated with maximal output (P_{max}) in both panels. (Right panel) The generally increasing response output is associated with inelastic demand for food and the relatively elastic demand for saccharin. The horizontal lines are the maximal levels of response output (O_{max}) for food and saccharin.

than about FR28. We call demand for the "necessity" of food pellets relatively inelastic and demand for the "luxury" good, saccharin-sweetened water, relatively elastic. This concept of elasticity as a fundamental property of reinforcement, separable from reinforcer magnitude, was introduced by Hursh (1984). It has become a part of the language of operant conditioning, characterizing the importance of a reinforcer within a specific context and the persistence of behavior to obtain that reinforcer in the face of constraints, such as cost, effort, or delays. In subsequent work, efforts were made to model demand with equations that yield a single parameter representing price sensitivity and explore conditions that change price sensitivity (see Hursh & Roma, 2016). In recent years, studies of substance use disorders have found that measures relating to price sensitivity or *persistence* are one of the two main factors that characterize demand for drugs and the amount of behavior dominated by drug seeking (González-Roz et al., 2018; Schwartz et al., 2022). The other major factor determining demand is related to the level or *amplitude* of demand, usually defined as the quantity of consumption with minimal or no constraint, Q_0 in Fig. 1.3, left panel (Hursh et al., 2005; Hursh & Winger, 1995).

Two-Commodity Studies and Reinforcer Interactions. A series of experiments looked at concurrent FR schedules for heterogeneous reinforcers such as food and water (Hursh, 1984, 1991; Hursh & Bauman, 1987), food and sucrose, or food and saccharin (Bauman et al., 1996). In the first case (Fig. 1.4, left panel), the price of food increased in the presence of a fixed price for water (FR10) in water-deprived subjects. As food consumption declined under increasing prices, water consumption declined even though its price was constant. This defined water, in this instance, as

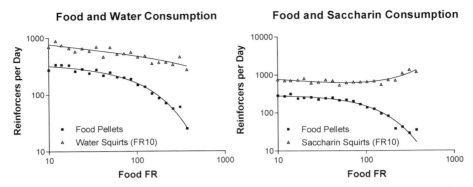

Figure 1.4 (Left panel) The consumption of food under increasing FR values and the decreasing consumption of water under a constant FR10 schedule, a complement to food. (Right panel) The decreasing level of consumption under increasing FR values for food and the increasing levels of consumption for saccharin-sweetened water under constant FR10, a substitute for food.

a "complement" to food; generally, when food consumption declines, animals drink less water. In another case (Fig. 1.4, right panel), the price of food increased in the presence of a fixed price (FR10) for saccharin-sweetened water in a non–water-deprived subject (Bauman et al., 1996). As the price of food increased and food consumption decreased, the consumption of saccharin-sweetened water increased. This defined sweet water as a substitute for food, even though it did not replace the calories lost from food. Similar and more dramatic effects occurred when the alternative was a caloric-rich sucrose solution (Bauman et al., 1996). These experiments became paradigmatic exemplars of substitution and complementarity observed under controlled laboratory conditions and closed economies. In later explorations of reinforcer interactions, we proposed that substitution was not necessarily symmetrical (Hursh, 1991). For example, drug A might fully substitute for drug B, but if drug B stimulates only a subset of physiological states stimulated by drug A, then drug B might not substitute for A as the price of A is increased. In subsequent models of reinforcer interactions, the interaction term is specific to the reinforcer and context (Hursh & Roma, 2013, 2016; Hursh & Schwartz, 2023). This realization has important policy implications as efforts are underway to find substitutes for harmful commodities, such as substitutes for cigarettes (Petry & Bickel, 1998; Smethells et al., 2018).

Open and Closed Economies. The original work with baboons working for concurrent food, water, and heroin was done in such a way that there was no other source of those reinforcers. It was a closed system, and I called it a Closed Economy (Hursh, 1980) as opposed to an Open Economy in which the experimenter provided additional access to the reinforcers to hold daily deprivation constant. This was a deliberate decision because drugs in the natural environment are part of a closed system where users must work for their access. To fairly compare the strength of drug reinforcement to food and water reinforcement, we arranged a similar closed system for them as well. As a result, we found that responding increased across a wide range of FR values up to an FR372, with daily levels as high as 18,000 responses (Fig. 1.3). Similar levels of responding have been found with rats and pigeons in a closed economy (Collier, 1983; Raslear et al., 1988; Zeiler, 1999). This was in contrast to studies with controlled deprivation in short sessions (open economies) that showed consistent decreases in responding with increases in FR value (Felton & Lyon, 1966; Zeiler, 1999). One way to think about this distinction is that an open economy provides a substitutable alternative source of food, and the availability of the substitute increases the elasticity of demand for the food used as a reinforcer in the test session. In subsequent studies, I sought to quantify the nature of the economic context on demand elasticity. In a series of experiments, the monkeys were given a 12-hour work session for food under the usual, increasing series of FR schedules that increased each day across several weeks. The degree of "openness" was manipulated by providing variable amounts of food at the end of the 12-hour session. In one experiment, varying amounts of food were delivered non-contingently. In another experiment, food was available under an FR1 for a short period after the 12-hour test session or intermittently after shorter test sessions. These arrangements resulted in progressive increases in the elasticity of demand for food, with P_{max} systematically moving to the left with increasing amount and immediacy of food external to the work session (Hursh, 1991; Hursh & Bauman, 1987), see Imam and Hursh (2000). An economic explanation of these findings is that the food provided external to the work session was a substitute for the food earned under increasing prices, and the substitution effect resulted in increased elasticity of demand. Another explanation for these findings and the similar findings of increased elasticity when the session ended after a fixed number of reinforcers (Hursh, 1978) is based on operant conditioning principles. Both arrangements weaken the dependency relationship between responding in the test session and daily food consumption (Imam & Hursh, 2000; Zeiler, 1999). These results establish that elasticity of demand is not an inherent property of the reinforcer but an emergent property of the reinforcer in the context of other reinforcers, as proposed in 1984 (Hursh, 1984).

The concept of open and closed economies has relevance for understanding the management of reinforcer access to modulate response rates in applied behavioral settings (Roane et al., 2005). This global concept of open and closed economics is also relevant to our understanding of the powerful effects of medication-assisted treatment, such as methadone maintenance treatment for opioid addiction. The medically provided opiate serves as a substitute for the drugs obtained in the community, weakens the contingency relationship, increases the elasticity of demand, and decreases overall drug seeking in the community (Hursh, 1991).

The Linear Elasticity Model of Demand. Over the course of many studies that mapped demand curves under a range of conditions, we began to see regularities in the shape of the curve and have proposed several mathematical models to fit those curves. These efforts were motivated by a desire to derive metrics describing the nonlinear shape of the demand curve as a way to scale the value of different reinforcers or conditions that impact the value of reinforcers. Starting from Hursh (1980), the concept of elasticity was an important feature of demand—roughly speaking, how sensitive consumption is to price constraints. Economists have already provided us with a general understanding of elasticity as a way to measure the importance or value of a commodity. The curves economists often drew for simplicity and, without the benefit of quantitative experiments, were generally linear in log-log coordinates, and the slope of that function was taken as a measure of elasticity. However, the wealth of experiments with animals, and more recently with humans, demonstrated that typical demand curves were not linear in log-log coordinates but showed increasing downward curvature with increasing price. This curvature created a problem for precisely characterizing elasticity across commodities and situations. Ideally, if a function could be fit to the demand curve with a single parameter that defined the rate of change in elasticity, then that parameter could be used to rank order elasticities. The first conjecture by Hursh et al. (1989) was that elasticity increased as a linear function of price. In other words, the first derivative of the log-log function was linear. The demand model was called the linear elasticity model, which was the dominant way to model demand until Hursh and Silberberg (2008) introduced the exponential demand model. The linear elasticity model is written as follows, in log units of consumption, log Q:

$$\log Q = \log I + b(\log P) - aP \tag{1.1}$$

Interpreting the model's parameters, I represented the level or intensity of demand, and the a and b parameters determine the rate of change in elasticity with increasing log price or price sensitivity. Since no single parameter represented price sensitivity (it was a two-parameter linear equation), that factor in demand was gauged by the price at unit elasticity, or P_{max}, or the price with maximum response output. Since elasticity, or the first derivative of Eq. (1.2), was a linear function of parameters a and b, finding P_{max} when elasticity equals -1 was straightforward:

$$P_{max} = \frac{1+b}{a} \tag{1.2}$$

P_{max} defined the boundary between inelastic and elastic demand and was the point of maximum response output. A commodity with a higher P_{max} was more valuable than a commodity with a lower P_{max}. Based on studies such as Hursh et al. (1988), price was defined as the number of responses per unit of reinforcement, such as responses per gram of food. This was termed the unit price conjecture and became a standard way to assess demand for drugs and other reinforcers.

Normalized demand

The conceptualization that demand could be scaled in terms of unit price and price sensitivity could be gauged by P_{max} began to run into trouble, starting with the study by Hursh and Winger (1995). That study summarized several experiments looking at the demand for various drugs self-administered by rhesus monkeys. The problem with P_{max} was that it assumed that the unit price was sufficient to scale the value of a drug.

But what was discovered in that study, and many studies since, is that the potency of drugs can vary wildly. The reinforcing value of the drug is not captured by the dose of the drug, which was a key ingredient in the definition of the price specified as the number of responses per mg/kg of the drug. If the unit price does not fully capture the "cost-benefit ratio" of a drug, then P_{max} will also be an inaccurate scale for drugs across doses and potencies. In 1995, it was proposed that demand curves be scaled in normalized terms, such that consumption declined from 100% at baseline with very low cost and that price be scaled in terms of the dose as a fraction of that baseline level. The assumption was that the baseline level would account for differences in potency. For example, a highly potent drug would be consumed in lower volumes than a less potent drug, but whatever that baseline level was found to be at the lowest price would be used to scale both consumption and price. That study and several after that time showed that once demand was normalized, the P_{max} stated in normalized units was a better reflection of the reinforcing value of a drug. Hursh and Winger (1995) still used the linear elasticity model scaled in normalized units of consumption and price to properly rank order drugs of known abuse potential.

Soon after that study's completion in 1995, I finished my career with the Army and left my primate laboratory at the WRAIR. What followed was a long and productive collaboration with Drs. Gail Winger and James Woods at the University of Michigan. From 1995 to 2007, we published nine articles that explored demand for nine self-administered drugs, each with at least three doses and three primates for over 80 separate demand curve determinations. In all those experiments, demand was plotted on normalized scales to account for differences in dose and potency. Hursh et al. (2005) summarized much of that work.

Interestingly, since demand was normalized, information pertaining to the level of demand at zero price (Q_0) was lost. Instead, the two parameters of demand used to compare drugs were P_{max} and the output of responses at that price, O_{max}. Those two parameters have been found to be meaningful aspects of demand in many subsequent studies of demand. The curves fit to the data in Fig. 1.5 are based on the linear elasticity model. The three drugs differ in speed of onset of action, rank ordered as ketamine, the fastest, and dizocilpine, the slowest. Note that the ketamine demand curve is shifted to the right (higher P_{max}) and has the highest response output, O_{max}. As a result, the differences in P_{max} were a linear decreasing function of time to onset of peak effect, implicating delay of reinforcement as a key pharmacological factor in determining the strength of demand for a drug.

It is not an overstatement that the many papers from the Winger and Woods collaboration have been fundamentally important in providing carefully determined demand data used to test various improvements in methods to model demand (Gilroy et al., 2021). In one of the last papers describing collaborative studies with the University of Michigan (Winger et al., 2007), I introduced a new model of demand, still using normalized units. It was a simple decreasing exponential:

$$\text{Log } Q = \log(100)e^{-aP} \qquad (1.3)$$

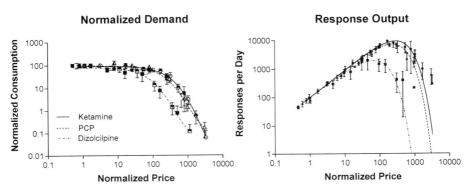

Figure 1.5 (Left panel) Three normalized demand curves for drugs of increasing elasticity—ketamine, PCP, and dizolcipine. (Right panel) The increasing responding for the three drugs with the point of maximal responding (P_{max}) moving progressively leftward to lower prices for the same drugs. The demand curves were fit with a simple exponential, Eq. (1.3).

The equation did a remarkably good job fitting the demand curves and allowed for a clear differentiation between demand for cocaine, ethanol, and their combination. A single "a" parameter differentiated between drugs and combinations based on the rate of change in elasticity. This article was a preview of the exponential model of demand introduced the following year in 2008 (Hursh & Silberberg, 2008).

Exponential demand and essential value

I became the president of the Institutes for Behavior Resources (IBR) in 2005, and the last collaborative study with the University of Michigan was published in 2007 (Winger et al., 2007). In 2008, Alan Silberberg and I set out to create an improved model for demand curves (Hursh & Silberberg, 2008) that leveraged the prior decade of work with primate self-administration of drugs. That 2008 paper detailed the shortcomings of the normalization procedure and the linear elasticity model previously used and set out to describe a new model with two prime objectives:

- Eliminate the need to normalize consumption and price to obtain a dose and potency-independent measure of price sensitivity.
- Provide a single parameter that represents the sensitivity of consumption to increases in price or the essential value of the drug.

The equation extended the simple exponential (Winger et al., 2007) in three significant ways. The equation is stated as follows:

$$\log Q = \log(Q_0) + k\left(e^{-\alpha \cdot Q_0 \cdot C} - 1\right) \tag{1.4}$$

Note first, instead of assuming that all consumption was normalized to 100%, the starting value was set as a free parameter, Q_0, to represent the level or *amplitude of demand*. Second, the rate constant "a" was replaced with α modulated by the independent variable of constraint (C). Third, to account for differences in drug dose and potency or reinforcer magnitude in general, the constraint term (C) in the exponent was multiplied by Q_0. Effectively, this converted the absolute price to what might be called "real price," or $Q_0 \cdot C$, that amount of responding at any level of constraint required to defend the baseline level of consumption at zero price, Q_0. To illustrate with an example, consider the experiment on the cost-benefit definition of price (Hursh et al., 1988) in which the reinforcer was either one food pellet or two. In practice, Q_0 (number of reinforcers at zero price) for one pellet would be about twice that for two pellets to maintain a roughly constant intake of food. Hence, for any given FR, say 100, the "real price" would be 100 x Q_0, and since Q_0 was twice as high for one pellet, real price at an FR of 100 for the one-pellet reinforcer would be double the real price of two pellets. In the case of food pellets, we know the objective size of the reinforcer. Whereas, for different drugs that vary in potency and reinforcing value, we cannot tell the size of the reinforcer from the objective dimensions of the reinforcer, such as dose, but it can be inferred from Q_0, just like one-pellet reinforcers are consumed in greater quantity to two-pellet reinforcers. The drug with a higher Q_0 is less potent than a drug with a lower Q_0 (it takes more of the less potent drug to achieve the same physiological effect as the more potent drug), and real price accounts for that difference. The ability of exponential demand to control for potency in the estimation of α has been confirmed by reexamining the data from the Winger and Woods experiments (Gilroy et al., 2021). Within limits, α tends to be constant across doses of a drug (holding the span parameter, k, constant). Exponential demand and a derivative form, the exponentiated demand model (Koffarnus et al., 2015, 2022), have remained popular models for assessing demand curves in both animal and human experiments, with over 700 citations of the original work (Hursh & Silberberg, 2008).

By using real price in the exponential exponent, the α parameter reflects the overall *sensitivity of consumption* to increases in constraint independent of differences in reinforcer magnitude scaled by Q_0. As defined in Hursh and Silberberg (2008), the reinforcer's essential value (EV) is inversely proportional to α. Unfortunately, since α and k tend to vary inversely, comparisons of α can only be done with a constant span parameter, k. In more recent accounts of exponential demand, EV has been defined such that it is independent of k and inversely proportional to α, either by approximation (Hursh & Roma, 2016) or analytically derived from the exact formula for P_{max} (Gilroy, 2023; Gilroy et al., 2019). Gilroy (2023) has shown that EV is inversely proportional to α and directly proportional to $P_{max} \cdot Q_0$; hence, EV can be stated as normalized P_{max}[1]:

---

[1] Note that EV is independent of Q_0 because embedded in the mathematical definition of Pmax is $1/Q_0$ which cancels Q_0 in the computation of normalized EV. Stated another way, EV is P_{max} scaled in terms of real price.

$$\text{EV} = \frac{P_{max} \cdot Q_0}{100} = P_{max} \cdot \frac{Q_0}{100} \tag{1.5}$$

The concept of EV is an important advance because it allows for the comparison of price sensitivity or demand *persistence* across studies and demand determinations that differ in the exponential span parameter, k. EV is an important trans-situational measure of demand persistence that can be used as a clinical indicator, a metric for abuse liability of drugs, and a public policy tool applied across many different contexts.

In economic terms, α reflects the rate of change in elasticity, and when Q_0 is constant, α is inversely proportional to P_{max}, the price at unit elasticity (Gilroy et al., 2019). In behavioral terms, EV is a measure of the persistence of consumption in the face of increasing constraints. It has been shown to be predictive of essential aspects of substance use disorder (Schwartz, Silberberg, & Hursh, 2021), while other studies have shown the predictive value of the inverse of α (Madden & Kalman, 2010; McClure et al., 2013; Secades-Villa et al., 2016). Several studies (Aston et al., 2017; Bidwell et al., 2012; Epstein et al., 2018; González-Roz et al., 2018; MacKillop et al., 2009; Schwartz et al., 2022) have shown that demand can be factored into two primary components, *amplitude* indexed primarily by Q_0 (and a less extent O_{max}) and *persistence* index primarily by $1/\alpha$ and P_{max}, and O_{max}. EV is directly related to $1/\alpha$ but is independent of k and Q_0 and could have important implications for future research on abuse liability that will be discussed later.

Despite the broad application of various forms of exponential demand, the model has several practical shortcomings. The first is the need to take the logarithm of the data to apply the model since it is a model of log-log demand. This is an important feature because the slope in log-log coordinates equates to elasticity, relative changes in consumption with relative changes in price; a key parameter, P_{max}, is defined as a point slope of -1 in log-log space, which defines the boundary between inelastic and elastic demand and the point of maximum response output. Fitting the data with this model stated in log terms ensures that the model, when fitted to actual data, is optimized for minimizing variance in the estimation of point elasticity, a measure of point slope in relative terms. In practice, this gives equal weighting to relative deviations along the price dimension (Gilroy et al., 2021). But that carries with it the limitation that zero values of consumption cannot be considered because the log of zero is undefined. This can be important because, in many experiments, the last price considered is the one that results in zero consumption and effectively represents the breakpoint. Ignoring that point may reduce the overall accuracy of the fits to the demand data. One solution is to convert the first zero value to a small nonzero value, but the size of that value is arbitrary and could impact the overall fit to the data (Koffarnus et al., 2015, 2022). Koffarnus et al. (2015) suggested exponentiating Eq. (1.2) so that the model is fit to the arithmetic data. This approach can often provide an adequate fit to the data but also has its limitations (Gilroy et al., 2021). First, exponentiation does not eliminate the fact that the exponential model cannot provide a solution for a zero-consumption level of demand, and it does not eliminate the other shortcoming of exponential demand, the span constant, k. The k parameter was required in Eq. (1.4) to provide a lower bound or establish a span of the consumption dimension, which in log values has no minimum. However, α and k are inversely related—a wider span will require a lower rate of change. To derive a value of α that reflects differences across conditions in an experiment, the k parameter is held constant across conditions. Usually, a single value of k can be found that fits all the data within an experiment, but since k is not necessarily constant across experiments in the literature, this can complicate comparisons of α from different studies.

Fortunately, there are several solutions to this problem. The first is to not compare α across experiments but rather compare EV because that value, computed either as an approximation (Hursh & Roma, 2016) or as an exact value (Gilroy, 2023) from Eq. (1.5), is independent of k, as discussed previously. The other solution is to use a log-like transform of the data that computes to zero when the data are zero but is otherwise equivalent to the log-transformed values at levels of consumption above some low level, such as 5. That approach was explained by Gilroy et al. (2021) using the log-like inverse hyperbolic sine (IHS) transform. With a data transformation that results in a zero floor, the overall exponential equation can be simplified because the k parameter is no longer needed, and the span is determined by Q_0. There are other log-like transforms bounded at zero that could be used, so for simplicity, I will define LT as the log-like transform. We can then simplify Eq. (1.4) as follows and call it the zero-bounded exponential (ZBE) model of demand (Gilroy et al., 2021).

$$LT(y) = LT(Q_0) * e^{-\frac{\alpha}{LT(Q_0)}Q_0 C} \quad (1.6)$$

In this formulation, only two free parameters, Q_0 and α, have the same meaning as in the original exponential equation. The span parameter, k, is unnecessary because $LT(Q_0)$ is the span of the function and can be factored out of the expression in Eq. (1.4). Note that α is normalized for changes in span by dividing by $LT(Q_0)$ to control for the known relationship between α and span (Gilroy et al., 2021). When the log-like transform is IHS, we have found that in most cases using Eq. (1.6), α is dose-independent, preserving one of the key properties of exponential demand with a simpler two-parameter model that can retain zero data. Using this two-parameter version of the exponential model, EV can be stated simply as $1/(100 \cdot \alpha)$.

Several other models have been proposed in recent years to fit demand data (Newman & Ferrario, 2020; Rzeszutek et al., 2023), and each has its applications for specific situations. One factor distinguishes exponential demand in its various forms (Gilroy, 2023; Gilroy et al., 2021; Hursh & Silberberg, 2008; Koffarnus et al., 2015): The measure of value, EV (or the inverse of α), is generally (within limits) independent of reinforcer magnitude making it an ideal model for rank ordering drugs for abuse liability independent of dose. Reviewing all the drugs tested during many years of collaboration with Winger and Woods, we can offer this rank ordering of drugs based on EV (Hursh & Roma, 2016) and the original exponential model (Table 1.1).

Abuse Liability Assessment. This methodology has great potential for FDA regulation of pharmaceuticals under the Controlled Substance Act that defines five schedules of controls, determined in part by the abuse liability of the substance. If a standardized method of abuse liability assessment based on demand curve testing using drug-self-administration procedures were developed and a standardized model for rank ordering

Table 1.1 The exponential demand model (Hursh & Silberberg, 2008) was applied to a range of drug and non-drug reinforcers using previously published data: food and saccharin (Hursh, 1991), remifentanil, alfentanil, and fentanyl (Ko et al. 2002), ketamine, phencyclidine, and dizocilpine (Winger et al. 2002), alfentanil, cocaine, methohexital, and nalbuphine (Hursh & Winger, 1995). The best fitting parameters of the exponential model provided an estimate of α. The commodities were rank ordered by EV using the formula from Hursh and Roma (2016).

Drug	EV
Food	825
Remifentanil	341
Alfentanil (2002)	315
Alfentanil (1995)	302
Ketamine	255
Phencyclidine	212
Cocaine (2 higher doses)	207
Fentanyl	187
Saccharin	118
Methohexital	78
Nalbuphine	72
Dizocilpine	39

Source: Winger, G., Hursh, S.R., Casey, K.L., & Woods, J.H. (2002). Relative reinforcing strength of three n-methyl-D-Aspartate antagonists with different onsets of action. *Journal of Pharmacology and Experimental Therapeutics*, *301*(2), 690-697.

drugs were developed (as shown in Table 1.1), then drugs could be more precisely differentiated based on the likely robustness of demand supported by the drug in the natural marketplace (Koffarnus, 2023). While many drugs may support consumption at a very low price, say FR10, the drugs listed earlier were all differentiated by sensitivity to prices greater than 10. This has important implications for public policy. A range of opioid-like substances have beneficial properties for pain relief but have become restricted by the FDA because of abuse liability concerns. This is understandable given the FDA's experience with opioid drugs like OxyContin that were excessively prescribed and resulted in large-scale misuse. But there are now many hybrid formulations with mixed-agonist and antagonist properties that might offer significant pain relief with reduced abuse liability. An assessment based on demand could differentiate those drugs from other highly abusable opioids, such as fentanyl.

One question might be whether the demand curve method and the estimates of EV are sufficiently robust to be used by the FDA for regulatory purposes. If the method were to be applied across experiments, labs, time, and companies, the FDA would want some assurance that a drug's evaluation would be consistent across all these conditions, provided the methods used were "standardized." To test that assumption, I looked at two demand determinations of alfentanil, one reported in 1995 (Hursh & Winger, 1995) and the other in 2002 (Ko et al., 2002), both from the primate lab at the University of Michigan. The seven demand curves are shown in Fig. 1.6, and

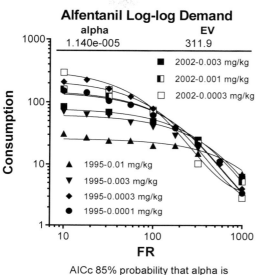

Figure 1.6 Demand curves for varying doses of alfentanil were determined first in 1995 and then replicated in 2002. Across all doses and years of study, there was a high probability that the α parameter was constant based on exponential demand (Eq. 1.4).

notice that the doses tend to have different Q_0 values, with the highest doses having the lowest Q_0 values. When the data were combined and fit with the exponential model, it turned out that for the four doses used in 1995 and the three doses used in 2002, there was an 85% probability that a common value for α and EV was appropriate for all those data series (AICc, 84.98%). The exponential model effectively controlled for a 10-fold swing in Q_0 across doses (and studies) to provide a single estimate of EV. This offers some retrospective evidence that the method has sufficient reproducibility to be used as a regulatory tool. Those laboratory studies with nonhuman primates have been confirmed with human subjects making hypothetical purchases (see Chapter 4) of drugs with varying doses. Berry et al. (2023) have demonstrated that exponential demand for cocaine and methamphetamine of varying doses resulted in a single estimate of α (and EV) for each drug independent of dose despite significant differences across doses in demand intensity (Q_0). Future studies across a range of drugs will be required to confirm the generality and limitations of these findings.

The concept of demand assessment has another policy implication. In the natural environment, drugs compete in the marketplace. Drugs that are marginally reinforcing but support highly elastic demand are likely to be noncompetitive in the community marketplace, given the availability of other drugs with greater EV. Creating a scaling system that reflects this reality could lead to a more precise scheduling system that restricts the drugs with the highest EV and lowers the restrictions on drugs with low EV. This will facilitate innovation by pharmaceutical companies to formulate new compounds with greater therapeutic value, lower EV, and minimal abuse potential.

Human demand analysis and hypothetical purchase tasks

Human demand studies involving subjects executing an operant to obtain a commodity demonstrated that the demand curve analysis perfected in laboratory studies did apply to humans (Greenwald & Hursh, 2006; Hursh & Roma, 2013; Spiga et al., 2005). However, studies with humans are technically difficult and prevent the study of drugs with potentially harmful effects. Jacobs and Bickel (1999) introduced a solution to that problem by showing that a reasonable demand curve could be mapped by simply offering a series of prices for a well-described product or outcome (reinforcer) and asking how much of that outcome the subjects would purchase. Other chapters in this book (Chapters 6 and 12) describes that entire line of research and innovation and its relevance for extending the behavioral economics of demand to understanding a range of health behaviors. One of the key programs at IBR is a behavioral health clinic that provides substance use disorder treatment. In collaboration with Lindsay Schwartz, we conducted several studies on the relevance of hypothetical purchase tasks for a range of drugs targeting substance use disorder treatment (Schwartz, Blank, & Hursh, 2021; Schwartz et al., 2019). One study demonstrated that demand indices, such as EV, were predictive of subsequent drug use. Another study (Schwartz et al., 2022) elucidated the latent factors in demand that are associated with drug demand, specifically demand amplitude (Q_0 and O_{max}) and demand persistence ($1/\alpha$, P_{max}, O_{max}, and breakpoint).

Reminiscent of animal experiments examining demand with two alternatives are studies of hypothetical demand that pose a choice between two commodities, one with an increasing price and the other at a constant price. Such studies can reveal the substitutable and complementary relationships between commodities in the context of human choices. The relationship is called cross-price demand because the level of consumption of the constant price alternative changes in response to the price of the other commodity, hence, "cross-price" demand. The exponential model of demand has been extended to that situation as the difference between two exponentials. Consider two commodities, A with an increasing price and B with a constant price. Demand for commodity B can be modeled as cross-price demand as a function of the price of commodity A using the following equation:

$$\mathrm{Log}\ Q_B = \mathrm{Log}(Q_{0B}) + I e^{-\beta \cdot C_A}$$

Q_{0B} is the asymptotic level of demand for commodity B at an infinite price for commodity A (zero consumption). I is the interaction constant, β is the sensitivity of commodity B demand to the price of commodity A (cross-price elasticity), and C_A is the cost of commodity A. The cross-price demand model can be applied to both substitutes and complements. The I parameter in the equation specifies the direction of interaction such that negative values imply substitution in which the constant commodity replaces the varying price commodity. Positive values of that same parameter have been shown to describe the cross-price relationships of complements, that is, commodities that vary in the same direction with changes in the price of one of them (Hursh et al., 2013). This cross-price demand model has been shown to be accurate for actual choices between commodities (Hursh & Roma, 2013; Smethells et al., 2018) and with hypothetical choices between alternatives (Amlung & MacKillop, 2019; Gelino et al., 2024). For example, demand for a fixed-price legal source of cannabis increased as the price of illegal cannabis increased, serving as a substitute (Amlung & MacKillop, 2019). Demand for a fixed price of cannabis decreased as the price of alcohol increased, serving as a complement (Dolan et al., 2022).

Behavioral economics and empirical public policy

Over the years, from 2013 to 2023, I have been very interested in the extensions of operant behavioral economics to empirical public policy (Hursh et al., 2020; Hursh & Roma, 2013; Reed et al., 2016; Strickland, Reed, Dayton, et al., 2022; Strickland, Reed, Hursh, et al., 2022; Strickland, Stoops, et al., 2022). In fact, the model presented in 1991 (Hursh, 1991) seems just as valid today as it was when originally presented, as adapted in Reed et al. (2022). Chapter 12 provides a more detailed discussion of the applications of operant behavioral economics to public policy. One of the key advantages of behavioral economics for policy design and evaluation is that the language of economics is familiar to policymakers (Strickland & Lacy, 2020). For example, in the realm of drug control policy, there is an established need to balance "supply side" measures to restrict the availability of illegal substances, which drives up market prices, and "demand side" policies to expand treatment and reduce the number of individuals who would fuel the illegal market as customers. Hence, a behavioral economic analysis provides guidance that policymakers can understand and readily incorporate into policy decisions.

For this story, I will focus on one aspect of public policy that merits greater attention. We commonly think of the monetary and effort cost of various policies: how much will a medical procedure cost, how often does one have to charge an electric vehicle, or how hard is it to install solar panels on my home. But equally important is the time cost associated with a policy: How long do I have to wait for an appointment, how long will it take to receive my benefits, and how soon will I get the results of a COVID-19 test (Reed et al., 2022; Schwartz & Hursh, 2022b), or how long will it take to recharge my electric car. The enormous power of reducing delays is demonstrated by Amazon online marketplace's success, which can promise Prime users next-day delivery of many items. Often, time costs are understood within a delay discounting framework, but that method generally is focused on the discount rate applied to the goods or services and provides less information about overall demand relative to alternatives. However, time is just another kind of constraint, and the same demand models used to examine money and effort costs can be applied to time costs (Schwartz & Hursh, 2022b). Recognizing that temporal costs behave like other kinds of constraints led me to explore whether choices framed as competing demand with variable time costs could be generalized as a framework to account for findings from studies of delay discounting, specifically the hyperbolic discount function (see Chapters 7 and 10). I created a simulation of a hypothetical choice between immediate access to one alternative versus delayed access to a larger alternative, each modeled as demand curves using a generalized version of the cross-price demand equation described previously (Hursh, 2014; Hursh et al., 2013; Hursh & Roma, 2013, 2016). The expansion of the model (Hursh & Schwartz, 2023) depicts demand for each alternative in a two-commodity simulation as the sum of two exponential demand equations. The formulation has terms for the relative size of the alternatives, the level of demand for each alternative (Q_0), the sensitivity of demand to time cost (α), and the degree of substitutability between an alternative and its context, or the interaction strength (I). For substitutes used in delay discounting, the I parameter is negative, and demand for the immediate alternative subtracts from demand for the larger alternative as it is increasingly delayed. The simulation results have been published as the *General Model of Demand and Discounting* (Hursh & Schwartz, 2023) and will not be discussed in detail here. But there are several intriguing implications of the simulation that await further empirical test:

1. For cases in which the delayed alternative was highly substitutable with the immediate alternative, hyperbolic discounting was the result.
2. The discount rate for the delayed alternative was controlled by the temporal sensitivity of demand for that alternative (α).
3. Increasing the amplitude of demand (Q_0) for delayed alternatives decreased the discount rate.
4. The discount rate was also related to the degree of substitutability with the context, such that higher discount rates occurred when substitutability was increased.
5. In the extreme cast, when the delayed alternative had no substitute from the context, the discount function was exponential, not hyperbolic.

Several of these implications are consistent with the extent of literature on cross-commodity discounting, but other relationships have yet to be studied (Hursh & Schwartz, 2023). The General Model has implications for the study of substance use disorders, testing of more effective treatments, and more comprehensive formulations of public policy that involve temporal costs. The General Model is the synthesis of many of the connected principles arising from my personal story of operant behavioral economics and hopefully serves as the impetus for empirical studies of actual concurrent choice to confirm or refine the model. In either case, the resulting experimentation will lead to progress toward applying operant behavioral economics to solving important social problems.

Retrospective and prospective views of behavioral economics

It has now been over 4 decades since the first experiments that formed the basis for operant behavioral economics. At about the same time, economists discovered that human choice behavior did not always conform to neoclassical economic theory based on an assumption of rational decision-making, a field we call cognitive-behavioral economics. As noted in several bibliometric analyses (Costa et al., 2019; Frid-Nielsen & Jensen, 2021), these two lines of thought coexisted over that time as two distinct constellations of studies with very view cross-references. In retrospect, I ask several questions about this historical accident:

- What was so surprising about cognitive-behavioral economics that excited economists but was largely ignored by behavior analysis?
- Are there lessons from cognitive-behavioral economics that can inform and enrich operant behavioral economics?
- Likewise, what lessons from operant behavioral economics might deserve more attention from cognitive-behavioral economists?

In this short discussion, I will not attempt an exhaustive discussion of cognitive-behavioral economics but will pick several classic "cognitive biases" that typify that line of reasoning. To understand and appreciate a cognitive bias, you first must understand that the theory and mathematics of neoclassical economics are based on calculations of optimal outcomes and that, with perfect knowledge, a rational person should always choose the outcome that maximizes monetary gains and minimizes losses. This assumption makes it possible for economists to predict how a person should invest, choose between two probabilistic outcomes, and, in turn, how the economic market should structure choices for the consumer. What cognitive-behavioral economists discovered when they offered such choices to people was that there tended to be consistent biases away from optimal long-term benefit. These biases were newsworthy in economics because they upset time-honored assumptions of rationality and forced a reformulation of the mathematics of economic theory. But, interestingly, many of the kinds of "biases" that surprised economists would not be surprising to persons schooled in behavior analysis.

If there is one thing behavior analysis has learned from schedules of reinforcement, it is that patterns of outcomes that "average" to the same rate of reinforcement do not have equivalent effects on behavior. Consider the basic differences between FR and fixed-interval schedules compared to variable-ratio and variable-interval schedules with the same average rate of reinforcement. It is well known that variable outcomes reinforce stronger and more consistent patterns of behavior. There is no assumption of "rationality" of the average outcome that underpins behavior analysis. Even within a single schedule type, like interval schedules, it is well known that short intervals are weighted more highly in the average than long intervals (Hursh & Fantino, 1974), perhaps because of the gradient of the strength of delayed reinforcement or more molecular reinforcement factors, such as differential reinforcement of short inter-response times. Whatever the reason, these findings are not particularly surprising, and they do not fundamentally upset the principles of operant conditioning because there is no first principle of rationality.

Consider "negativity bias" in that adverse outcomes disproportionately impact decisions compared to positive outcomes. For example, one is likely to prefer a treatment that is described as resulting in 90% success compared to one that is described as having a 10% failure rate, even though the two treatments are objectively identical. From a behavior-analytic perspective, this is not particularly surprising. The basic theory of conditioned reinforcement predicts that positive outcomes lead to effective conditioned reinforcers, and negative outcomes do not. Several studies of the reinforcing effects of "good and bad news" in both animals and humans confirm that good news is more reinforcing than bad, but that bad news may be reinforcing if it provides information that can ultimately lead to good news. In other words, knowing which treatment has the worst outcomes can lead to finding a treatment with a better outcome. But the point is, there is no assumption of symmetry between good and bad news, even if, from a logical perspective, they are of equal value (Fantino & Stolarz-Fantino, 2013; Sears et al., 2022; Silberberg & Fantino, 2010).

Edmund Fantino has considered cognitive biases and nonoptimal human reasoning and how they can be understood from a behavioral perspective (Fantino, 2012; Fantino & Stolarz-Fantino, 2013). But, that does not mean that the work of cognitive-behavioral economists to document and catalog these biases is not useful. While we might be able to "explain" them based on the first principles of operant conditioning, we might not apply those lessons in everyday decision-making without the useful tips from cognitive science. However, these revelations do not shake the foundations of behavior analysis as they did economics because they do not challenge fundamental assumptions, which may explain why those studies have attracted so much less attention from behavior analysts.

While various forms of nonoptimal behavior are common observations in the behavioral laboratory, another aspect of this discussion is worth remembering. Most examples cited in the behavioral literature illustrate how contingency-shaped behavior may contradict a rational explanation. I would venture to say that economists would still expect human reasoning to be more robust than the natural inclinations of conditioned responses. Consider the "near-miss effect" in gambling. The near-miss effect refers to a losing situation that is (or perceived to be) close to a win by the gambler (Parke et al., 2004). Because these negative (losing) outcomes are perceived by gamblers as close to winning, they are positively reinforcing and can result in continued gambling. As a result, near-misses can encourage obsessive gambling in vulnerable individuals at no cost to the casino (Clark et al., 2009; Reid, 1986). In fact, Dores et al. (2020) showed that the physiological effect of a near-miss could be more similar to a win than a loss. One explanation, of course, is stimulus generalization—the arrangement of slot machine symbols of a near-miss is similar to the arrangement of a "win." In addition, because the symbols rotate to display various combinations just before a "win," the near-miss arrangement may occur immediately before a win, creating the conditions for the formation of a conditioned reinforcer. From an economic perspective, a near-miss is no better than a clear loss, but from a behavioral perspective, they may be perceived as similar and have reinforcing properties. This explanation from the point of view of stimulus control and conditioning is in stark contrast to a verbal description of the situation made outside the emotional experience that concludes that a near-miss has zero value. So, in a sense, a person can be both rational and irrational, depending on the situation, and this underscores the behavioral view of verbal behavior. Sometimes, immediate reinforcement causes a person to violate the direction of their own verbal behavior. And verbal descriptions and explanations of ourselves are no more perfect than our ability to observe and explain the behavior of others. For operant behavioral economists, verbal behavior that results in illogical and irrational conclusions is merely a reflection of our conditioning history—verbal behavior is not a special class of behavior. It can be just as illogical as schedule-controlled behavior evaluated in terms of optimal gains and losses.

This distinction between behavior that is primarily under contingency control and may lead to different outcomes compared to rule-governed behavior or behavior guided by verbal behavior is very similar to what the noted cognitive-behavioral economist Kahneman (2011) has described as fast and slow thinking. In the context of the gambling example, fast thinking reacts to the physiological and emotional effects of the near-miss, whereas slow thinking steps back from the situation and applies cool logic (self-instruction) to evaluate near-misses as equivalent to losses. Which "person" will win out will probably depend on social and collateral reinforcers that either keep the person in the fast mode or encourage a shift into the slow mode.

For the economist, this problem of irrational verbal behavior is important because many economic decisions are not under direct contingency control, but rather are based on a verbal description of the alternatives and the perceived outcomes. When a person signs a contract, the terms of the agreement specify the contingencies, but the ultimate outcome is in the future. How well those outcomes are evaluated in relation to the effort or costs demanded of the contract may be subject to various forms of cognitive bias embedded in the verbal behavior we bring to the situation. Hence, knowing the common fallacies of reasoning or cognitive biases that can enter into that decision-making can help to avoid nonoptimal or harmful future outcomes, but only when a person is in "slow thinking" mode.

It is interesting to note that there is some evidence that cognitive-behavioral economics is discovering the principles of reinforcement and response cost. The book *Nudge* (Thaler & Sunstein, 2009) suggests that choice architectures can be arranged that lead to more optimal choices by capitalizing on certain automatic tendencies (i.e., operant conditioning principles). For example, when an employee is offered the opportunity to participate in a retirement savings account, the default option should be to enroll, and a specific action is required to opt out. From a behavioral perspective, the "better choice" should involve less effort than the less optimal choice. This arrangement is a kind of "nudge" to do the better thing, even though both options are available, and the person is not "forced" to participate. We can debate whether such an arrangement is unnecessarily "paternalistic," but the fact is that such arrangements do result in more participation in retirement and health insurance programs. These kinds of outcomes are newsworthy, partly because they are effective and partly because they might be surprising for the average person. For a behavior analyst, the success of such arrangements is probably not surprising.

Despite the foregoing examples, cognitive-behavioral economics does offer operant behavioral economics some important lessons and concepts. First, we should not fall victim to the same assumption of "rationality" as economists. I have made a strong point that the best way to conceptualize price is as a cost-benefit ratio. I have also emphasized the value of the exponential demand equation for controlling for "real-price" in the analysis of demand and EV. But those principles are not without their own limits. For example, not all doses of a drug will result in the same α; constancy is within certain pharmacological limits, and to be conducted properly, demand assessment of drugs should start with a dose-response curve to define the range of reinforcing doses. Violations of unit price constancy have also been found when comparing demand under random-ratio versus FR series of prices, with random-ratio schedules resulting in more persistent consumption and lower values of α, even when the numerical average unit price was constant (Lagorio & Winger, 2014). Similar nonlinearities apply to the cost component of the cost-benefit ratio when time delays are the cost. We have found that the time scale is not necessarily linear in its impact on demand. Based on Steven's power law, it was found that time in Eq. (1.6) resulted in more accurate representations of demand when time was raised to a power and the best value of the exponent varying from 0.4 to 0.8 depending on the commodity (Schwartz & Hursh, 2022b).

Second, in the realm of hypothetical demand, the first step in obtaining estimates of consumption across a range of prices is to describe the nature of the outcome. But fundamentally, hypothetical demand is an experiment in verbal behavior. No costs are actually applied, and no reinforcers are actually offered. The system relies on the ability of the person to accurately describe their own behavior as it might occur under verbally described circumstances. While those estimates have been validated (Mackillop et al., 2016), it is also true that the quality of the description of the outcome and the subject's familiarity with the outcome are important determiners of the resulting demand curves. For example, when determining the impact of tamper-proof formulations on demand for opioid pills, it was important that the subjects had prior experience with manipulating pills (Schwartz et al., 2019). Strickland, Reed, Dayton, et al. (2022) point out that the verbal framing of the scenario and consequences can impact the ultimate amplitude and persistence of demand, like seeking a COVID-19 vaccination. In this context, some of the lessons from cognitive-behavioral economics regarding framing and cognitive bias may be useful in the formulation of public messaging in response to future infectious disease crises to optimize acceptance of recommended public health behaviors. Nevertheless, the value of these lessons in cognitive-behavioral economics is demonstrated with the quantitative methods of operant behavioral economics.

Hence, I will conclude with speculation regarding the value of operant behavioral economics for economics in general. Cognitive-behavioral economics arose out of human research and studies in game theory (Smith, 1992). Reviewing the entirety of experimental economics is beyond the scope of this chapter, but I would suggest that economic experimentation does not rival the detailed and quantitative determinations of demand curves and the careful experimental exploration of factors that impact demand that characterize operant behavioral economics. While most of the work so far in operant behavioral economics has been directed at understanding health-related behaviors, a few studies have extended the methods to the larger arena of consumer goods (Roma et al., 2015; Schwartz & Hursh, 2022a). There is the potential that in the future, a melding of behavior analysis and experimental economics could lead to more realistic and predictive behavioral economic models.

References

Allison, J., Miller, M., & Wozny, M. (1979). Conversation in behavior. *Journal of Experimental Psychology: General, 108*(1), 4–34. https://doi.org/10.1037/0096-3445.108.1.4

Amlung, M., & MacKillop, J. (2019). Availability of legalized cannabis reduces demand for illegal cannabis among Canadian cannabis users: Evidence from a behavioural economic substitution paradigm. *Canadian Journal of Public Health, 110*(2), 216–221. https://doi.org/10.17269/s41997-018-0160-4

Aston, E. R., Farris, S. G., MacKillop, J., & Metrik, J. (2017). Latent factor structure of a behavioral economic marijuana demand curve. *Psychopharmacology, 234*(16), 2421–2429. https://doi.org/10.1007/s00213-017-4633-6

Bauman, R. A., Raslear, T. G., Hursh, S. R., Shurtleff, D., & Simmons, L. (1996). Substitution and caloric regulation in a closed economy. *Journal of the Experimental Analysis of Behavior, 65*(2), 401–422. https://doi.org/10.1901/jeab.1996.65-401

Berry, M. S., Naudé, G. P., Johnson, P. S., & Johnson, M. W. (2023). The blinded-dose purchase task: Assessing hypothetical demand based on cocaine, methamphetamine, and alcohol administration. *Psychopharmacology, 240*, 921–933. https://doi.org/10.1007/s00213-023-06334-6

Bidwell, L. C., MacKillop, J., Murphy, J. G., Tidey, J. W., & Colby, S. M. (2012). Latent factor structure of a behavioral economic cigarette demand curve in adolescent smokers. *Addictive Behaviors, 37*(11), 1257–1263. https://doi.org/10.1016/j.addbeh.2012.06.009

Catania, A. C. (1963). Concurrent performances: Reinforcement interaction and response independence. *Journal of the Experimental Analysis of Behavior, 6*(2), 253–263. https://doi.org/10.1901/jeab.1963.6-253

Catania, A. C., & Reynolds, G. S. (1968). A quantitative analysis of the responding maintained by interval schedules of reinforcement. *Journal of the Experimental Analysis of Behavior, 11*(3S2), 327–383. https://doi.org/10.1901/jeab.1968.11-s327

Chung, S. H., & Herrnstein, R. J. (1967). Choice and delay of reinforcement. *Journal of the Experimental Analysis of Behavior, 10*(1), 67–74. https://doi.org/10.1901/jeab.1967.10-67

Clark, L., Lawrence, A. J., Astley-Jones, F., & Gray, N. (2009). Gambling near-misses enhance motivation to gamble and recruit win-related brain circuitry. *Neuron, 61*(3), 481–490. https://doi.org/10.1016/j.neuron.2008.12.031

Collier, G. H. (1983). Life in a closed economy: The ecology of learning and motivation. In M. D. Z. P. Harzem (Ed.), *Advances in analysis of behavior: Vol. 3. Biological factors in learning* (pp. 223–274). Wiley.

Costa, D. F., Carvalho, F.d. M., & Moreira, B. C.d. M. (2019). Behavioral economics and behavioral finance: A bibliometric analysis of the scientific fields: Bibliometric analysis of behavioral economics and behavioral finance. *Journal of Economic Surveys, 33*(1), 3–24. https://doi.org/10.1111/joes.12262

Dolan, S. B., Spindle, T. R., Vandrey, R., & Johnson, M. W. (2022). Behavioral economic interactions between cannabis and alcohol purchasing: Associations with disordered use. *Experimental and Clinical Psychopharmacology, 30*(2), 159–171. https://doi.org/10.1037/pha0000397

Dores, A. R., Rocha, A., Paiva, T., Carvalho, I. P., Geraldo, A., Griffiths, M. D., & Barbosa, F. (2020). Neurophysiological correlates of the near-miss effect in gambling. *Journal of Gambling Studies, 36*(2), 653–668. https://doi.org/10.1007/s10899-020-09937-2

Elsmore, T. F., Fletcher, G. V., Conrad, D. G., & Sodetz, F. J. (1980). Reduction of heroin intake in baboons by an economic constraint. *Pharmacology, Biochemistry and Behavior, 13*(5), 729–731. https://doi.org/10.1016/0091-3057(80)90018-0

Epstein, L. H., Stein, J. S., Paluch, R. A., MacKillop, J., & Bickel, W. K. (2018). Binary components of food reinforcement: Amplitude and persistence. *Appetite, 120*, 67–74. https://doi.org/10.1016/j.appet.2017.08.023

Fantino, E. (2012). Optimal and non-optimal behavior across species. *Comparative Cognition & Behavior Reviews, 8*, 44–54. https://doi.org/10.3819/ccbr.2012.70003

Fantino, E., & Stolarz-Fantino, S. (2013). The logic and illogic of human reasoning. In G. J. Madden, W. V. Dube, T. D. Hackenberg, G. P. Hanley, & K. A. Lattal (Eds.), *APA handbook of behavior analysis, Vol. 1: Methods and principles* (pp. 439–461). American Psychological Association.

Felton, M., & Lyon, D. O. (1966). The post-reinforcement pause. *Journal of the Experimental Analysis of Behavior, 9*(2), 131–134. https://doi.org/10.1901/jeab.1966.9-131

Frid-Nielsen, S. S., & Jensen, M. D. (2021). Maps of behavioural economics: Evidence from the field. *Journal of Interdisciplinary Economics, 33*(2), 226–250. https://doi.org/10.1177/0260107920925675

Gelino, B. W., Graham, M. E., Strickland, J. C., Glatter, H. W., Hursh, S. R., & Reed, D. D. (2024). Using behavioral economics to optimize safer undergraduate late-night transportation. *Journal of Applied Behavior Analysis, 57*(1), 117–130. https://doi.org/10.1002/jaba.1029

Gilroy, S. P. (2023). Interpretation (s) of essential value in operant demand. *Journal of the Experimental Analysis of Behavior, 119*(3), 554–564. https://doi.org/10.1002/jeab.845

Gilroy, S. P., Kaplan, B. A., Reed, D. D., Hantula, D. A., & Hursh, S. R. (2019). An exact solution for unit elasticity in the exponential model of operant demand. *Experimental and Clinical Psychopharmacology, 27*(6), 588–597. https://doi.org/10.1037/pha0000268

Gilroy, S. P., Kaplan, B. A., Schwartz, L. P., Reed, D. D., & Hursh, S. R. (2021). A zero-bounded model of operant demand. *Journal of the Experimental Analysis of Behavior, 115*(3), 729–746. https://doi.org/10.1002/jeab.679

González-Roz, A., Secades-Villa, R., Weidberg, S., García-Pérez, Á., & Reed, D. D. (2018). Latent structure of the cigarette purchase task among treatment-seeking smokers with depression and its predictive validity on smoking abstinence. *Nicotine & Tobacco Research, 22*(1), 74–80. https://doi.org/10.1093/ntr/nty236

Greenwald, M. K., & Hursh, S. R. (2006). Behavioral economic analysis of opioid consumption in heroin-dependent individuals: Effects of unit price and pre-session drug supply. *Drug and Alcohol Dependence, 85*(1), 35–48. https://doi.org/10.1016/j.drugalcdep.2006.03.007

Guilkey, M., Shull, R. L., & Brownstein, A. J. (1975). Response-rate invariance in concurrent schedules: Effects of different changeover contingencies. *Journal of the Experimental Analysis of Behavior, 24*(1), 43–52. https://doi.org/10.1901/jeab.1975.24-43

Herrnstein, R. J. (1961). Relative and absolute strength of response as a function of frequency of reinforcement. *Journal of the Experimental Analysis of Behavior, 4*(3), 267–272. https://doi.org/10.1901/jeab.1961.4-267

Herrnstein, R. J. (1970). On the law of effect. *Journal of the Experimental Analysis of Behavior, 13*(2), 243–266. https://doi.org/10.1901/jeab.1970.13-243

Hill, W. L., & Collier, G. H. (1978). *The economics of response rate as a feeding strategy*. Washington, D.C: Eastern Psychological Association.

Hursh, S. R. (1978). The economics of daily consumption controlling food- and water-reinforced responding. *Journal of the Experimental Analysis of Behavior, 29*(3), 475–491. https://doi.org/10.1901/jeab.1978.29-475

Hursh, S. R. (1980). Economic concepts for the analysis of behavior. *Journal of the Experimental Analysis of Behavior, 42*(2), 219–238. https://doi.org/10.1901/jeab.1980.34-219

Hursh, S. R. (1984). Behavioral economics. *Journal of the Experimental Analysis of Behavior, 42*(3), 435–452. https://doi.org/10.1901/jeab.1984.42-435

Hursh, S. R. (1991). Behavioral economics of drug self-administration and drug abuse policy. *Journal of the Experimental Analysis of Behavior, 56*(2), 377–393. https://doi.org/10.1901/jeab.1991.56-377

Hursh, S. R. (2014). Behavioral economics and the analysis of consumption and choice. In F. K. McSweeney, & E. S. Murphy (Eds.), *Wiley Blackwell handbook of operant classical conditioning* (pp. 275–305). Wiley-Blackwell. https://doi.org/10.1002/9781118468135.ch12

Hursh, S. R., & Bauman, R. A. (1987). The behavioral economic analysis of demand. In L. Green, & J. H. Kagel (Eds.), *Vol 1. Advances of behavioral economics* (pp. 117–165). Ablex.

Hursh, S. R., & Fantino, E. (1974). An appraisal of preference for multiple versus mixed schedules. *Journal of the Experimental Analysis of Behavior, 22*(1), 31–38. https://doi.org/10.1901/jeab.1974.22-31

Hursh, S. R., Galuska, C. M., Winger, G., & Woods, J. H. (2005). The economics of drug abuse: A quantitative assessment of drug demand. *Molecular Interventions, 5*(1), 20–28. https://doi.org/10.1124/mi.5.1.6

Hursh, S. R., Madden, G. J., Spiga, R., DeLeon, I. G., & Francisco, M. T. (2013). The translational utility of behavioral economics: The experimental analysis of consumption and choice. In G. J. Madden, W. V. Dube, T. D. Hackenberg, G. P. Hanley, & K. A. Lattal (Eds.), *APA handbook of behavior analysis, Vol. 2: Translating principles into practice* (pp. 191–224). American Psychological Association.

Hursh, S. R., Raslear, T. G., Bauman, R., & Black, H. (1989). The quantitative analysis of economic behavior with laboratory animals. In K. G. Grunert, & F. Ölander (Eds.), *Understanding economic behaviour* (pp. 393–407). Netherlands: Springer.

Hursh, S. R., Raslear, T. G., Shurtleff, D., Bauman, R., & Simmons, L. (1988). A cost-benefit analysis of demand for food. *Journal of the Experimental Analysis of Behavior, 50*(3), 419–440. https://doi.org/10.1901/jeab.1988.50-419

Hursh, S. R., & Roma, P. G. (2013). Behavioral economics and empirical public policy. *Journal of the Experimental Analysis of Behavior, 99*(1), 98–124. https://doi.org/10.1002/jeab.7

Hursh, S. R., & Roma, P. G. (2016). Behavioral economics and the analysis of consumption and choice. *Managerial and Decision Economics, 37*(4–5), 224–238. https://doi.org/10.1002/mde.2724

Hursh, S. R., & Schwartz, L. P. (2023). A general model of demand and discounting. *Psychology of Addictive Behaviors, 37*(1), 37–56. https://doi.org/10.1037/adb0000848

Hursh, S. R., & Silberberg, A. (2008). Economic demand and essential value. *Psychological Review, 115*(1), 186–198. https://doi.org/10.1037/0033-295X.115.1.186

Hursh, S. R., Strickland, J. C., Schwartz, L. P., & Reed, D. D. (2020). Quantifying the impact of public perceptions on vaccine acceptance using behavioral economics. *Frontiers in Public Health, 8*, Article 608852. https://doi.org/10.3389/fpubh.2020.608852

Hursh, S. R., & Winger, G. (1995). Normalized demand for drugs and other reinforcers. *Journal of the Experimental Analysis of Behavior, 64*(3), 373–384. https://doi.org/10.1901/jeab.1995.64-373

Imam, A. A., & Hursh, S. R. (2000). Molar effects of increasing amounts and immediacy to external food sources in 4-hr sessions. *Psychological Record, 50*(1), 155–172. https://doi.org/10.1007/BF03395348

Jacobs, E. A., & Bickel, W. K. (1999). Modeling drug consumption in the clinic using simulation procedures: Demand for heroin and cigarettes in opioid-dependent outpatients. *Experimental and Clinical Psychopharmacology, 7*(4), 412−426. https://doi.org/10.1037/1064-1297.7.4.412

Kahneman, D. (2011). *Thinking, fast and slow*. Farrar, Straus and Giroux.

Killeen, P. R. (2009). An additive-utility model of delay discounting. *Psychological Review, 116*(3), 602−619. https://doi.org/10.1037/a0016414

Killeen, P. R. (2015). The arithmetic of discounting. *Journal of the Experimental Analysis of Behavior, 103*(1), 249−259. https://doi.org/10.1002/jeab.130

Ko, M. C., Terner, J., Hursh, S., Woods, J. H., & Winger, G. (2002). Relative reinforcing effects of three opioids with different durations of action. *Journal of Pharmacology and Experimental Therapeutics, 301*(2), 698−704. https://doi.org/10.1124/jpet.301.2.698

Koffarnus, M. N. (2023). Recommendations for the use of behavioral economic demand as an abuse liability assessment for drug scheduling. *Behavioral and Brain Sciences, 10*(1), 113−120. https://doi.org/10.1177/23727322221150197

Koffarnus, M. N., & Bickel, W. K. (2014). A 5-trial adjusting delay discounting task: Accurate discount rates in less than one minute. *Experimental and Clinical Psychopharmacology, 22*(3), 222−228. https://doi.org/10.1037/a0035973

Koffarnus, M. N., Franck, C. T., Stein, J. S., & Bickel, W. K. (2015). A modified exponential behavioral economic demand model to better describe consumption data. *Experimental and Clinical Psychopharmacology, 23*(6), 504−512. https://doi.org/10.1037/pha0000045

Koffarnus, M. N., Kaplan, B. A., Franck, C. T., Rzeszutek, M. J., & Traxler, H. K. (2022). Behavioral economic demand modeling chronology, complexities, and considerations: Much ado about zeros. *Behavioural Processes, 199*, Article 104646. https://doi.org/10.1016/j.beproc.2022.104646

Lagorio, C. H., & Winger, G. (2014). Random-ratio schedules produce greater demand for i.v. drug administration than fixed-ratio schedules in rhesus monkeys. *Psychopharmacology, 231*(15), 2981−2988. https://doi.org/10.1007/s00213-014-3477-6

Lea, S. E. (1978). The psychology and economics of demand. *Psychological Bulletin, 85*(3), 441−466. https://doi.org/10.1037/0033-2909.85.3.441

Mackillop, J., Murphy, C. M., Martin, R. A., Stojek, M., Tidey, J. W., Colby, S. M., & Rohsenow, D. J. (2016). Predictive validity of a cigarette purchase task in a randomized controlled trial of contingent vouchers for smoking in individuals with substance use disorders. *Nicotine & Tobacco Research, 18*(5), 531−537. https://doi.org/10.1093/ntr/ntv233

MacKillop, J., Murphy, J. G., Tidey, J. W., Kahler, C. W., Ray, L. A., & Bickel, W. K. (2009). Latent structure of facets of alcohol reinforcement from a behavioral economic demand curve. *Psychopharmacology, 203*(1), 33−40. https://doi.org/10.1007/s00213-008-1367-5

Madden, G. J., & Kalman, D. (2010). Effects of bupropion on simulated demand for cigarettes and the subjective effects of smoking. *Nicotine & Tobacco Research, 12*(4), 416−422. https://doi.org/10.1093/ntr/ntq018

McClure, E. A., Vandrey, R. G., Johnson, M. W., & Stitzer, M. L. (2013). Effects of varenicline on abstinence and smoking reward following a programmed lapse. *Nicotine & Tobacco Research, 15*(1), 139−148. https://doi.org/10.1093/ntr/nts101

Myerson, J., & Green, L. (1995). Discounting of delayed rewards: Models of individual choice. *Journal of the Experimental Analysis of Behavior, 64*(3), 263−276. https://doi.org/10.1901/jeab.1995.64-263

Newman, M., & Ferrario, C. R. (2020). An improved demand curve for analysis of food or drug consumption in behavioral experiments. *Psychopharmacology, 237*(4), 943−955. https://doi.org/10.1007/s00213-020-05491-2

Parke, A., Griffiths, M., & Irwing, P. (2004). Personality traits in pathological gambling: Sensation seeking deferment of gratification and competitiveness as risk factors. *Addiction Research and Theory, 12*(3), 201−212. https://doi.org/10.1080/1606635310001634500

Petry, N. M., & Bickel, W. K. (1998). Polydrug abuse in heroin addicts: A behavioral economic analysis. *Addiction, 93*(3), 321−335. https://doi.org/10.1046/j.1360-0443.1998.9333212.x

Pliskoff, S. S., & Brown, T. G. (1976). Matching with a trio of concurrent variable-interval schedules of reinforcement. *Journal of the Experimental Analysis of Behavior, 25*(1), 69−73. https://doi.org/10.1901/jeab.1976.25-69

Rachlin, H. (2006). Notes on discounting. *Journal of the Experimental Analysis of Behavior, 85*(3), 425−435. https://doi.org/10.1901/jeab.2006.85-05

Rachlin, H., & Burkhard, B. (1978). The temporal triangle: Response substitution in instrumental conditioning. *Psychological Review, 85*(1), 22−47. https://doi.org/10.1037/0033-295X.85.1.22

Rachlin, H., Green, L., Kagel, J. H., & Battalio, R. C. (1976). Economic demand theory and psychological studies of choice. In , *Vol 10. Psychology of learning and motivation* (pp. 129−154). Elsevier.

Raslear, T. G., Bauman, R. A., Hursh, S. R., Shurtleff, D., & Simmons, L. (1988). Rapid demand curves for behavioral economics. *Animal Learning & Behavior, 16*(3), 330−339. https://doi.org/10.3758/BF03209085

Reed, D. D., Kaplan, B. A., Becirevic, A., Roma, P. G., & Hursh, S. R. (2016). Toward quantifying the abuse liability of ultraviolet tanning: A behavioral economic approach to tanning addiction. *Journal of the Experimental Analysis of Behavior, 106*(1), 93−106. https://doi.org/10.1002/jeab.216

Reed, D. D., Strickland, J. C., Gelino, B. W., Hursh, S. R., Jarmolowicz, D. P., Kaplan, B. A., & Amlung, M. (2022). Applied behavioral economics and public health policies: Historical precedence and translational promise. *Behavioural Processes, 198*, Article 104640. https://doi.org/10.1016/j.beproc.2022.104640

Reid, R. L. (1986). The psychology of the near miss. *Journal of Gambling Behavior, 2*(1), 32−39. https://doi.org/10.1007/BF01019932

Roane, H. S., Call, N. A., & Falcomata, T. S. (2005). A preliminary analysis of adaptive responding under open and closed economies. *Journal of Applied Behavior Analysis, 38*(3), 335−348. https://doi.org/10.1901/jaba.2005.85-04

Roma, P. G., Hursh, S. R., & Hudja, S. (2015). Hypothetical purchase task questionnaires for behavioral economic assessments of value and motivation. *Managerial and Decision Economics, 37*(4−5), 306−323. https://doi.org/10.1002/mde.2718

Rzeszutek, M. J., Franck, C. T., Traxler, H. K., Kaplan, B. A., & Koffarnus, M. N. (2023). Notes on demand: Conceptual and empirical benefits of applying Rachlin's discounting equation to demand data. *Psychology of Addictive Behaviors, 37*(1), 57−71. https://doi.org/10.1037/adb0000889

Samuelson, P. A. (1976). *Economics* (10th ed.). McGraw-Hill.

Schwartz, L. P., Blank, L., & Hursh, S. R. (2021). Behavioral economic demand in opioid treatment: Predictive validity of hypothetical purchase tasks for heroin, cocaine, and benzodiazepines. *Drug and Alcohol Dependence, 221*, Article 108562. https://doi.org/10.1016/j.drugalcdep.2021.108562

Schwartz, L. P., & Hursh, S. R. (2022a). A behavioral economic analysis of smartwatches using internet-based hypothetical demand. *Managerial and Decision Economics, 43*(7), 2729−2736. https://doi.org/10.1002/mde.3558

Schwartz, L. P., & Hursh, S. R. (2022b). Time cost and demand: Implications for public policy. *Perspectives on Behavior Science*, 1−16. https://doi.org/10.1007/s40614-022-00349-8

Schwartz, L. P., Roma, P. G., Henningfield, J. E., Hursh, S. R., Cone, E. J., Buchhalter, A. R., Fant, R. V., & Schnoll, S. H. (2019). Behavioral economic demand metrics for abuse deterrent and abuse potential quantification. *Drug and Alcohol Dependence, 198*, 13−20. https://doi.org/10.1016/j.drugalcdep.2019.01.022

Schwartz, L. P., Silberberg, A., & Hursh, S. R. (2021). Purchase task sensitivity to drug and nondrug reinforcers in opioid-agonist treatment patients. *Journal of the Experimental Analysis of Behavior, 115*(3), 717−728. https://doi.org/10.1002/jeab.681

Schwartz, L. P., Toegel, F., Devine, J. K., Holtyn, A. F., Roma, P. G., & Hursh, S. R. (2022). Latent factor structure of behavioral economic heroin and cocaine demand curves. *Experimental and Clinical Psychopharmacology, 31*(2), 378−385. https://doi.org/10.1037/pha0000594

Sears, B., Dunn, R. M., Pisklak, J. M., Spetch, M. L., & McDevitt, M. A. (2022). Good news is better than bad news, but bad news is not worse than no news. *Learning & Behavior, 50*(4), 482−493. https://doi.org/10.3758/s13420-021-00489-y

Secades-Villa, R., Pericot-Valverde, I., & Weidberg, S. (2016). Relative reinforcing efficacy of cigarettes as a predictor of smoking abstinence among treatment-seeking smokers. *Psychopharmacology, 233*(17), 3103−3112. https://doi.org/10.1007/s00213-016-4350-6

Silberberg, A., & Fantino, E. (2010). Observing responses: Maintained by good news only? *Behavioural Processes, 85*(1), 80−82. https://doi.org/10.1016/j.beproc.2010.06.002

Smethells, J. R., Harris, A. C., Burroughs, D., Hursh, S. R., & LeSage, M. G. (2018). Substitutability of nicotine alone and an electronic cigarette liquid using a concurrent choice assay in rats: A behavioral economic analysis. *Drug and Alcohol Dependence, 185*, 58−66. https://doi.org/10.1016/j.drugalcdep.2017.12.008

Smith, V. L. (1992). Game theory and experimental economics: Beginnings and early influences. *History of Political Economy, 24*(Suppl. ment), 241−282. https://doi.org/10.1215/00182702-24-Supplement-241

Spiga, R., Martinetti, M. P., Meisch, R. A., Cowan, K., & Hursh, S. R. (2005). Methadone and nicotine self-administration in humans: A behavioral economic analysis. *Psychopharmacology, 178*(2−3), 223−231. https://doi.org/10.1007/s00213-004-2020-6

Strickland, J. C., & Lacy, R. T. (2020). Behavioral economic demand as a unifying language for addiction science: Promoting collaboration and integration of animal and human models. *Experimental and Clinical Psychopharmacology, 28*(4), 404−416. https://doi.org/10.1037/pha0000358

Strickland, J. C., Reed, D. D., Dayton, L., Johnson, M. W., Latkin, C., Schwartz, L. P., & Hursh, S. R. (2022). Behavioral economic methods predict future COVID-19 vaccination. *Translational Behavioral Medicine, 12*(10), 1004−1008. https://doi.org/10.1093/tbm/ibac057

Strickland, J. C., Reed, D. D., Hursh, S. R., Schwartz, L. P., Foster, R. N. S., Gelino, B. W., LeComte, R. S., Oda, F. S., Salzer, A. R., Schneider, T. D., Dayton, L., Latkin, C., & Johnson, M. W. (2022). Behavioral economic methods to inform infectious disease response: Prevention, testing, and vaccination in the COVID-19 pandemic. *PLoS One, 17*(1), Article e0258828. https://doi.org/10.1371/journal.pone.0258828

Strickland, J. C., Stoops, W., Banks, M. G., & Gipson-Reichardt, C. D. (2022). Logical fallacies and misinterpretations that hinder progress in translational addiction neuroscience. *Journal of the Experimental Analysis of Behavior, 117*(3), 384−403. https://doi.org/10.1002/jeab.757

Thaler, R. H., & Sunstein, C. R. (2009). *Nudge*. Penguin.

Watson, D. S. H.,M. A. (1977). *Price theory and its uses* (4th ed.). Houghton Mifflin.

Winger, G., Galuska, C. M., & Hursh, S. R. (2007). Modification of ethanol's reinforcing effectiveness in rhesus monkeys by cocaine, flunitrazepam, or gamma-hydroxybutyrate. *Psychopharmacology, 193*(4), 587−598. https://doi.org/10.1007/s00213-007-0809-9

Winger, G., Hursh, S. R., Casey, K. L., & Woods, J. H. (2002). Relative reinforcing strength of three n-methyl-D-Aspartate antagonists with different onsets of action. *Journal of Pharmacology and Experimental Therapeutics, 301*(2), 690−697.

Zeiler, M. D. (1999). Reversed schedule effects in closed and open economies. *Journal of the Experimental Analysis of Behavior, 71*(2), 171−186. https://doi.org/10.1901/jeab.1999.71-171

Introduction to operant demand

Derek D. Reed[1], Madison E. Graham[2] and Samuel F. Acuff[3]
[1]Institutes for Behavior Resources, Inc., Baltimore, MD, United States; [2]University of Kansas, Department of Applied Behavioral Science, Lawrence, KS, United States; [3]Recovery Research Institute, Center for Addiction Medicine, Massachusetts General Hospital and Harvard Medical School, Boston, MA, United States

Introduction to operant demand

Operant psychology is an approach to understanding and affecting behavior via consequences (Staddon & Cerutti, 2003). Operant behavioral economics is a subspecialization of operant psychology concerned with how the constraint of consequences impacts behavior (Reed et al., 2013). Operant demand—hereafter termed demand unless otherwise specified—is a specialized application of operant behavioral economics concerned with how an organism behaves to defend its consumption of reinforcers amid increased constraints on the reinforcing consequences (Hursh & Roma, 2016). In demand applications, these reinforcement constraints are typically operationalized by differing "costs" inherent in meeting the reinforcement contingency, such as financial prices, effort manipulations, time costs, or response requirements. Such costs are defined as "unit prices" wherein there is a ratio of costs to benefits (Hursh et al., 1988)—that is, the ratio of behavioral output to reinforcer magnitude (e.g., a response requirement of 20 button presses to return a reinforcer of $5 would equal a ratio of 20/5 or a unit price of 4.00).

This chapter provides a general description of demand and the factors modulating it. Later chapters will discuss the methods used to collect demand data, the analyses used to analyze these data, and the technical applications of these procedures and analyses in greater detail. Thus we aim to provide a layperson primer on the general concept of demand in operant behavioral economics; readers interested in this concept's scientific nuances and academic applications are encouraged to read the chapters specific to these topics.

We next provide an example of demand theory to which almost anyone can relate. Consider the following scenario: You wake up one morning and find that gasoline for your internal combustion car has increased from $3.48/gallon to $3.51/gallon. If you are like most gasoline consumers, this 0.80% increase is unlikely to spur any change in gasoline consumption. You spend the remainder of the week driving your gasoline-powered car just as you typically do, despite paying more—albeit a fraction more—per gallon. *You have defended* (kept your baseline rate of driving) *your consumption* (of fuel) *amid increasing constraints* ($/gallon). A week later, you awake to hear of political unrest in a major oil-producing region of the world, quadrupling the cost of crude oil and resulting in gasoline prices around $10/gallon. You cancel your forthcoming road trip, dust off your bicycle, and pedal to the nearest electric vehicle dealership to test drive a new car.

The example previously illustrates what happens when costs become too high to maintain the consummatory status quo (i.e., you can no longer maintain baseline rates of reinforcement consumption). While this example is somewhat extreme, it is essentially what happened during the fuel crisis of the early 1970s (Corbett, 2013). This example illustrates the central concept of demand: *The Law of Demand* (Samuelson, 1937). According to the Law of Demand, consumption of a commodity will decrease when prices increase above a tolerable threshold. What is "tolerable" to one organism may not be tolerable to another based on their histories consuming that commodity or experiencing those kinds of costs, or the context in which consumption must occur—these factors that modulate demand are explored later in this chapter. An economist interpreting the "tolerability" of costs for a given commodity would discuss its "utility": How the consumer's satisfaction with that commodity changes as a function of cost. A behavior analyst's interpretation, however, would view "tolerability" as an operationalized measure of relative reinforcer efficacy—that is, the value of that commodity as measured by operant response patterns across changing prices, amid open and closed economies, and interacting with motivating operations elicited by environmental variables.

Origins of operant demand

The concept of operant demand has been present in psychology since the early days of operant behaviorism. Indeed, one of Skinner's first papers (Skinner, 1930) examined the rate of rats' consumption of reinforcers (food pellets) as a function of context (time passing across an "eating period"). Like a demand analysis, Skinner was interested in consumption as a reinforcer. Moreover, Skinner's analysis included a power function equation and logarithmically transformed scales in his visual displays—commensurate with the classical approach to examining demand functions and curves (Shepherd, 1936).

Skinner did not, however, persist in his use of demand-like analyses, choosing to emphasize rates of behavior rather than consumption as the primary dependent variable (Skinner, 1938). Skinner also focused on "context" in terms of reinforcement schedules, eventually cataloging the robust predictability of response patterns associated with varying components of schedule types (Ferster & Skinner, 1957). Early efforts to describe relative reinforcer efficacy—that is, the reinforcing "power" or "value" of a consequence—relied on response rate, based on Skinner's emphasis on this dependent variable. However, Ferster and Skinner's accounts of schedule-induced responding clearly showed that minor manipulations to a schedule (e.g., moving from a fixed-ratio [FR] to a variable-ratio [VR]) dramatically impact the overall response rate. Thus the same reinforcer (often a food pellet or grain with nonhuman animals) would have differing measures of efficacy despite the putative commodity being the same, and even after controlling for global reinforcement rates (e.g., the same number of reinforcers delivered in 1 hour would produce different response patterns if programmed using fixed-vs. variable-ratio schedules).

As reinforcement schedule research evolved, so did their applications, leading to one of the most monumental discoveries in the analysis of reinforcement value and choice: Herrnstein's matching law (Herrnstein, 1961, 1970). The matching law states that relative reinforcement rates predict relative response rates, assuming that reinforcement effects are relative to differing response rates across two response alternatives, ceteris paribus. A benefit to Herrnstein's approach is quantitative descriptors and a formalized behavioral model in a mathematical function. Thus matching law analyses provide objective quantitative markers of how sensitive behavior is to reinforcement and whether a bias to response alternative exists irrespective of schedule values. The model's mathematical form enjoys all the benefits of quantitative modeling, but in a behavior-prediction enterprise (Critchfield & Reed, 2009), opening the door for more sophisticated translations to important research questions. The downside, however, is that matching analyses are most useful if using one kind of schedule (variable-interval [VI]) and comparing the same reinforcer across different response alternatives, using concurrent but independent VI schedules. Thus there is no objective way to compare relative reinforcer efficacy between *different* reinforcers—often the goal of a reinforcer assessment. Put simply, prototypical matching analyses can only tell you the relative reinforcing efficacy of apples relative to apples but cannot tell you that of apples relative to oranges.

While Skinner and Herrnstein were busy advancing basic research in the experimental analysis of behavior (EAB), other behavior analysts were beginning to put their EAB training to use in the burgeoning field of behavioral pharmacology. Specifically, behavior scientists such as Travis Thompson and Charles Schuster were translating EAB procedures to assess the pharmacological effects of drugs on operant responding, providing an early proxy to measuring drugs' relative reinforcement effects, which ultimately helped inform abuse liability testing (Thompson & Schuster, 1968). The most prominent method to emerge from this work was the use of progressive ratio (PR (Jarmolowicz & Lattal, 2010)) schedules to render a "breaking point" (Hodos, 1961) that quantified the highest PR response requirement that yielded reinforcement (i.e., the last response requirement met in the progression). The interpretation of the breakpoint metric is intuitive: A high breaking point means the organism emitted a higher number of responses to access one unit of the reinforcer. This breakpoint thereby became an attractive outcome variable for assessing the abuse potential of drugs (and even cited by the FDA as a recommended metric for drug developers; [FDA, 2017]), and this use generalized to more common reinforcer assessments in the broader field of behavior analysis (Roane, 2008).

Despite its intuitive advantages, the PR breakpoint remains an insufficient metric for two major reasons. First, breakpoints are dependent on the ratio requirements assessed—large step sizes between progressions impact the resolution of analysis and may provide highly inaccurate estimates of an organism's motivation to earn a reinforcer. For example, suppose you assess responding at ratio requirements progressing through the following values: FR1, FR10, FR100, and FR1000. An organism exhibiting a breakpoint of FR100 may have emitted 999 additional responses into the FR1000 requirement, falling just one response shy of the reinforcer. The researcher can only conclude, then, that the breakpoint is 100. Another organism may have stopped responding after the first response to the FR1000 requirement. Yet those two organisms have the same breakpoint of FR100. Second, the breakpoint value is unfaceted. That is, the breakpoint value tells you just that: the value at which responding last produced a reinforcer. This metric does not capture information regarding the organism's response across the potential parametric continuum of costs, the total number of responses emitted, the persistence of responding amid extinction, etc. This is due to the binary nature of the response outcome at each ratio requirement: That is, whether it (yes/no) resulted in reinforcement. For these limitations, PR breakpoints cannot provide a sufficient metric of relative reinforcer efficacy, particularly when different PR step sizes are used across different reinforcers or with differing doses/magnitudes of a reinforcer.

In 1980, Hursh published the first operant account of behavioral economics, attempting to address many of the aforementioned concerns regarding the operationalization of reinforcer value. His work translated ideas from microeconomics into the EAB, resulting in the proposal that behavioral scientists ought to conceptualize the economics of operant behavior—that is, how unit prices and economy types might influence operant responses (for a full historical account, see Chapter 1 of this volume). Hursh subsequently refined these ideas into a quantitative model of reinforcer demand from an operant perspective (Hursh et al., 1989). This model-based approach seemingly corrected for the many limitations associated with the previously described attempts at quantifying the "value" of a reinforcer. First, the model was conceptually linked to the broader interpretation of "consumer demand," which integrates the notion that the cost–benefit tradeoff (i.e., the unit price) of response requirements and a reinforcer should govern the behavioral outcomes. Second, the use of model-fitting permitted a robust nonlinear account of operant responding across the entire range of parametric values. That is, the demand function could interpolate ratio requirements not assessed within the range of experienced ratio requirements. Third, the demand curve is multifaceted, providing additional information into variables such as consumption when there is a minimal cost, total response output across the demand curve, and the degree to which an organism will defend its baseline consumption of reinforcement as unit prices increase (i.e., demand elasticity). The operant demand model has been subjected to intense reanalyses, reconceptualizations, and revisions since Hursh's first proposal in 1989. The discussion of this evolution is outside the scope of this chapter, so we invite readers to consult Chapter 1 of this volume, along with other papers on this matter (Gilroy et al., 2018, 2021; Hursh & Schwartz, 2022; Kaplan et al., 2019, 2021; Koffarnus et al., 2022).

Capturing "demand"

Chapters 5 and 6 provide much greater detail on the various ways demand assays are used in academic research and experimentation. This section, however, provides a primer on the most general approach to capturing the construct of operant "demand." As defined previously, operant demand is the act of an organism defending its consumption of a reinforcer amid increasing constraints. The operant interpretation of this definition is that an organism must respond proportionally to some schedule of reinforcement imposed on a reinforcer. Thus the "constraint" of the reinforcer is operationalized as some reinforcement schedule imposed on a target response. The economic view of this arrangement is that an organism transacts with its environment by spending its responses on attaining one unit of reinforcement, where the cost is the unit price scheduled by the reinforcement contingency. Higher costs translate to higher unit prices. Thus in its simplest form, a demand assay (i.e., a procedure used to quantify operant demand) must present a series of differing unit prices to an organism and record the number of responses emitted and the number of reinforcers "purchased" in the transactions.

Unit price

Unit price is a simple concept but warrants discussion. When introducing the unit price above, we defined it as a cost-benefit ratio of response requirements to reinforcer amount. The demand assay requires a range of unit prices to examine how behavior adjusts as the unit prices increase. The exact number of unit prices depends on one's research question. If the goal is a simple parametric comparison, at least 3 unit prices should be used—a very low unit price, a unit price that is commensurate with the natural contingencies in the environment, and a very high unit price that ought to suppress demand. If the goal is to fit a demand function, at least 6 unit price amounts should be used. No matter the number of unit prices assessed, there should always be a very low unit price that should be an easy response requirement to meet (e.g., FR1), a very high unit price that should reduce responding to near zero levels (e.g., FR 1000), with the median unit price set to a value commensurate with the natural contingencies in the organism's environment. Researchers typically use arithmetic (i.e., adding a constant number to each iteration of the unit price) or geometric (e.g., a set multiplicative pattern to the differences in unit prices, such as doubling each unit price or using exponential changes) approaches to programming the range of unit price values.

As a cost-benefit ratio, unit price values can be arranged by manipulating either the cost or the benefit component. Typically, researchers hold the amount of reinforcement ("benefit") constant (e.g., a fixed portion size of food) and gradually increase the response requirement ("cost") across the unit price sequence (Raslear et al., 1988). However, the reader should note that the same unit prices can be achieved by holding the response requirement fixed and varying the amount of reinforcement (Bentzley et al., 2013)—this approach is well-suited for within-session arrangements to quickly assess demand. Fig. 2.1 shows various ways to arrive at the same unit price values. In approaches A and B, the response requirement varies while the reinforcement amount is fixed to arrive at the unit price. In approaches B and C, the response requirement is fixed across unit prices, with varying reinforcement amounts to render the unit price. Looking at a unit price of 10 (middle column), we can see that each of the four approaches arrives at that unit price via differing manipulations of costs or benefits.

	Unit Price					Responses	Reinforcers
Approach	1	5	10	50	100		
A	1 response for 1 reinforcer	5 responses for 1 reinforcer	10 responses for 1 reinforcer	50 responses for 1 reinforcer	100 responses for 1 reinforcer	Varied	Fixed
B	10 responses for 10 reinforcers	50 responses for 10 reinforcers	100 responses for 10 reinforcers	500 responses for 10 reinforcers	1000 for 10 reinforcers		
C	1 response for 1 reinforcer	1 response for .20 reinforcer	1 response for .10 reinforcer	1 response for .02 reinforcer	1 response for .01 reinforcer	Fixed	Varied
D	100 responses per 100 reinforcers	100 responses per 20 reinforcers	100 responses per 10 reinforcers	100 responses per 2 reinforcers	100 responses per 1 reinforcer		

Figure 2.1 Unit price parity across differing manipulation approaches.

Research suggests that no matter how the unit price is manipulated, demand effects should be similar and sensitive to the unit prices rather than the approach used to arrive at the unit price sequences or manipulations to the cost or benefit aspects of its calculation (Degrandpre et al., 1993; Delmendo et al., 2009; Madden et al., 2000). However, it should be noted that most of the unit price research conducted to date—regardless of species—have either compared approaches similar to A and B in Fig. 2.1, or similar to approaches C and D in Fig. 2.1. There appears to be a gap in the literature comparing approaches such as A and C from Fig. 2.1.

Demand curves

As discussed in the introduction of this chapter, a substantial advantage of the demand approach to quantifying reinforcer efficacy is the multifaceted nature of this construct. Described plainly, operant demand is represented as consumption plotted as a function of unit price, where consumption: (A) begins at "baseline" levels as measured by a minimal price, then (B) remains high despite initial increases in unit price, then (C) declines rapidly until consumption ceases. Across this demand curve, one can also track the behavioral output of the organism. "Output" corresponds to the behavior expended by an organism to meet the unit price requirements to obtain reinforcement. Behavioral economists typically discuss output as "work" or "expenditure." Regardless of nomenclature, output is simply the number of responses made at each unit price level. This metric is typically quantified by simply multiplying the unit price by the number of reinforcers consumed at that price. For example, if we see an organism consumed 10 reinforcers at an FR20 response requirement, we know there were *at least* 200 responses (i.e., they met the FR20 response requirement at least 10 times, so 10 × 20 = 200), so 200 may conservatively be used as the output at FR20. Note the emphasis on the words "at least." There may be instances where an organism began emitting responses to meet an FR requirement but ceased responding before earning a reinforcer. The organism with the output = 200 at FR20 had at least 10 bouts of responding at that response requirement. That organism may have begun an 11th bout, emitting 19 responses toward the FR20 requirement before ceasing responding, resulting in no reinforcer earned. In this case, the organism's *actual* response output was 219, rather than 200. Readers should be aware of these distinctions when reading methods sections, and authors should be precise in describing their calculations. We again emphasize that "output" be interpreted conservatively, given these nuances.

Using the components A, B, and C in the preceding description of demand curves, we can note that at the A phase of the demand curve (see Fig. 2.2), there is minimal behavioral output, given there is essentially no cost. Again, Component A of the demand curve represents the amount of consumption when no constraint is imposed. This baseline level of behavior under optimal conditions represents the maximum demand *intensity*, similar to the notion of a "bliss" point for that organism (i.e., the amount of reinforcement consumed in the absence of any constraint [Staddon, 1979]). The intensity thereby serves as the anchor of comparison when unit price increases.

Component B of the demand curve (see Fig. 2.2) begins with the first unit price experienced following the intensity measurement. As unit prices increase, the behavioral output must increase proportionally to continue meeting the reinforcement contingencies to consume the reinforcer—that is, the organism must increase its output to defend consumption at its intensity level. At this juncture, we advise the reader to notice the use of logarithmic scaling on the x- (Unit Price) and y- (Consumption) axes. The use of logarithmic scales is advantageous to behavioral economists for two main reasons. First, unit price is defined as a ratio of costs and benefits (i.e., the

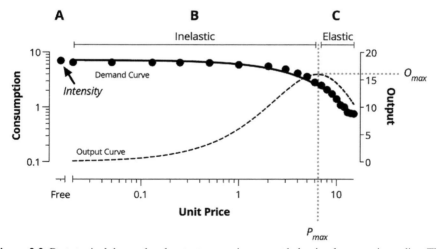

Figure 2.2 Prototypical demand and output curves in operant behavioral economic studies. The *x*-axis represents the unit price (note the log scale). The demand curve function is plotted as a solid line against the left *y*-axis (note the log scale), while the output curve function is plotted as a dashed line against the right *y*-axis. The vertical dotted line represents the point of P_{max}, while the horizontal dotted line represents O_{max} (see text). Across the top of the figure, Component A represents responding at intensity (price = free). Component B represents consumption at all prices up to P_{max} (i.e., inelastic demand), while component C represents consumption at all prices past P_{max} (i.e., elastic demand).

proportion of costs to benefits), so unit price changes across the axis are necessarily proportional. The demand curve seeks to measure whether proportional changes in unit price produce proportional changes in consumption as a way to standardize our interpretation of the demand function and cost-behavior relations. Logarithmic scaling permits proportional comparisons when absolute changes may be inappropriate. For example, increases in a response requirement from a unit price of 1−2 is an absolute change of 1, but is a 100% increase, doubling the cost. This change in cost may affect behavior more than increasing the unit price of 998−999—still an absolute change of 1, but which constitutes just a 0.1% proportional increase. The logarithmic scaling represents these differences in meaningful ways. Second, the "unit change" aspect of the logarithmic scale makes intuitive sense when understanding the impact of unit price on consumption. Does a 1 unit change in unit price produce a 1 unit change in consumption? The logarithmic scale puts unit price and consumption on equal axes, permitting an answer to that question. In economics, the rate of change in consumption across a change in price constitutes a metric known as *elasticity* (Gilroy et al., 2020). In logarithmic space, we can calculate the slope of consumption between 2 unit prices to derive a measure of elasticity.

As evidenced in Fig. 2.2, Component B corresponds with the range of *inelastic* demand. Leveraging the logarithmic scales, we can quantify inelastic demand as the range of unit prices featuring elasticity values > -1.00. In plain English, inelastic demand is when a one-unit increase in unit price is met with *less than* one-unit decrease in consumption. In addition, visualized in Fig. 2.2 is the rapid increase in response output as the unit prices increase. This output curve peaks at the end of the inelastic range, showing that maximum output is attained at the end of the inelastic range.

The inelastic range of demand (Component B of Fig. 2.2 demand curve) switches to *elastic* (Component C) at the peak level in the output curve. The level of maximum output is termed "Output$_{max}$" and abbreviated as O_{max} in behavioral economic parlance. The price associated with O_{max} is thereby the maximum price that maintains demand (i.e., the price at which demand shifts from inelastic to elastic) and is termed "Price$_{max}$" and abbreviated to P_{max}. In terms of elasticity, O_{max} and P_{max} occur when the elasticity exactly equals -1.00 in logarithmic space—perfect *unit elasticity*. Put in plain English, unit elasticity (the point of O_{max} and P_{max}) occurs when a 1 unit increase in unit price produces exactly 1 unit decrease in consumption. The P_{max} value thereby quantifies the exact price at which demand shifts from inelastic to elastic (Gilroy et al., 2019).

Component C of the demand curve in Fig. 2.2 is the area of elastic demand, wherein a 1 unit increase in unit price produces >1 unit decrease in consumption. Another way to interpret inelastic demand is the range where consumption is significantly price-sensitive. Thus as unit prices increase beyond P_{max}, responding significantly reduces, producing a rapid decline in the output curve as unit prices increase further.

The astute reader will no doubt notice that Fig. 2.2 contains a series of closed data points through which the solid black nonlinear demand curve is plotted. Decades of research confirm that operant demand curves are exponential-like in function. The practice of fitting nonlinear models to demand data is routine, but discussion of this

Validity of demand analyses

As mentioned earlier, the behavior analyst interprets demand as an operationalized measure of relative reinforcer efficacy, elsewhere referred to as the value of a commodity or of the organism's motivation to consume that commodity. In other words, responding in a demand paradigm is presumed to reflect how an organism may respond in the real world. Researchers have evaluated the validity of such paradigms by examining the correspondence between demand indices and indicators of real-world behavior. Though beyond the scope of this introductory chapter to comprehensively detail the research demonstrating a connection between demand and clinically relevant outcomes, demand for relevant commodities predicts a range of behavior, including alcohol and other drug use (Martínez-Loredo et al., 2021), problematic internet use (Acuff et al., 2018), ultraviolet indoor tanning (Reed et al., 2016), gambling (Weinstock et al., 2016), vaccine hesitancy (Hursh et al., 2020), and safe sex (Harsin et al., 2021).

Despite the intuitive nature of indices P_{max} and breakpoint, in practice, these indices have not been as consistently associated with real-world behavior. As discussed earlier, this may be in part due to the large unit price gaps that occur, which can increase noise and reduce granularity. Intensity, elasticity, and O_{max} have consistently demonstrated robust associations with clinically relevant outcomes (Kiselica et al., 2016; Strickland et al., 2020; Zvorsky et al., 2019). Analyses examining correspondence between demand and clinical outcomes typically use what is referred to as a "trait" task that attempts to generalize responding by setting parameters that (1) close the economy, and (2) emulate typical conditions in a respondent's environment (Kaplan et al., 2018). Thus, such analyses assume a degree of stability in both responding and the environment (Miller et al., 2023).

Factors that govern demand

Although responding to such tasks is often used to indicate a trait reinforcing the efficacy of a commodity for an organism, the task designs also inherently demonstrate within-subject variability across varying degrees of a constraint. In most studies, "constraints" are unidimensionally defined as the response requirement. In preclinical studies, cost is typically represented by something like pulling a lever. In clinical studies, cost may be represented by a similar physical action (clicking a button) or through monetary expenditures. Paradigms progressively increase the overall "cost" of the commodity, and response rates reduce as costs increase. However, constraints may be more broadly defined as any factor that modulates demand (Acuff & Murphy, 2021), and studies have shown that manipulating constraints beyond response requirements can impact responding. For example, studies demonstrate that those who smoke daily have a lower demand for cigarettes with reduced nicotine content compared to cigarettes with levels of nicotine consistent with cigarettes that are commercially available (Higgins et al., 2017).

Other studies have manipulated the context, instead of the characteristics of the reinforcer, in such a way that theoretically affects the value of the commodity. For example, studies have begun to examine how the presence of others impacts the demand for drugs. In general, these studies demonstrate the demand for either drugs or food in a social versus a solitary setting (Acuff, Soltis, & Murphy, 2020; Epstein et al., 1991). More broadly, a robust body of research (Acuff et al., 2024), particularly in the area of substance use, have begun to document similar effects (or in some cases, a lack thereof) when manipulating other constraints including opportunity cost (Ferguson et al., 2021; Gilbert et al., 2014; Teeters & Murphy, 2015), available income (Carroll, 1999; Koffarnus et al., 2015), purchasing hour windows (Kaplan et al., 2017), and pain (Moskal et al., 2018). Shifting constraints that influence behavioral responding in demand paradigms are theoretically impacting the value of the commodity. In the case of the modulation of alcohol demand by the social environment, for example, the social environment is somehow increasing the value of alcohol.

Demand paradigms often measure responding across shifting constraints for a single commodity in isolation, yet organisms frequently emit responding in the context of two or more commodities. Studies demonstrate that additional reinforcers in an environment can influence the output of another reinforcer. In a choice context with two or more reinforcers, reinforcement from option A may be either independent or dependent upon the schedule of reinforcement for option B; in other words, commodities available concurrently can either be independent or may operate as either substitutes or complements (Green & Freed, 1993; Hursh, 1984). Such relationships can be elucidated in paradigms that increase the price of one commodity while holding another commodity constant. These relationships, called cross-commodity relationships, are represented conceptually in Fig. 2.3.

Using the demand curve framework, the cross-commodity relations can be understood by examining how demand for one commodity changes in the presence of a concurrently available commodity. The typical approach to measuring cross-commodity relations is to measure baseline demand for Commodity A amid increasing prices (left column of Fig. 2.3). After a baseline demand curve is rendered, demand for Commodity A is again measured, but this time an organism can also emit responses toward a concurrently available Commodity B, which is present at a fixed price. That is, as prices for Commodity A increase, the price of Commodity B remains constant. What happens in these demand curves defines the kind of cross-commodity relation.

The top row of Fig. 2.3 depicts a substitution relation. Two commodities are substitutes when consumption of Commodity B increases as the price for choice A increases, and vis-a-versa (e.g., coffee and tea). A stronger effect is evidenced when the consumption of Commodity B nearly matches peak baseline consumption of Commodity A at the highest price of Commodity A in the cross-commodity arrangement (e.g., Brand X coffee and Brand Y coffee). A partial substitute (e.g., tea substituting for coffee) is evidenced in weaker effects. Notice also that the demand for Commodity

Introduction to operant demand

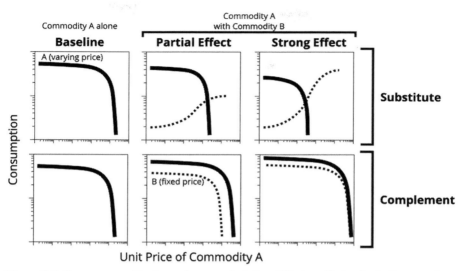

Figure 2.3 Cross-commodity demand curves depicting differing effects of substitutes and complements.

A is shifted downward (intensity is lower and elasticity is greater) in the presence of a substitute, and is most impacted when there is a better substitute available (i.e., the stronger effect in the right column of Fig. 2.3).

Two commodities are complements when consumption of Commodity B decreases as the price for choice A increases, and vis-a-versa (e.g., coffee and creamer). The demand rendering of a complementary relation is evidenced in the bottom row of Fig. 2.3. The presence of Commodity B *increases* demand for Commodity A above its baseline levels—that is, Commodity B interacts with Commodity A making Commodity A even more valuable to the organism in the cross-commodity arrangement. Finally, two commodities are independent when changes in the price of Commodity A have no influence on the price of Commodity B (e.g., coffee and ketchup).

In practice, cross-commodity demand models are useful for understanding decisions between using reinforcers and other, nonprogrammed reinforcer alternatives. For example, in substance use concerns, there may be some classes of activities that have complementary associations with alcohol use (spending time with friends and attending football games), other classes of activities that serve as substitutes for alcohol use (preparing for an exam or attending religious services), and other classes of activities that may have an independent association with alcohol use (grooming and watching TV).

More broadly, studies demonstrating modulating effects of the context or the introduction of additional reinforcers on demand for a commodity highlight the complexity of defining the experimental arrangements that help decide the outcome. All choice research, in addition to real-world decision making, occurs within the confines of experimental arrangements or constraints that reflect, in the language of behavioral economics, closed versus open economic systems, depending on the level of independence between the schedule of reinforcement and consumption of the commodity (Imam, 1993; Kearns, 2019). In a perfect closed economy, consumption of a commodity is a direct function of the organism's interaction with the schedule of reinforcement. In other words, receipt of the reward is only possible through engagement with the schedule of reinforcement, which thereby drives a stronger demand for that reward. Recall the run on products such as toilet paper and hand sanitizer during the peak of the COVID-19 pandemic. Retailers could not keep items in stock, substantially closing the economies for these goods. During that time, consumers paid substantially more to obtain these goods, commensurate with the closed economy interpretation (Reed et al., 2023).

An open economy may be defined as any of a variety of experimental arrangements that provide some degree of independence between daily consumption and a schedule of reinforcement for a single commodity. In such open economies, there is ample availability of reinforcers that substitute for one another, making demand more sensitive to pricing since cheaper substitutes can be pursued. Commensurate with Fig. 2.3, responding under open economies is typically more sensitive to price and thereby more elastic; such findings have been reported in the preclinical (Kearns, 2019), clinical (Greenwald & Hursh, 2006), and applied domains (Roane et al., 2005). Most research using the demand paradigms in humans has used closed economies or strictly defined open economies, such as cross-commodity purchase tasks (Gelino et al., 2024; Weinsztok et al., 2022). The effect of contexts, cross-commodity research, and the difference between open and closed economies represent critical research gaps with a small but growing body of literature.

Importantly, while studies demonstrating a stable association between trait-level indices of demand and clinically relevant outcomes are useful and important, studies demonstrating the malleability of behavioral responding under different manipulable conditions provide equally viable information that can be used to shape clinical outcomes. Such paradigms have been used to test the efficacy of interventions (Acuff, Amlung, et al., 2020), both pharmacological (Green & Ray, 2018; Murphy et al., 2017) and psychosocial (Stein et al., 2018), and may be useful for determining the efficacy of public health level decisions and interventions (Reed et al., 2022).

Conclusion

Operant demand curves provide a unique yet robust account of the effects of constraints on the responding to and consumption of reinforcers. While the study of operant demand emanates from preclinical work in behavioral pharmacology, this approach is now widely used across basic and applied pursuits in behavior analysis (Madden et al., 2024) and has demonstrated sufficient psychometric properties. This work can also be extended to examine cross-commodity interactions such as substitution or complementary relations. Chapters 3 and 4 will expand on operant demand methods for nonhuman and human research, respectively, while Chapters 5 and 6 will describe quantitative approaches to modeling demand and their practical applications, respectively.

References

Acuff, S. F., Amlung, M., Dennhardt, A. A., MacKillop, J., & Murphy, J. G. (2020). Experimental manipulations of behavioral economic demand for addictive commodities: A meta-analysis. *Addiction, 115*(5), 817–831. https://doi.org/10.1111/ADD.14865

Acuff, S. F., MacKillop, J., & Murphy, J. G. (2018). Applying behavioral economic theory to problematic Internet use: An initial investigation. *Psychology of Addictive Behaviors, 32*(7), 846–857. https://doi.org/10.1037/ADB0000404

Acuff, S. F., & Murphy, J. G. (2021). Commentary on Martínez-Loredo et al.: Where do we go from here? Increasing the clinical utility of alcohol purchase tasks by expanding our definition of constraint. *Addiction, 116*(10), 2651–2652. https://doi.org/10.1111/ADD.15481

Acuff, S. F., Oddo, L. E., Johansen, A. N., & Strickland, J. C. (2024). Contextual and psychosocial factors influencing drug reward in humans: The importance of non-drug reinforcement. *Pharmacology Biochemistry and Behavior, 241*, Article 173802. https://doi.org/10.1016/J.PBB.2024.173802

Acuff, S. F., Soltis, K. E., & Murphy, J. G. (2020). Using demand curves to quantify the reinforcing value of social and solitary drinking. *Alcoholism: Clinical and Experimental Research, 44*(7), 1497–1507. https://doi.org/10.1111/ACER.14382

Bentzley, B. S., Fender, K. M., & Aston-Jones, G. (2013). The behavioral economics of drug self-administration: A review and new analytical approach for within-session procedures. *Psychopharmacology, 226*(1), 113–125. https://doi.org/10.1007/s00213-012-2899-2

Carroll, M. E. (1999). Income alters the relative reinforcing effects of drug and nondrug reinforcers. *NBER Chapters*, 311–326. https://ideas.repec.org/h/nbr/nberch/11164.html.

Corbett, M. (2013). Oil shock of 1973–74. *Federal Reserve History, 22*. https://www.federalreservehistory.org/essays/oil-shock-of-1973-74.

Critchfield, T. S., & Reed, D. D. (2009). What are we doing when we translate from quantitative models? *The Behavior Analyst, 32*(2), 339–362.

Degrandpre, R. J., Bickel, W. K., Hughes, J. R., Layng, M. P., & Badger, G. (1993). Unit price as a useful metric in analyzing effects of reinforcer magnitude. *Journal of the Experimental Analysis of Behavior, 60*(3), 641–666. https://doi.org/10.1901/jeab.1993.60-641

Delmendo, X., Borrero, J. C., Beauchamp, K. L., & Francisco, M. T. (2009). Consumption and response output as a function of unit price: Manipulation of cost and benefit components. *Journal of Applied Behavior Analysis, 42*(3), 609–625. https://doi.org/10.1901/jaba.2009.42-609

Epstein, L. H., Smith, J. A., Vara, L. S., & Rodefer, J. S. (1991). Behavioral economic analysis of activity choice in obese children. *Health Psychology: Official Journal of the Division of Health Psychology, American Psychological Association, 10*(5), 311–316. https://doi.org/10.1037/0278-6133.10.5.311

FDA, Food & Drug Administration. (2017). Assessment of abuse potential of drugs guidance for industry. http://www.fda.gov/Drugs/GuidanceComplianceRegulatoryInformation/Guidances/default.htm.

Ferguson, E., Bush, N., Yurasek, A., & Boissoneault, J. (2021). The effect of next day responsibilities and an adaptive purchase task on cannabis demand. *Drug and Alcohol Dependence, 227*, Article 108919. https://doi.org/10.1016/J.DRUGALCDEP.2021.108919

Ferster, C. B., & Skinner, B. F. (1957). *Schedules of reinforcement*. East Norwalk, CT: Appleton-Century-Crofts. https://doi.org/10.1037/10627-000

Gelino, B. W., Graham, M. E., Strickland, J. C., Glatter, H. W., Hursh, S. R., & Reed, D. D. (2024). Using behavioral economics to optimize safer undergraduate late-night transportation. *Journal of Applied Behavior Analysis, 57*(1), 117–130. https://doi.org/10.1002/jaba.1029

Gilbert, L. J., Murphy, J. G., & Dennhardt, A. A. (2014). A behavioral economic analysis of the effect of next-day responsibilities on drinking. *Psychology of Addictive Behaviors, 28*(4), 1253–1258. https://doi.org/10.1037/A0038369

Gilroy, S. P., Kaplan, B. A., & Reed, D. D. (2020). Interpretation(s) of elasticity in operant demand. *Journal of the Experimental Analysis of Behavior, 114*(1), 106–115. https://doi.org/10.1002/jeab.610

Gilroy, S. P., Kaplan, B. A., Reed, D. D., Hantula, D. A., & Hursh, S. R. (2019). An exact solution for unit elasticity in the exponential model of operant demand. *Experimental and Clinical Psychopharmacology, 27*(6), 588–597. https://doi.org/10.1037/pha0000268

Gilroy, S. P., Kaplan, B. A., Reed, D. D., Koffarnus, M. N., & Hantula, D. A. (2018). The Demand Curve Analyzer: Behavioral economic software for applied research. *Journal of the Experimental Analysis of Behavior, 110*(3), 553–568. https://doi.org/10.1002/jeab.479

Gilroy, S. P., Kaplan, B. A., Schwartz, L. P., Reed, D. D., & Hursh, S. R. (2021). A zero-bounded model of operant demand. *Journal of the Experimental Analysis of Behavior, 115*(3), 729–746. https://doi.org/10.1002/jeab.679

Green, L., & Freed, D. E. (1993). The substitutability of reinforcers. *Journal of the Experimental Analysis of Behavior, 60*(1), 141–158. http://www.ncbi.nlm.nih.gov/pubmed/16812696.

Green, R. J., & Ray, L. A. (2018). Effects of varenicline on subjective craving and relative reinforcing value of cigarettes. *Drug and Alcohol Dependence, 188*, 53–59. https://doi.org/10.1016/J.DRUGALCDEP.2018.03.037

Greenwald, M. K., & Hursh, S. R. (2006). Behavioral economic analysis of opioid consumption in heroin-dependent individuals: Effects of unit price and pre-session drug supply. *Drug and Alcohol Dependence, 85*(1), 35–48. https://doi.org/10.1016/j.drugalcdep.2006.03.007

Harsin, J. D., Gelino, B. W., Strickland, J. C., Johnson, M. W., Berry, M. S., & Reed, D. D. (2021). Behavioral economics and safe sex: Examining condom use decisions from a reinforcer pathology framework. *Journal of the Experimental Analysis of Behavior, 116*(2), 149–165. https://doi.org/10.1002/jeab.706

Herrnstein, R. J. (1961). Relative and absolute strength of response as a function of frequency of reinforcement. *Journal of the Experimental Analysis of Behavior, 4*(3), 267–272. https://doi.org/10.1901/jeab.1961.4-267

Herrnstein, R. J. (1970). On the law of effect. *Journal of the Experimental Analysis of Behavior, 13*(2), 243–266. https://doi.org/10.1901/jeab.1970.13-243

Higgins, S. T., Heil, S. H., Sigmon, S. C., Tidey, J. W., Gaalema, D. E., Hughes, J. R., Stitzer, M. L., Durand, H., Bunn, J. Y., Priest, J. S., Arger, C. A., Miller, M. E., Bergeria, C. L., Davis, D. R., Streck, J. M., Reed, D. D., Skelly, J. M., & Tursi, L. (2017). Addiction potential of cigarettes with reduced nicotine content in populations with psychiatric disorders and other vulnerabilities to tobacco addiction. *JAMA Psychiatry, 74*(10), 1056–1064. https://doi.org/10.1001/JAMAPSYCHIATRY.2017.2355

Hodos, W. (1961). Progressive ratio as a measure of reward strength. *Science, 134*(3483), 943–944. http://www.ncbi.nlm.nih.gov/pubmed/13714876.

Hursh, S. R. (1984). Behavioral economics. *Journal of the Experimental Analysis of Behavior, 42*(3), 435−452. https://doi.org/10.1901/jeab.1984.42-435

Hursh, S. R., Raslear, T. G., Bauman, R., & Black, H. (1989). The quantitative analysis of economic behavior with laboratory animals. In K. G. Grunert, & F. Olander (Eds.), *Understanding economic behavior* (pp. 117−165). Kluwer Academic Publishers. https://doi.org/10.1007/978-94-009-2470-3. Theory and Decision Library.

Hursh, S. R., Raslear, T. G., Shurtleff, D., Bauman, R., & Simmons, L. (1988). A cost-benefit analysis of demand for food. *Journal of the Experimental Analysis of Behavior, 50*(3), 419−440. https://doi.org/10.1901/jeab.1988.50-419

Hursh, S. R., & Roma, P. G. (2016). Behavioral economics and the analysis of consumption and choice. *Managerial and Decision Economics, 37*(4−5), 224−238. https://doi.org/10.1002/mde.2724

Hursh, S. R., & Schwartz, L. P. (2022). A general model of demand and discounting. *Psychology of Addictive Behaviors, 37*(1), 37−56. https://doi.org/10.1037/ADB0000848

Hursh, S. R., Strickland, J. C., Schwartz, L. P., & Reed, D. D. (2020). Quantifying the impact of public perceptions on vaccine acceptance using behavioral economics. *Frontiers in Public Health, 8*, Article 608852. https://doi.org/10.3389/FPUBH.2020.608852/BIBTEX

Imam, A. A. (1993). Response-reinforcer independence and the economic continuum: A preliminary analysis. *Journal of the Experimental Analysis of Behavior, 59*(1), 231−243. http://www.ncbi.nlm.nih.gov/pubmed/16812684.

Jarmolowicz, D. P., & Lattal, K. A. (2010). On distinguishing progressively increasing response requirements for reinforcement. *Behaviour Analysis, 33*(1), 119−125. http://www.ncbi.nlm.nih.gov/pubmed/22479130.

Kaplan, B. A., Foster, R. N. S., Reed, D. D., Amlung, M., Murphy, J. G., & MacKillop, J. (2018). Understanding alcohol motivation using the alcohol purchase task: A methodological systematic review. *Drug and Alcohol Dependence, 191*, 117−140. https://doi.org/10.1016/j.drugalcdep.2018.06.029

Kaplan, B. A., Franck, C. T., McKee, K., Gilroy, S. P., & Koffarnus, M. N. (2021). Applying mixed-effects modeling to behavioral economic demand: An introduction. *Perspectives on Behavior Science, 44*(2), 333−358. https://doi.org/10.1007/S40614-021-00299-7

Kaplan, B. A., Gilroy, S. P., Reed, D. D., Koffarnus, M. N., & Hursh, S. R. (2019). The R package beezdemand: Behavioral economic easy demand. *Perspectives on Behavior Science, 42*(1), 163−180. https://doi.org/10.1007/s40614-018-00187-7

Kaplan, B. A., Reed, D. D., Murphy, J. G., Henley, A. J., DiGennaro Reed, F. D., Roma, P. G., & Hursh, S. R. (2017). Time constraints in the alcohol purchase task. *Experimental and Clinical Psychopharmacology, 25*(3), 186−197. https://doi.org/10.1037/pha0000110

Kearns, D. N. (2019). The effect of economy type on reinforcer value. *Behavioural Processes, 162*, 20−28. https://doi.org/10.1016/J.BEPROC.2019.01.008

Kiselica, A. M., Webber, T. A., & Bornovalova, M. A. (2016). Validity of the alcohol purchase task: A meta-analysis. *Addiction, 111*(5), 806−816. https://doi.org/10.1111/add.13254

Koffarnus, M. N., Kaplan, B. A., Franck, C. T., Rzeszutek, M. J., & Traxler, H. K. (2022). Behavioral economic demand modeling chronology, complexities, and considerations: Much ado about zeros. *Behavioural Processes, 199*, Article 104646. https://doi.org/10.1016/J.BEPROC.2022.104646

Koffarnus, M. N., Wilson, A. G., & Bickel, W. K. (2015). Effects of experimental income on demand for potentially real cigarettes. *Nicotine & Tobacco Research, 17*(3), 292−298. https://doi.org/10.1093/NTR/NTU139

Madden, G. J., Bickel, W. K., & Jacobs, E. A. (2000). Three predictions of the economic concept of unit price in a choice context. *Journal of the Experimental Analysis of Behavior, 73*(1), 45−64. https://doi.org/10.1901/jeab.2000.73-45

Madden, G. J., Reed, D. D., & Lerman, D. C. (2024). Behavioral economics for applied behavior analysts. In H. S. Roane, A. R. Craig, V. Saini, & J. Ringdahl (Eds.), *Behavior analysis: Translational Perspectives and clinical practice* (pp. 457−481). The Guilford Press. https://psycnet.apa.org/record/2024-33130-021.

Martínez-Loredo, V., González-Roz, A., Secades-Villa, R., Fernández-Hermida, J. R., & MacKillop, J. (2021). Concurrent validity of the alcohol purchase task for measuring the reinforcing efficacy of alcohol: An updated systematic review and meta-analysis. *Addiction, 116*(10), 2635−2650. https://doi.org/10.1111/ADD.15379

Miller, B. P., Reed, D. D., & Amlung, M. (2023). Reliability and validity of behavioral-economic measures: A review and synthesis of discounting and demand. *Journal of the Experimental Analysis of Behavior, 120*(2), 263−280. https://doi.org/10.1002/JEAB.860

Moskal, D., Maisto, S. A., De Vita, M., & Ditre, J. W. (2018). Effects of experimental pain induction on alcohol urge, intention to consume alcohol, and alcohol demand. *Experimental and Clinical Psychopharmacology, 26*(1), 65−76. https://doi.org/10.1037/PHA0000170

Murphy, C. M., MacKillop, J., Martin, R. A., Tidey, J. W., Colby, S. M., & Rohsenow, D. J. (2017). Effects of varenicline versus transdermal nicotine replacement therapy on cigarette demand on quit day in individuals with substance use disorders. *Psychopharmacology, 234*(16), 2443−2452. https://doi.org/10.1007/S00213-017-4635-4/METRICS

Raslear, T. G., Bauman, R. A., Hursh, S. R., Shurtleff, D., & Simmons, L. (1988). Rapid demand curves for behavioral economics. *Animal Learning & Behavior, 16*(3), 330−339. https://doi.org/10.3758/Bf03209085

Reed, D. D., Kaplan, B. A., Becirevic, A., Roma, P. G., & Hursh, S. R. (2016). Toward quantifying the abuse liability of ultraviolet tanning: A behavioral economic approach to tanning addiction. *Journal of the Experimental Analysis of Behavior, 106*(1), 93−106. https://doi.org/10.1002/JEAB.216

Reed, D. D., Kaplan, B. A., Oda, F. S., & Strickland, J. C. (2023). Extra-experimental scarcity impacts hypothetical operant demand: A natural SARS-CoV-2 eperiment. *Behavioural Processes, 205*. https://doi.org/10.1016/J.BEPROC.2022.104817

Reed, D. D., Niilleksela, C. R., & Kaplan, B. A. (2013). Behavioral economics: A tutorial for behavior analysis in practice. *Behavior Analysis in Practice, 6*(1), 34−54. http://search.proquest.com/docview/1400135232?accountid=14556.

Reed, D. D., Strickland, J. C., Gelino, B. W., Hursh, S. R., Jarmolowicz, D. P., Kaplan, B. A., & Amlung, M. (2022). Applied behavioral economics and public health policies: Historical precedence and translational promise. *Behavioural Processes, 198*, Article 104640. https://doi.org/10.1016/J.BEPROC.2022.104640

Roane, H. S. (2008). On the applied use of progressive-ratio schedules of reinforcement. *Journal of Applied Behavior Analysis, 41*(2), 155. https://doi.org/10.1901/JABA.2008.41-155

Roane, H. S., Call, N. A., & Falcomata, T. S. (2005). A preliminary analysis of adaptive responding under open and closed economies. *Journal of Applied Behavior Analysis, 38*(3), 335−348. https://doi.org/10.1901/JABA.2005.85-04

Samuelson, P. A. (1937). A note on measurement of utility. *The Review of Economic Studies, 4*(2), 155−161. https://doi.org/10.2307/2967612

Shepherd, G. (1936). Vertical and horizontal shifts in demand curves. *Econometrica, 4*(4), 361. https://doi.org/10.2307/1905614

Skinner, B. F. (1930). On the conditions of elicitation of certain eating reflexes. *Proceedings of the National Academy of Sciences of the United States of America, 16*(6), 433. https://doi.org/10.1073/PNAS.16.6.433

Skinner, B. F. (1938). *The behavior of organisms: An experimental analysis.* Oxford: Appleton-Century. http://search.proquest.com/docview/615079530?accountid=14556.

Staddon, J. E. (1979). Operant behavior as adaptation to constraint. *Journal of Experimental Psychology: General, 108*(1), 48−67. https://doi.org/10.1037/0096-3445.108.1.48

Staddon, J. E. R., & Cerutti, D. T. (2003). Operant conditioning. *Annual Review of Psychology, 54*, 115. https://doi.org/10.1146/ANNUREV.PSYCH.54.101601.145124

Stein, J. S., Tegge, A. N., Turner, J. K., & Bickel, W. K. (2018). Episodic future thinking reduces delay discounting and cigarette demand: An investigation of the good-subject effect. *Journal of Behavioral Medicine, 41*(2), 269−276. https://doi.org/10.1007/S10865-017-9908-1/METRICS

Strickland, J. C., Campbell, E. M., Lile, J. A., & Stoops, W. W. (2020). Utilizing the commodity purchase task to evaluate behavioral economic demand for illicit substances: A review and meta-analysis. *Addiction, 115*(3), 393−406. https://doi.org/10.1111/ADD.14792

Teeters, J. B., & Murphy, J. G. (2015). The behavioral economics of driving after drinking among college drinkers. *Alcoholism: Clinical and Experimental Research, 39*(5), 896−904. https://doi.org/10.1111/ACER.12695

Thompson, T., & Schuster, C. R. (1968). *Behavioral pharmacology.* Prentice-Hall. https://psycnet.apa.org/record/1968-35032-000.

Weinstock, J., Mulhauser, K., Oremus, E. G., & D'Agostino, A. R. (2016). Demand for gambling: Development and assessment of a gambling purchase task. *International Gambling Studies, 16*(2), 316−327. https://doi.org/10.1080/14459795.2016.1182570

Weinsztok, S. C., Reed, D. D., & Amlung, M. (2022). Substance-related cross-commodity purchase tasks: A systematic review. *Psychology of Addictive Behaviors, 37*(1), 72−86. https://doi.org/10.1037/ADB0000851

Zvorsky, I., Nighbor, T. D., Kurti, A. N., DeSarno, M., Naudé, G., Reed, D. D., & Higgins, S. T. (2019). Sensitivity of hypothetical purchase task indices when studying substance use: A systematic literature review. *Preventive Medicine, 128*, Article 105789. https://doi.org/10.1016/J.YPMED.2019.105789

Nonhuman research methods and procedures for studying operant demand

Cassandra D. Gipson[1], Christa L. Corley[1], Ashley Craig[1], Mikhail N. Koffarnus[2] and Joshua S. Beckmann[3]
[1]Department of Pharmacology and Nutritional Sciences, University of Kentucky, Lexington, KY, United States; [2]Department of Family and Community Medicine, University of Kentucky, Lexington, KY, United States; [3]Department of Psychology, University of Kentucky, Lexington, KY, United States

Introduction

Preclinical (nonhuman) animal models which incorporate methodologies that allow for evaluation of behavioral processes can be leveraged to determine the complex bidirectional relationship between the environment and behavior. This is important because, in the context of substance use, this relationship is critical in driving the use of drugs of dependence. The effects of preclinical reinforcement models can be applied to different types of reinforcers, including natural reinforcers (e.g., food and social interaction) and drug reinforcers (e.g., cocaine and opioids). The strength of this approach is that these analyses allow for a high level of translatability between human behavior and nonhuman animals and allow for more mechanistic dissections of behavior and underlying biology from a preclinical perspective. Throughout this chapter, we will first define schedules of reinforcement and highlight those commonly used to manipulate unit prices in preclinical demand studies. Next, we will describe the history of preclinical modeling of demand with a focus on natural reinforcers. We will then describe the implementation of demand models to nonhuman animal models of drugs of dependence and focus on mechanistic factors that may underlie demand processes for drugs as reinforcers.

Schedules of reinforcement

Behavior reinforcement schedules can be categorized into continuous reinforcement (CR) or intermittent reinforcement (IR), and more specifically, fixed ratio (FR), variable ratio (VR), fixed interval (FI), variable interval (VI), or progressive ratio (PR). CR reinforces behavior every time the behavior is present. On the other hand, IR only sometimes reinforces behavior when it is present. Here, we define the different schedules of reinforcement commonly used in preclinical studies, highlight those most commonly implemented in studies where unit price is manipulated, and describe generalized reinforcers often utilized in demand models.

Ratio reinforcement schedules

FR reinforcement schedules depend on a fixed number of responses emitted by the subject (Killeen et al., 2009). For example, an FR schedule of one would yield one reinforcer (e.g., one food pellet) for one response (e.g., one lever press). Killeen et al. define VR reinforcement as a schedule that does not have fixed intervals but rather varies between responses to achieve an average response rate (Killeen et al., 2009). VR reinforcement schedules utilize randomization based on probability for the delivery of reinforcement. In VR schedules, there is a predefined list of potential ratios which are chosen at random at the start of each trial. In another variation, random ratio (RR) schedules utilize a random chance of being rewarded in each trial. In humans, one example of RR reinforcement is gambling; the behavior is reinforced after a variable number of attempts (Scott, 2024). In the preclinical field, VR reinforcement schedules are often based on an average number of responses on an operandum such as a lever or a nose poke. PR reinforcement schedules differ from VR schedules in that they involve stepwise increases in the ratio of reinforcement between trials (Killeen et al., 2009; e.g., FR-1 increases to FR-2, then 4, then 8, and so on). An example of this schedule type would be described as increasing the ratio size by 5 after each response (Derenne, 2020). In this study, the initial ratio was five responses, which then increased to 10 responses, which then increased to 15, and so on until the animal reached 250 responses or stopped responding for 5 minutes (Derenne, 2020). FR schedules of reinforcement are regularly implemented in demand studies to evaluate unit price (described in more detail in the following section (DeFulio et al., 2014; McSweeney & Swindell, 1999)).

Interval reinforcement schedules

FI schedules reinforce behavior after a certain amount of time has elapsed. In FI schedules, the intervals stay the same from trial to trial. For example, in a study with pigeons using FI reinforcement schedules, subjects received food pellet reinforcement with intervals of 180 seconds (Dews, 1969). Similarly, VI schedules reinforce behavior through time intervals; however, in VI schedules, an array of intervals are utilized that average to the set interval time of the schedule (one example would be a VI-10 seconds schedule, which may incorporate 4, 6, 12, and 18 seconds intervals are randomly selected from the array average to 10). In a published example, Long Evans rats received reinforcement by intervals that were drawn randomly from an array with replacement and included time points of 1 minute, 2 minutes, 4 minutes, 8 minutes, 0.5 minutes, 0.25 minutes, and so on (Shull et al., 2004).

Generalized reinforcers: Using schedules of reinforcement to earn tokens

One commonly utilized reinforcer in demand models is tokens, which are generalized reinforcers that retain their reinforcing efficacy across a wide range of motivational conditions. One example of a generalized reinforcer is money, which retains its value across a range of contexts. Similarly, tokens can be used in preclinical models. In token economies, subjects receive a token on a schedule of reinforcement (e.g., a token-production FR schedule [DeFulio et al., 2014]) that functions as a conditioned reinforcer to elicit a certain behavior. Subjects often trade in their tokens for a primary reinforcer such as food or water (DeFulio et al., 2014; Ivy et al., 2017). Token economies can be utilized to determine how environmental contingencies (such as controlled environments including restricted budgets) impact demand elasticity for generalized reinforcers, which can be used to model generalized reinforcers in humans.

Preclinical models of demand using natural reinforcers: A historical perspective

Behavioral economics is a concept or field of study that evaluates the choice and value of a commodity. In a preclinical laboratory setting, behavioral economics combines operant behavior with microeconomics to quantify choice and value allowing for better evaluation of factors that influence consumption of reinforcers and can be leveraged to evaluate both natural reinforcers and drugs of dependence as reinforcers. Behavioral economics began in the 1970s and 1980s using nonhuman animal subjects. One of the first documented studies was conducted by Steven Hursh in 1978 with two rhesus monkeys (Hursh, 1978), which was an extension of earlier pigeon studies from the 1960s indicating that the absolute rate of an operant is directly proportional to the rate of presentation of a reinforcer for that operant (Catania & Reynolds, 1968; Herrnstein, 1961). In the 1978 paper, two experiments were conducted to determine preference for the different schedules as the rate of presentations was manipulated. In the first experiment, the daily intakes of food and water were not ensured. Next, two concurrent variable-interval schedules of food presentations and one of water presentations were implemented and the maximum rate of food presentations was varied. As the rate of presentations increased, the level of responding on the two food schedules decreased yet the level of responding on the water schedule increased. Here, the preference for the variable food schedule matched the proportion of reinforcers that were obtained from it. In the next experiment, the constant daily intakes of food and water were ensured, and the absolute response rates under the two food schedules combined and the water schedule no longer changed when the rate of food was increased during the sessions. Here, the author concluded that behavior emitted to obtain non-substitutable commodities (in this case, food and water) is controlled by the economic conditions of consumption of these commodities. Notably, food and water are natural reinforcers, and thus future work extends natural reinforcement to drugs of dependence (in Section Utilizing preclinical demand models for drugs of dependence).

In 1980, Hursh described four points regarding schedules of reinforcement, response rates, and choice, stating that (1) behavioral experiments are economic systems that can be influenced by whether the economy is open or closed; (2) reinforcers can be differentiated by their elasticity; (3) reinforcers can have different relationships with each other, for example, they can function as complements or substitutes; and (4) choice behavior cannot simply be accounted for by matching (Hursh, 1980). To the first point, there is an argument that open versus closed economies impact behavior. In an open economy, the daily consumption of food by an animal is not the result of the subject's interaction with the environment during a session but is rather arbitrarily controlled by the experimenter. By contrast, in a closed economy, no extra food is provided to an animal outside of a session. It was argued in this paper that the closed economy can be described in economic terms whereby the behavior of the consumer reflects an equilibrium between the supply of a commodity and the demand of the consumer for the commodity. It was further described that this equilibrium can be described by a demand curve, which is the amount of a commodity the subject will consume at a given price. Indeed, a closed economy is an ideal state whereby the daily consumption of a commodity is the result of the equilibrium between supply and demand, which cannot be applied in an open economy.

Manipulation of unit price (i.e., increases in the cost or unit price of the commodity) in a closed economy can result in a downward slope of the demand curve, although this does not extend to all reinforcers. For example, one study evaluated three rats that lived in operant chambers (24 hours/day) whereby one lever provided electrical brain stimulation, and the other lever provided food pellets on variable-interval schedules (Hursh & Natelson, 1981). As the schedule increased, the response rate for electrical brain stimulation was a decreasing function that resembled a food function in an open economy, rather than the response rate being an increasing function. It was argued that this was an example of the second point, that reinforcers are distinguishable by their elasticity of demand, which can be differentiated from their differences in value. Put more simply, not all commodities are equally important to the consumer, and some are more essential to a consumer than others. Applied to the shape of the demand curve, a curve that has a steep decay as price increases indicates that a small change in the price of the commodity has a large effect on the quantity of the commodity that is consumed.

To the third point above that reinforcers can have different relationships with each other, there is a large body of literature indicating that reinforcers can act as substitutes or complements (Green & Freed, 1993), or have no such relationship for each other and therefore function as independents (Green & Rachlin, 1991). For example, one study found that pigeons will exchange generalized tokens (tokens that are exchangeable for either food or water reinforcers, as described in section Schedules of Reinforcement above) in a closed token economy for more expensive reinforcers when token prices for the reinforcers (food = green tokens or water = red tokens) were manipulated (Andrade & Hackenberg, 2017). When food and water were freely available outside of the session (in an open economy), token production and exchange decreased significantly. In another example evaluating the economic substitutability of electric brain stimulation, food, and water, Green and Rachlin found that when concurrent variable-ratio schedules of electric brain stimulation, food and water reinforcement were paired in different combinations in rats, economic substitutability of electric brain stimulation for food and water reinforcers was found, although food and water did not serve as economic substitutes for each other (Green & Rachlin, 1991).

Demand curves are calculated as the measure of consumption as a function of unit price, whereby consumption of the commodity is then plotted against the unit price of the commodity. In the context of drugs as reinforcers (described in the section below), this is calculated as the response requirement to earn an infusion divided by the dose. The exponential demand equation (Hursh & Silberberg, 2008) shown below is often used whereby it is fit to the consumption-by-unit price data. The following equation fits demand data well and generally accounts for a large amount of the variance in consumption data from a variety of studies including from different species and procedures:

$$\log Q = \log Q_0 + k\left(e^{-\alpha \cdot Q_0 \cdot C} - 1\right)$$

Here, Q_0 represents the "intensity" of demand, whereas α represents "essential value" (Bickel et al., 1990). Higher α values produce steeper curves (more elastic) and represent decreased commodity value. k is a scalar constant. Demand curves are calculated by this equation, which are then analyzed using a best-fit exponential demand function (Hursh & Silberberg, 2008; Tucker et al., 2017). Parameters are further defined in Table 3.1.

Since the original Hursh and Silberberg equation was established and regularly implemented in demand studies, issues arose that required modification of the original equation. Specifically, the equation above requires log-transformation of consumption values (as $\log Q$ above), which cannot be done with zero value (in other words, if an animal consumes zero drugs at a specific price, the consumption value would be zero and this could not be log transformed). As described in depth in Koffarnus et al. (2015), there are typically three alternative approaches implemented by researchers who collect datasets that contain zero values. The first approach is to omit the zero values from analysis, and only fit the curve to nonzero values. The drawback of this approach is that it omits legitimate data points from the curves. The second approach is to replace the zero values with small nonzero values (e.g., 0.1 or 0.01 [Galuska et al., 2011]). However, replacing these values can have an outsized influence on curve fits, as described in detail by Koffarnus and colleagues (Koffarnus et al., 2015). Finally, Koffarnus and colleagues describe restricting the analysis to group models that contain a large number of zero values. However, group models rely on mean data, and thus do not allow for between-subject variability in the data. To address

Table 3.1 Parameters in calculating demand curves.

Parameter	Definition
Q_0	Maximum consumption at zero price
k	Scalar constant
α	Rate of change of consumption with increases in unit price
c	Price

this critical issue, Koffarnus and colleagues tested a new, modified version of the exponential equation; termed the "exponentiated equation," originally mentioned in Yu et al. (2014) but validated in Koffarnus et al. (2015):

$$Q = Q_0 * 10k\left(e^{-\alpha \cdot Q_0 \cdot C} - 1\right)$$

This equation allows for the inclusion of zero values in demand functions and better fits the data as it does not require modification of zero values from individual subjects. This equation has been utilized at the clinical level for cannabis demand (Schultz et al., 2023) as well as e-cigarette demand (Rzeszutek et al., 2023), and has been utilized in combination with brain reactivity measures in the context of cocaine demand (Webber et al., 2023), among other areas. Preclinically, this equation has been utilized in the context of demand data from operant studies evaluating drugs of dependence as reinforcers, including nicotine (Powell et al., 2019) and cocaine (Powell, Namba, et al., 2020). In the following sections, we will describe the implementation of economic demand of drugs as reinforcers in preclinical models and provide examples of its application.

Utilizing preclinical demand models for drugs of dependence

Preclinical studies of drug self-administration (SA) have important value for the field as they are highly rigorous, controlled, can be conducted quickly, and are generalizable to humans. Behavioral economic paradigms model addiction-like behaviors at both the clinical (Bickel & Madden, 1999; Smith et al., 2017) and preclinical (Grebenstein et al., 2013, 2015) levels of analysis, illustrating translational value (Bentzley et al., 2014; Cox et al., 2017; Tucker et al., 2017). Further, demand modeling has been utilized preclinically across drug classes, including nicotine (Powell, Beckmann, et al., 2020; Powell et al., 2019), cocaine (Yates et al., 2019), opioids (Mattox & Carroll, 1996), among others across a number of nonhuman species, including nonhuman primates (Cosgrove & Carroll, 2003; Mattox et al., 1997) and rodents (Bentzley et al., 2013, 2014; Christensen, Silberberg, Hursh, Huntsberry, & Riley, 2008). This approach involves varying price (or effort) to generate demand curves to allow estimations of free consumption (Q_0), demand elasticity (α; sensitivity of demand to changes in price), and motivation for drug and nondrug reinforcers (Christensen, Silberberg, Hursh, Huntsberry, & Riley, 2008; Christensen, Silberberg, Hursh, Roma, & Riley, 2008; Hursh, 1980; Hursh & Silberberg, 2008). Importantly, α and Q_0 predict addiction-related behavior in humans and animals, and therefore, may represent an effective translational model to inform and guide nicotine and tobacco regulatory policy (Fowler et al., 2018; Hatsukami et al., 2010; Powell, Beckmann, et al., 2020) as well as other clinical applications. Generating demand curves traditionally requires individuals to stabilize responding at multiple prices (including the number of lever presses required to receive a reinforcer and reinforcer magnitude (Bickel et al.,

1990) over multiple weeks of testing (Oleson & Roberts, 2009), limiting the ability of the model to assess neurobiological and behavioral mechanisms involved in demand. Consequently, a within-session threshold procedure was developed to assess cocaine and methamphetamine SA (Bentzley et al., 2014; Cox et al., 2017; Oleson & Roberts, 2012), and we extended this to nicotine by validating both within- and between-session threshold procedures in nicotine SA (Powell et al., 2019). In the between-session threshold procedure that we developed, rats received descending doses of nicotine in daily 2-hour sessions following a nicotine SA acquisition phase. In other words, the dose of nicotine delivered was decreased in each subsequent session, which reflected an increase in the unit price of nicotine each day. The training dose (0.06 mg/kg/infusion) served as the highest nicotine dose, and the unit price of this dose was set to 1. The next day, the nicotine dose was halved to 0.03 mg/kg/infusion, and thus the unit price of this dose was calculated to be 2. A total of nine doses were tested, which allowed for demand curves to be generated as consumption as a function of unit price. As mentioned previously, the between-session threshold procedure (which is sensitive to biological sex and factors of cross-price elasticity such as environmental enrichment; see Powell et al., 2019) has limitations with respect to neuroscience research efforts as manipulating neurobiological mechanisms often requires same-day testing procedures. Thus we developed the within-session threshold procedure which utilizes the same unit prices of nicotine as the between-session procedure; however, price is manipulated in 10-minute blocks within the same session. This procedure allows for same-day evaluations of all unit prices of nicotine (also see Powell et al., 2019). For additional methodological details on the within- and between-session threshold procedures, please see our prior publications (Maher et al., 2021; Powell et al., 2019, 2020).

An example of demand data derived from our between-session intravenous nicotine threshold procedure in rats (see Fig. 3.1A for a timeline) is shown in Fig. 3.1B.

Here, rats were injected with heroin (3 mg/kg, subcutaneous injections) or saline (subcutaneous injections) prior to daily 2-hour operant sessions during 10 sessions of acquisition of intravenous 0.06 mg/kg/infusion nicotine SA. Acquisition criteria typically consist of a threshold amount of drug that an animal self-administers for a specified amount of time (e.g., above 1 mg/kg for three consecutive sessions) to reflect stable intake, as well as a lever press criterion above a threshold for active versus inactive lever presses. One response on a lever (FR-1) resulted in the delivery of one nicotine infusion (0.1 mL across 5.9 seconds). Following acquisition, heroin and saline injections ceased and nicotine demand was evaluated during heroin withdrawal, as opioid withdrawal is associated with increased nicotine use at the clinical level (Mannelli et al., 2013); it should be noted that rats in this experiment did not receive naloxone injections to precipitate withdrawal). The demand phase of the experiment included nine daily 2-hour sessions of descending nicotine doses whereby the dose decreased in each subsequent session. Unit price was calculated with the highest dose being set to a unit price of 1, and the unit price of each subsequent lower dose was calculated by dividing 0.06 by that dose. Thus unit price increased as nicotine dose decreased (Table 3.2). Of note, unit price can either be manipulated through altering the drug dose or changing the response requirement.

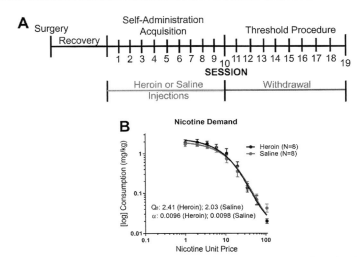

Figure 3.1 (A) Experimental timeline. (B) Heroin withdrawal does not alter nicotine demand parameters (α or Q_0) in a rat between-session threshold procedure. All procedures were approved by the IACUC at Arizona State University (Gipson protocol #18−1642R).

Table 3.2 Calculation of unit price as a function of drug dose during self-administration.

Nicotine dose (mg/kg/infusion)	Infusion length (s)	Unit price
0.06	6	1
0.03	3	2
0.017	1.7	3.53
0.01	1	6
0.0056	0.56	10.71
0.003	0.3	20
0.0017	0.17	35.29
0.001	0.1	60
0.00056	0.056	107.14

The unit price was calculated with the highest dose being set to 1, and each subsequent dose calculated as 0.06 divided by that lower dose. Dose was manipulated by reducing the time of the nicotine infusion (in seconds).

Pretreatments with heroin or saline ceased during the demand phase, and thus rats underwent experimenter-imposed withdrawal from heroin during nicotine demand manipulations. Using nonlinear mixed effect modeling (NLME), there were no differences in Q_0 or α as a function of heroin withdrawal; however, these data demonstrate that controlled manipulations can be conducted in preclinical rodent models of drug demand. As mentioned earlier, we have also validated this procedure with a within-session threshold procedure, using 10-minute blocks at each unit price as manipulations of unit price can be done either between sessions or within a session (Weatherly et al., 2004). Literature indicates that within-session changes in response rates in pigeons and rats responding to FR schedules of reinforcement can be implemented and should involve short sessions (McSweeney & Swindell, 1999). The benefit of this approach is that it allows for neurobiological manipulations prior to or during the session where all unit prices are presented to the subject.

As mentioned in the previous section, reinforcers can have substitution, complementary, or independent relationships with each other, and this can be extended to drugs as reinforcers. One example of a complementary relationship between drug and nondrug reinforcers was demonstrated in a rat choice study, where cocaine and heroin were evaluated for their economic relationship with two nondrug reinforcers, a negative reinforcer of timeout from avoidance (TOA; i.e., a lever press resulted in a period of safety from footshock), and also saccharin (Beasley et al., 2023). In the first experiment, rats chose between either cocaine and TOA or heroin and TOA. When the relative prices of the reinforcers were manipulated, rats in the cocaine condition allocated responding to the more expensive option and therefore consumed a relatively proportional intake of cocaine and TOA. These results suggest a complementary relationship between cocaine and TOA. In the heroin condition, rats allocated responses to heroin as it became cheaper and away from TOA, suggesting that heroin substituted for safety from footshock. When saccharin was tested as the nondrug reinforcer, heroin and saccharin demonstrated a complementary relationship. The results from this clever study demonstrate that drug-taking behavior at the clinical level likely depends on the type of drug and also other contexts such as the type of nondrug reinforcer(s) available. These results also underscore the importance of evaluations of drugs of dependence with nondrug alternative reinforcers incorporated into experimental designs.

Preclinical studies have evaluated how factors such as the level of enrichment provided during development can impact drug demand elasticity and intensity, and this has been evaluated with both cocaine (Yates et al., 2019) and nicotine (Powell et al., 2019). Generally, environmental enrichment reduces drug SA in rat models as compared to rats raised in an isolated environment (Alvers et al., 2012; Bardo et al., 2001; Gipson et al., 2011). These environments are manipulated such that enriched rats receive novel toys that are replaced regularly, live in larger cages, and are raised with other rats that are the same age (usually from postnatal day 21 until adulthood, and often continuing into experimentation). Isolated rats, however, live in small cages and are individually housed throughout experimentation. In the Yates study, enriched rats were less willing to respond to cocaine as the price increased as compared to isolated rats (Yates et al., 2019), consistent with the literature indicating that environmental enrichment protects against drug SA. Similarly, rats raised in an enriched environment self-administer less nicotine during acquisition and display reductions in nicotine demand intensity (Powell et al., 2019). Together, these studies demonstrate the additional information that can be gleaned from preclinical procedures that incorporate evaluations of more than one dose (price) of a drug commodity, and that these procedures are sensitive to factors such as environmental enrichment.

Additional examples of the utility of preclinical demand models come from prior research from our lab evaluating the contributions of ovarian and contraceptive hormones on nicotine demand. Using between and within-session threshold procedures, we have previously shown that steroid hormones significantly shift demand intensity (Q_0). In the first study, we investigated the effects of estrogens, either natural or synthetic, on nicotine SA, demand, and reinstatement (Maher et al., 2021). In this study, demand intensity was highest in ovary-intact rats (a sham group) when compared to an ovariectomized group given vehicle injections (sesame oil). Two groups were supplemented daily with either the contraceptive synthetic estrogen, ethinyl estradiol (EE), or exogenous injections of the endogenous estrogen, 17β-estradiol (E2); both groups showed increased demand intensity compared to vehicle, but these estrogen-supplemented groups did not reach ovary-intact levels of nicotine demand intensity. Importantly, these results were specific because there was no effect on demand elasticity (α), demonstrating that hormone manipulations only impacted one parameter. Finally, the lever press discriminability remained unaffected by changes in the unit price of nicotine, demonstrating that although the hormone manipulations reduced nicotine consumption, they did not impair learning the operant task.

Another study from our lab investigated the effects of synthetic contraceptive hormone treatments (EE with or without the synthetic progestin, levonorgestrel, or LEVO) on the co-use of ethanol (EtOH) and nicotine in ovary-intact female rats (Maher et al., 2023). This study provides evidence that EtOH and nicotine can act as substitute reinforcers for each other, which has also been supported by other studies (Chandler et al., 2020). In the Maher study, when an alternative reinforcer (nicotine) was introduced in a sequential session during the day (following morning EtOH drinking in the dark, or DID), EtOH consumption decreased. In addition, in a water control group that self-administered nicotine, when nicotine sessions were no longer available and the rats were presented with a two-bottle preference test (EtOH vs. water), these rats strongly preferred EtOH despite having no experience with drinking it. Importantly, the preclinical EtOH field has struggled with outbred rat strains drinking significant amounts of and/or preferring EtOH without extended training or special breeding schemes (e.g., EtOH-preferring rat strains (Dyr & Kostowski, 2000);), and thus our results underscore a potentially important relationship between EtOH and other drug reinforcers such as nicotine, which may have translational value to individuals who drink alcohol and also smoke nicotine-containing products. We further found that rats treated with LEVO or EE + LEVO did not show a decrease in nicotine or EtOH consumption when the drugs were co-used, demonstrating that supplementation with synthetic contraceptive hormone combinations occludes the ability of these reinforcers to act as economic substitutes. Our study further evaluated nicotine demand as a function of synthetic hormone treatment using a within-session threshold procedure in rats who either also drank EtOH or water during morning DID sessions. While our results were preliminary, NLME revealed a significant effect of day on Q_0 and α, with increasing trends in Q_0 and decreasing trends in α. These results reflect greater nicotine valuation across days. Further, there was a significant main effect of EtOH drinking experience and hormone on α, demonstrating that synthetic hormone manipulations may impact demand elasticity in an ovary-intact system. Together, these two studies show that threshold procedures can be implemented to evaluate the relationships between different reinforcers and are sensitive to translationally relevant biological manipulations such as synthetic hormones.

Neurobiological mechanisms of operant demand: Implications for drugs of dependence

The decades of research utilizing operant processes to understand reinforcement laid a foundation upon which drugs were then defined as reinforcers (Meisch, 1987). Since those early studies, neuroscience techniques have evolved significantly and that has allowed us to better understand neurobiological mechanisms underlying drugs of dependence and how they function as reinforcers. Drugs of dependence alter neurophysiology both through direct pharmacological action (e.g., nicotine is an agonist at nicotinic acetylcholine receptors, or nAChRs; Marks et al., 1983), and also through constitutive changes in neural circuits and cellular physiology following extended use (Russo et al., 2010). Decades ago, it was found that electrical brain stimulation could serve as a reinforcer and could substitute for water. Indeed, septal stimulation did not increase water intake; however, it was preferred to water as a reinforcer until an animal was sufficiently dehydrated (Falk, 1961). These results implicate neural systems in behavior and underscore the role of neurobiological processes in reinforcement. However, an overwhelming majority of studies evaluating the neurobiology of drugs of dependence typically focus on drugs in isolation, without alternative reinforcers present. It is posited that substance use disorder is in part due to allocation of choice toward a drug reinforcer relative to nondrug alternatives (Heyman, 2013), thus models of choice continue to be incorporated in neuroscience studies as the field moves forward.

A growing body of literature has evaluated drug versus nondrug choice and has found that when these alternative reinforcers are available concurrently, preference is determined by relative differences in the dimensions of the reinforcers (e.g., magnitude, price, delay to reinforcement, and frequency of reinforcement consistent with generalized matching [Anderson et al., 2002; Grace, 1994]). Indeed, choice for a drug alternative over a nondrug alternative can be manipulated by manipulating the price (dose) of the drug, and this has been repeatedly demonstrated (Anderson et al., 2002; Beckmann et al., 2019; Panlilio et al., 2017). One issue with digging for neurobiological mechanisms underlying substance use disorders is that the choice between different reinforcers (including drug vs. nondrug reinforcers) can be manipulated by varying unit prices of the commodity (Chow et al., 2022). For decades, a prevailing narrative has been that drugs "rewire" or "hijack" the brain (Dong & Nestler, 2014; Neill, 2022). In contrast to this description of substance use disorder, individuals who have been clinically diagnosed with substance use disorder often "age out" of problematic substance use (Heyman, 2013), and the ability to shift choice to nondrug alternatives directly undermines the idea that compulsive drug use reflects a permanent shift in neurobiology, which causes this behavioral change (Strickland et al., 2022). In addition, contingency management, a behavioral therapy that reinforces individuals with substance use disorder for positive behavioral changes (e.g., negative urine samples) is a highly effective treatment (Petry, 2011). The idea that abstinence can be achieved through behavioral therapy contradicts that the use of drugs induces stable brain changes causing chronic compulsion in the context of drugs of dependence. There are instances in the preclinical literature in which neurobiological changes in the reward pathway after drug SA (specifically, the nucleus accumbens) are transient (see one such example in (Gipson et al., 2013) related to transient changes in glutamate plasticity during a cocaine reinstatement task). However, a large majority of studies in the neuroscience field are designed to identify novel neural substrates with the goal of developing novel pharmacotherapeutics to treat substance use, and the overwhelming majority of these neurobiological studies do not incorporate evaluations of price or choice for the drug over nondrug alternatives (including the Gipson et al., 2013 example study earlier). Thus it is not clear if the vast amount of information on the neuroscience of drugs of dependence translates to the clinical condition, or if the drug-associated neurobiological changes found in one context would persist if the context were altered.

Although little work has been done evaluating neurobiology in the context of drug choice or demand, there has been some literature in this domain. For example, one study evaluated ventral tegmental area (VTA) orexin-1 receptor (Ox1R) involvement in cocaine demand using a within-session demand procedure (Pantazis et al., 2021). In this study, rats were trained to lever press for sucrose pellets or cocaine, where cues (light and tone) were paired with the delivery of the sucrose pellet reinforcer in one condition, and in another condition, no cues were delivered. For the sucrose experiment, rats began on an FR-1 schedule of reinforcement, which was then increased every 3 days to FR-3, FR-10, FR-32, and FR-100. Following acquisition, rats underwent a behavioral economics phase in which the order of the FR schedules was reversed (in a descending FR order), with 10-minute periods for each unit price (FR). Intra-VTA microinfusions of artificial cerebral spinal fluid (aCSF) or the Ox1R antagonist, SB-334867, occurred prior to demand sessions. For the cocaine experiment, rats were trained to self-administer cocaine on a FR-1 schedule followed by a demand phase where the duration of the infusion of cocaine decreased every 10 minutes (383.5, 215.6, 121.3, 68.2, 38.3, 21.6, 12.1, 6.8, 3.8, 2.2, and 1.2 ug per infusion). The results indicate that intra-VTA SB injections increased the percent baseline α value, with no impact on Q_0 only in rats trained with conditioned cues. This was interpreted as indicating that SB injections in the VTA "lowered motivation for cocaine paired with discrete cues." It is important to note that this paper did not utilize NLME to evaluate group differences in α or Q_0. Rather, two-way repeated measures or mixed-effects ANOVAs were utilized here, which present statistical limitations (Kaplan et al., 2021). In a paper by Young and colleagues, a series of Monte Carlo simulations unequivocally demonstrate that both LME and NLME are vastly superior to ANOVA (Young et al., 2009). Thus studies incorporating demand should implement these superior statistical analyses to better interpret experimental interventions such as neurobiological manipulations on demand parameters.

In addition, another study evaluated the effect of corticotropin-releasing factor (CRF), an endogenous stress neuropeptide that mediates endocrine, physiological, and behavioral responses to stress, in the relationship between stress and drug dependence using a within-session behavioral paradigm (Leonard et al., 2017). In this study, CRF was microinjected into the VTA prior to sessions. This was utilized as an artificial stress model and was compared to animals that were subjected to social defeat stress, which is a model that exposes subjects to an aggressive encounter. The goal of this study was to evaluate how the simulation of CRF release into the VTA, which occurs during intermittent social defeat stress, impacts economic demand for cocaine. Here, the subjects were placed in a cage with another rat. First, the rats were placed in a protective wire mesh cage for the instigation phase. After 10 minutes they were placed directly into the cage and an aggressive encounter was allowed to ensue with the other rat. The fight was stopped by researchers after 6 seconds of supine posture of the intruder rat. Both animals then self-administered intravenous cocaine. Animals began in an acquisition phase of FR-1 where one lever press resulted in one intravenous infusion of cocaine (0.75 mg/kg) and was also accompanied by light and sound cues and followed by a 30-second timeout period. Animals moved out of the acquisition phase once they reached 15 infusions or 5 hours, whichever came first, for two consecutive days. The next phase slowly increased to an FR-5 where five lever presses resulted in one intravenous cocaine infusion. Animals self-administered cocaine on an FR-5 reinforcement schedule for a minimum of five sessions. After these sessions, animals were given a 24-hour binge period where they had unlimited access to cocaine infusions (FR-5, 0.3 mg/kg/infusion). The total number of lever presses for these 24 hours was then recorded, and results showed that rats exposed to intra-VTA CRF injections consumed more cocaine during the 24-hour binge period than CRF control rats. Analyses also indicated the amount of CRF microinjected did not affect intake. Although animals exposed to social defeat stress also had elevated levels of cocaine consumption and a similar overall number of lever presses, the 24-hour binge period indicated different patterns of consumption. CRF animals typically stopped responding 18–20 hours into the 24-hour period while social defeat animals tended to consume for the entire 24 hours. Results indicate that rats exposed to either social defeat or intra-VTA CRF microinfusions have protracted yet distinct impacts on cocaine consumption across a 24-hour binge period. Individual demand curves were produced for each rat with stable performance, and no correlations were found between Q_0 and α. These results support the assumption that Q_0 and α represent independent and dissociable components of demand. Importantly, few preclinical studies have evaluated the relationship between these two parameters, especially in the context of neurobiological manipulations. At the group level, intra-VTA-CRF microinjections were sufficient to change demand elasticity but not intensity for cocaine through selectively reducing α but having no effect on Q_0, respectively. These results indicate that intra-VTA CRF induced a less steep consumption curve as cocaine unit price was increased, and thus increased commodity value. Contrary to the original hypothesis, however, social defeat had no effect on either parameter. These results suggest that infusions of CFR have a prolonged effect on demand elasticity for cocaine, whereas social defeat does not. Together, these studies demonstrate that preclinical evaluations of neurobiological mechanisms can be combined with threshold and choice procedures in the context of drugs of dependence, allowing for a better mechanistic understanding of drug demand and drug choice for better translatability beyond preclinical models.

Conclusions

Here we provide a historical context of preclinical economic demand analysis of operant behavior in the context of natural reinforcers and have extended this to drug reinforcers. We further provide evidence that threshold procedures in the context of drugs of dependence are sensitive to biological, environmental, and translationally relevant manipulations. As mentioned earlier, the majority of preclinical animal studies in the addiction field have incorporated schedules of reinforcement in operant tasks utilizing one unit price of a drug of dependence and evaluated neurobiology utilizing the same experimental parameters from study to study. Here we provide examples of studies that have incorporated economic demand analyses, which have shown translational utility between human behavior and nonhuman animals. Incorporating experimental methodologies that evaluate possible contexts where effects occur and boundary conditions of these effects defined by contexts where they do not (Gipson & Beckmann, 2022), such as in evaluations of unit price, allows for clarity regarding mechanisms of behavior and underlying biology. Although the exemplar studies cited previously have incorporated techniques that allow for biological manipulations with demand procedures, a large majority of neuroscience studies that incorporate behavior have not utilized these more complex behavioral approaches. Recent advancements in neuroscience techniques allow for granular evaluations of neurobiology; however, these techniques are often difficult to implement, have a high level of attrition, and can be laborious to successfully execute. Regardless, future studies should incorporate more complex behavioral tasks with advanced neuroscience techniques to better understand neurobiological mechanisms of behavior as this relates to the use of drugs of dependence.

References

Alvers, K. M., Marusich, J. A., Gipson, C. D., Beckmann, J. S., & Bardo, M. T. (2012). Environmental enrichment during development decreases intravenous self-administration of methylphenidate at low unit doses in rats. *Behavioural Pharmacology, 23*(7), 650–657. https://doi.org/10.1097/FBP.0b013e3283584765

Anderson, K. G., Velkey, A. J., & Woolverton, W. L. (2002). The generalized matching law as a predictor of choice between cocaine and food in rhesus monkeys. *Psychopharmacology, 163*(3–4), 319–326. https://doi.org/10.1007/s00213-002-1012-7

Andrade, L. F., & Hackenberg, T. D. (2017). Substitution effects in a generalized token economy with pigeons. *Journal of the Experimental Analysis of Behavior, 107*(1), 123–135. https://doi.org/10.1002/jeab.231

Bardo, M. T., Klebaur, J. E., Valone, J. M., & Deaton, C. (2001). Environmental enrichment decreases intravenous self-administration of amphetamine in female and male rats. *Psychopharmacology, 155*(3), 278–284. http://www.ncbi.nlm.nih.gov/pubmed/11432690.

Beasley, M. M., Amantini, S., Gunawan, T., Silberberg, A., & Kearns, D. N. (2023). Cocaine and heroin interact differently with nondrug reinforcers in a choice situation. *Experimental and Clinical Psychopharmacology*. https://doi.org/10.1037/pha0000674

Beckmann, J. S., Chow, J. J., & Hutsell, B. A. (2019). Cocaine-associated decision-making: Toward isolating preference. *Neuropharmacology, 153*, 142−152. https://doi.org/10.1016/j.neuropharm.2019.03.025

Bentzley, B. S., Fender, K. M., & Aston-Jones, G. (2013). The behavioral economics of drug self-administration: A review and new analytical approach for within-session procedures. *Psychopharmacology, 226*(1), 113−125. https://doi.org/10.1007/s00213-012-2899-2

Bentzley, B. S., Jhou, T. C., & Aston-Jones, G. (2014). Economic demand predicts addiction-like behavior and therapeutic efficacy of oxytocin in the rat. *Proceedings of the National Academy of Sciences of the United States of America, 111*(32), 11822−11827. https://doi.org/10.1073/pnas.1406324111

Bickel, W. K., DeGrandpre, R. J., Higgins, S. T., & Hughes, J. R. (1990). Behavioral economics of drug self-administration. I. Functional equivalence of response requirement and drug dose. *Life Sciences, 47*(17), 1501−1510. http://www.ncbi.nlm.nih.gov/pubmed/2250566.

Bickel, W. K., & Madden, G. J. (1999). A comparison of measures of relative reinforcing efficacy and behavioral economics: Cigarettes and money in smokers. *Behavioural Pharmacology, 10*(6−7), 627−637. http://www.ncbi.nlm.nih.gov/pubmed/10780504.

Catania, A. C., & Reynolds, G. S. (1968). A quantitative analysis of the responding maintained by interval schedules of reinforcement. *Journal of the Experimental Analysis of Behavior, 11*(3), 327−383. https://doi.org/10.1901/jeab.1968.11-s327

Chandler, C. M., Maggio, S. E., Peng, H., Nixon, K., & Bardo, M. T. (2020). Effects of ethanol, naltrexone, nicotine and varenicline in an ethanol and nicotine co-use model in Sprague-Dawley rats. *Drug and Alcohol Dependence, 212*, Article 107988. https://doi.org/10.1016/j.drugalcdep.2020.107988

Chow, J. J., Beacher, N. J., Chabot, J. M., Oke, M., Venniro, M., Lin, D. T., & Shaham, Y. (2022). Characterization of operant social interaction in rats: Effects of access duration, effort, peer familiarity, housing conditions, and choice between social interaction vs. food or remifentanil. *Psychopharmacology, 239*(7), 2093−2108. https://doi.org/10.1007/s00213-022-06064-1

Christensen, C. J., Silberberg, A., Hursh, S. R., Huntsberry, M. E., & Riley, A. L. (2008). Essential value of cocaine and food in rats: Tests of the exponential model of demand. *Psychopharmacology, 198*(2), 221−229. https://doi.org/10.1007/s00213-008-1120-0

Christensen, C. J., Silberberg, A., Hursh, S. R., Roma, P. G., & Riley, A. L. (2008). Demand for cocaine and food over time. *Pharmacology Biochemistry and Behavior, 91*(2), 209−216. https://doi.org/10.1016/j.pbb.2008.07.009

Cosgrove, K. P., & Carroll, M. E. (2003). Effects of a non-drug reinforcer, saccharin, on oral self-administration of phencyclidine in male and female rhesus monkeys. *Psychopharmacology, 170*(1), 9−16. https://doi.org/10.1007/s00213-003-1487-x

Cox, B. M., Bentzley, B. S., Regen-Tuero, H., See, R. E., Reichel, C. M., & Aston-Jones, G. (2017). Oxytocin acts in nucleus accumbens to attenuate methamphetamine seeking and demand. *Biological Psychiatry, 81*(11), 949−958. https://doi.org/10.1016/j.biopsych.2016.11.011

DeFulio, A., Yankelevitz, R., Bullock, C., & Hackenberg, T. D. (2014). Generalized conditioned reinforcement with pigeons in a token economy. *Journal of the Experimental Analysis of Behavior, 102*(1), 26−46. https://doi.org/10.1002/jeab.94

Derenne, A. (2020). Performance on a progressive-ratio schedule of food reinforcement during concurrent access to a sucrose solution or tap water. *Behavioural Processes, 173*, Article 104040. https://doi.org/10.1016/j.beproc.2020.104040

Dews, P. B. (1969). Studies on responding under fixed-interval schedules of reinforcement: The effects on the pattern of responding of changes in requirements at reinforcement. *Journal of* the *Experimental Analysis of Behavior, 12*(2), 191−199. https://doi.org/10.1901/jeab.1969.12-191

Dong, Y., & Nestler, E. J. (2014). The neural rejuvenation hypothesis of cocaine addiction. *Trends in Pharmacological Sciences, 35*(8), 374−383. https://doi.org/10.1016/j.tips.2014.05.005

Dyr, W., & Kostowski, W. (2000). Animal model of ethanol abuse: Rats selectively bred for high and low voluntary alcohol intake. *Acta Poloniae Pharmaceutica, 57*(Suppl. l), 90−92.

Falk, J. L. (1961). Septal stimulation as a reinforcer of and an alternative to consumatory behavior. *Journal of the Experimental Analysis of Behavior, 4*(3), 213−217. https://doi.org/10.1901/jeab.1961.4-213

Fowler, C. D., Gipson, C. D., Kleykamp, B. A., Rupprecht, L. E., Harrell, P. T., Rees, V. W., Gould, T. J., Oliver, J., Bagdas, D., Damaj, M. I., Schmidt, H. D., Duncan, A., De Biasi, M., & Basic Science Network of the Society for Research on, Nicotine and Tobacco. (2018). Basic science and public policy: Informed regulation for nicotine and tobacco products. *Nicotine & Tobacco Research, 20*(7), 789−799. https://doi.org/10.1093/ntr/ntx175

Galuska, C. M., Banna, K. M., Willse, L. V., Yahyavi-Firouz-Abadi, N., & See, R. E. (2011). A comparison of economic demand and conditioned-cued reinstatement of methamphetamine-seeking or food-seeking in rats. *Behavioural Pharmacology, 22*(4), 312−323. https://doi.org/10.1097/FBP.0b013e3283473be4

Gipson, C. D., & Beckmann, J. S. (2022). Compulsion and substance use disorder: Potential importance of boundary conditions. *Neuropsychopharmacology: Official Publication of the American College of Neuropsychopharmacology*. https://doi.org/10.1038/s41386-022-01462-7

Gipson, C. D., Beckmann, J. S., El-Maraghi, S., Marusich, J. A., & Bardo, M. T. (2011). Effect of environmental enrichment on escalation of cocaine self-administration in rats. *Psychopharmacology, 214*(2), 557−566. https://doi.org/10.1007/s00213-010-2060-z

Gipson, C. D., Kupchik, Y. M., Shen, H., Reissner, K. J., Thomas, C. A., & Kalivas, P. W. (2013). Relapse induced by cues predicting cocaine depends on rapid, transient synaptic potentiation. *Neuron*. https://doi.org/10.1016/j.neuron.2013.01.00

Grace, R. C. (1994). A contextual model of concurrent-chains choice. *Journal of the Experimental Analysis of Behavior, 61*(1), 113−129. https://doi.org/10.1901/jeab.1994.61-113

Grebenstein, P. E., Burroughs, D., Roiko, S. A., Pentel, P. R., & LeSage, M. G. (2015). Predictors of the nicotine reinforcement threshold, compensation, and elasticity of demand in a rodent model of nicotine reduction policy. *Drug and Alcohol Dependence, 151*, 181−193. https://doi.org/10.1016/j.drugalcdep.2015.03.030

Grebenstein, P., Burroughs, D., Zhang, Y., & LeSage, M. G. (2013). Sex differences in nicotine self-administration in rats during progressive unit dose reduction: Implications for nicotine regulation policy. *Pharmacology Biochemistry and Behavior, 114*−*115*, 70−81. https://doi.org/10.1016/j.pbb.2013.10.020

Green, L., & Freed, D. E. (1993). The substitutability of reinforcers. *Journal of the Experimental Analysis of Behavior, 60*(1), 141−158. https://doi.org/10.1901/jeab.1993.60-141

Green, L., & Rachlin, H. (1991). Economic substitutability of electrical brain stimulation, food, and water. *Journal of the Experimental Analysis of Behavior, 55*(2), 133−143. https://doi.org/10.1901/jeab.1991.55-133

Hatsukami, D. K., Perkins, K. A., Lesage, M. G., Ashley, D. L., Henningfield, J. E., Benowitz, N. L., Backinger, C. L., & Zeller, M. (2010). Nicotine reduction revisited: Science and future directions. *Tobacco Control, 19*(5), e1−e10. https://doi.org/10.1136/tc.2009.035584

Herrnstein, R. J. (1961). Relative and absolute strength of response as a function of frequency of reinforcement. *Journal of the Experimental Analysis of Behavior, 4*(3), 267−272. https://doi.org/10.1901/jeab.1961.4-267

Heyman, G. M. (2013). Addiction and choice: Theory and new data. *Frontiers in Psychiatry, 4*, 31. https://doi.org/10.3389/fpsyt.2013.00031

Hursh, S. R. (1978). The economics of daily consumption controlling food- and water-reinforced responding. *Journal of the Experimental Analysis of Behavior, 29*(3), 475−491. https://doi.org/10.1901/jeab.1978.29-475

Hursh, S. R. (1980). Economic concepts for the analysis of behavior. *Journal of the Experimental Analysis of Behavior, 34*(2), 219−238. https://doi.org/10.1901/jeab.1980.34-219

Hursh, S. R., & Natelson, B. H. (1981). Electrical brain stimulation and food reinforcement dissociated by demand elasticity. *Physiology & Behavior, 26*(3), 509−515. https://doi.org/10.1016/0031-9384(81)90180-3

Hursh, S. R., & Silberberg, A. (2008). Economic demand and essential value. *Psychological Review, 115*(1), 186−198. https://doi.org/10.1037/0033-295X.115.1.186

Ivy, J. W., Meindl, J. N., Overley, E., & Robson, K. M. (2017). Token economy: A systematic review of procedural descriptions. *Behavior Modification, 41*(5), 708−737. https://doi.org/10.1177/0145445517699559

Kaplan, B. A., Franck, C. T., McKee, K., Gilroy, S. P., & Koffarnus, M. N. (2021). Applying mixed-effects modeling to behavioral economic demand: An introduction. *Perspectives on Behavior Science, 44*(2−3), 333−358. https://doi.org/10.1007/s40614-021-00299-7

Killeen, P. R., Posadas-Sanchez, D., Johansen, E. B., & Thrailkill, E. A. (2009). Progressive ratio schedules of reinforcement. *Journal of Experimental Psychology: Animal Behavior Processes, 35*(1), 35.

Koffarnus, M. N., Franck, C. T., Stein, J. S., & Bickel, W. K. (2015). A modified exponential behavioral economic demand model to better describe consumption data. *Experimental and Clinical Psychopharmacology, 23*(6), 504−512. https://doi.org/10.1037/pha0000045

Leonard, M. Z., DeBold, J. F., & Miczek, K. A. (2017). Escalated cocaine "binges" in rats: Enduring effects of social defeat stress or intra-VTA CRF. *Psychopharmacology, 234*(18), 2823−2836. https://doi.org/10.1007/s00213-017-4677-7

Maher, E. E., Overby, P. F., Bull, A. H., Beckmann, J. S., Leyrer-Jackson, J. M., Koebele, S. V., Bimonte-Nelson, H. A., & Gipson, C. D. (2021). Natural and synthetic estrogens specifically alter nicotine demand and cue-induced nicotine seeking in female rats. *Neuropharmacology, 198*, Article 108756. https://doi.org/10.1016/j.neuropharm.2021.108756

Maher, E. E., White, A. M., Craig, A., Khatri, S., Kendrick, P. T., Jr., Matocha, M. E., Bondy, E. O., Pallem, N., Breakfield, G., Botkins, M., Sweatt, O., Griffin, W. C., Kaplan, B., Weafer, J. J., Beckmann, J. S., & Gipson, C. D. (2023). Synthetic contraceptive hormones occlude the ability of nicotine to reduce ethanol consumption in ovary-intact female rats. *Drug and Alcohol Dependence, 252*, Article 110983. https://doi.org/10.1016/j.drugalcdep.2023.110983

Mannelli, P., Wu, L. T., Peindl, K. S., & Gorelick, D. A. (2013). Smoking and opioid detoxification: Behavioral changes and response to treatment. *Nicotine & Tobacco Research: Official Journal of the Society for Research on Nicotine and Tobacco, 15*(10), 1705−1713. https://doi.org/10.1093/ntr/ntt046

Marks, M. J., Burch, J. B., & Collins, A. C. (1983). Effects of chronic nicotine infusion on tolerance development and nicotinic receptors. *Journal of Pharmacology and Experimental Therapeutics, 226*(3), 817−825.

Mattox, A. J., & Carroll, M. E. (1996). Smoked heroin self-administration in rhesus monkeys. *Psychopharmacology, 125*(3), 195−201. http://www.ncbi.nlm.nih.gov/pubmed/8815953.

Mattox, A. J., Thompson, S. S., & Carroll, M. E. (1997). Smoked heroin and cocaine base (speedball) combinations in rhesus monkeys. *Experimental and Clinical Psychopharmacology, 5*(2), 113−118. http://www.ncbi.nlm.nih.gov/pubmed/9234046.

McSweeney, F. K., & Swindell, S. (1999). Behavioral economics and within-session changes in responding. *Journal of the Experimental Analysis of Behavior, 72*(3), 355−371. https://doi.org/10.1901/jeab.1999.72-355

Meisch, R. A. (1987). Factors controlling drug reinforced behavior. *Pharmacology Biochemistry and Behavior, 27*(2), 367−371. https://doi.org/10.1016/0091-3057(87)90584-3

Neill, U. S. (2022). A conversation with nora volkow. *The Journal of Clinical Investigation, 132*(3). https://doi.org/10.1172/jci157462

Oleson, E. B., & Roberts, D. C. (2009). Behavioral economic assessment of price and cocaine consumption following self-administration histories that produce escalation of either final ratios or intake. *Neuropsychopharmacology, 34*(3), 796−804. https://doi.org/10.1038/npp.2008.195

Oleson, E. B., & Roberts, D. C. (2012). Cocaine self-administration in rats: Threshold procedures. *Methods in Molecular Biology, 829*, 303−319. https://doi.org/10.1007/978-1-61779-458-2_20

Panlilio, L. V., Secci, M. E., Schindler, C. W., & Bradberry, C. W. (2017). Choice between delayed food and immediate opioids in rats: Treatment effects and individual differences. *Psychopharmacology, 234*(22), 3361−3373. https://doi.org/10.1007/s00213-017-4726-2

Pantazis, C. B., James, M. H., O'Connor, S., Shin, N., & Aston-Jones, G. (2021). Orexin-1 receptor signaling in ventral tegmental area mediates cue-driven demand for cocaine. *Neuropsychopharmacology: Official Publication of the American College of Neuropsychopharmacology*. https://doi.org/10.1038/s41386-021-01173-5

Petry, N. M. (2011). Contingency management: What it is and why psychiatrists should want to use it. *Psychiatrist, 35*(5), 161−163. https://doi.org/10.1192/pb.bp.110.031831

Powell, G. L., Beckmann, J. S., Marusich, J. A., & Gipson, C. D. (2020). Nicotine reduction does not alter essential value of nicotine or reduce cue-induced reinstatement of nicotine seeking. *Drug and Alcohol Dependence*. , Article 108020. https://doi.org/10.1016/j.drugalcdep.2020.108020

Powell, G. L., Cabrera-Brown, G., Namba, M. D., Neisewander, J. L., Marusich, J. A., Beckmann, J. S., & Gipson, C. D. (2019). Economic demand analysis of within-session dose-reduction during nicotine self-administration. *Drug and Alcohol Dependence, 201*, 188−196. https://doi.org/10.1016/j.drugalcdep.2019.03.033

Powell, G. L., Namba, M. D., Vannan, A., Bonadonna, J. P., Carlson, A., Mendoza, R., Chen, P. J., Luetdke, R. R., Blass, B. E., & Neisewander, J. L. (2020). The long-acting D3 partial agonist MC-25-41 attenuates motivation for cocaine in sprague-dawley rats. *Biomolecules, 10*(7). https://doi.org/10.3390/biom10071076

Russo, S. J., Dietz, D. M., Dumitriu, D., Morrison, J. H., Malenka, R. C., & Nestler, E. J. (2010). The addicted synapse: Mechanisms of synaptic and structural plasticity in nucleus accumbens. *Trends in Neurosciences, 33*(6), 267−276. https://doi.org/10.1016/j.tins.2010.02.002

Rzeszutek, M. J., Kaplan, B. A., Traxler, H. K., Franck, C. T., & Koffarnus, M. N. (2023). Hyperbolic discounting and exponentiated demand: Modeling demand for cigarettes in three dimensions. *Journal of the Experimental Analysis of Behavior, 119*(1), 169−191. https://doi.org/10.1002/jeab.818

Schultz, N. R., Frohe, T., Correia, C. J., & Ramirez, J. J. (2023). Why get high? Coping and enjoyment motives mediate elevated cannabis demand and cannabis-related outcomes.

Psychology of Addictive Behaviors: Journal of the Society of Psychologists in Addictive Behaviors, 37(6), 796−808. https://doi.org/10.1037/adb0000937

Scott, H. (2024). Behavior modification. *Behavior modification*. StatPearls Publishing. PMID: 29083709.

Shull, R. L., Grimes, J. A., & Bennett, J. A. (2004). Bouts of responding: The relation between bout rate and the rate of variable-interval reinforcement. *Journal of the Experimental Analysis of Behavior, 81*(1), 65−83. https://doi.org/10.1901/jeab.2004.81-65

Smith, T. T., Cassidy, R. N., Tidey, J. W., Luo, X., Le, C. T., Hatsukami, D. K., & Donny, E. C. (2017). Impact of smoking reduced nicotine content cigarettes on sensitivity to cigarette price: Further results from a multi-site clinical trial. *Addiction, 112*(2), 349−359. https://doi.org/10.1111/add.13636

Strickland, J. C., Stoops, W. W., Banks, M. L., & Gipson, C. D. (2022). Logical fallacies and misinterpretations that hinder progress in translational addiction neuroscience. *Journal of the Experimental Analysis of Behavior*. https://doi.org/10.1002/jeab.757

Tucker, M. R., Laugesen, M., & Grace, R. C. (2017). Estimating demand and cross-price elasticity for very low nicotine content (VLNC) cigarettes using a simulated demand task. *Nicotine & Tobacco Research*. https://doi.org/10.1093/ntr/ntx051

Weatherly, J. N., McSweeney, F. K., & Swindell, S. (2004). Within-session rates of responding when reinforcer magnitude is changed within the session. *The Journal of General Psychology, 131*(1), 5−16. https://doi.org/10.3200/genp.131.1.5-17

Webber, H. E., Yoon, J. H., de Dios, C., Suchting, R., Dang, V., Versace, F., Green, C. E., Wardle, M. C., Lane, S. D., & Schmitz, J. M. (2023). Assessing cocaine motivational value: Comparison of brain reactivity bias toward cocaine cues and cocaine demand. *Experimental and Clinical Psychopharmacology, 31*(4), 861−867. https://doi.org/10.1037/pha0000622

Yates, J. R., Bardo, M. T., & Beckmann, J. S. (2019). Environmental enrichment and drug value: A behavioral economic analysis in male rats. *Addiction Biology, 24*(1), 65−75. https://doi.org/10.1111/adb.12581

Young, M. E., Clark, M. H., Goffus, A., & Hoane, M. R. (2009). Mixed effects modeling of Morris water maze data: Advantages and cautionary notes. *Learning and Motivation, 40*(2), 160−177.

Yu, J., Liu, L., Collins, R. L., Vincent, P. C., & Epstein, L. H. (2014). Analytical problems and suggestions in the analysis of behavioral economic demand curves. *Multivariate Behavioral Research, 49*(2), 178−192. https://doi.org/10.1080/00273171.2013.862491

Human research methods for studying operant demand

Sarah Weinsztok[1,3], Brandon Miller[1], Elizabeth Aston[2] and Michael Amlung[1]
[1]University of Kansas, Lawrence, KS, United States; [2]Brown University, Providence, RI, United States; [3]Rutgers, The State University of New Jersey, New Brunswick, NJ, United States

Introduction

Human behavior is complex, multifaceted, and, from the perspective of the operating organism, always in one's best interest. The concept of "irrationality" may, therefore, be considered a misnomer; the organism predictably responds as a function of both reinforcement history and present environmental circumstances. Humans tend to prefer immediacy over delay, guarantees over probabilistic outcomes, and maximizing consumption as a function of unit price (Rachlin, 1978; Rachlin et al., 1976). However, these preferences may shift depending on environmental circumstances, individual learning history, and momentary changes in motivation. In this chapter, we will focus on the changes in defense of the consumption of a particular reinforcer or commodity as a function of environmental changes. This phenomenon is widely conceptualized as *the law of demand*—that is, the observation that as a commodity or reinforcer increases in unit price, we tend to observe subsequent decreases in consumption. However, myriad other variables impact this relation, including the availability of alternative commodities. Using behavioral economic frameworks to help conceptualize demand for commodities as molar changes in reinforcer value—that is, broad patterns of behavior as opposed to momentary shifts in responding (Hursh, 1980; Rachlin, 1978). A molar account of behavior is necessary to describe, predict, and control human behavior that our science seeks to explore. It may arguably be a more useful account when examining the consumption of commodities such as drugs, alcohol, or other behaviors that have pathological tendencies.

The law of demand has been most extensively studied and has subsequently become invaluable in the assessment and treatment of substance use disorders and other maladaptive behaviors. The law of demand is also a central component of the reinforcer pathology model of addiction, which states that individuals who engage in hazardous alcohol or drug use or who have substance use disorder (SUD) or alcohol use disorder (AUD) excessively value the immediacy of rewards and display persistent demand for substances (Bickel et al., 2014). Assessments and experimental manipulations of operant demand have been implemented to determine how individuals with substance use and other maladaptive disorders value rewards and how this valuation can be changed by introducing other stimuli.

This chapter will describe past and present methods of studying operant demand in human subject research. As most research advancements have been in substance and alcohol use disorders, this will be the chapter's primary focus. However, assessments of demand for other behavior patterns will also be included. We will begin by introducing the reader to historical perspectives of operant demand and conceptual foundations underlying this area of study. We will move on to a now-common method for assessing hypothetical demand in human subjects: The commodity purchase task. We will describe the purposes behind its historical design and its uses and benefits. Finally, we will provide the reader with a toolkit that can be used when designing their purchase tasks, and identifying when and how to make modifications. We will conclude this chapter by exploring further refinements and applications of the purchase task.

Historical perspectives on measuring behavior under constraint

Behavior analysts have long been concerned with relative reinforcing efficacy (RRE)—an intervening variable (MacCorquodale & Meehl, 1948) that describes a reinforcer's behavior-strengthening or behavior-maintaining effectiveness under given constraints. Behavior analysts have been interested in RRE because of its utility in understanding drug-taking and drug-seeking behavior (see Bickel et al., 2000; Griffiths et al., 1978; Katz, 1990 for perspectives on RRE). The earliest attempts to examine the RRE of addictive commodities often involved first imposing an obstacle (e.g., an electrified grid) between a nonhuman organism and the substance of interest and then measuring breakpoint, or the number of crossings during a fixed period (see Warden, 1931 for review). Unfortunately, exposure to repeated shocks often produced highly variable responses that were difficult to interpret using a single-case design. Due to concerns regarding variability and threats to internal validity, three alternative methods of measuring RRE became popular over the proceeding decades: (a) Progressive ratio (PR) breakpoint, (b) peak response output, and (c) relative preference under concurrent schedules.

The first two methods stem from Hodos (1961), in which a novel method called the PR schedule was proposed as a direct response to the problems produced by earlier methods involving repeated shocks. The term "progressive ratio" has since been adapted to refer to several arrangements that involve an increasingly greater response requirement (or unit price) for obtaining a reinforcer over successive trials in both humans and nonhuman organisms (Jarmolowicz & Lattal, 2010; Richardson & Roberts, 1996). In the traditional within-session PR arrangement (henceforth referred to as arrangement "A"), researchers progressively increase the response requirement for reinforcer delivery (e.g., the number of lever presses, button presses, nose pokes, key pecks, or Lindsley-plunger pulls) with each reinforcer delivery (e.g., Hodos, 1961; Meisch & Thompson, 1973). Of note, PR arrangements allow for both within-ratio and post-reinforcement pauses, which refer to pauses in responding during the middle of the ratio requirement and pauses after the organism obtains the reinforcer, respectively. The progressive response requirement most often increases arithmetically, meaning that the change in response requirements occurs at a constant rate (e.g., 2, 4, 6, 8, 10, and 12). In other instances, this progression happens geometrically, where researchers determine the response requirement by multiplying the previous requirement by a constant value (e.g., 2, 4, 8, 16, 32, and 64). Though researchers often use PR schedules to determine the RRE of addictive commodities using preclinical models, there are some notable exceptions. As an example of arrangement A using a unique non-substance−based commodity and response requirement, Stinson et al. (2021) had participants "purchase" 30-second access to their smartphones by requiring an escalating number of computer mouse clicks (i.e., 2, 4, 9, 20, 40, 77, 95, 118, 145, and 250) to access each successive 30-second interval.

Like arrangement A, arrangement B—the intermittent arrangement—involves adjusting the response requirement within a session; however, unlike the first arrangement, the response requirement increases intermittently (i.e., more gradually). As such, the ratio requirement may remain an FR4 for five trials before increasing to an FR9. The specific type of PR arrangement a researcher employs will depend on the research questions they are attempting to answer. Not all PR arrangements involve changes in response requirements that happen within-session. Therefore an alternative to arrangements A and B is to increase the response requirement between sessions (i.e., arrangement C) rather than within sessions. For instance, McLeod and Griffiths (1983) exposed five participants with a history of sedative drug use to PR schedules of pentobarbital self-administration. In McLeod and Griffiths (1983), the number of button presses or time required to pedal a bike increased across the session rather than within the session. Notably, the only reinforcement associated with responding to arrangement C is the reinforcer delivered to complete the ratio requirement. Arrangement C is, therefore, typically associated with lower response rates and higher breakpoints than arrangement A or B (Foster et al., 1997).

Two indices can be derived from PR schedules regardless of the procedure used. The first index is the PR breakpoint, the greatest response requirement that sustains behavior under a given reinforcement schedule. The second index generated from PR schedules is the peak response rate or the maximum number of responses observed under a given reinforcement schedule. To understand how researchers calculate both indices, consider an organism that completes an FR 30 schedule but then ceases responding after 35 lever presses during the next session when the researcher increases the response requirement to an FR 40. In this instance, the organism's breakpoint would be 30, while the peak response output would be 35.

Despite the usefulness of PR arrangements, they have some limitations. One problem is that different arrangements may have different variables that control breakpoints (Jarmolowicz & Lattal, 2010; Li et al., 2003; Reed et al., 2015; Stafford et al., 1999). While responding to the within-session arrangements is likely strengthened by reinforcer delivery and session continuation, responding to the between-session arrangement is influenced less by session duration. In other words, the organism controls session duration in the within-session arrangement, while the experimenter controls session duration in the between-session arrangement. Therefore the influences on the primary outcome variable (i.e., breakpoint) will differ depending on the methodology employed, and researchers should interpret comparisons across studies using different PR arrangements cautiously. Regardless of the chosen arrangement, the second problem with PR schedules is that they only produce two indices of RRE—breakpoint and peak response rate. A third drawback to using PR breakpoint and peak response rate is that PR arrangements generally have lower external validity, as they often only present a single response option. Having a single response option is problematic, given that several response options are always available at any given time in environments outside of a human operant laboratory. A fourth and final limitation is that PR schedules cannot identify steady-state responses, which threatens internal validity.

An alternative method to studying RRE is measuring drug preferences under concurrent reinforcement schedules. Researchers can do this by using either differing doses of the same drug, two different drugs, or a drug and a nondrug alternative (see Brady & Griffiths, 1976; Iglauer & Woods, 1974; Johanson & Schuster, 1975, for example). Regardless of the chosen reinforcers, the methodologies remain consistent. For example, one method is through a concurrent operant arrangement. In a concurrent operant arrangement, two or more response options are made available with different schedules of reinforcement associated with each option (Baum & Rachlin, 1969). As an example, consider an operant chamber consisting of two levers. A researcher might program schedules so that responding on lever 1 produces food pellets on an FR3 schedule while responding on lever 2 results in an intravenous injection of cocaine on an FR9. In this example, an organism with a larger response rate on lever 2 would indicate greater RRE for cocaine over food.

An alternative choice procedure is a concurrent chain procedure (Autor, 1960). A typical current chain procedure involves two or more concurrently available reinforcement schedules with corresponding discriminative stimuli associated with each schedule. Completing the initial requirement in either "initial links" leads to access to a secondary schedule or a "terminal link." Thus the relative allocation of behavior on an initial link indicates a preference for the corresponding terminal link stimulus (see Hughes et al., 2022; Jimenez-Gomez & Shahan, 2012). Though concurrent chains provide an advantage by allowing for choice allocation among multiple response options, these procedures are also complicated by the possibility of bringing behavior under the control of confounding factors like changeover delays. In short, choice procedures compare the relative frequency of responding as a measure of RRE instead of PR breakpoint or peak response output.

One advantage of using a choice procedure over PR breakpoint or peak response output is that it is the only method that emphasizes the importance of relative response engagement across alternatives at similar or different schedules of reinforcement. Furthermore, since multiple response options are freely available, greater allocation of behavior among one option demonstrates greater RRE than the other option. In contrast, directly comparing the RRE of two different reinforcers (e.g., cocaine and alcohol) within a single organism using two different PR arrangements does not allow an accurate ranking to be determined, given that several alternative variables may be responsible for the observed differences in RRE (e.g., order effects). In summary, the history of assessing RRE is complex and involves several methods, each with unique strengths and weaknesses. Notably, all the methods we have mentioned so far are limited by their inability to generate more than two indices of RRE.

Purchase task methodology as a novel alternative to operant choice tasks

The preceding section discussed several approaches to studying human and animal choice behavior using operant choice tasks. While these methods have numerous advantages, they are not without limitations.

Cost is an important consideration when deciding which behavioral paradigm to implement in a research study. In this context, "cost" includes both financial costs as well as costs on the individual's responding in terms of time and effort. Indeed, many choice paradigms involve numerous trials that may require a substantial amount of time. This raises important considerations about participant burden, fatigue, and concerns regarding maintaining proper attention to the task. In addition, important financial limitations exist when using these tasks as they may frequently require the delivery of monetary incentives or other reinforcers.

With the above limitations in mind, behavior analysts and behavioral economists sought to develop new ways of examining the reinforcing value of substances that minimize the cost, time, and ethical constraints of operant choice tasks. These efforts resulted in the development of the *hypothetical purchase task* approach. In this procedure, individuals make a series of hypothetical choices for how much of a specific commodity they would purchase at a range of unit prices, given certain conditions (e.g., that all of the commodity must be consumed within the given hypothetical time frame). This methodology is described in greater detail below; for now, it is important to emphasize how it circumvents many of the abovementioned issues. First, because purchase tasks are frequently hypothetical (i.e., no money or commodities are provided), there are limited constraints from a financial standpoint. These measures also allow for assessing a much larger range of unit prices, which often would not be practical if real money were involved using a conventional PR schedule. Assessing a broad range of unit prices enhances the precision of pinpointing various aspects of demand (i.e., elasticity, P_{max}, and O_{max}) from the results of the purchase task. The hypothetical nature of these tasks allows researchers to recruit a broader range of participants for whom actual delivery of reinforcers (e.g., alcohol or drugs) would be unsafe, illegal, or otherwise unethical. For example, participants who are pregnant or in treatment/recovery for substance use would not be eligible for a study using an actual outcome task for alcohol or drug rewards due to medical and ethical concerns, but they would qualify for a study that uses hypothetical outcomes.

Similarly, underage participants who cannot legally purchase alcohol or other drugs can complete a hypothetical measure for these commodities. Providing drugs to participants also poses unique logistical and safety concerns for researchers, including careful screening for potential contraindications of use and the need to closely monitor participants for adverse reactions. This typically involves building in additional time in the lab to recover from the acute effects of use and providing transportation home from a study, both of which can be taxing on financial and staff resources from the researchers' standpoint and may require a considerably longer duration of testing for participants. A final advantage to the purchase task approach is the generation of several unique indices of substance demand, as opposed to the single PR breakpoints generated from several of the measures reviewed previously. These indices capture distinct aspects of the reinforcing value of a commodity (e.g., unrestricted consumption, maximum expenditure, and price sensitivity), which can provide novel insights into choice behavior in healthy and clinical samples.

Progression of purchase task methodology: Verification and applications

Purchase tasks are a cost-effective, ethical, and reasonably efficient method of assessing demand for a particular commodity in the face of various environmental constraints. The utility of purchase task methodology rests on the extent to which the results of self-reported consumption correspond to traditional behavior observed in laboratory self-administration, thereby demonstrating concurrent validity (Jacobs & Bickel, 1999). Purchase tasks demonstrate close correspondence to these methods (e.g., Jacobs & Bickel, 1999; Petry & Bickel, 1998). Much of purchase task research, as aforementioned, has been conducted in the context of drug use.

The first example of purchase task methodology was a multiple-choice procedure, in which participants selected between varying amounts of a drug and an alternative monetary reinforcer (Griffiths et al., 1993). At the end of the assessment, one outcome was randomly chosen to be administered to participants. Hypothetical purchase tasks were then expanded from this methodology. The hypothetical purchase task is similar to the original purchase task in which a random outcome is administered, except that no outcomes are provided at the end of the task. Hypothetical purchase tasks involve instructing the participant to imagine the outcomes that would occur based on their behavior and to act as if their responses would result in the actual outcome. Behavioral economic indices were first derived from hypothetical purchase task data of cigarettes and illicit drugs (heroin; Valium; Jacobs & Bickel, 1999; Petry & Bickel, 1998). The advancement of hypothetical purchase task methodology has included the development of vignettes to simulate real-world circumstances under which purchasing may occur. These vignettes are best demonstrated in the alcohol purchase task: A systematic and structured hypothetical task that was developed to measure alcohol consumption and which provided predetermined contexts for the participant in the form of a structured vignette and purchase units (Murphy & MacKillop, 2006).

The alcohol purchase task has been consistently validated since its conception almost 20 years ago, demonstrating good internal reliability, construct validity, and convergent validity despite consistent heterogeneity in methodology and analysis (Kaplan et al., 2018). Modifications have been made to the vignette of the alcohol purchase task to accommodate the researcher's specific study purposes; however, the general overview remains the same. A sample vignette of an alcohol purchase task is displayed in Box 4.1. Participants are asked to imagine that they are in either a typical situation in which they normally drink or a specific situation tailored to the researcher's study purpose. Participants are instructed to identify how many standard-sized drinks (6 oz of wine, 12 oz of beer, and 1 oz of hard liquor) they would consume in a given time period across a range of prices, with the understanding that they cannot stockpile the alcohol for later and that the varying prices do not indicate a change in the quality of the alcohol. The range of prices may be small or large, in ascending/descending cost sequence or randomized, and the density of prices may be close together or spread farther apart. Following the completion of the purchase task, a *demand curve* can be plotted from the individual participant or group-level data, and demand indices of intensity, elasticity, and breakpoint can be derived from this curve. The demand curve is a quantitative embodiment of the law of demand: as price increases, consumption tends to decline, inevitably hitting a breakpoint, in which consumption ceases.

Box 4.1 Sample purchase task vignette

In the questionnaire that follows we would like you to pretend to purchase and consume alcohol during a 5-hour period. Imagine you are in a situation in which you usually drink alcohol (at a bar, at a party, at home, with friends, etc.). Imagine that you do not have any obligations the next day (i.e., no work or classes). The following questions ask how many drinks you would purchase at various prices. The available drinks are standard-size beers (12 oz.), wine (5 oz.), shots of hard liquor/distilled spirits (1.5 oz.), or mixed drinks containing one shot of liquor/distilled spirits. Assume that you did not drink alcohol or use drugs before and that you will not drink or use drugs after. You do not have access to any other alcohol than what is available for purchase here and assume you have the same income/savings that you do now*. Also, assume that the alcohol you are about to purchase is for your consumption only and you would consume every drink you request. In other words, you cannot sell the drinks or give them to anyone else. You also can't stockpile the drinks for later. Everything you buy is, therefore, for your own personal use during the 5-hour period. Please respond to these questions honestly, as if you were actually in this situation.

Remember:

You are in a situation in which you usually drink alcohol (at a bar, at a party, at home, with friends, etc.)

You have no access to alcohol other than what is available for purchase here.

Everything you buy is for your own personal use during the 5-hour period.

There are no "right" or "wrong" responses. Please answer all questions honestly, thoughtfully, and to the best of your understanding, as if you were actually in this situation.

The methodology of the alcohol purchase task has been adapted to assess demand for other commodities of interest. While mostly drug-related (e.g., marijuana purchase task, cocaine purchase task, and cigarette purchase task; Aston et al., 2015; Bruner & Johnson, 2014; Collins et al., 2014; Field et al., 2006), these extensions have also included nondrug commodities (e.g., tanning purchase task, pornography purchase task; Reed et al., 2016; Mulhauser et al., 2018). Studies show that, while further refinements across substances are often necessary due to the differences in choosing an optimal unit of purchase, the application of purchase task methodology produces valid demand data (e.g., Aston et al., 2021).

As purchase task methodology grew in appeal and the frequency of its use in research, it became necessary to determine the optimal methodological procedures that would enhance the measures' content, as well as the ecological and internal validity. Price sequence methodology (i.e., fixed ascending or descending prices vs. random price sequences) was a component of interest in research. Though price sequence appeared to differentially impact response consistency (Amlung & MacKillop, 2012), fixed versus random price sequences both result in high response consistency overall (Amlung & MacKillop, 2012; Salzer et al., 2021). In addition, the implementation of real versus hypothetical rewards also does not appear to result in differences in responding (Amlung et al., 2012; Amlung & MacKillop, 2015). These results hold important implications for researchers who plan to employ purchase tasks to assess demand; they demonstrate that flexibility in price sequence and in using real versus hypothetical rewards do not differentially impact responding in a significant way. Therefore a researcher may choose what methods to use based on risk constraints, environmental supports, research questions, and ethical concerns.

Roma et al. (2016) conducted several studies and made several methodological recommendations, including the number of prices at which respondents report hypothetical consumption per task (price density) and quantity versus probability format. Based on the results of their series of studies, the authors recommended that at least nine prices be used in an HPT to prevent distortion of demand curves and stated that 17 prices are preferable. Roma et al. (2016) also proposed a novel probability format for HPTs and recommended continued study of that format. This format has been evaluated more recently, with some researchers arguing for its utility while others pointing to methodological and quantitative concerns when deriving demand indices using the probability format (e.g., Brown et al., 2021). We recommend that researchers familiarize themselves with both the potential benefits and pitfalls of varying price densities and probability versus quantity formats and weigh the costs and benefits when designing their own HPT.

The question of how to handle and eliminate (when applicable) nonsystematic demand data from purchase tasks has been evaluated by several research groups (Bruner & Johnson, 2014; Stein et al., 2015). Using preset guidelines for identifying nonsystematic data may be helpful in making comparisons across studies and heterogeneous groups. Stein et al. (2015) established three criteria to evaluate nonsystematic data: Trend, bounce, and reversals from zero. The authors recommended that researchers adopt these methods and remove data when necessary and when those data do not reflect a crucial purpose or novel methodology and thus would warrant inclusion despite nonsystematic responding.

Purchase Task Toolkit

When preparing to conduct purchase tasks for your research endeavors, you must make several ad hoc determinations of the components that will make up the assessment. These components should be made based on the following considerations: (1) What is the purpose of your study? (2) What outcomes are you hoping to measure? (3) What resource constraints in your environment may preclude using one or more types of purchase task components (e.g., actual vs. hypothetical outcomes due to monetary and laboratory resource constraints)? (4) What are the ethical considerations of each component of the purpose task based on your study's purpose? (5) What background research and training have you undergone to ensure that you can appropriately weigh the costs and benefits of the purchase task methodology and design a purchase task that answers your research question accurately?

To help guide you in this process, the authors of this chapter have devised a Purchase Task Toolkit (Fig. 4.1). This toolkit aims to provide you with an easy-to-read

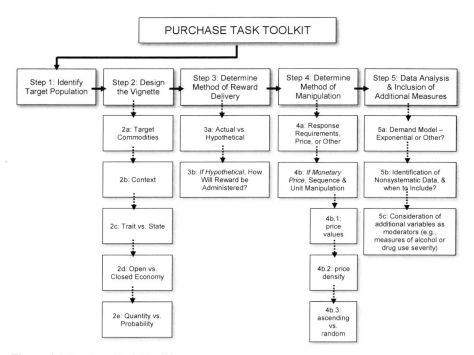

Figure 4.1 Purchase Task Toolkit.

flowchart of considerations for developing each component of your purchase task. This toolkit is intended to guide you as you develop purchase tasks; however, it is important to note that not every consideration specific to your study's purpose may be included in this toolkit. While some aspects of the toolkit are expanded upon briefly in this chapter (e.g., price density, hypothetical vs. real rewards), in-depth components of design and analysis are beyond the scope of this introductory chapter. We recommend that readers familiarize themselves with the literature base appropriate to the type of purchase task or types of commodities they would like to use and receive additional training to ensure competence if necessary. A list of recommended resources for each portion of Steps 2–5 of the toolkit is located in Table 4.1.

Table 4.1 Recommended resources for Toolkit steps.

Steps	Step components	Sample references (not exhaustive list)
Step 2: Design and vignette	Target commodities	(Aston et al., 2021; Strickland et al., 2021)
	Context	(Kaplan et al., 2018; Reed et al., 2020)
	Trait versus state	(Kaplan et al., 2018; Reed et al., 2020)
	Open versus closed economy	(Hursh, 1980; Hursh, 2014; Hursh, 1993)
	Quantity versus probability	(Roma et al., 2016; Brown et al., 2021)
Step 3: Determine method of reward delivery	Actual versus hypothetical	(Amlung et al., 2012; Amlung & MacKillop, 2015)
	If actual, how will reward be administered?	(Stein et al., 2018; Pope et al., 2019; Shahan et al., 1999; DeGrandpre et al., 1994)
Step 4: Determine method of manipulation	Monetary price, response requirements, other	(Johnson & Bickel, 2003; Shahan et al., 2000)
	Price sequence and unit manipulation	(Roma et al., 2016)
Step 5: Data analysis & inclusion of additional measures	Demand model	(Hursh & Silberberg, 2008 (exponential); Koffarnus et al., 2015 (exponentiated))
	Identification/use of nonsystematic data	(Stein et al., 2015; Bruner & Johnson, 2014)

Further refinements and applications of purchase tasks: Utilization of qualitative methods to improve assessment of behavioral economic substance demand

Qualitative methods are used to identify and understand a research question or line of scientific inquiry from the perspective of the population involved. This type of research is particularly valuable in obtaining population-specific data regarding behaviors, beliefs, and contextual factors that are critical in accurately describing, assessing, and answering the question of interest (Foley & Timonen, 2015; Mack et al., 2005). Qualitative work has many strengths, including the ability to provide very detailed portrayals of how the population of interest experiences a given issue, including the many contradictions that may be involved. Moreover, such methods are uniquely suited to expound upon less tangible factors that influence behavior and decision-making, including emotions, relationships, roles, and norms (Mack et al., 2005; Tenny et al., 2022). From a scientific perspective, all of these variables have the propensity to influence all aspects of research, including study design, proper assessment techniques, appropriate language, and nuanced terminology, among many others.

As explained earlier in this chapter, hypothetical substance purchase tasks are typically used to assess demand for a particular substance and comprised vignettes and questions asking individuals to decide how much substance they would purchase under specified conditions over escalating price points. There are substantial differences across tasks in terms of substance, unit of purchase, price, number of price points, timing of use, and most importantly, within instructional vignettes (Aston & Cassidy, 2019; Kaplan et al., 2018). The aforementioned variations across substances typically require adaptations across purchase task formats to produce the most optimized assessment of relative value specific to a given substance. Importantly, qualitative approaches have shown great promise in improving, optimizing, and tailoring such measures (Aston et al., 2021). Qualitative techniques can be used to provide invaluable information regarding central issues and concepts to be investigated in subsequent quantitative research (Neale et al., 2005). One such area amenable to qualitative inquiry is measure development, refinement, and improvement. Qualitative methods can be used to improve and enhance existing assessments by obtaining feedback from members of the population of interest via focus groups, individual interviews, and cognitive interviews. In this regard, measures assessing behavioral economic cannabis demand have undergone substantial improvement by implementing qualitative methodology (Aston et al., 2021).

Purchase task formats and instructions have historically been designed by researchers (e.g. Aston et al., 2015; Collins et al., 2014; MacKillop et al., 2008; Murphy & MacKillop, 2006), and thus may not accurately reflect terminology, concepts, appropriate language, norms, and contextual factors cited by the group of interest; all of which may impact performance on these measures. Individual interviews and focus groups can be quite valuable for measuring development and refinement as discussions with individuals who endorse substance use can better demonstrate overall task comprehension, probe appropriate terminology, and uncover complex concepts that may critically influence task performance.

Purchase task vignettes typically place the respondent in a hypothetical situation wherein they are asked to purchase and consume a given substance; critical components of this instructional set include the setting wherein the substance use will take place, the duration of time allowed for substance use following purchase, the unit of substance purchase, the substance quality or type, and other stipulations specific to the commodity, including but not limited to substance stockpiling, abstinence from substance use prior to task initiation, sharing of the commodity, financial conditions, proscription of additional substance purchase following task completion, and description of any responsibilities that the respondent must maintain at a designated time following completion of substance use, among others (Aston & Cassidy, 2019; Kaplan et al., 2018). Even small changes in these dimensions can impact demand (Kaplan et al., 2017; Vincent et al., 2017), dramatically altering purchase task performance. Some substances, such as cannabis, have complex units, modes of administration, broad ranges in quality, and unclear legality, all of which impact demand. What is more, we, as researchers are likely unaware of other variables simultaneously impacting demand within a given population. Taken together, purchase task instructional sets and vignettes can be tremendously complex and are often fraught with eccentricities specific to a given substance. Consequently, the benefits of using a qualitative approach to investigate each component in turn, among individuals endorsing the use of the said substance are clear.

Qualitative approaches are extensive, though several methodological techniques hold much promise for behavioral economic assessment development and improvement, specifically focus groups, individual interviews, and cognitive interviews (Punch, 2013). The objective of a focus group is to provide breadth on a particular topic or set of behaviors (Mack et al., 2005). A focus group usually comprises six to eight individuals from a group of interest, though researchers may choose to hold groups with more or fewer participants. Groups must have at least four individuals, however, as triads and dyads are characterized by different dynamics. Similarly, it is inadvisable to hold groups with greater than eight individuals as conversations may become unrulily or result in some individuals speaking and contributing less frequently—or not at all—to the discussion (Mack et al., 2005). Researchers are intentionally trying to collect wide-ranging opinions, beliefs, and personal experiences from a given group, with particular emphasis on the differences and similarities in responses. While a set of questions or interview guide is not required, it may be highly beneficial to develop a semi-structured interview agenda before group commencement to ensure that questions are open-ended, not leading, and all topics of interest are covered. For substance purchase tasks, focus groups may be ideal for novel substances for which there is currently less data (e.g., delta-8 THC, kratom, and spice). Such groups may be used to provide a broad, comprehensive picture of such substances, including their subjective effects, price, effect duration, co-use with other substances, consequences, and societal stigma surrounding their use. In addition, focus groups may be beneficial in collecting information about substances that are better understood but have changed in their legality (e.g., tobacco) (Friedman & Wu, 2020), availability (e.g., opiates) (Manchikanti et al., 2012), formulation (e.g., cannabis) (Spindle et al., 2019), or have displayed an uptick in popularity and use (e.g., psychedelics) (Kelmendi et al., 2022). Generally, focus groups should be conducted until saturation has been reached in the data (Morse, 1995), meaning that little to no new information is generated in subsequent groups. Thus researchers should plan to conduct a range of groups depending on the saturation of the data; this may occur in as few as three or four or as many as eight or nine. Planning for conduction of five to six groups is usually sufficient, however.

Individual interviewing is a related but distinct qualitative technique (Mack et al., 2005). An individual interview aims to provide depth on a particular subject or area of focus. Individual interviews are ideal when gathering information on more sensitive topics about which respondents may be less comfortable sharing as part of a larger group. For example, research questions about medical conditions, treatments, illegal activities, or traumatic events are likely better suited to more private interviewing approaches as respondents' confidentiality is more easily protected and concerns about judgment or stigmatization are more easily alleviated. Similar to focus groups, individual interviews may benefit from pre-generation of a semi-structured interview agenda to informally guide the conversation. Again, the number of interviews required should be determined by saturation of the data; this may occur after 12 interviews (Guest et al., 2006) or after the completion of 25. Generally, a range of 20 to 30 interviews is considered a reasonable number for which to aim (Dworkin, 2012; Marshall et al., 2013; Morse, 2000).

Concerning hypothetical purchase task improvement and adaptation, cognitive interviewing may be one of the most valuable tools in the qualitative repertoire. Cognitive interviewing can assess the appropriateness and comprehension of any behavioral economic vignette or instructional set. This technique appreciates that the thought process required for individuals to answer questions is complex and often convoluted, comprising multiple cognitive steps, including question comprehension, retrieval of pertinent information from memory, assembling and integrating memorized information to select an answer, and ultimately planning and executing a response (McNeely et al., 2014; Willis, 2005). Cognitive interviewing may begin with training individuals to "think aloud" when completing a task. This may be done by asking them to verbally describe the number of windows in their home; for example, absent further instruction or specifications. Participants usually begin to speak aloud their thought process as they count and quickly begin to verbalize questions or issues with the task, such as "Does an attic window count?" or "I have a detached garage, so those windows aren't technically part of my home" or "My basement window was broken so I am not sure whether that counts?" and so forth. Ultimately, the individual understands the process by which they should evaluate the behavioral economic measure of interest and are ready to begin using the same technique on a substance purchase task. Taking one line of the vignette at a time, the participants can describe what they think each instruction means and why, and the researcher may probe their understanding further throughout the interview. Hypothetical purchase task vignettes may be divided into singular instructions, each of which the participant will evaluate in turn, including the phrasing within the actual items asking about the number of desired units per price increase. The researcher may wish to count how many participants appear to comprehend each point of interest to decide what adaptations may improve comprehension for most individuals.

Ultimately, researchers may wish to integrate qualitative and quantitative methods using a sequential explanatory mixed methods design (Ivankova et al., 2006). This design typically begins with qualitative method and analysis, followed by initial measure refinement and adaptation. Such adapted measures are then assessed using cognitive interviewing techniques, after which the measure is further refined. This process may be repeated until task comprehension peaks across most of a given qualitative sample. Finally, any modified hypothetical purchase task should be validated using an appropriately powered sample before its introduction to the field (see Fig. 4.2).

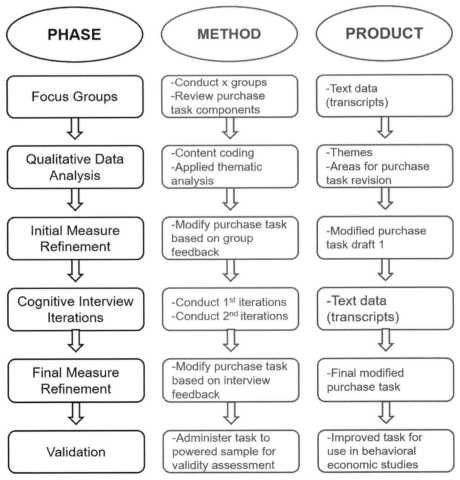

Figure 4.2 Modifications and refinements to hypothetical purchase tasks: A flowchart.

Notably, the qualitative approaches delineated herein are by no means exhaustive; myriad techniques may be combined with quantitative methods to adapt behavioral economic assessments. Using these tools in concert may arguably yield superior tasks, resulting in more accurate data that better reflects choices concerning substance use and allocation of financial resources, ultimately yielding indices that are better predictors, mediators, or outcomes within the substance use field.

References

Amlung, M. T., Acker, J., Stojek, M. K., Murphy, J. G., & MacKillop, J. (2012). Is talk "cheap"? An initial investigation of the equivalence of alcohol purchase task performance for hypothetical and actual rewards. *Alcoholism: Clinical and Experimental Research, 36*(4), 716−724. https://doi.org/10.1111/j.1530-0277.2011.01656.x

Amlung, M., & MacKillop, J. (2012). Consistency of self-reported alcohol consumption on randomized and sequential alcohol purchase tasks. *Frontiers in Psychiatry, 3*, 65. https://doi.org/10.3389/fpsyt.2012.00065

Amlung, M., & MacKillop, J. (2015). Further evidence of close correspondence for alcohol demand decision making for hypothetical and incentivized rewards. *Behavioural Processes, 113*, 187−191. https://doi.org/10.1016/j.beproc.2015.02.012

Aston, E. R., & Cassidy, R. N. (2019). Behavioral economic demand assessments in the addictions. *Current Opinion in Psychology, 30*, 42−47. https://doi.org/10.1016/j.copsyc.2019.01.016

Aston, E. R., Metrik, J., & MacKillop, J. (2015). Further validation of a marijuana purchase task. *Drug and Alcohol Dependence, 152*, 32−38.

Aston, E. R., Metrik, J., Rosen, R. K., Swift, R., & MacKillop, J. (2021). Refining the marijuana purchase task: Using qualitative methods to inform measure development. *Experimental and Clinical Psychopharmacology, 29*(1), 23. https://doi.org/10.1037/pha0000355

Autor, S. M. (1960). *The strength of conditioned reinforcers as a function of frequency and probability of reinforcement*. Unpublished doctoral dissertation. Harvard University.

Baum, W. M., & Rachlin, H. C. (1969). Choice as time allocation. *Journal of the Experimental Analysis of Behavior, 12*, 861−874. https://doi.org/10.1901/jeab.1969.12-861

Bickel, W. K., Johnson, M. W., Koffarnus, M. N., MacKillop, J., & Murphy, J. G. (2014). The behavioral economics of substance use disorders: Reinforcement pathologies and their repair. *Annual Review of Clinical Psychology, 10*, 641−677. https://doi.org/10.1146/annurev-clinpsy-032813-153724

Bickel, W. K., Marsch, L. A., & Carroll, M. E. (2000). Deconstructing relative reinforcing efficacy and situating the measures of pharmacological reinforcement with behavioral economics: A theoretical proposal. *Psychopharmacology, 153*(1), 44−56. https://doi.org/10.1007/s002130000589

Brady, J. V., & Griffiths, R. R. (1986). Behavioral procedures for evaluating the relative abuse potential of CNS drugs in primates. *Federation Proceedings, 35*, 2245−2253.

Brown, J., Washington, W. D., Stein, J. S., & Kaplan, B. A. (2021). The gym membership purchase task: Early evidence towards establishment of a novel hypothetical purchase task. *Psychological Record*, 1−11. https://doi.org/10.1007/s40732-021-00475-w

Bruner, N. R., & Johnson, M. W. (2014). Demand curves for hypothetical cocaine in cocaine-dependent individuals. *Psychopharmacology, 231*(5), 889−897. https://doi.org/10.1007/s00213-013-3312-5

Collins, R. L., Vincent, P. C., Yu, J., Liu, L., & Epstein, L. H. (2014). A behavioral economic approach to assessing demand for marijuana. *Experimental and Clinical Psychopharmacology, 22*(3), 211.

DeGrandpre, R. J., Bickel, W. K., Higgins, S. T., & Hughes, J. R. (1994). A behavioral economic analysis of concurrently available money and cigarettes. *Journal of the Experimental Analysis of Behavior, 61*(2), 191−201.

Dworkin, S. L. (2012). Sample size policy for qualitative studies using in-depth interviews. *Archives of Sexual Behavior, 41*(6), 1319−1320. https://doi.org/10.1007/s10508-012-0016-6

Field, M., Santarcangelo, M., Sumnall, H., Goudie, A., & Cole, J. (2006). Delay discounting and the behavioural economics of cigarette purchases in smokers: The effects of nicotine deprivation. *Psychopharmacology, 186*(2), 255−263. https://doi.org/10.1007/s00213-006-0385-4

Foley, G., & Timonen, V. (2015). Using grounded theory method to capture and analyze health care experiences. *Health Services Research, 50*(4), 1195−1210. https://doi.org/10.1111/1475-6773.12275

Foster, T. M., Temple, W., Cameron, B., & Poling, A. (1997). Demand curves for food in hens: Similarity under fixed-ratio and progressive-ratio schedules. *Behavioural Processes, 39*, 177−185.

Friedman, A. S., & Wu, R. J. (2020). Do local tobacco-21 laws reduce smoking among 18 to 20 year-olds? *Nicotine & Tobacco Research, 22*(7), 1195−1201. https://doi.org/10.1093/ntr/ntz123

Griffiths, R. R., Brady, J. V., & Bradford, L. D. (1978). Predicting the abuse liability of drugs and animal drug self-administration procedures: Psychomotor stimulants and hallucinogens. In T. Thompson, & P. B. Dews (Eds.), *Advances in behavioral pharmacology* (Vol 2, pp. 163−208). N. Y.: Academic Press.

Griffiths, R., Troisi II, J., Silvermanê, K., & Mumford[o], G. (1993). Multiple-choice procedure: An efficient approach for investigating drug reinforcement in humans. *Behavioural Pharmacology, 4*, 3−13.

Guest, G., Bunce, A., & Johnson, L. (2006). How many interviews are enough?: An experiment with data saturation and variability. *Field Methods, 18*(1), 59−82. https://doi.org/10.1177/1525822X05279903

Hodos, W. (1961). Progressive ratio as a measure of reward strength. *Science, 134*(3483), 943−944. https://doi.org/10.1126/science.134.3483.943

Hughes, C. E., Langford, J. S., Van Heukelom, J. T., Blejewski, R. C., & Pitts, R. C. (2022). A method for studying reinforcement factors controlling impulsive choice for use in behavioral neuroscience. *Journal of the Experimental Analysis of Behavior, 117*(3), 363−383. https://doi.org/10.1002/jeab.751

Hursh, S. R. (1980). Economic concepts for the analysis of behavior. *Journal of the Experimental Analysis of Behavior, 34*(2), 219−238. https://doi.org/10.1901/jeab.1980.34-219

Hursh, S. R. (1993). Behavioral economics of drug self-administration: An introduction. *Drug and Alcohol Dependence, 33*(2), 165−172. https://doi.org/10.1016/0376-8716(93)90058-X

Hursh, S. R. (2014). Behavioral economics and the analysis of consumption and choice. In F. K. McSweeney, & E. S. Murphy (Eds.), *The Wiley Blackwell handbook of operant and classical conditioning* (pp. 275−305). Hoboken, NJ: John Wiley & Sons. https://doi.org/10.1002/9781118468135.ch12

Hursh, S. R., & Silberberg, A. (2008). Economic demand and essential value. *Psychological Review, 115*(1), 186−198. https://doi.org/10.1037/0033-295X.115.1.186

Iglauer, C., & Woods, J. H. (1974). Concurrent performances: Reinforcement by different doses of intravenous cocaine in rhesus monkeys. *Journal of the Experimental Analysis of Behavior, 22*(1), 179−196. https://doi.org/10.1901/jeab.1974.22-179

Ivankova, N. V., Creswell, J. W., & Stick, S. L. (2006). Using mixed-methods sequential explanatory design: From theory to practice. *Field Methods, 18*(1), 3−20. https://doi.org/10.1177/1525822X05282260

Jacobs, E. A., & Bickel, W. K. (1999). Modeling drug consumption in the clinic using simulation procedures: Demand for heroin and cigarettes in opioid-dependent outpatients. *Experimental and Clinical Psychopharmacology, 7*(4), 412. https://doi.org/10.1037/1064-1297.7.4.412

Jarmolowicz, D. P., & Lattal, K. A. (2010). On distinguishing progressively increasing response requirements for reinforcement. *The Behavior Analyst, 33*(1), 119−125. https://doi.org/10.1007/BF03392207

Jimenez-Gomez, C., & Shahan, T. A. (2012). Concurrent-chains schedules as a method to study choice between alcohol-associated conditioned reinforcers. *Journal of the Experimental Analysis of Behavior, 97*(1), 71−83.

Johanson, C. E., & Schuster, C. R. (1975). A choice procedure for drug reinforcers: Cocaine and methylphenidate in the rhesus monkey. *Journal of Pharmacology and Experimental Therapeutics, 193*, 676−688.

Johnson, M. W., & Bickel, W. K. (2003). The behavioral economics of cigarette smoking: The concurrent presence of a substitute and an independent reinforcer. *Behavioural Pharmacology, 14*(2), 137−144. https://doi.org/10.1097/00008877-200303000-00005

Kaplan, B. A., Foster, R. N., Reed, D. D., Amlung, M., Murphy, J. G., & MacKillop, J. (2018). Understanding alcohol motivation using the alcohol purchase task: A methodological systematic review. *Drug and Alcohol Dependence, 191*, 117−140. https://doi.org/10.1016/j.drugalcdep.2018.06.029

Kaplan, B. A., Reed, D. D., Murphy, J. G., Henley, A. J., Reed, F. D. D., Roma, P. G., & Hursh, S. R. (2017). Time constraints in the alcohol purchase task. *Experimental and Clinical Psychopharmacology, 25*(3), 186−197. https://doi.org/10.1037/pha0000110

Katz, J. L. (1990). Models of relative reinforcing efficacy of drugs and their productive utility. *Behavioural Pharmacology*, (1), 283−301.

Kelmendi, B., Kaye, A. P., Pittenger, C., & Kwan, A. C. (2022). Psychedelics. *Current Biology, 32*(2), R63−R67. https://doi.org/10.1016/j.cub.2021.12.009

Koffarnus, M. N., Franck, C. T., Stein, J. S., & Bickel, W. K. (2015). A modified exponential behavioral economic demand model to better describe consumption data. *Experimental and Clinical Psychopharmacology, 23*(6), 504−512. https://doi.org/10.1037/pha0000045

Li, N., He, S., Parrish, C., Delich, J., & Grasing, K. (2003). Differences in morphine and cocaine reinforcement under fixed and progressive ratio schedules; effects of extinction, reacquisition and schedule design. *Behavioural Pharmacology, 14*, 619−630. https://doi.org/10.1097/01.fbp.0000104883.69384.e3

MacCorquodale, K., & Meehl, P. E. (1948). On a distinction between hypothetical constructs and intervening variables. *Psychological Review, 55*(2), 95−107. https://doi.org/10.1037/h0056029

Mack, N., Woodsong, C., MacQueen, K. M., Guest, G., & Namey, E. (2005). *Qualitative research methods: A data collector's field guide*. Family Health International.

MacKillop, J., Murphy, J. G., Ray, L. A., Eisenberg, D. T. A., Lisman, S. A., Lum, J. K., & Wilson, D. S. (2008). Further validation of a cigarette purchase task for assessing the relative reinforcing efficacy of nicotine in college smokers. *Experimental and Clinical Psychopharmacology, 16*(1), 57−65. https://doi.org/10.1037/1064-1297.16.1.57

Manchikanti, L., Helm Ii, S., Fellows, B., Janata, J. W., Pampati, V., Grider, J. S., & Boswell, M. V. (2012). Opioid epidemic in the United States. *Pain Physician, 15*(3 Suppl. l), ES9−ES38.

Marshall, B., Cardon, P., Poddar, A., & Fontenot, R. (2013). Does sample size matter in qualitative research?: A review of qualitative interviews in is research. *Journal of Computer Information Systems, 54*(1), 11−22. https://doi.org/10.1080/08874417.2013.11645667

McLeod, D. R., & Griffiths, R. R. (1983). Human progressive-ratio performance: Maintenance by pentobarbital. *Psychopharmacology, 79*, 4−9. https://doi.org/10.1007/BF00433007

McNeely, J., Halkitis, P. N., Horton, A., Khan, R., & Gourevitch, M. N. (2014). How patients understand the term "nonmedical use" of prescription drugs: Insights from cognitive interviews. *Substance Abuse, 35*(1), 12−20. https://doi.org/10.1080/08897077.2013.789463

Meisch, R. A., & Thompson, T. (1973). Ethanol as a reinforcer: Effects of fixed-ratio size and food deprivation. *Psychopharmacologia, 28*(2), 171−183. https://doi.org/10.1007/BF00421402

Morse, J. M. (1995). The significance of saturation. *Qualitative Health Research, 5*(2), 147−149. https://doi.org/10.1177/104973239500500201

Morse, J. M. (2000). Determining sample size. *Qualitative Health Research, 10*(1), 3−5. https://doi.org/10.1177/104973200129118183

Mulhauser, K., Miller Short, E., & Weinstock, J. (2018). Development and psychometric evaluation of the pornography purchase task. *Addictive Behaviors, 84*, 207−214. https://doi.org/10.1016/j.addbeh.2018.04.016

Murphy, J. G., & MacKillop, J. (2006). Relative reinforcing efficacy of alcohol among college student drinkers. *Experimental and Clinical Psychopharmacology, 14*(2), 219. https://doi.org/10.1037/1064-1297.14.2.219

Neale, J., Allen, D., & Coombes, L. (2005). Qualitative research methods within the addictions. *Addiction, 100*(11), 1584−1593. https://doi.org/10.1111/j.1360-0443.2005.01230.x

Petry, N. M., & Bickel, W. K. (1998). Polydrug abuse in heroin addicts: A behavioral economic analysis. *Addiction, 93*(3), 321−335. https://doi.org/10.1046/j.1360-0443.1998.9333212.x

Pope, D. A., Poe, L., Stein, J. S., Kaplan, B. A., Heckman, B. W., Epstein, L. H., & Bickel, W. K. (2019). Experimental tobacco marketplace: Substitutability of e-cigarette liquid for cigarettes as a function of nicotine strength. *Tobacco Control, 28*(2), 206−211. https://doi.org/10.1136/tobaccocontrol-2017-054024

Punch, K. F. (2013). *Introduction to social research: Quantitative and qualitative approaches* (3rd ed.). SAGE Publications Ltd.

Rachlin, H. (1978). A molar theory of reinforcement schedules. *Journal of the Experimental Analysis of Behavior, 30*(3), 345−360. https://doi.org/10.1901/jeab.1978.30-345

Rachlin, H., Green, L., Kagel, J. H., & Battalio, R. C. (1976). Economic demand theory and psychological studies of choice. *Psychology of Learning and Motivation, 10*, 129−154. https://doi.org/10.1016/S0079-7421(08)60466-1

Reed, D. D., Kaplan, B. A., & Becirevic, A. (2015). Basic research on the behavioral economics of reinforcer value. In F. D. D. Reed, & D. D. Reed (Eds.), *Autism service delivery: Bridging the gap between science and practice* (pp. 279−306). Springer Science + Business Media. https://doi.org/10.1007/978-1-4939-2656-5_10

Reed, D. D., Kaplan, B. A., Becirevic, A., Roma, P. G., & Hursh, S. R. (2016). Toward quantifying the abuse liability of ultraviolet tanning: A behavioral economic approach to tanning addiction. *Journal of the Experimental Analysis of Behavior, 106*(1), 93−106. https://doi.org/10.1002/jeab.216

Reed, D. D., Naudé, G. P., Salzer, A. R., Peper, M., Monroe-Gulick, A. L., Gelino, B. W., Harsin, J. D., Foster, R. N. S., Nighbor, T. D., Kaplan, B. A., Koffarnus, M. N., & Higgins, S. T. (2020). Behavioral economic measurement of cigarette demand: A descriptive review of published approaches to the cigarette purchase task. *Experimental and Clinical Psychopharmacology, 28*(6), 688−705. https://doi.org/10.1037/pha0000347

Richardson, N. R., & Roberts, D. C. S. (1996). Progressive ratio schedules in drug self-administration studies in rats - a method to evaluate reinforcing efficacy. *Journal of Neuroscience Methods, 66*, 1−11.

Roma, P. G., Hursh, S. R., & Hudja, S. (2016). Hypothetical purchase task questionnaires for behavioral economic assessments of value and motivation. *Managerial and Decision Economics, 37*(4−5), 306−323. https://doi.org/10.1002/mde.2718

Salzer, A. R., Strickland, J. C., Stoops, W. W., & Reed, D. D. (2021). An evaluation of fixed and randomized price sequence on the alcohol purchase task. *Experimental and Clinical Psychopharmacology, 29*(4), 295.

Shahan, T. A., Bickel, W. K., Madden, G. J., & Badger, G. J. (1999). Comparing the reinforcing efficacy of nicotine containing and de-nicotinized cigarettes: A behavioral economic analysis. *Psychopharmacology, 147*, 210−216. https://doi.org/10.1007/s002130051162

Shahan, T. A., Odum, A. L., & Bickel, W. K. (2000). Nicotine gum as a substitute for cigarettes: A behavioral economic analysis. *Behavioural Pharmacology, 11*(1), 71−79. https://doi.org/10.1097/00008877-200002000-00008

Spindle, T. R., Bonn-Miller, M. O., & Vandrey, R. (2019). Changing landscape of cannabis: Novel products, formulations, and methods of administration. *Current Opinion in Psychology, 30*, 98−102. https://doi.org/10.1016/j.copsyc.2019.04.002

Stafford, D., LeSage, M. G., & Glowa, J. R. (1999). Effects of phentermine on responding maintained by progressive-ratio schedules of cocaine and food delivery in rhesus monkeys. *Behavioural Pharmacology, 10*, 775−784.

Stein, J. S., Koffarnus, M. N., Snider, S. E., Quisenberry, A. J., & Bickel, W. K. (2015). Identification and management of nonsystematic purchase task data: Toward best practice. *Experimental and Clinical Psychopharmacology, 23*(5), 377. https://doi.org/10.1037/pha0000020

Stein, J. S., Koffarnus, M. N., Stepanov, I., Hatsukami, D. K., & Bickel, W. K. (2018). Cigarette and e-liquid demand and substitution in e-cigarette naïve smokers. *Experimental and Clinical Psychopharmacology, 26*(3), 233−243. https://doi.org/10.1037/pha0000192

Stinson, L. A., Prioleau, D., Laurenceau, I., & Dallery, J. (2021). Correspondence between responses on an internet purchase task and a laboratory progressive ratio task. *Psychological Record, 71*(2), 247−255. https://doi.org/10.1007/s40732-021-00463-0

Strickland, J. C., Vsevolozhskaya, O. A., & Stoops, W. W. (2021). E-cigarette demand: Impact of commodity definitions and test−retest reliability. *Nicotine & Tobacco Research, 23*(3), 557−565. https://doi.org/10.1093/ntr/ntaa139

Tenny, S., Brannan, J. M., & Brannan, G. D. (2022). Qualitative study. In *StatPearls*. StatPearls Publishing. http://www.ncbi.nlm.nih.gov/books/NBK470395/.

Vincent, P. C., Collins, R. L., Liu, L., Yu, J., De Leo, J. A., & Earleywine, M. (2017). The effects of perceived quality on behavioral economic demand for marijuana: A web-based experiment. *Drug and Alcohol Dependence, 170*, 174–180. https://doi.org/10.1016/j.drugalcdep.2016.11.013

Warden, C. J. (1931). *Animal motivation: Experimental studies on the albino rat.* Columbia University Press. https://doi.org/10.5962/bhl.title.82146

Willis, G. B. (2005). *Cognitive interviewing: A tool for improving questionnaire design.* Sage Publications.

Quantitative models of operant demand

Brent A. Kaplan [1,2]
[1]Codedbx, United States; [2]Innovation Department, Advocates for Human Potential, Inc., Sudbury, MA, United States

Quantitative models of operant demand

The field of behavioral economic demand focuses on quantifying the value of a reinforcer or outcome. As we will see, methods for quantifying value are vast and there is no single "correct" approach. This chapter is written assuming you, the reader, have some cursory knowledge of behavioral economic demand methods. If you have picked up this chapter without knowing much about demand, I encourage you to peruse Chapter 2 *Introduction to Operant Demand* and either Chapter 3 *Nonhuman Research Methods/Procedures for Studying Operant Demand* or Chapter 4 *Human Research Methods for Studying Operant Demand*. These chapters will provide the background knowledge necessary to understand how the quantitative approaches fit within the broader backdrop and framework of demand methodology.

The chapter is organized as follows. I will first provide a brief primer on regression methods, including linear and nonlinear regression, and the various approaches to analyzing demand data. This primer should give you some intuitive ideas about what happens when we try to fit a model to the data and a better understanding of the differences between regression approaches. I will then highlight a few of the more popular and frequently used demand models (don't worry, I will sprinkle in citations to direct further reading). Then, similar to Chapter 10 *Quantitative Models of Discounting*, I will outline and walk through the steps of analyzing demand data using the R Statistical Software and demonstrate several approaches to modeling demand data using freely available data. Then, I will finish the chapter by discussing some issues and considerations when modeling demand data and providing suggestions for resources.

A quick note about this chapter before moving on: this chapter is written using Quarto (Allaire et al., 2024), an "open-source scientific and technical publishing system built on Pandoc," and the source code and supporting files are available in my repository: https://github.com/brentkaplan/quant-demand. I *highly encourage* you to look at the source file, especially when navigating through some of the R code (while I expose some of the R code used in this document, there is plenty more that you cannot see). This chapter would be much more tedious to write if it were not for the developers of the apaquarto extension (Schneider, 2025), which allows for a seamless process of creating documents following the American Psychological Association's 7th Edition style requirements.

Important terms

Before diving into the numerous quantitative models proposed to describe demand data, there are a handful of terms with which familiarity will be helpful while navigating the chapter. Adapted in part from Koffarnus et al. (2022), Table 5.1 lists some of these terms and their definitions. These terms will be used throughout the chapter when referencing different aspects of demand and its analysis, and they are helpful generally when working with behavioral economic demand data and analyses.

A note on regression

Regression is the statistical process of investigating the relationship between two or more variables. Typically, regression aims to understand the effect of some independent variable (in other words, some variable that the experimenter manipulates or some variable that may causally affect the outcome) on a dependent variable (i.e., the outcome variable). Regression can take many forms, but for this chapter, we will distinguish between linear and nonlinear regression and spend most of the focus on the latter.

Linear regression versus nonlinear regression

If you have learned about or conducted any regression modeling, you have probably heard of or performed linear regression. General linear regression models the relationship between the independent and dependent variables and, importantly, assumes this relationship is linear and the residuals (i.e., the difference between what the model predicts and the observed data) follow a conditionally normal distribution. This means that no matter what, one unit increase in the value of the independent variable (e.g., age) will result in the same amount of change in the dependent variable (e.g., salary). The general linear model is simply a specific case of the class of models known as *generalized* linear models, where the assumptions about the residual structure are not so strict. Nonlinear regression models, on the other hand, can hold the assumption of conditionally normally distributed residuals, but is not necessarily inherent and, potentially more importantly, the distinction between the aforementioned linear regression and nonlinear regression lies in the relation of the predictor variables — they are expressed as a *nonlinear* combination. As such, nonlinear models can be highly flexible in their ability to bend and curve. Because behavioral economic demand methods attempt to model some consummatory behavior (or the self-report of such behavior) by capturing both the inelastic and elastic relationship with price, nonlinear models are especially useful for describing this pattern. Historically, numerous models have been proposed to describe how consumption decreases as a function of increasing costs, starting as far back as 1988 (Hursh et al., 1988).

Quantitative models of operant demand

Table 5.1 Important behavioral economic demand terms.

Term	Similar terms	Definition
Cost	Price, Unit Price, Effort	The response effort or monetary expenditure associated with obtaining one unit of a commodity. It represents the price, effort, or number of responses required, or a combination of these factors.
Consumption		The amount of a commodity earned or obtained and then consumed at a specific cost.
Purchasing		The quantity of a commodity obtained or earned, typically equal to consumption but particularly relevant in hypothetical scenarios or tasks where not all purchased items are consumed.
Demand Intensity	Q_0	The level of consumption associated with minimal or zero cost. This may be measured directly (such as free consumption) or derived from demand models.
Demand Elasticity		Reflects the reduction in consumption when cost increases by a single unit. Elasticity often changes with cost, following a curvilinear demand curve. It is generally derived from model parameters, making interpretation dependent on the specific model used and often requiring multiple parameters for precision.
Change in Elasticity	α	As elasticity is cost-dependent and demand is curvilinear, some models measure the rate of elasticity change as cost rises. Like elasticity, this parameter is derived from model-based parameters, which influences interpretation and makes it contextually dependent.
Omax	Max Expenditure	The peak amount spent or maximum effort exerted for any given price. This value can be computed by identifying Pmax and then multiplying it by the consumption level at that price point.
Pmax		The cost associated with the Omax value. Calculated by determining where the demand curve has a slope of -1 in log-log space, irrespective of the specific demand model used.
Breakpoint		The cost threshold that brings consumption down to zero. It can be derived from raw data or model-based equations, though models with exponential decay functions may not reach zero, requiring specialized estimation methods.

Regression approaches to demand

I want to highlight three regression approaches commonly used to analyze demand data. I will briefly describe each approach but the reader is encouraged to read Kaplan et al. (2021) for a more in-depth discussion of each.

Fit-to-group approach

This first approach can be conducted in two ways. The first way is fitting a model to preaggregated averaged data. In this approach, data at each price is first averaged across individuals (or organisms) and then a line is fit to these averaged data. Because all the variability in the data is compressed into a singular point for each price, this approach ignores the intraprice variability and is typically not appropriate for statistical inference. However, this approach may be useful for descriptive, graphical, or theoretical equation testing. The second approach is fitting a curve to all data without aggregation, also known as a pooled approach. Under typical circumstances, the resulting point estimates from the regression will be the same regardless of either of these fit-to-group approaches. However, in the case of this pooled approach, the standard errors are likely to be incorrect because all data points are treated as independent observations when there is dependence within an individual or condition.

Two-stage approach

This two-stage approach is quite common for analyzing demand data. In this approach, a demand model is fit to each individual's data separately. This approach results in parameter estimates for each individual and condition. We have called this the two-stage approach because the modeling serves as the first stage, and the resulting demand metrics are used in the second stage of statistical analysis to make some sort of inference or comparison (e.g., a t-test, correlation). One downside to this approach is that the model effectively overfits the individual's data and ignores any information about how other individuals in the sample respond to the same experimental conditions.

Mixed-effects modeling

Both of the approaches mentioned above are considered "fixed-effects" only approaches. Fixed-effects parameter estimates that are constant or unchanging across different observations (i.e., they are "fixed" across individuals or conditions). In the approaches above, these fixed effects are Q_0 and α; for example, in the fit-to-means approach only one sample level Q_0 and α is estimated so each individual inherits those values. Random effects, on the other hand, account for variability that differs across individuals or experimental sessions. They allow the model to recognize that there may be differences between subjects or conditions that are not captured by the fixed effects. You can think of mixed-effects models broadly as the ability to simultaneously estimate "population-level" effects (akin to the fit-to-group approaches) and "subject-level" effects (akin to the two-stage approach), with the model taking into account *all the data* provided. As such, mixed-effects models combine both fixed and random effects to capture both the within-subject variability and between-subject variability. This approach allows the researcher to properly account for the nested and crossed nature that is typical of demand data. For example, prices are often nested *within* an individual and the same individuals typically participate in multiple conditions, which is a classic example of crossed random effects. For a much more thorough and detailed discussion of these regression approaches including the numerous benefits of mixed-effects models, see Kaplan et al. (2021).

Brief overview of models of demand

This section will provide a brief overview of some of the more frequently used demand models, and a new model that appears promising in simplifying demand analyses. There are certainly many other models not discussed here and while they could be afforded an entire chapter, that focus would detract from that of the current chapter on implementing the quantitative techniques of fitting these models. As such, a comprehensive review of all models is beyond the scope of the current chapter. Instead, I direct you toward Koffarnus et al. (2022) for a thorough discussion of the various models, including the advantages and disadvantages of each. For a quick reference to the seminal papers and model formulations, see Table 5.2.

Table 5.2 Quantitative models of demand.

Citation	Model formulation
Hursh et al. (1988)	$\log(Q) = \log(L) + b(\log(P)) - aP$
Winger et al. (2006)	$\log(Q) = \log(L)e^{-aP}$
Hursh and Silberberg (2008)	$\log(Q) = \log(Q_0) + k\left(e^{-\alpha Q_0 C} - 1\right)$
Yu et al. (2014)	$Q = L \cdot P^b \cdot e^{-aP}$
Koffarnus et al. (2015)	$Q = Q_0 \cdot 10^{k(e^{-\alpha Q_0 C} - 1)}$
Newman and Ferrario (2020)	$Q = Q_0 \left[1 + \left(\frac{P}{P_0}\right)^b\right]^{-a/b}$
Gilroy et al. (2021)	$\mathrm{IHS}(Q) = \mathrm{IHS}(Q_0) + \mathrm{IHS}(Q_0) \cdot e^{-\alpha Q_0 P} - 1$ where $\mathrm{IHS}(Q_0) = \log_{10}\left(0.5 \cdot Q_0 + \sqrt{0.25 \cdot Q_0^2 + 1}\right)$
Rzeszutek et al. (in press)	$Q_j = Q_0 \cdot e^{(-\alpha \cdot Q_0 \cdot C_j)}$

As noted in previous works, such as Kaplan et al. (2021), many original model formulations did not provide explicit error terms; Error terms describe deviations from a regression line, so they have not been included here.

Linear elasticity

The linear elasticity model (Eq. 5.1), proposed in 1988 by Hursh et al. (1988), jointly describes changes in elasticity as a function of a (change in slope with increases in price) and b (the initial slope of the curve). L is analogous to the intercept, or estimated consumption when the price is infinitesimally small. In this model, changes in elasticity are assumed to be linear. Later equations improved upon the primary limitations of this model, where the idea of elasticity is jointly described by two parameters (instead of one) and where the model sometimes predicts increases in consumption at very small prices.

$$\log(Q_j) = \log(L) + b \cdot (\log(P)) - a \cdot P_j + \varepsilon_j, j = 1, ..., k \tag{5.1}$$

Exponential

The exponential model of demand (Eq. 5.2), introduced in 2008 by Hursh and Silberberg (2008), utilizes an exponential decay function to describe the relationship between price and consumption. Contrasted with earlier models, this model describes the rate at which elasticity changes across the demand curve in the free parameter α and the "intercept" or consumption when there is no price is Q_0. In this model, the parameter k governs how high and low the curve is allowed to go; generally, smaller values of k will restrict the range of consumption, while larger values of k will allow for wider ranges of consumption. Due to the logarithmic transformations, especially for the dependent variable (y values), this model cannot incorporate zeros as data unless those zero values are manually transformed into a small positive value. Changing these values is not recommended as the decision of *what* "small" value to use may quite substantially affect the resulting parameter estimates (Koffarnus et al., 2015; Yu et al., 2014).

$$\log(Q_j) = \log(Q_0) + k\left(e^{-\alpha \cdot Q_0 \cdot C_j} - 1\right) + \varepsilon_j, j = 1, ..., k \tag{5.2}$$

Exponentiated

The exponentiated model (Eq. 5.3), introduced in 2015 by Koffarnus et al. (2015), serves as a simple mathematical transformation of Eq. (5.2) (both sides of the model are exponentiated), where all the parameters from Eq. (5.2) have the same interpretations. This model has been used frequently in the literature and is often preferred to the original formulation because no logarithmic transformations of y-values are required – the data can be fit directly.

$$Q_j = Q_0 \cdot 10^{k\left(e^{-\alpha \cdot Q_0 \cdot C_j} - 1\right)} + \varepsilon_j, j = 1, ..., k \tag{5.3}$$

Simplified exponential with normalized decay

The simplified exponential with normalized decay (Eq. 5.4) is a modification of Eq. (5.3) that functionally removes the need to include the span parameter k. One benefit of this model is that some of the derived metrics (e.g., essential value) have a closed-form solution compared to other models that require approximations. This is a newly proposed model, and studies may benefit from demonstrating its utility compared to other models (e.g., Eqs. 5.2 and 5.3).

$$Q_j = Q_0 \cdot e^{(-\alpha \cdot Q_0 \cdot C_j)} + \varepsilon_j, j = 1, ..., k \tag{5.4}$$

Tools for demand analysis

Several tools and software exist for modeling demand. GraphPad Prism (GraphPad Software, n.d.) is one popular program for conducting demand analysis. While Prism is also a popular software for statistical analysis and data visualization (especially in the field of biostatistics), it is proprietary and costs money to license and use. Other free software languages you can use to run demand analyses (essentially any program that can perform nonlinear regression) include but are not limited to, software such as R and Python. This chapter will primarily focus on using the R Statistical Programming Language (R Core Team, 2024) to analyze demand data. R is a free, open-source programming language and environment for statistical computing and graphics and is a popular language for statistical analysis and data visualization. R has "packages," which are collections of functions that can be used to perform specific tasks. For example, the *nlmrt* and *nlme* packages (Nash, 2016; Pinheiro et al., 2023) contain functions that are used to run nonlinear fixed-effects and mixed-effects models, respectively. For this chapter, we will use collections of packages such as *tidyverse* (Wickham et al., 2019) and *easystats* (Lüdecke et al., 2022), as well as individual packages such as *nlmrt* and *nlme*. I have developed a specific R package called *beezdemand* [Behavioral Economic Easy Demand; Kaplan et al. (2019), Kaplan (2023)] that contains many helper functions that can be used to conduct various aspects related to demand analyses. Although I will not rely on the *beezdemand* package for everything in this chapter, I will use some functions and highlight others that may make analyses easier.

One other tool that I have made recently available is *shinybeez* (Kaplan & Reed, 2025), which is an R Shiny application that can be used to conduct behavioral economic demand and discounting analyses. A Shiny application is essentially a web application that can be run locally or on the web and allows the user to conduct analyses without having to write any code. The *shinybeez* application is (currently) available at https://brentkaplan.shinyapps.io/shinybeez/, and the source code is available at https://github.com/brentkaplan/shinybeez (this repository will always contain up-to-date web URLs). In addition to being completely free, *shinybeez* relies on *beezdemand* to perform the core functionality of the demand analyses. This allows *transparency* and *replicability* in conducting demand analyses regardless of whether you are using the *beezdemand* package as part of a broader R workflow or using the *shinybeez* application. Please consult Kaplan and Reed (2025) for more detailed information about *shinybeez*. Finally, you will find many of the papers I have published and referenced in this chapter, as well as tools that I have created on my website: https://codedbx.com. Visit that website to always find the most up-to-date versions of the tools and code that I create.

General steps for demand analysis

Here, I will outline the general steps that can be used to conduct demand analysis. These steps are not necessarily the only way to conduct demand analysis, but they are a good starting point for those new to these analyses, and I will generally follow these steps in this chapter. An important note for these steps is that I highly recommend using them to outline the decision rules used to conduct the analyses a priori. This is important because it will help you to be more transparent and replicable in your analyses and, importantly, decrease the likelihood of getting lost in the garden of forking paths (Gelman & Loken, 2013).

- Step 0: Analysis development. This step involves developing a plan for the analysis, including the specific demand model and regression approach to be used, the criteria for model selection, and the criteria for model validation. This step should include laying out the decision rules you will use for each of the following seven steps, including contingency plans for if something does not go as planned (e.g., if a model you choose does not converge, what changes will you make?).
- Step 1: Data preparation and initial examination. This step involves preparing the data for analysis, including checking for missing values, outliers, and data transformations. Practical approaches include creating a table of descriptive statistics and potentially creating visualizations such as scatterplots or histograms.
- Step 2: Use criteria to examine systematicity. This step involves using systematic criteria to examine how data conform to our preexisting expectations of demand functions.
- Step 3: Model fitting. Select the demand model and use nonlinear regression to plot the demand curve. This step involves analyzing the data according to the chosen regression method specified in Step 0 (i.e., fit-to-group, two-stage, and mixed-effects models).
- Step 4: Visual analysis and interpretation. Plot the demand curve using semi- or double-logarithmic scales to create demand (and/or work) functions visually depicting the model. Overlay model fit lines and data points to visually examine how closely the model accurately represents the data points.
- Step 5: Model comparison and refinement. If more than one demand model is applicable, compare their fit indices (e.g., R^2 values) to select the most accurate data representations. Adjust parameters (e.g., k) to improve the fit and interpretability of the demand curve. Repeat steps 3 through 5 as needed or based on the a priori decision rules.
- Step 6: Calculate important metrics. Calculate metrics from the demand curve, including Q_0 (model-based intensity), elasticity, and model-based O_{max} and P_{max}. Other metrics that may not be reliant on fitting the demand curve include observed intensity, observed O_{max} and P_{max}, and breakpoint.
- Step 7: Interpret and report findings. Explain what key measures mean in the analysis context and broader research question. For example, whether specific reinforcers maintain behavior longer or are more resistant to price increases. Provide a detailed summary of the model

parameters, including the goodness-of-fit, and discuss any observed deviations or patterns in the demand curve. Report all decisions made during this seven-step process and, ideally, provide the code and data to facilitate replication.

Step 1. Data preparation and initial examination of example demand data

In this chapter, we will work with a dataset I have previously made publicly available in the GitHub repository: https://github.com/brentkaplan/mixed-effects-demand. The data we will use was used previously by Kaplan et al. (2021), where we introduced concepts about mixed-effects models for behavioral economic demand; however, here, I will provide a more step-by-step approach for conducting demand analyses in general according to the steps outlined before.

The dataset is human self-report response data on the Alcohol Purchase Task (APT) from Kaplan and Reed (2018). This study used "happy hour" alcohol pricing to explore how different promotional price frames (e.g., buy-one-get-one-free vs. half-price deals) influence alcohol demand. We found that these frames significantly affected consumption patterns, with the buy-one-get-one-free format generating a higher demand. The data we will use here is a subset of the data from this study from one experimental condition.

Alcohol purchase task

The alcohol purchase task consisted of 17 prices: $0, $0.25, $0.5, $1, $1.5, $2, $2.5, $3, $4, $5, $6, $7, $8, $9, $10, $15, $20 and had a standard vignette:

In the questionnaire that follows we would like you to pretend to purchase and consume alcohol for 5 hours. Imagine that you and your friends are at a bar on a weekend night from **9:00** p.m. **until 2:00** a.m. to see a band. Imagine that you do not have any obligations the next day (i.e., no work or classes). The following questions ask how many drinks you would purchase at various prices. The available drinks are standard-size domestic beers (12 oz.), wine (5 oz.), shots of hard liquor (1.5 oz.), or mixed drinks containing one shot of liquor. Assume that you did not drink alcohol or use drugs before you went to the bar and that you will not drink or use drugs after leaving the bar. You cannot bring your alcohol or drugs to the bar. Also, assume that the alcohol you are about to purchase is for your consumption only. In other words, you cannot sell the drinks or give them to anyone else. You also cannot bring the drinks home and you have no other alcohol at home. Everything you buy is, therefore, for your personal use within the **5 hours** that you are at the bar. Please respond to these questions honestly, as if you were actually in this situation. To verify you understand the pretend scenario, you must correctly answer the next three questions before moving on to the questionnaire.

Then, participants were asked to correctly answer three multiple-choice questions before going forward: (a) "In this pretend scenario, how many hours do you have to consume the drinks?", (b) "In this pretend scenario, how much did you drink before the bar?", and (c) "In this pretend scenario, what is the drink special?"

Importance of exploring data before fitting

```
apt |>
  # select only x and y columns
  select(x, y) |>
  # for each unique x value
  group_by(x) |>
  # calculate the following statistics
  summarise(
    Mean = mean(y),
    `Std. Dev` = sd(y),
    Min = min(y),
    `25%` = quantile(y, .25),
    Median = median(y),
    `75%` = quantile(y, .75),
    Max = max(y)
  ) |>
  ungroup() |>
  mutate(x = paste0("$", x)) |>
  rename(
    "Price" = "x"
  )
```

When collecting demand data, I recommend visualizing or plotting consumption values as a function of the prices. This is done to examine the range of the data and determine whether specific values are *too extreme*. Table 5.3 shows descriptive statistics such as mean, standard deviation, and quantiles at each price. As Table 5.3 shows, the maximum number of drinks a participant reported was 50, which corresponds to 10 alcoholic drinks per hour for 5 hours. These numbers, and numbers that you see, may seem unrealistic and should be investigated. At a minimum, the responses by these participant(s) should be examined and at most removed if there is a justifiable and compelling reason for doing so. These decisions should be outlined in Step 0 when creating the analysis plan. Table A5.1 shows the descriptive table output from the

Table 5.3 Descriptive statistics for the Alcohol Purchase Task data.

Price	Mean	Std. Dev	Min	25%	Median	75%	Max
$0	5.86	4.71	0	3	5	8	50
$0.25	5.43	4.31	0	3	5	8	40
$0.5	5.26	4.20	0	2	5	8	30
$1	5.05	3.94	0	2	5	7	30
$1.5	4.72	3.71	0	2	4	7	30
$2	4.40	3.42	0	2	4	6	30
$2.5	4.08	3.27	0	2	4	6	30
$3	3.69	3.02	0	1	3	5	30
$4	3.16	2.81	0	1	3	5	30
$5	2.66	2.41	0	1	2	4	20
$6	2.17	2.26	0	0	2	3	25
$7	1.80	2.35	0	0	1	3	44
$8	1.43	1.78	0	0	1	2	19
$9	1.12	1.74	0	0	0	2	30
$10	0.92	1.70	0	0	0	1	30
$15	0.49	1.19	0	0	0	1	25
$20	0.35	0.90	0	0	0	0	16

GetDescriptives() function in the *beezdemand* package.[1] This table provides similar information to Table 5.3 which I manually created.

Sometimes, it is helpful to examine the data by plotting the relative distribution of responses for each price. Fig. 5.1 shows such data for the APT. In this figure, the gray boxplots represent the 25th to 75th percentile, with the horizontal lines representing the median values, the red line (light gray in print version) representing the mean, and the green (gray in print version) and red (dark gray in print version) dots representing the minimum and maximum values, respectively. You can see that there is quite a bit of variability in the first couple of prices. Overall, the average and median number of self-reported drinks purchased *decreases* as the price per drink increases, typical of demand data. Plotting data in this way can help you see big-picture trends in the data to identify extreme values or patterns counter to expectations. However, it is also important to attempt to quantify the extent to which demand data are considered "systematic".

Step 2: Use criteria to examine systematicity

Stein et al. (2015) proposed a set of three criteria for examining and identifying the extent to which demand data (e.g., responses) are deemed "systematic." These three criteria include trend, bounce, and reversals from zero. Trend assumes that consumption from the first price to the last price should go down (with a suggested default value of at least 0.025 log-unit reduction per log-unit range in price). Bounce is a measure of

---

[1] *shinybeez* automatically creates a descriptive table for you when you load your data.

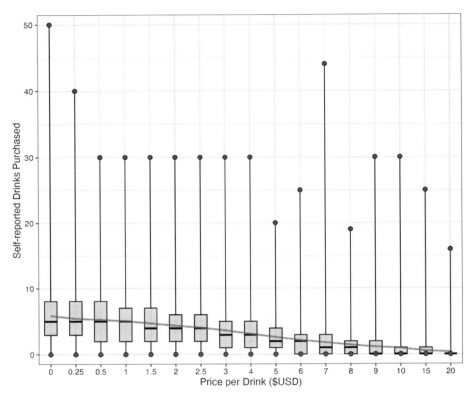

Figure 5.1 Descriptive statistics for the Alcohol Purchase Task data. Boxplots represent the 25%–75% interquartile range, horizontal lines within the boxplots represent the median, high and low points represent the maximum and minimum values, and the red line (light gray in print version) represents the mean.

price-to-price increases/decreases in consumption, as the general expectation is that consumption should decrease overall and not result in frequent price increases. Stein and colleagues suggest a detection limit of 0.10, meaning the criteria is flagged when increases occur for more than 10% of the price increments. Finally, reversals from zero occur when a nonzero response follows two or more consecutive zero responses. Readers are encouraged to consult Stein et al. (2015) for a more detailed discussion of these criteria. Important to note is that these criteria are for *identification* and are not to be used automatically or thoughtlessly for exclusion.

Although I recommend researchers screen for systematicity and report these numbers, the decision to retain these response sets in subsequent analyses is in the researcher's hands. If the researcher decides to remove or exclude some response sets based on these criteria, I recommend analyzing both the full dataset and the restricted dataset and reporting the extent to which excluding those response sets affected the results and interpretations.

```
# pass the dataframe `apt` to the `CheckSystematic` function from the
# beezdemand package. default values are used for the three criteria.
apt_unsys <- beezdemand::CheckUnsystematic(apt)
```

Here, I use the `checkUnsystematic` function from the *beezdemand* package. This function outputs a data frame with the total number of criteria passed, each criteria's value and whether that criterion was met, and the number of positive values. The number of positive values is helpful because, in some regression approaches (e.g., two-stage), these datasets cannot be fit. Table 5.4 shows the output from this function.[2] You can see that the criteria values all differ and that only among this small subset, id = 5 passes only two criteria. Numbers and percentages of the number of response sets that pass the three criteria, as well as how these respondents are treated should be reported. For example, Table A5.2 shows the number and percentage of response sets associated with the number of criteria passed.

Step 3: Model fitting

Approaches for handling k values

The k value in Eqs. (5.2) and (5.3) generally reflect a "range" of the data and functionally constrain the upper and lower bounds of the demand model, such that a higher k value will result in a relatively higher and lower asymptote and a lower k value will result in a relatively lower upper bound and a relatively higher lower bound. There are several different ways of calculating k values. One approach does not rely on solving it as a free parameter and is instead calculated based on the observed range of the data. Then, this value is inserted as a constant into the model during the fitting process. Sometimes, a value of 0.5 is added to the calculated observed range because of the potential that an estimated Q_0 value might exceed the range of the observed data. Such changes should be reported when describing the method of calculating k. Another approach is to treat k as a free parameter in the model process. In the two-stage approach, this can be done by solving for k *differently* for each participant or by *sharing* a singular (i.e., global) k value across all participants. The former approach typically results in estimates highly specific to each participant, whereas the latter approach considers the entire range of the data.

---

[2] *shinybeez* automatically creates a table of unsystematic criteria similar to Table 5.4. Criteria values can be specified in the application.

Table 5.4 First 10 rows from the checkUnsystematic function from the beezdemand package.

id	TotalPass	DeltaQ	DeltaQPass	Bounce	BouncePass	Reversals	ReversalsPass	NumPosValues
1	3	0.30	Pass	0.00	Pass	0	Pass	17
2	3	0.82	Pass	0.00	Pass	0	Pass	12
3	3	0.91	Pass	0.00	Pass	0	Pass	16
4	3	0.84	Pass	0.00	Pass	0	Pass	16
5	2	0.00	Fail	0.00	Pass	0	Pass	0
6	3	0.88	Pass	0.00	Pass	0	Pass	14
7	3	0.82	Pass	0.00	Pass	0	Pass	15
8	3	0.84	Pass	0.00	Pass	0	Pass	15
9	3	0.70	Pass	0.06	Pass	0	Pass	5
10	3	0.88	Pass	0.00	Pass	0	Pass	13

```
# manual k calculation
apt_k <- log10(max (apt$y[apt$y > 0]) / min(apt$y[apt$y > 0])) + 0.5


# beezdemand k calculation specifying using the full range of data
apt_k_beez <- beezdemand::GetK(apt, mnrange = FALSE)


# identical results
apt_k
[1] 2.19897
apt_k_beez
[1] 2.19897
```

In any case, treating k as a free parameter can cause issues with model convergence (i.e., finding an optimal solution based on a set of reasonable parameters). In my experience, when this occurs, the model estimates a very high k value that is many magnitudes higher than the actual range of the data in logarithmic units. For this chapter, I will use the first approach by calculating the observed range in logarithmic units and then adding 0.5 to that range. This approach is equivalent to the *beezdemand* function GetK with mnrange = FALSE.[3] The resulting k value is 2.199. See the code chunk.

A note on model specification

Entering the parameters to be solved into the model can be done in one of two ways. In the first, the parameters are entered directly into the model without any "transformation" such that Q_0 and α are optimized in their natural units (e.g., Q_0 in the units of consumption and α in the inverse units of price). Essentially, these units are on different scales. Small changes in Q_0 and α can lead to disproportionately large changes in the predicted demand curve, especially at extreme values (e.g., very high prices where consumption drops sharply). The other method – reexpressing Q_0 and α as logarithms of Q_0 and α during the fitting process – can help make parameter estimation more stable and less susceptible to outliers or noise in the data. For this chapter, I will express the models and the Q_0 and α parameters in the model as logarithms.

---

[3] *shinybeez* and *beezdemand* allow several different options for calculating k values, including treating k as a free parameter.

Fit to group

Two "fit-to-group" approaches will be mentioned here briefly. The first is what we have termed the "fit to means," and the second is what we have termed "pooling data" (or "fit-to-pooled").

Fit to means

```
# nlmrt::wrapnls version
apt_averaged <- apt |>
  # for each x value (i.e., price)
  group_by(x) |>
  # calculate the mean of y
  summarise(mn = mean(y)) |>
  # fit the nonlinear model
  nlmrt::wrapnls(
    # specify the model by Koffarnus et al.
    mn ~ 10^(q0) * 10^(apt_k * (exp(-10^(alpha) * 10^(q0) * x) - 1)),
    # find starting values that appear feasible based on the data
    start = list(q0 = 1, alpha = -1),
    data = _,
    control = list(maxiter = 1000)
  )


# minpack.lm::nlsLM version
apt_averaged_nlsLM <- apt |>
  # for each x value (i.e., price)
  group_by(x) |>
  # calculate the mean of y
  summarise(mn = mean(y)) |>
  # fit the nonlinear model
  minpack.lm::nlsLM(
    mn ~ 10^(q0) * 10^(apt_k * (exp(-10^(alpha) * 10^(q0) * x) - 1)),
    start = list(q0 = 1, alpha = -1),
    data = _,
    control = list(maxiter = 1000)
  )
```

```
# beezdemand::FitCurves version

apt_averaged_beez <- beezdemand::FitCurves(

    dat = apt,

    # specify the equation

    equation = "koff",

    # specify the k value

    k = apt_k,

    # specify how the data should be aggregated

    agg = "Mean"

)
```

Here, I have conducted the fit-to-means approach in three different ways. The first two use nonlinear regression packages *nlmrt* and *minpack.lm*. The functions from these two packages, compared to `nls` from base R, tend to be more robust in convergence and identify sensible initial values to start the optimization. The fit-to-means approach *typically* results in the easiest convergence and optimization (i.e., this approach tends to work well and does not frequently throw errors). The third approach I use is the `FitCurves` function from the *beezdemand* package. Instead of having to specify an equation, this function allows you to specify the equation to fit the data (currently supports Eqs. 5.2 and 5.3) and the aggregation method (NULL for two-stage, "Mean" for fit-to-means, and "Pooled" for the fit-to-pooled approach).

We can see the $\widehat{Q_0}$ and $\widehat{\alpha}$ (the hats indicated predicted values) estimates are expressed in the logarithmic units. $\widehat{Q_0} = 0.777$ and $\widehat{\alpha} = -2.207$. When transformed back onto the parameter's original scale, these values are 5.977 and 0.006. Notice how these are very similar to the results of the *beezdemand* package (identical to three decimal places): 5.977 and 0.006.

Fig. 5.2 graphically displays the fit-to-means approach. As the figure shows, the line tracks the data points reasonably well. This is a typical, normal-looking demand curve when fit to averaged data. This approach is a simple way to examine how closely the predicted line tracks the data. The *beezdemand* package has functions to plot the data after fitting the data using the `FitCurves` function.[4]

---

[4] *shinybeez* automatically creates a plot of the data depending on the regression method used (e.g., fit-to-group or two stage).

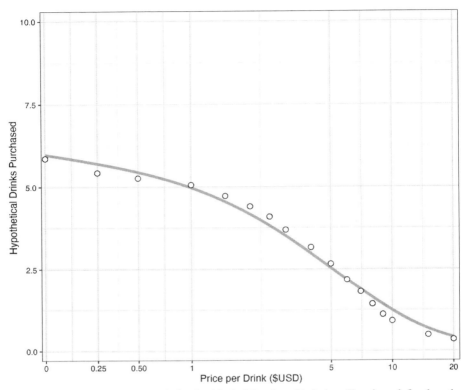

Figure 5.2 Fit-to-means approach for the Alcohol Purchase Task data. Zero is undefined on the log scale, so this plot uses a pseudo-log scale to visualize zero.

Pooling data

```
# nlmrt::wrapnls version

apt_pooled <- apt |>
  nlmrt::wrapnls(
    y ~ 10^(q0) * 10^(apt_k * (exp(-10^(alpha) * 10^(q0) * x) - 1)),
    start = list(q0 = 1, alpha = -1),
    data = _,
    control = list(maxiter = 1000)
  )

# minpack.lm::nlsLM version

apt_pooled_nlsLM <- apt |>
  # fit the nonlinear model
  minpack.lm::nlsLM(
    y ~ 10^(q0) * 10^(apt_k * (exp(-10^(alpha) * 10^(q0) * x) - 1)),
    start = list(q0 = 1, alpha = -1),
    data = _,
    control = list(maxiter = 1000)
  )

# beezdemand::FitCurves version

apt_pooled_beez <- beezdemand::FitCurves(
  dat = apt,
  equation = "koff",
  k = apt_k,
  agg = "Pooled"
)
```

Like the fit-to-means approach, I fit the data using the fit-to-pooled approach via three different methods. As mentioned earlier, both fit-to-group approaches result in highly similar parameter estimates. The standard errors of the estimates and goodness-of-fit statistics differ between the two approaches. Table 5.5 shows the differences in the model estimates.

Table 5.5 Parameter estimates from the fit-to-group approaches for the Alcohol Purchase Task data.

Parameter	Estimate	Std. error	t value	P value	Approach
q0	0.7765	0.0083	93.33	0.0000	Fit-to-Mean
alpha	−2.2069	0.0160	−137.74	0.0000	Fit-to-Mean
q0	0.7765	0.0036	214.14	0.0000	Fit-to-Pooled
alpha	−2.2069	0.0070	−316.03	0.0000	Fit-to-Pooled

Estimates and standard errors are expressed in log(10) units.

Fig. 5.3 graphically displays the fit-to-pooled approach. Although all data points fit to this model, I only show the data points between 0 and 30 on the y-axis. Furthermore, given the transparency of the points, more points in the x-y coordinate reflect a darker mass of points. As is often the case, the curve is nearly indistinguishable from the fit-to-mean approach.

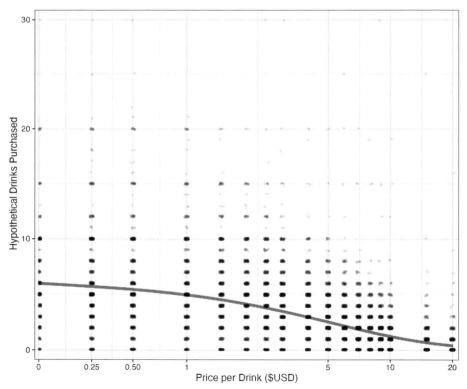

Figure 5.3 Fit-to-pooled approach for the Alcohol Purchase Task data. All data points within 0−30 on the y-axis are shown, even though all data are used to fit the model. Data points are transparent so the darker the mass of points, the more data points are located at that price–consumption combination. Zero is undefined on the log scale, so this plot uses a pseudo-log scale to visualize zero.

Two-stage approach to modeling

```
# fit a single wrapnls function for use with apt data
nls_fit <- function(df, kval) {
  fit <- try(nlmrt::wrapnls(
    y ~ 10^(q0) * 10^(apt_k * (exp(-10^(alpha) * 10^(q0) * x) - 1)),
    start = list(q0 = 1, alpha = -1),
    data = df,
    control = list(maxiter = 1000)
  ), silent = T)
  return(fit)
}


# fit a single nlsLM function for use with apt data
nlsLM_fit <- function(df, kval) {
  fit <- try(minpack.lm::nlsLM(
    y ~ 10^(q0) * 10^(apt_k * (exp(-10^(alpha) * 10^(q0) * x) - 1)),
    start = list(q0 = 1, alpha = -1),
    data = df,
    control = list(maxiter = 1000)
  ), silent = T)
  return(fit)
}


# needs workaround because any datasets that do not converge results
# in a logical NA instead of a tibble
# create two replacement tibbles for any NAs; tidied and glanced
# and use these for the `otherwise` argument in the next code block
tidied_na <- tibble(
  `term` = c("q0", "alpha"),
  `estimate` = c(NA, NA),
  `std.error` = c(NA, NA),
```

```r
  `statistic` = c(NA, NA),
  `p.value` = c(NA, NA)
)


glanced_na <- tibble(
  `sigma` = NA,
  `isConv` = NA,
  `finTol` = NA,
  `logLik` = NA,
  `AIC` = NA,
  `BIC` = NA,
  `deviance` = NA,
  `df.residual` = NA,
  `nobs` = NA
)


# nlmrt::wrapnls version
apt_twostage <- apt |>
  nest(data = c(x, y)) |>
  group_by(id) |>
  mutate(
    # we fit the model here using the function we defined above
    fit = map(data, nls_fit, kval),
    # broom-specific functions to extract the model estimates and
    tidied = map(fit, possibly(broom::tidy, otherwise = tidied_na)),
    # goodness-of-fit statistics
    glanced = map(fit, possibly(broom::glance, otherwise = glanced_na))
  ) |>
  unnest(cols = c("data")) |>
  filter(x %in% 0) |>
  unnest(cols = "tidied")
```

```r
# minpack.lm::nlsLM version
apt_twostage_nlsLM <- apt |>
  nest(data = c(x, y)) |>
  group_by(id) |>
  mutate(
    fit = map(data, nlsLM_fit, kval),
    tidied = map(fit, possibly(broom::tidy, otherwise = tidied_na)),
    glanced = map(fit, possibly(broom::glance, otherwise = glanced_na))
  ) |>
  unnest(cols = c("data")) |>
  filter(x %in% 0) |>
  unnest(cols = "tidied")


# beezdemand version
apt_twostage_beez <- beezdemand::FitCurves(
  dat = apt,
  equation = "koff",
  k = apt_k,
)
```

Table 5.6 shows the estimates from the two-stage approach for the first 10 participants in the sample (ids 1−10). You can see that each participant has a specific $\widehat{Q_0}$ and $\widehat{\alpha}$ estimates, and for participant id = 5, the estimates result in NA values because this participant has no positive consumption values so the model cannot be fit.

Table 5.6 Two-stage approach to modeling the Alcohol Purchase Task data showing the first five participants' estimates.

id	Parameter	Estimate	Std. error	t value	P value
1	q0	1.0515	0.0173	60.72	0.0000
1	alpha	−2.7218	0.0401	−67.80	0.0000
2	q0	0.7779	0.0367	21.18	0.0000
2	alpha	−2.1152	0.0676	−31.28	0.0000
3	q0	1.0638	0.0253	42.09	0.0000
3	alpha	−2.5226	0.0495	−50.97	0.0000
4	q0	0.8307	0.0208	39.98	0.0000
4	alpha	−2.2015	0.0388	−56.71	0.0000
5	q0	NA	NA	NA	NA
5	alpha	NA	NA	NA	NA

Fig. 5.4 shows the two-stage approach to modeling the APT data for the first 10 response sets in the sample (ids 1−10). The figure shows how well each curve tracks each response set's data. The curve closely tracks the data because each model is optimized to that response set. Response set five (id = 5) has no line because there are no positive consumption values.

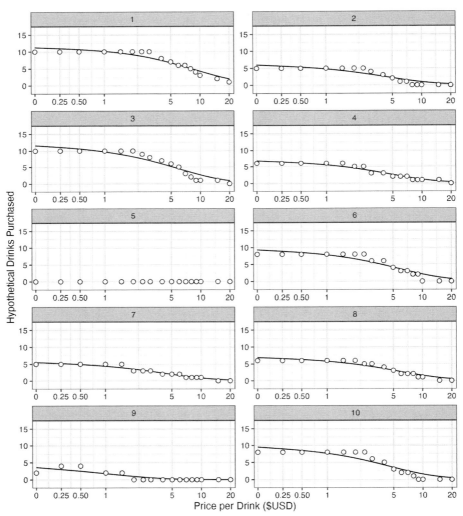

Figure 5.4 Two-stage approach to modeling the Alcohol Purchase Task data. Figure shows the first 10 response sets. The fifth response set (id = 5) does not have a curve because the model cannot be fit to all zeros. Zero is undefined on the log scale, so this plot uses a pseudo-log scale to visualize zero.

Mixed-effects modeling

```r
apt_nlme <- nlme::nlme(
  # specify the equation
  y ~ 10^(q0) * 10^(apt_k * (exp(-10^(alpha) * 10^(q0) * x) - 1)),
  # add column for the k value constant being used
  data = apt |>
    mutate(apt_k = apt_k),
  # specify fixed effects
  fixed = list(
    q0 ~ 1,
    alpha ~ 1
  ),
  # specify random effects
  random = list(nlme::pdDiag(q0 + alpha ~ 1)),
  # starting values from the fixed effects only model
  start = list(fixed = c(
    coef(apt_averaged)[1],
    coef(apt_averaged)[2]
  )),
  groups = ~id,
  method = "ML",
  verbose = 2,
  # specify control parameters for fitting
  control = list(
    msMaxIter = 5000,
    niterEM = 5000,
    maxIter = 5000,
    pnlsTol = .001,
    tolerance = .01,
    apVar = T,
    minScale = .0000001,
    opt = "optim"
  )
)
```

Fig. 5.5 shows the results of the mixed-effects modeling approach. This figure shows that the mixed-effect model can predict curves for each response set (the semi-transparent black lines; analogous to the two-stage approach) while also predicting the population fixed effects (the solid red line (dark gray in print version); analogous to the fit-to-group approach).

Fig. 5.6 shows the results of the mixed-effects modeling approach except for each participant. The black line, again, shows the predicted lines generated from the random effects and the red line (dark gray in print version), which is identical across plots, shows the group-level effects. Notice how the black lines *deviate* higher and lower compared to the red line (dark gray in print version). The mixed-effects model takes into account all the data simultaneously to estimate both individual and group-level effects.

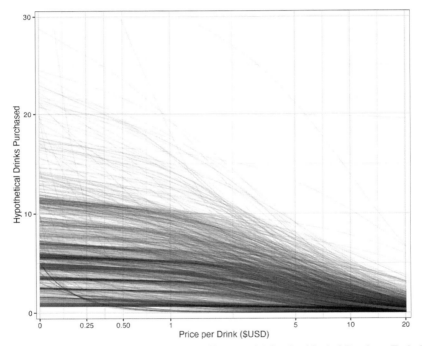

Figure 5.5 Predicted values from the mixed-effects model for the Alcohol Purchase Task data. Semitransparent black lines indicate predicted values (random effects) for each participant while the solid red line (dark gray in print version) indicates the predictions (fixed effects) for the entire sample. Zero is undefined on the log scale, so this plot uses a pseudo-log scale to visualize zero.

Quantitative models of operant demand

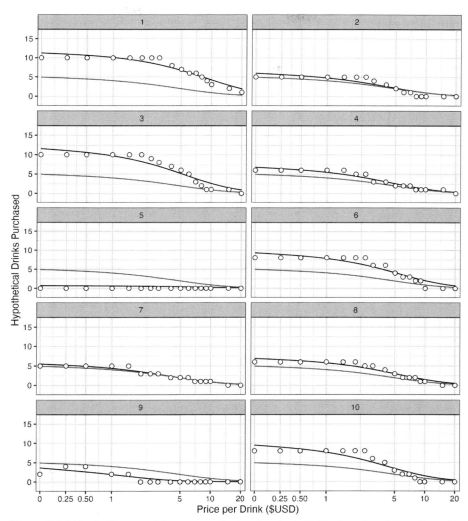

Figure 5.6 Mixed-effects modeling approach showing the individual predicted lines from the random effects in black and the predicted line from the population fixed effects in red (dark gray in print version). Note that the fifth response set (id = 5) now has an individual predicted line because the model leverages information from the entire sample to assign a "best guess" for that response set. Zero is undefined on the log scale, so this plot uses a pseudo-log scale to visualize zero.

Step 4: Visual analysis and interpretation

We have analyzed the models visually and examined how well they describe the data using the three regression approaches. Overall, we have seen that Eq. (5.3) describes the data well in all approaches. Provided our mixed-effects regression approach and current model adequately fit the data, we can use the results of this model to conduct any model comparisons (i.e., fit a different model using the mixed-effects regression approach) going forward and according to whatever predefined analysis steps are outlined from Step 0.

Step 5: Model comparison and refinement

This step involves comparing the model(s), refining the model(s) (e.g., choosing a different k value, using more informative initial values, choosing which response sets to include), and ultimately choosing the model that will be used to calculate key metrics and interpret the results. Therefore, Steps 3 through 5 may be repeated as necessary, and remember, all these decisions should be considered and outlined in Step 0. If decisions are made at this point *sans* any analysis plan, then decisions could be made based on what you think might be most likely to produce the results you want, not necessarily based on what is most appropriate and justifiable based on the existing literature and research question. For example, I have fitted and plotted both Eqs. (5.3) and (5.4) using the different approaches discussed in this chapter, shown in Figs. A5.1—A5.2.

Step 6: Calculate important metrics

Step 6 involves calculating critical metrics related to the data and model chosen. These metrics typically fall into two buckets: observed metrics (those metrics calculated directly from the data) and derived metrics (those metrics calculated based on model fitting). I will explain the metrics in each section and provide helpful functions from the *beezdemand* package to help calculate them so they do not have to be calculated manually. For ease, I will demonstrate obtaining metrics based on the two-stage approach (using Eq. 5.3) because oftentimes we will want to use the metrics in some second-stage analysis (e.g., *t*-tests, correlations). Both the *beezdemand* R package and *shinybeez* will support automatic calculation of these metrics for mixed-effects models in the future.

Observed metrics

```
apt_beez_obs <- beezdemand::GetEmpirical(dat = apt)
```

Depending on the analysis plan, this step involves generating the important metrics of interest and reporting them in a digestible format, such as a table or a figure. Table 5.7 shows the observed metrics calculated for the first 10 ids using the *beezdemand* package.

Table 5.7 Observed metrics for the Alcohol Purchase Task data generated from the beezdemand package.

id	Intensity	BP0	BP1	Omaxe	Pmaxe
1	10	NA	20.00	42.00	7.00
2	5	8.00	7.00	12.50	2.50
3	10	20.00	15.00	30.00	6.00
4	6	20.00	15.00	15.00	15.00
5	0	NA	NA	0.00	0.00
6	8	10.00	9.00	24.00	4.00
7	5	15.00	10.00	12.00	6.00
8	6	15.00	10.00	16.00	8.00
9	2	2.00	1.50	3.00	1.50
10	8	9.00	8.00	20.00	4.00

Table shows the first 10 response sets.

The `GetEmpirical()` function from the *beezdemand* package calculates the following observed metrics directly from the data[5]:

- Intensity: Intensity is the consumption (i.e., y value) associated with the lowest price (i.e., x value) in the data. Depending on the task, this could be when the price is free or when the price is some small value.
- Breakpoint 0 ($BP\sim0$): The first and lowest price at which consumption is zero.
- Breakpoint 1 ($BP\sim1$): The last and highest price at which consumption is nonzero.
- $Omax_e$: Represents the maximum expenditure (e.g., effort or cost) an organism is willing to exert to obtain the reinforcer, indicating the peak of "spending" for that commodity. This is calculated by the peak of the expenditure curve by multiplying each x value by its corresponding y value
- $Pmax_e$: The price (i.e., x value) associated with where $Omax_e$ occurs.

Derived metrics

The `FitCurves()` function from the *beezdemand* package calculates the following derived metrics based on the model chosen.[6] Table 5.8 shows the derived metrics calculated for the first 10 ids using the *beezdemand* package.

- $Q0_d$: The estimated consumption (i.e., y value) when the price is zero. This is analagous to the observed metric of intensity but has an associated standard error provided in the output.
- α: The estimated *rate of change in elasticity* across the entire demand curve.
- Essential Value (*EV*): Essential value quantifies the relative reinforcing efficacy of a commodity, representing how strongly an organism maintains consumption of a commodity even as price increases or access is restricted, and is inversely related to elasticity. The goal of EV is to be comparable across all commodities (and models).

---

[5] *shinybeez* automatically creates a table of observed metrics for you when you load your data.
[6] *shinybeez* returns a table of derived metrics for you automatically when you run the demand analysis.

Table 5.8 Derived metrics for the Alcohol Purchase Task data generated from the beezdemand package.

id	Equation	Q0d	K	Alpha	R2	Q0se	Alphase	N	AbsSS	SdRes	EV	Omaxd	Pmaxd	Omaxa	Pmaxa	Notes
1	koff	11.26	2.20	0.00190	0.92	0.45	0.00018	17	13.00	0.93	1.62	42.99	11.95	42.99	11.93	converged
2	koff	6.00	2.20	0.00767	0.86	0.51	0.00119	17	11.56	0.88	0.40	10.64	5.55	10.64	5.54	converged
3	koff	11.58	2.20	0.00300	0.90	0.67	0.00034	17	23.50	1.25	1.02	27.18	7.34	27.18	7.33	converged
4	koff	6.77	2.20	0.00629	0.94	0.32	0.00056	17	4.91	0.57	0.49	12.98	6.00	12.98	5.98	converged
5	koff	−0.00	2.20	0.02000	NA	NA	NA	17	0.00	0.00	0.15	4.08	−89,554, 659,598, 886.59	4.08	−89,383, 368,470, 915.56	wrapnls failed to converge, reverted to nlxb
6	koff	9.32	2.20	0.00379	0.89	0.59	0.00047	17	17.90	1.09	0.81	21.53	7.23	21.53	7.22	converged
7	koff	5.53	2.20	0.00834	0.95	0.25	0.00070	17	2.87	0.44	0.37	9.78	5.54	9.78	5.53	converged
8	koff	6.91	2.20	0.00512	0.92	0.36	0.00052	17	6.53	0.66	0.60	15.92	7.21	15.92	7.20	converged
9	koff	3.60	2.20	0.04074	0.74	0.58	0.01139	17	8.47	0.75	0.08	2.00	1.74	2.00	1.74	converged
10	koff	9.52	2.20	0.00462	0.87	0.73	0.00066	17	24.59	1.28	0.66	17.65	5.80	17.65	5.79	converged

Table shows the first 10 response sets and a subset of the derived metrics reported.

- $Omax_{d/a}$: Similar to Observed *Omax*, except this is (d)erived/(a)nalytic because it is computed after calculating (d)erived/(a)nalytic *Pmax*.
- $Pmax_{d/a}$: (D)erived/(A)nalytic *Pmax* is the price at which the slope of the tangent line of the demand curve is equal to -1 (also known as unit elasticity).

Step 7: Interpret and report findings

The final step is to interpret and report the findings of the demand curve analysis. This step involves taking the observed and/or derived metrics, reporting them either in text or a table, and interpreting them in the context of the research question. This step is crucial for communicating the demand curve analysis findings to others and ensuring that the findings are accurate, reliable, and understandable. This step should also involve reporting the goodness-of-fit metrics used to assess the adequacy of the model reported (e.g., R2, Root mean square error, AIC, BIC) depending on what was specified in Step 0.

Issues and considerations for demand curve analyses

k

In my experience, one of the most common (and frustrating) issues in conducting demand curve analyses is dealing with the k parameter. Conceptually, we may want always to try and model k as a free parameter to let the model determine the best "range" of the data. However, in practice, this can lead to issues, with the most common problem being that the model attempts to estimate an astronomically high k value. While the model may technically converge, estimates of α tend to be quite different (because in Eqs. (5.2) and (5.3), k is intricately linked with α) than if using a more "reasonable" k value that more closely reflects the range of the data. As I have done here, one straightforward way of dealing with this is to determine a reasonable k value from the observed data and enter that value as a constant into the model. This approach tends to work quite well, and I believe it can be justifiable during the analysis. Another consideration is to test out Eq. (5.4) recently proposed by Rzeszutek et al. (in press), where k is removed from the model entirely. I encourage the reader to consult Rzeszutek et al. (in press) for a technical discussion of this model if you want to use it. Both *beezdemand* and *shinybeez* will have the functionality to fit this model along with Eqs. (5.2) and (5.3).

Modeling probabilities

Another methodological approach to assessing "demand" is using probability-based purchase tasks (Gelino et al., 2023; Harsin et al., 2021; Reed et al., 2016; Reed et al., 2022; Roma et al., 2016). In these purchase tasks, instead of the respondent responding with a quantity of the outcome being purchased, the respondent responds with a probability of purchasing the outcome (e.g., 0%–100% likelihood of buying the outcome or engaging in the behavior). On the face of it, these tasks appear to resemble typical quantity-based purchase tasks. However, there are several aspects to consider, not only about the task itself but also about the analysis methods and the interpretations of the model results.

The first consideration is whether probability-based purchase tasks are measuring demand in the conventional sense of what quantity-based purchase tasks attempt to measure. While self-report quantity-based purchase tasks are in and of themselves a slight departure from traditional experiential paradigms (e.g., self-administration), literature has shown adequate correspondence between these types of tasks (Kaplan et al., 2018; Kiselica et al., 2016; Strickland et al., 2020; Martínez-Loredo et al., 2021; Wilson et al., 2015). Probability-based purchase tasks, while also being self-reported, appear relatively newer, and evidence for adequate correspondence between these types of tasks and conventional quantity-based purchase tasks has not yet been firmly established. Taking a step back, the general concept of demand quantifies the extent to which an organism *defends its baseline consumption* in the face of increasing costs. Translating this to probability-based purchase tasks, should the interpretation be the extent to which an organism (i.e., human) defends its baseline likelihood of engaging in the behavior? Also, how sensitive are respondents to differences in probabilities? For example, is there a meaningful difference between someone responding with a likelihood of 62% versus 69% or 18% versus 23%? This will depend somewhat on the task but may inject an artificial degree of accuracy into the data.

The second consideration is when modeling these types of data, what should the interpretation of Q_0 be if it is estimated to exceed one (or 100%)? Is it possible for someone to be more than 100% likely to engage in a behavior? This parameter could be constrained at a group or individual level basis leaving only one (i.e., α) or two (i.e., α and k) parameters to be estimated, but this assumption may be too restrictive depending on the research question.

Two considerations for addressing these issues are to reconceptualize the purchase task as a dichotomous choice task (i.e., "yes" or "no" at each price point) and consider using a logistic regression model. When conceptualizing a probability-based purchase task, it may be helpful to consider that, in reality, the respondent can only make one choice: they either engage in the behavior or they do not. Therefore, a dichotomous choice task may more accurately reflect the individual's actual behavior in the real world. Data from such a task lends itself well to logistic regression models where the outcome is a binary variable. The logistic regression model, therefore, is used to estimate the *probability* of engaging in the behavior at each price point rather than relying on the respondent to report these probabilities with an unknown degree of accuracy.

Recommended resources and readings

This chapter is not exhaustive of the demand curve literature (including demand curve analysis), regression modeling, or working in R. There are numerous other resources that serve as valuable resources for these topics. For the demand of curve literature, I recommend the reader look at papers by some of the following authors (in no specific order): Reed et al. (2013), Strickland et al. (2020), Roma et al. (2016), Reed et al. (2022), Aston and Meshesha (2020), Reed et al. (2020), Zvorsky et al. (2019), Weinsztok et al. (2023), Kiselica et al. (2016), and Kaplan et al. (2018).

Concerning statistics and the intersection of statistics and behavioral economics, I recommend the reader look at resources by some of the following authors: Young (2018), Yu et al. (2014), Kaplan et al. (2021), Ho et al. (2018), McElreath (2018), and James et al. (2023).

To learn more about R, many fantastic resources exist online such as Wickham and Grolemund (2016) and Wickham (2019), https://swirlstats.com, and the R journal. Another good resource for new users of R who are interested in conducting demand curve analyses is the paper by Kaplan et al. (2019) and the associated document "Introduction to R and beezdemand" available at: https://github.com/brentkaplan/beezdemand/tree/master/pobs along with Gilroy and Kaplan (2019) (which introduces and explains GitHub). The former document provides beginner-friendly steps for using R and recommends resources for learning its fundamental functionalities.

Conclusion

Quantitative analysis of behavioral economic demand data continues to evolve with new models, methods, and tools becoming available to researchers. In this chapter, I provided a general approach to conducting demand analyses through seven key steps, from initial planning through final interpretation. I demonstrated various regression approaches including fit-to-group, two-stage, and mixed-effects modeling, and their implementation using freely-available tools like R and the *beezdemand* package. By following these systematic approaches and leveraging modern analytical tools, researchers can produce more robust and replicable demand analyses. The field continues to advance with new methodological developments, offering exciting opportunities for future research. As these methods become more accessible through open-source tools, the quality and sophistication of behavioral economic demand analyses will continue to improve. Understanding how these models work is just a first step in advancing the field.

Appendix

Table A5.1 Descriptive statistics for the Alcohol Purchase Task data generated from the beezdemand package.

Price	Mean	Median	SD	PropZeros	NAs	Min	Max
0	5.86	5	4.71	0.08	0	0	50
0.25	5.43	5	4.31	0.13	0	0	40
0.5	5.26	5	4.20	0.15	0	0	30
1	5.05	5	3.94	0.14	0	0	30
1.5	4.72	4	3.71	0.17	0	0	30
2	4.40	4	3.42	0.17	0	0	30
2.5	4.08	4	3.27	0.19	0	0	30
3	3.69	3	3.02	0.19	0	0	30
4	3.16	3	2.81	0.22	0	0	30
5	2.66	2	2.41	0.25	0	0	20
6	2.17	2	2.26	0.31	0	0	25
7	1.80	1	2.35	0.37	0	0	44
8	1.43	1	1.78	0.43	0	0	19
9	1.12	0	1.74	0.50	0	0	30
10	0.92	0	1.70	0.56	0	0	30
15	0.49	0	1.19	0.71	0	0	25
20	0.35	0	0.90	0.76	0	0	16

Table A5.2 Breakdown of number of response sets with the number of criteria passed.

TotalPass	n	Percentage (%)
0	36	3.27
1	66	6
2	52	4.73
3	946	86

Quantitative models of operant demand

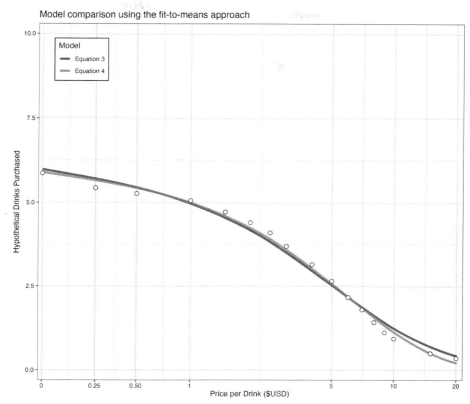

Figure A5.1 Model comparison using the fit-to-means approach. Zero is undefined on the log scale, so this plot uses a pseudo-log scale to visualize zero.

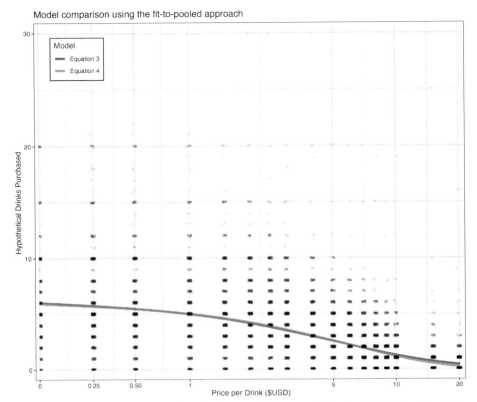

Figure A5.2 Model comparison using the fit-to-pooled approach for the Alcohol Purchase Task data. All data points within 0–30 on the y-axis are shown, even though all data are used to fit the model. Data points are transparent so the darker the mass of points, the more data points are located at that price—consumption combination. Zero is undefined on the log scale, so this plot uses a pseudo-log scale to visualize zero.

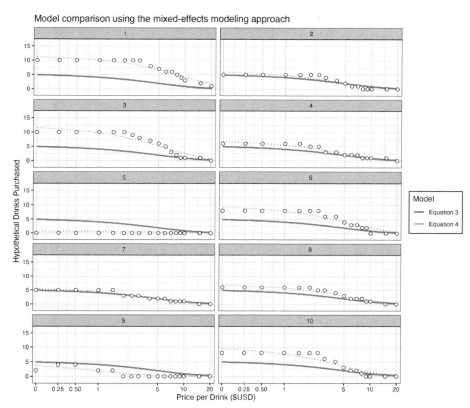

Figure A5.3 Model comparison using the mixed-effects model approach. Zero is undefined on the log scale, so this plot uses a pseudo-log scale to visualize zero.

Biography

Brent A. Kaplan http://orcid.org/0000-0002-3758-6776

The code to recreate this chapter is located at https://github.com/brentkaplan/quant-demand. Please visit the GitHub repository or https://codedbx.com for the most current version of this chapter. The author has no conflicts of interest to declare.

Correspondence concerning this article should be addressed to Brent A. Kaplan, Innovation Department, Advocates for Human Potential, Inc., 490-B Boston Post Road, Sudbury, MA, Email: bkaplan@ahpnet.com; bkaplan.ku@gmail.com

References

Allaire, J. J., Teague, C., Scheidegger, C., Xie, Y., & Dervieux, C. (2024). *Quarto*. https://doi.org/10.5281/zenodo.5960048

Aston, E. R., & Meshesha, L. Z. (2020). Assessing cannabis demand: A comprehensive review of the marijuana purchase task. *Neurotherapeutics, 17*(1), 87–99. https://doi.org/10.1007/s13311-019-00819-z

Gelino, B. W., Kaplan, B. A., & Reed, D. D. (2023). A behavioral economic analysis of carbon-neutral home energy enrollment. *Behavior and Social Issues, 32*(2), 517–533. https://doi.org/10.1007/s42822-023-00143-4

Gelman, A., & Loken, E. (2013). *The garden of forking paths: Why multiple comparisons can be a problem, even when there is no "fishing expedition" or "p-hacking" and the research hypothesis was posited ahead of time.*

Gilroy, S. P., & Kaplan, B. A. (2019). Furthering open science in behavior analysis: An introduction and tutorial for using GitHub in research. *Perspectives on Behavior Science, 42*(3), 565–581. https://doi.org/10.1007/s40614-019-00202-5

Gilroy, S. P., Kaplan, B. A., Schwartz, L. P., Reed, D. D., & Hursh, S. R. (2021). A zero-bounded model of operant demand. *Journal of the Experimental Analysis of Behavior, 115*(3), 729–746. https://doi.org/10.1002/jeab.679

GraphPad Software. (n.d.). GraphPad software.

Harsin, J. D., Gelino, B. W., Strickland, J. C., Johnson, M. W., Berry, M. S., & Reed, D. D. (2021). Behavioral economics and safe sex: Examining condom use decisions from a reinforcer pathology framework. *Journal of the Experimental Analysis of Behavior, 116*(2), 149–165. https://doi.org/10.1002/jeab.706

Ho, Y.-Y., Nhu Vo, T., Chu, H., Luo, X., & Le, C. T. (2018). A Bayesian hierarchical model for demand curve analysis. *Statistical Methods in Medical Research, 27*(7), 2038–2049. https://doi.org/10.1177/0962280216673675

Hursh, S. R., Raslear, T. G., Shurtleff, D., Bauman, R., & Simmons, L. (1988). A cost-benefit analysis of demand for food. *Journal of the Experimental Analysis of Behavior, 50*(3), 419–440. https://doi.org/10.1901/jeab.1988.50-419

Hursh, S. R., & Silberberg, A. (2008). Economic demand and essential value. *Psychological Review, 115*(1), 186–198. https://doi.org/10.1037/0033-295X.115.1.186

James, G., Witten, D., Hastie, T., Tibshirani, R., & Taylor, J. (2023). *An introduction to statistical learning: With applications in Python*. Springer International Publishing. https://doi.org/10.1007/978-3-031-38747-0

Kaplan, B.A. (2023). Beezdemand: Behavioral economic easy demand. R package version 0.1.2, https://github.com/brentkaplan/beezdemand; https://cran.r-project.org/web/packages/beezdemand/.

Kaplan, B. A., Foster, R. N. S., Reed, D. D., Amlung, M., Murphy, J. G., & MacKillop, J. (2018). Understanding alcohol motivation using the alcohol purchase task: A methodological systematic review. *Drug and Alcohol Dependence, 191*, 117–140. https://doi.org/10.1016/j.drugalcdep.2018.06.029

Kaplan, B. A., Franck, C. T., McKee, K., Gilroy, S. P., & Koffarnus, M. N. (2021). Applying mixed-effects modeling to behavioral economic demand: An introduction. *Perspectives on Behavior Science, 44*(2), 333–358. https://doi.org/10.1007/s40614-021-00299-7

Kaplan, B. A., Gilroy, S. P., Reed, D. D., Koffarnus, M. N., & Hursh, S. R. (2019). The R package beezdemand: Behavioral economic easy demand. *Perspectives on Behavior Science, 42*(1), 163–180. https://doi.org/10.1007/s40614-018-00187-7

Kaplan, B. A., & Reed, D. D. (2018). Happy hour drink specials in the alcohol purchase task. *Experimental and Clinical Psychopharmacology, 26*(2), 156−167. https://doi.org/10.1037/pha0000174

Kaplan, B. A., & Reed, D. D. (2025). *shinybeez*: A shiny app for behavioral economic easy demand and discounting. *Journal of the Experimental Analysis of Behavior, 123*(2). https://doi.org/10.1002/JEAB.70000. https://github.com/brentkaplan/shinybeez

Kiselica, A. M., Webber, T. A., & Bornovalova, M. A. (2016). Validity of the alcohol purchase task: A meta-analysis. *Addiction, 111*(5), 806−816. https://doi.org/10.1111/add.13254

Koffarnus, M. N., Franck, C. T., Stein, J. S., & Bickel, W. K. (2015). A modified exponential behavioral economic demand model to better describe consumption data. *Experimental and Clinical Psychopharmacology, 23*(6), 504−512. https://doi.org/10.1037/pha0000045

Koffarnus, M. N., Kaplan, B. A., Franck, C. T., Rzeszutek, M. J., & Traxler, H. K. (2022). Behavioral economic demand modeling chronology, complexities, and considerations: Much ado about zeros. *Behavioural Processes, 199*, Article 104646. https://doi.org/10.1016/j.beproc.2022.104646

Lüdecke, D., Ben-Shachar, M. S., Patil, I., Wiernik, B. M., Bacher, E., Thériault, R., & Makowski, D. (2022). *Easystats: Framework for easy statistical modeling, visualization, and reporting.* https://doi.org/10.32614/CRAN.package.easystats

Martínez-Loredo, V., González-Roz, A., Secades-Villa, R., Fernández-Hermida, J. R., & MacKillop, J. (2021). Concurrent validity of the Alcohol Purchase Task for measuring the reinforcing efficacy of alcohol: An updated systematic review and meta-analysis. *Addiction, 116*(10), 2635−2650. https://doi.org/10.1111/add.15379

McElreath, R. (2018). *Statistical rethinking: A bayesian course with examples in R and stan* (1st ed.). Chapman and Hall/CRC. https://doi.org/10.1201/9781315372495

Nash, J. C. (2016). *Nlmrt: Functions for nonlinear least squares solutions. R package version 2016.3.2.*

Newman, M., & Ferrario, C. R. (2020). An improved demand curve for analysis of food or drug consumption in behavioral experiments. *Psychopharmacology, 237*(4), 943−955. https://doi.org/10.1007/s00213-020-05491-2

Pinheiro, J., Bates, D., & R Core Team. (2023). *Nlme: Linear and nonlinear mixed effects models. R package version 3.1-164.* https://CRAN.R-project.org/package=nlme.

R Core Team. (2024). *R: A language and environment for statistical computing* [Manual]. R Foundation for Statistical Computing.

Reed, D. D., Naudé, G. P., Salzer, A. R., Peper, M., Monroe-Gulick, A. L., Gelino, B. W., Harsin, J. D., Foster, R. N. S., Nighbor, T. D., Kaplan, B. A., Koffarnus, M. N., & Higgins, S. T. (2020). Behavioral economic measurement of cigarette demand: A descriptive review of published approaches to the cigarette purchase task. *Experimental and Clinical Psychopharmacology, 28*(6), 688−705. https://doi.org/10.1037/pha0000347

Reed, D. D., Niileksela, C. R., & Kaplan, B. A. (2013). Behavioral economics: A tutorial for behavior analysts in practice. *Behavior Analysis in Practice, 6*(1), 34−54. https://doi.org/10.1007/BF03391790

Reed, D. D., Kaplan, B. A., Becirevic, A., Roma, P. G., & Hursh, S. R. (2016). Toward quantifying the abuse liability of ultraviolet tanning: A behavioral economic approach to tanning addiction. *Journal of the Experimental Analysis of Behavior, 106*(1), 93−106. https://doi.org/10.1002/jeab.216

Reed, D. D., Strickland, J. C., Gelino, B. W., Hursh, S. R., Jarmolowicz, D. P., Kaplan, B. A., & Amlung, M. (2022). Applied behavioral economics and public health policies: Historical precedence and translational promise. *Behavioural Processes, 198*, Article 104640. https://doi.org/10.1016/j.beproc.2022.104640

Roma, P. G., Hursh, S. R., & Hudja, S. (2016). Hypothetical purchase task questionnaires for behavioral economic assessments of value and motivation. *Managerial and Decision Economics, 37*(4−5), 306−323. https://doi.org/10.1002/mde.2718

Rzeszutek, M. J., Regnier, S. D., Franck, C. T., & Koffarnus, M. N. (2025). Overviewing the exponential model of demand and introducing a simplification that solves issues of span, scale, and zeros. *Experimental and Clinical Psychopharmacology*.

Schneider, W.J. (2025). *Apaquarto*. Version 1.2. https://github.com/wjschne/apaquarto [Software].

Stein, J. S., Koffarnus, M. N., Snider, S. E., Quisenberry, A. J., & Bickel, W. K. (2015). Identification and management of nonsystematic purchase task data: Toward best practice. *Experimental and Clinical Psychopharmacology, 23*(5), 377−386. https://doi.org/10.1037/pha0000020

Strickland, J. C., Campbell, E. M., Lile, J. A., & Stoops, W. W. (2020). Utilizing the commodity purchase task to evaluate behavioral economic demand for illicit substances: A review and meta-analysis. *Addiction, 115*(3), 393−406. https://doi.org/10.1111/add.14792

Weinsztok, S. C., Reed, D. D., & Amlung, M. (2023). Substance-related cross-commodity purchase tasks: A systematic review. *Psychology of Addictive Behaviors, 37*(1), 72−86. https://doi.org/10.1037/adb0000851

Wickham, H. (2019). *Advanced R* (2nd ed.). CRC Press/Taylor & Francis Group.

Wickham, H., Averick, M., Bryan, J., Chang, W., McGowan, L. D., François, R., Grolemund, G., Hayes, A., Henry, L., Hester, J., Kuhn, M., Pedersen, T. L., Miller, E., Bache, S. M., Müller, K., Ooms, J., Robinson, D., Seidel, D. P., Spinu, V., ... Yutani, H. (2019). Welcome to the tidyverse. *Journal of Open Source Software, 4*(43), 1686. https://doi.org/10.21105/joss.01686

Wickham, H., & Grolemund, G. (2016). *R for data science: Import, tidy, transform, visualize, and model data* (1st ed.). O'Reilly Media.

Wilson, A. G., Franck, C. T., Koffarnus, M. N., & Bickel, W. K. (2015). Behavioral economics of cigarette purchase tasks: Within-subject comparison of real, potentially real, and hypothetical cigarettes. *Nicotine & Tobacco Research, 18*(5), 524−530. https://doi.org/10.1093/ntr/ntv154

Winger, G., Galuska, C. M., Hursh, S. R., & Woods, J. H. (2006). Relative reinforcing effects of cocaine, remifentanil, and their combination in rhesus monkeys. *Journal of Pharmacology and Experimental Therapeutics, 318*(1), 223−229. https://doi.org/10.1124/jpet.105.100461

Young, M. E. (2018). A place for statistics in behavior analysis. *Behaviour Analysis: Research and Practice, 18*(2), 193−202. https://doi.org/10.1037/bar0000099

Yu, J., Liu, L., Collins, R. L., Vincent, P. C., & Epstein, L. H. (2014). Analytical problems and suggestions in the analysis of behavioral economic demand curves. *Multivariate Behavioral Research, 49*(2), 178−192. https://doi.org/10.1080/00273171.2013.862491

Zvorsky, I., Nighbor, T. D., Kurti, A. N., DeSarno, M., Naudé, G., Reed, D. D., & Higgins, S. T. (2019). Sensitivity of hypothetical purchase task indices when studying substance use: A systematic literature review. *Preventive Medicine, 128*, Article 105789. https://doi.org/10.1016/j.ypmed.2019.105789

Practical applications of the Operant Demand Framework

Shawn P. Gilroy
Louisiana State University, Baton Rouge, LA, United States

> *Economics is, at root, the study of incentives*
> Steven Levitt, Freakonomics.

The field of economics broadly refers to how individuals and groups allocate their time and resources to outcomes of personal and societal interest (Samuelson & Nordhaus, 2009). Similarly, fields such as behavior analysis also research factors underpinning rational and 'irrational' patterns of choice (Francisco et al., 2009; Reed et al., 2013). The rise of behavioral economics has led to an increasing overlap between various fields studying choice phenomena (Camerer & Loewenstein, 2004).

The past several decades have produced substantial advancements in statistical methods and experimental methodology. For example, carefully designed studies in economics increasingly highlight the importance of ecological factors when characterizing individual decision-making—optimal or suboptimal (Samuelson & Nordhaus, 2009). Despite differences in scientific terminology, research on ecological factors and their effects on individual behavior between the two fields has revealed several areas in which the two fields complement one another (Hursh, 1980, 1984).

Economics and behavior analysis

A short introduction and review of economics are provided in this chapter to assist behavior analytic readers in orienting to similarities and differences between fields as well as introduce practices traditionally subsumed under the broader domain of economics. In economics, there are various methods and approaches are available and dependent on whether the unit of interest is individual or group-level behavior (e.g., choice behaviour measured at the region or national level Samuelson & Nordhaus, 2009). Specifically, certain methods are employed when the unit is the behavior of an individual (microeconomics) or some larger group or subgroup of individuals (macroeconomics). Whereas macroeconomic methods and practices are typically directed toward studies of broader choice and consumption (e.g., research on the consumption of goods/services across regions over time), the methods featured in microeconomics most relate to how individual consumers to various immediate ecological and contextual factors (e.g., pricing of goods, income-level effects; Samuelson & Nordhaus, 2009). Among the various areas of economics and behavioral economics, methods for understanding and influencing individual behavior are most aligned with microeconomic approaches.

Experimental microeconomics and behavior analysis

The experimental microeconomic domain of economic research shares considerable overlap with many common features of behavior analytic research (see Hursh, 1980, 1984); however, many of these links are often obscured due to distinct terminologies (e.g., reinforcer value vs. utility) and methodologies (e.g., direct behavior recording vs. self-report methods). With regards to the phenomenon of individual *preference*, each domain conducts but may introduce terms in which there is no comparable equivalent for the other. For instance, Iyengar and Lepper (2000) speak of 'choice overload' whereby those presented with a wide range of choices generally report lower levels of satisfaction than those with fewer choices. Researchers in behavior analysis have similarly reproduced this phenomenon, though the term used to characterize this phenomenon is framed in terms of ecological factors rather than individual constructs (e.g., effort discounting; see Reed et al., 2011 for a discussion).

Both fields also differ regarding what it means for some item or event to have some "value" to an individual. Within behavior analysis, "value" is something that is traditionally inferred and quantified from the responding necessary to produce it (see Heinicke et al., 2019, for a review). Such practices are well represented in applied behavior analysis due to commitments to including items and practices that are valued by the individual (i.e., social validity; Hanley, 2010; Wolf, 1978). Interpreted in the terminology of economics, this manner of assessment could similarly be described as stimuli linked to higher rates of selection providing superior "benefit" or "satisfaction" to the individual (i.e., top-rated item contributed greater satisfaction to the individual). A simplified visual account of these terms illustrated within an inspection of individual preference is provided in Fig. 6.1.

Applications of behavioral economics in applied behavior analysis

There is a rich and growing literature exploring how behavioral economics methods and accounts can extend basic and applied behavioral science. For applied readers, a review by Gilroy et al. (2018) presents a range of applied behavior analytic research that incorporates behavioral economics concepts and methods to support practices for individuals with developmental disabilities (e.g., autism). Specifically, the results of this review outlined how interpretations such as demand (i.e., the sensitivity of reinforcer effects to changes in schedule requirements or *Price*) and reinforcer economies (i.e., open or closed reinforcer markets) have influenced behavior analytic assessment and intervention. Results indicated that various economic methods and concepts had either been successfully replicated in single-case experimental design research or used as a means of advancing some aspects of behavioral assessment or intervention.[1]

---

[1] Note: There is a rich research tradition in the experimental analysis of behavior including nonhuman animals (e.g., pigeons), though these are not reviewed here due to a focus on methods with practical use to applied clinicians.

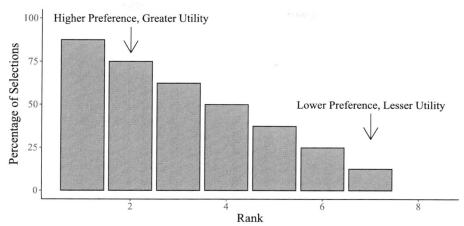

Figure 6.1 Quantifying preference and individual utility.

Results of the earlier review highlighted a range of economic concepts and approaches that have begun to be more represented in research completed by behavior analysts. Among these, economic concepts and methods have been useful for extending behavior analytic methods associated with how preference is quantified and defined. For example, Goldberg et al. (2017) evaluated preference for social and nonsocial stimuli and how the strength of these preferences for autistic and nonautistic matched peers. Regarding evaluations of reinforcer effects more broadly, early work such as Tustin (1994) revealed that differences in reinforcer performances at FR1 schedule requirements are generally not predictive of differences at later schedule requirements (i.e., preferences may switch in more lean arrangements, such as FR10). Additionally, research on understanding the "markets" for programmed reinforcers has highlighted how the availability of alternatives (i.e., functionally similar stimuli/events) or alternative means of producing access to reinforcers can influence reinforcer effects. Kodak et al. (2007) simulated the effects of an "open" reinforcer economy by providing individuals with a means of accessing programmed reinforcers outside of sessions either for free or at a minimal *price* (i.e., simply asking for them). These findings indicated that overall *demand* for reinforcers (i.e., the number of reinforcers purchased via responding across schedules) was lower in open economy arrangements, which is consistent with economic predictions related to demand.

The goals of this chapter are to present the available research specific to the economic concept of demand and the myriad ways in which this interpretation and approach correspond with active and historical behavior analytic research. The sections that follow will provide a general overview of broader concepts as well as specific implementations of the Operant Demand Framework relevant to applied behavior analysis.

Defining the Operant Demand Framework

The umbrella term "Operant Demand Framework" is used to describe a variety of methods and interpretations specific to how the economic concept of demand can be applied to operant behavior. More directly, much of this framework is derived from pioneering work by Hursh and colleagues with human and nonhuman animals (see Hursh, 1980). The Framework is not presented as a replacement for established behavior concepts and definitions and instead presents a flexible and dynamic view of reinforcement. Several economic concepts are presented and expanded upon in the sections that follow.

Reinforcement and the open or closed economy

Specific behavioral terminology for distinguishing between open and closed economies has been presented Hursh, and is as follows:

> The total daily consumption of food was not the result of the subjects' interaction with the environment during the sessions but was arbitrarily controlled by the experimenter. This is what I call an open economy.
> Hursh, S. R. (1980). Economic concepts for the analysis of behavior. Journal of the Experimental Analysis of Behavior, 34(2), 219−238. https://doi.org/10.1901/jeab. 1980.34-219, p. 221.

Unpacking this quote, arrangements wherein the delivery of some reinforcer is arbitrarily controlled by some experimenter (e.g., clinician, parent, teacher) represents a *closed* economy arrangement. Said a bit more simply, a closed economy reflects a context wherein all alternative pathways to produce a reinforcer remain closed to the organism. In contrast, the *open* economy reflects a context wherein there is more than one pathway open for producing access to a reinforcer (i.e., outside of programmed contingencies).

The type of reinforcer economy has applied relevance for several reasons. First, organisms able to freely access a reinforcer outside of a specific context (i.e., without "paying" in terms of responding) would not have to work as extensively to maintain their base level of consumption. In short, the overall *demand* curve becomes more elastic and more heavily impacted as schedule requirements increase. Fig. 6.2 provides a hypothetical example wherein a reinforcer in an *open* economy is associated with work performed peaking at a lower schedule requirement (i.e., more elastic) and at a lower overall level of responding.

Reinforcement and elasticity of demand

The term *elasticity* is represented in economics as well as other domains (e.g., pure maths, physics), though its definition and application in behavioral economics are highly contextualized to response and reinforcement rates. The definition provided by Hursh is as follows:

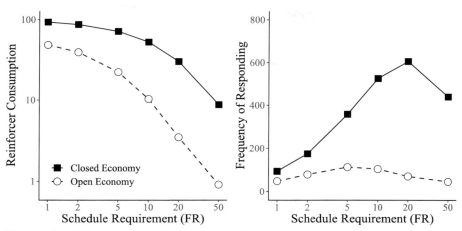

Figure 6.2 Reinforcer consumption across hypothetical economy types.

> *... reinforcers can be distinguished by their demand elasticity apart from differences in value, where value is inferred from response rate in a standard defining situation. Hursh, S. R. (1980). Economic concepts for the analysis of behavior.* Journal of the Experimental Analysis of Behavior, *34(2), 219—238. https://doi.org/10.1901/jeab. 1980.34-219, p. 226.*

An interpretation of reinforcer effects in terms of elasticity (η) differs from the more traditional approach of comparing reinforcer effects in several ways. First, traditional methods often quantify and compare reinforcer performances using some feature or aspect of responding (e.g., response rate, reinforcer breakpoint; Katz, 1990). For example, the reinforcer breakpoint (i.e., the leanest schedule upon which reinforcement was produced) is often used as an absolute quantity from which to compare multiple reinforcers. This overall strategy is historically referenced as a means of evaluating relative reinforcer efficacy, which is distinct from the broader Operant Demand Framework (see Johnson & Bickel, 2006, for a historical discussion). Second, an approach to understanding reinforcer effects in terms of elasticity emphasizes *changes in reinforcer consumption*. Changes across the "curve" of performances at varying schedule requirements are calculated in relative terms, with changes in reinforcer consumption (ΔQ) and schedule requirements (i.e., price; ΔP) providing the quantitative basis for determining elasticity. This overall calculation is provided in its entirety in the space below.

$$\eta = \frac{\frac{\Delta Q}{Q}}{\frac{\Delta P}{P}} = \frac{\Delta Q \frac{1}{Q}}{\Delta P \frac{1}{P}} = \frac{\Delta Q}{\Delta P} \frac{P}{Q} = \frac{\%\Delta Q}{\%\Delta P}$$

Various terms associated with elasticity include P_{MAX} and O_{MAX} and each is illustrated in Fig. 6.3. Quantity P_{MAX} represents a price value that distinguishes prices in the inelastic and elastic ranges. Elasticity associated with the inelastic range is typically described as having a value lower than 1, and this essentially means that the relative changes in consumption (%ΔQ) do not outpace relative changes in increasing price (%ΔP).[2] These values for elasticity are associated with increasing expenditure up to a point (P_{MAX}). In contrast, prices in the elastic range are associated with elasticity values greater than 1, which means that the relative changes in consumption (%ΔQ) outpace relative changes in increasing price (%ΔP). The result of this is rapid drops in observed consumption, which are associated with decreasing expenditure.

An elasticity-based account of reinforcement provides a dynamic interpretation of reinforcer effects across contexts and schedule arrangements. The overall responsiveness to changes in schedule requirements has been referred to as *essential value* (Gilroy, 2023; Hursh & Silberberg, 2008) and the focus on *relative* change provides a means of drawing comparisons within and between various reinforcers (e.g., efficacy of a reinforcer across prices and magnitudes).

Reinforcement and reinforcer complement/substitutes

> ... no simple, unidimensional rule of choice such as strict matching can explain interactions between reinforcers if some interact as substitutes and others interact as complements.
> Hursh, S. R. (1980). Economic concepts for the analysis of behavior. Journal of the Experimental Analysis of Behavior, 34(2), 219—238. https://doi.org/10.1901/jeab.1980.34-219, p. 235.

The economic concept of the open economy provides a useful framework for examining choice behavior in context. Hursh (1980) highlighted several challenges associated with applying the matching law when one or more choices may *interact* with one another. For example, certain types of consumption may be more likely as a result of consuming other reinforcers (i.e., a complementary relationship; e.g., the purchase of popcorn is related to abundant access to movies). Additionally, reinforcer preferences may *shift* as schedule requirements increase and individuals substitute a previously preferred reinforcer with a previously less preferred alternative (e.g., substituting a "premium" coffee beverage with a more basic alternative due to an increased cost).

Most examples provided thus far illustrate the demand for a reinforcer in isolation (i.e., Alone-Price demand for a reinforcer). In these arrangements, the goal is to examine the demand for a reinforcer in a specific context (i.e., absent any other alternatives; Closed Economy). However, it is often the case that multiple reinforcers are concurrently available, and the Operant Demand Framework provides a methodology for examining how individuals consume *alternatives* to a specific reinforcer (see Fig. 6.4).

---

[2] Note: Price elasticity of demand is typically a negative value but values are presented unsigned to simplify the overall ratio to the reader.

Practical applications of the Operant Demand Framework   137

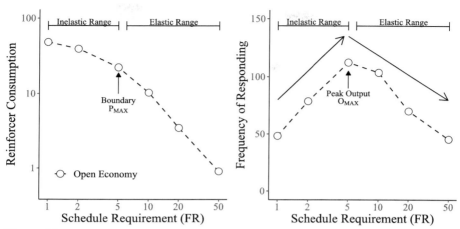

Figure 6.3 Ranges of elasticity and associated characteristics.

Cross-price analyses of demand consist of exploring how the demand for some *alternative* reinforcer (Cross-Price Demand) available at a fixed schedule requirement (e.g., FR2) changes as the demand for a *primary* reinforcer inevitably decreases across increasing schedule requirements (Own-Price Demand). The behavior of the alternative in this arrangement provides a basis for determining the relationship between reinforcers. An arrangement whereby demand for both reinforcers declines suggests that the two reinforcers *complement* one another (i.e., the utility of the alternative reinforcer is influenced by the availability of the primary reinforcer). In contrast, if the demand for the alternative reinforcer *increases* as the demand for the primary reinforcer falls, this suggests that there is a relationship based on a *substitution* relationship. Lastly, no

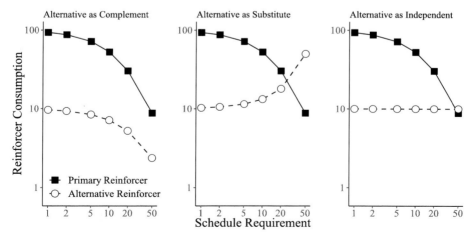

Figure 6.4 Functional relations among reinforcer options.

systematic relationship may exist, and this would be referred to as an *independent* relationship.

Various aspects of the Operant Demand Framework were introduced prior to describing how the framework has added constructively to behavior analytic research and practice. Each of the sections that follow will focus on a core domain of practice and how economic theory and concepts can support behavior analytic procedures or interpretations of data.

Applications of demand to preference assessment

Assessments of individual preference are typically included in behavior analytic research and practice for several reasons. Principal among these is to explore the degree to which aspects of the intervention (i.e., preference for intervention; Auten et al., 2024) or specific materials included in the intervention have value to the individual (e.g., items likely to have reinforcing effects; Fisher et al., 1992). Various assessments exist, and the particulars of each are not reviewed here (for reviews, see Cannella et al., 2005; Tullis et al., 2011), though most practices consist of sampling choice behavior with items either freely available (e.g., stimulus exposure) or contingent on some low-effort response (e.g., selection response; Fisher & Mazur, 1997).

Items or activities ranked highly on stimulus preference assessments have been linked to reinforcing effects; however, empirical evaluations of these effects have been restricted almost entirely to effects on FR1 schedules (Fisher et al., 1992; Piazza et al., 1996). Methods from the Operant Demand Framework have been introduced to study reinforcer preference and reinforcing effects and explore how these phenomena *scale* as a function of increasing response requirements (i.e., effects at FR1 vs. on FR5 or FR10).

Reinforcer preferences and varying schedule arrangements

Some of the earliest applied behavior analytic work evaluating how individual preference and reinforcer performance scales across *prices* was done by Tustin (1994). Tustin (1994) evaluated the demand for various types of reinforcers (e.g., auditory, visual, attention) in both isolated (Alone-Price methods) and concurrent arrangements (Cross-Price methods). A total of three adults with an intellectual disability demonstrated varying preferences across schedules that both conformed with demand theory (i.e., decreasing reinforcer consumption with increasing price) as well as illustrated the presence of functional relations among distinct reinforcers (e.g., presence of functional substitutes).

The overall approach presented by Tustin (1994) has been replicated and extended in various subsequent works (Deleon et al., 1997; Gilroy et al., 2021; Glover et al., 2008; Roane et al., 2001). More recent works have featured the use of Progressive Ratio (PR) schedules as a means of examining reinforcer effects as response requirements increase (Hodos, 1961). Various implementations of PR schedules exist in the literature (see Jarmolowicz & Lattal, 2010, for a review of multiple classifications), though most function by subsequently increasing (e.g., doubling) the amount of responding necessary to produce the reinforcer following each delivery of the reinforcer (e.g., PR1 → PR2 → PR4). Regardless of the specific mechanism by which response effort increased, works in this area revealed that preferences are inevitably influenced by both context (e.g., availability of alternative reinforcers) as well as the acts by which access to specific items is granted. Put simply, an item or event may be preferable when easily and readily produced (e.g., on FR1 schedules) but less so when the response necessary to produce it (i.e., work) increases beyond a simple act or selection response (e.g., FR2, FR10, etc.).

Applications of the Operant Demand Framework for preference assessment

The most direct evaluation of the Operant Demand Framework in the context of stimulus preference was presented by Gilroy et al. (2021). In this study, the authors conducted a stimulus preference assessment consistent with methods from Fisher et al. (1992) and evaluated the degree to which preference assessment rankings predicted reinforcing effects in terms of overall work performance. Findings from this study replicated those from Fisher et al. (1992), whereby items ranked highly (i.e., selected in >80% of opportunities) demonstrated a reinforcing effect when made contingent on behavior (e.g., FR1). Results from Gilroy et al. (2021) replicated the findings from Fisher et al. (1992) that items selected frequently (i.e., >80% of opportunities) demonstrated a reinforcing effect; however, evaluations of individual reinforcers using the Operant Demand Framework revealed that relative rankings were not predictive of reinforcer superiority on either sustained work at low prices (i.e., FR1) or the maximum amount of work an individual would perform to sustain preferred reinforcer levels (i.e., P_{MAX}, see Fig. 6.5).

Findings from Gilroy et al. (2021) highlight the complexities of choice, and preference, and how these phenomena scale uniquely as a function of schedule requirements. Indeed, choice and preference are inevitably influenced by the organism (e.g., preference), its history with various stimuli in the environment (e.g., prior history with preferred items/events), and various aspects of the present context (e.g., response requirements, availability of alternatives, reinforcer—reinforcer relations). The Operant Demand Framework provides a structured approach and molar interpretation of individual choice behavior that can add to the existing behavior analytic literature.

Applications of demand to reinforcer evaluations

Formal evaluations of reinforcer effects have been similarly well-represented in behavior analytic literature (Mason et al., 1989). The term "reinforcer effects" broadly refers to some characterization of how reinforcers affect behavior (e.g., response rate, level of consumption) and has been referenced previously in several ways (e.g.,

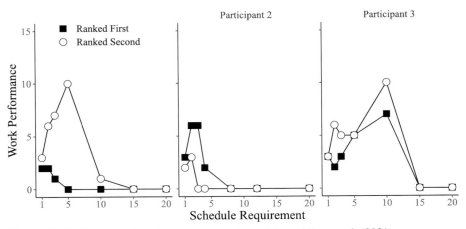

Figure 6.5 Preference and performance data extracted from Gilroy et al. (2021).

reinforcer potency, reinforcer efficacy). For the purposes of this section, reinforcer effects refer to the degree to which reinforcers sustain at least some level of responding and how these phenomena scale across various schedule arrangements (e.g., FR1 → FR2 → FR10) or changes in contexts (e.g., close → open economy).

Whereas studies of preference are often quantified simply as a percentage (e.g., percentage of times selected) or rank (e.g., ranked first, ranked last), the continuous nature of reinforcer effects presents a challenge to representing these effects on behavior. For example, attempts to compare reinforcers on some specific basis (i.e., studies of relative reinforcer efficacy [RRE]) may draw comparisons using features such as reinforcer breakpoint, response rates, and some other aspect of reinforcer consumption (e.g., number of reinforcers produced; Katz, 1990). Although straightforward and easily calculated, several researchers have highlighted how individual representations of RRE can provide conflicting information (e.g., breakpoint and unit elasticity; Madden et al., 2007), and various researchers have instead suggested representing reinforcer effects as a molar *curve* rather than any specific point (Johnson & Bickel, 2006). Johnson and Bickel (2006) made a case for moving from *specific* types of reinforcer comparisons and toward a *broader* interpretation based on the concept of economic demand.

The most popular and contemporary approaches for understanding the demand for reinforcers are based on the framework presented by Hursh and Silberberg (2008). The particulars of statistical modeling are not presented in this chapter, and instead, the focus of the approach highlighted in Hursh and Silberberg (2008) is limited to two key dimensions of reinforcer consumption: *demand intensity* and *elasticity of demand*. Regardless of the statistical approach adopted, if any, each dimension has practical implications for behavior analysts.

Demand intensity and reinforcer magnitude

References to demand intensity are localized to reinforcer consumption in a particular context (e.g., single vs. concurrent arrangements). Specifically, demand intensity represents the organism's behavior when a reinforcer can be accessed freely without having to work to "purchase" such access. As reinforcer consumption here is not dependent on purchase via work, it is represented on a figure where Price = 0 (i.e., intercept of the demand curve).

The concept of demand intensity has been a useful tool for understanding how a specific reinforcer influences an organism. For example, two individuals may similarly prefer to consume certain reinforcers (e.g., caffeinated beverages) but differ in their overall daily consumption (e.g., heavy-vs. low-volume consumers). Likewise, an individual may demonstrate a high consumption and preference for a reinforcer in one context but not in another. Furthermore, changes in the availability of a reinforcer (or others) can similarly influence preference and patterns of consumption (see Mangum et al., 2012 for a demonstration).

Demand intensity and the total consumption of a certain reinforcer is inevitably linked to certain *units*, such as the size of a specific reinforcer (e.g., 30s vs. 60s of toy access). In behavior analysis, such units are often referenced in terms of the *magnitude* of the reinforcer delivered (e.g., "large" = 60s, "small" = 30s; Trosclair-Lasserre et al., 2008). Demand intensity is interpreted in the *units* of reinforcers consumption, and due to this, reinforcer consumption would naturally *decrease* were the magnitude of reinforcers provided to *increase* (see Hursh et al., 1988, for an empirical demonstration). For example, an individual who enjoys roughly 1 hour of screentime in a day would consume approximately 60 units of reinforcement if delivered in 1 min intervals or 12 units of reinforcement if delivered in 5 min intervals. For this reason, interpretations of demand intensity are also interpreted with regard to the units applied (e.g., differences in magnitude, concentration/dosage, etc.).

The intensity of reinforcer demand has been linked to various aspects of context, or in economic terms, the *type* of economy (i.e., on a continuum from fully open to fully closed). For example, it stands to reason that the intensity of demand is greatest in a *closed* economic context where there are neither functional alternatives (e.g., comparable reinforcers) nor alternative methods for producing the reinforcer (i.e., not available elsewhere for free or at a lower "price"; Kearns, 2019). Various research studies have supported findings that the availability of substitutable reinforcer alternatives can influence both preferences as well as the intensity of demand for specific reinforcers (Green & Freed, 1993; Kodak et al., 2007; Roane et al., 2005).

One of the clearest demonstrations of this effect is illustrated in Kodak et al. (2007). In this study, the authors evaluated consumption patterns in conditions where a reinforcer could only be produced in programmed session conditions (i.e., closed economy) to conditions where the reinforcer could be freely accessed outside of programmed session conditions (i.e., open economy). These findings mirror common challenges encountered by applied behavior analysts, who often find that programmed reinforcers appear less "durable" when there is a possibility that individuals may consume them elsewhere via some alternative means.

Elasticity of demand and reinforcer durability

Whereas the intensity of demand is an indicator of overall "bliss point" consumption (i.e., consumption when able to consume freely), the *elasticity* of demand refers to how reinforcer consumption scales with increases in reinforcer price (i.e., schedule or response requirements). There has been considerable behavior analytic research finding that individual preferences shift or vary as a function of schedule requirements (Deleon et al., 1997; Gilroy et al., 2021; Glover et al., 2008; Roane et al., 2001).

Although relevant to behavior analytic work and research, the elasticity of demand for reinforcers is a dimension that is relatively less explored. One of the clearest demonstrations of this concept with severe and challenging behavior is presented in Borrero et al. (2007). In this study, the authors evaluated the elasticity of demand for reinforcement-maintaining forms of problematic behavior. Specifically, these authors evaluated how proportional changes in the response were related to proportional changes in the amount of reinforcement delivered (i.e., reinforcement determined via functional analysis). Also, descriptive findings from Borrero et al. (2007) most increases in the molar unit price (i.e., number of responses required divided by the duration of reinforcement delivered) were elastic ($\eta < -1$; i.e., relative decreases in consumption outpaced relative increases in unit price).

A study by Gilroy et al. (2021) explored elasticity in regard to work completion and reinforcing effects across different ranges of elasticity. In this study, a brief within-session assessment of reinforcer performance was used to identify schedules of reinforcement likely to be reflective of inelastic, elastic, and unit elastic prices. Results indicated that schedules associated with the elastic region of the demand curve maintained lower overall responding and greater variability; see Fig. 6.6.

Applications of demand to token economies

The token economy is one of the clearest analogs of the general everyday economy predicated on generalized conditioned reinforcers (e.g., cash). In these arrangements, responding on some schedule produces the delivery of some token or currency (token production schedule) which is subsequently exchanged on some schedule (i.e., exchange production schedule) for some established token price (i.e., token exchange schedule; Hackenberg, 2009). The Operant Demand Framework has good utility for examining how the combination of these various interlocking schedules jointly contributes to behavior change.

Many of the earliest works related to token economies and their application emerged in basic research with nonhuman animals (see Levins & Gilroy, 2024, for a relevant overview); however, delivering contingent reinforcement in the context of a simulated economy was readily incorporated into various supportive contexts (e.g., "Achievement Place" and other therapeutic settings; Phillips, 1968). Much of this research has examined how various economic concepts, such as reinforcer effects scaling as a function of price, have been examined and replicated in context (see Hayden et al., 1974, for an early example).

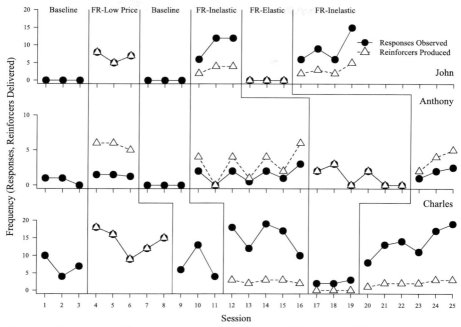

Figure 6.6 Reinforcer effects across elasticity range from Gilroy et al. (2021).

Specific to the economic concept of demand, a recent study by Levins and Gilroy (2024), presented an experiment that blended the framework outlined in Hackenberg (2009) with methods and concepts reflected in the Operant Demand Framework. Like that of Hayden et al. (1974), the reinforcing effects of token reinforcement systems were consistent with various economic concepts and expectations regarding the effects of price (i.e., the exchange production as well as token exchange schedules, see Fig. 6.6).

Challenges associated with applications of demand

This chapter outlined several areas in which the economic concept of demand can supplement existing behavior analytic research and applied practice. These new concepts and methods provide exciting new opportunities, especially for practical applications, but also introduce new challenges and considerations.

These methods and concepts are most often comprised of reinforcer evaluations, which are necessary as a means of testing reinforcer value (i.e., value in terms of work performed). Ethically, this can lead to scenarios in which programmed conditions simulate contexts in which work may not consistently be aligned with equitable reinforcer delivery (see Poling, 2010, for a relevant discussion related to PR schedules). Practically, the applied use of these methods with humans (who are often historically vulnerable populations) presents a risk of inducing considerable frustration when assessments probe excessively high response requirements (i.e., prices) while attempting to characterize various aspects of a demand curve.

Aside from evaluating schedules unlikely to be of clear relevance to intervention design, there is a balance between identifying information that is pragmatically useful in intervention and exploring various dimensions of reinforcer performance as a pursuit in and of itself. For example, many evaluations of reinforcer effects using the Operant Demand Framework use long-running intervals in which assessments run for several days (i.e., between-session price evaluations). Such evaluations would inevitably provide more representative data; however, the use of such practices with humans (especially vulnerable populations) introduces more challenges than they hope to solve. Shorter, within-session procedures (e.g., evaluations of schedules in a single session) lessen such risks, but likely provide more conservative and less precise estimates of reinforcer effects (i.e., more likely to encounter satiation a lower/earlier price points).

As a final point, the introduction of advanced economic concepts (e.g., quantitative concepts based on calculus, such as elasticity) further complicates practices that are often already challenging to communicate to lay audiences (e.g., teachers) and researchers not steeped in basic and applied research. This is especially problematic in efforts to characterize behavioral economic performance statistically, as there is little consensus regarding which approaches, practices, or models constitute best practices.

Future directions in research

Research on the effects of reinforcers has clear basic and applied research applications and methods in the Operant Demand Framework providing a means for exploring how various individual-level factors (e.g., preference) interact with complex contextual arrangements that are often encountered in real-world situations (e.g., open economy arrangements, availability of multiple reinforcer alternatives).

Various researchers and labs have been exploring how economic concepts can supplement strategies related to evaluating individual preference (Deleon et al., 1997; Goldberg et al., 2017), programming and subsequently thinning reinforcement schedules (e.g., unit prices for programmed reinforcement; Gilroy et al., 2019; Roane et al., 2007), evaluating aspects of token economy arrangements (Levins & Gilroy, 2024), and exploring factors contributing to resurgence and other extinction phenomena (Lambert et al., 2024).

References

Auten, E. M., Van Camp, C., & Ferguson, A. B. (2024). A review of the concurrent-chains arrangement to assess intervention choice: 2018−2023. *Journal of Applied Behavior Analysis, 57*(2), 319−330. https://doi.org/10.1002/jaba.1059

Borrero, J. C., Francisco, M. T., Haberlin, A. T., Ross, N. A., & Sran, S. K. (2007). A unit price evaluation of severe problem behavior. *Journal of Applied Behavior Analysis, 40*(3), 463. https://doi.org/10.1901/jaba.2007.40-463

Camerer, C. F., & Loewenstein, G. (2004). Behavioral economics: Past, present, future. In C. F. Camerer, G. Loewenstein, & M. Rabin (Eds.), *Advances in behavioral economics* (pp. 3–52). Princeton University Press. https://doi.org/10.1515/9781400829118-004

Cannella, H. I., O'Reilly, M. F., & Lancioni, G. E. (2005). Choice and preference assessment research with people with severe to profound developmental disabilities: A review of the literature. *Research in Developmental Disabilities, 26*(1), 1–15. https://doi.org/10.1016/j.ridd.2004.01.006

Deleon, I. G., Iwata, B. A., Goh, H.-L., & Worsdell, A. S. (1997). Emergence of reinforcer preference as a function of schedule requirements and stimulus similarity. *Journal of Applied Behavior Analysis, 30*(3), 439–449. https://doi.org/10.1901/jaba.1997.30-439

Fisher, W. W., & Mazur, J. E. (1997). Basic and applied research on choice responding. *Journal of Applied Behavior Analysis, 30*(3), 387–410. https://doi.org/10.1901/jaba.1997.30-387

Fisher, W. W., Piazza, C. C., Bowman, L. G., Hagopian, L. P., Owens, J. C., & Slevin, I. (1992). A comparison of two approaches for identifying reinforcers for persons with severe and profound disabilities. *Journal of Applied Behavior Analysis, 25*(2), 491–498. https://doi.org/10.1901/jaba.1992.25-491

Francisco, M. T., Madden, G. J., & Borrero, J. (2009). Behavioral economics: Principles, procedures, and utility for applied behavior analysis. *Behavior Analyst Today, 10*(2), 277–294. https://doi.org/10.1037/h0100671

Gilroy, S. P. (2023). Interpretation(s) of essential value in operant demand. *Journal of the Experimental Analysis of Behavior, 119*(3), 554–564. https://doi.org/10.1002/jeab.845

Gilroy, S. P., Ford, H. L., Boyd, R. J., O'Connor, J. T., & Kurtz, P. F. (2019). An evaluation of operant behavioural economics in functional communication training for severe problem behaviour. *Developmental Neurorehabilitation, 22*(8), 553–564.

Gilroy, S. P., Kaplan, B. A., & Leader, G. (2018). A systematic review of applied behavioral economics in assessments and treatments for individuals with developmental disabilities. *Review Journal of Autism and Developmental Disorders, 5*, 247–259. https://doi.org/10.1007/s40489-018-0136-6

Gilroy, S. P., Waits, J. A., & Feck, C. (2021). Extending stimulus preference assessment with the operant demand framework. *Journal of Applied Behavior Analysis, 54*(3), 1032–1044. https://doi.org/10.1002/jaba.826

Glover, A. C., Roane, H. S., Kadey, H. J., & Grow, L. L. (2008). Preference for reinforcers under progressive- and fixed-ratio schedules: A comparison of single and concurrent arrangements. *Journal of Applied Behavior Analysis, 41*(2), 163. https://doi.org/10.1901/jaba.2008.41-163

Goldberg, M. C., Allman, M. J., Hagopian, L. P., Triggs, M. M., Frank-Crawford, M. A., Mostofsky, S. H., Denckla, M. B., & DeLeon, I. G. (2017). Examining the reinforcing value of stimuli within social and non-social contexts in children with and without high-functioning autism. *Autism, 21*(7), 881–895. https://doi.org/10.1177/1362361316655035

Green, L., & Freed, D. E. (1993). The substitutability of reinforcers. *Journal of the Experimental Analysis of Behavior, 60*(1), 141. https://doi.org/10.1901/jeab.1993.60-141

Hackenberg, T. D. (2009). Token reinforcement: A review and analysis. *Journal of the Experimental Analysis of Behavior, 91*(2), 257–286. https://doi.org/10.1901/jeab.2009.91-257

Hanley, G. P. (2010). Toward effective and preferred programming: A case for the objective measurement of social validity with recipients of behavior-change programs. *Behavior Analysis in Practice, 3*(1), 13−21. https://doi.org/10.1007/BF03391754

Hayden, T., Osborne, A. E., Hall, S. M., & Hall, R. G. (1974). Behavioral effects of price changes in a token economy. *Journal of Abnormal Psychology, 83*(4), 432−439. https://doi.org/10.1037/h0036926

Heinicke, M. R., Carr, J. E., & Copsey, C. J. (2019). Assessing preferences of individuals with developmental disabilities using alternative stimulus modalities: A systematic review. *Journal of Applied Behavior Analysis, 52*(3), 847−869. https://doi.org/10.1002/jaba.565

Hodos, W. (1961). Progressive ratio as a measure of reward strength. *Science, 134*(3483), 943−944. https://doi.org/10.1126/science.134.3483.943

Hursh, S. R. (1980). Economic concepts for the analysis of behavior. *Journal of the Experimental Analysis of Behavior, 34*(2), 219−238. https://doi.org/10.1901/jeab.1980.34-219

Hursh, S. R. (1984). Behavioral economics. *Journal of the Experimental Analysis of Behavior, 42*(3), 435−452. https://doi.org/10.1901/jeab.1984.42-435

Hursh, S. R., Raslear, T. G., Shurtleff, D., Bauman, R., & Simmons, L. (1988). A cost-benefit analysis of demand for food. *Journal of the Experimental Analysis of Behavior, 50*(3), 419. https://doi.org/10.1901/jeab.1988.50-419

Hursh, S. R., & Silberberg, A. (2008). Economic demand and essential value. *Psychological Review, 115*(1), 186.

Iyengar, S. S., & Lepper, M. R. (2000). When choice is demotivating: Can one desire too much of a good thing? *Journal of Personality and Social Psychology, 79*(6), 995−1006. https://doi.org/10.1037/0022-3514.79.6.995

Jarmolowicz, D. P., & Lattal, K. A. (2010). On distinguishing progressively increasing response requirements for reinforcement. *The Behavior Analyst, 33*(1), 119−125. https://doi.org/10.1007/BF03392207

Johnson, M. W., & Bickel, W. K. (2006). Replacing relative reinforcing efficacy with behavioral economic demand curves. *Journal of the Experimental Analysis of Behavior, 85*(1), 73−93. https://doi.org/10.1901/jeab.2006.102-04

Katz, J. L. (1990). Models of relative reinforcing efficacy of drugs and their predictive utility. *Behavioural Pharmacology, 1*(4), 283.

Kearns, D. N. (2019). The effect of economy type on reinforcer value. *Behavioural Processes, 162*, 20−28. https://doi.org/10.1016/j.beproc.2019.01.008

Kodak, T., Lerman, D. C., & Call, N. (2007). Evaluating the influence of postsession reinforcement on choice of reinforcers. *Journal of Applied Behavior Analysis, 40*(3), 515−527. https://doi.org/10.1901/jaba.2007.40-515

Lambert, J. M., Osina, M. A., & Copeland, B. A. (2024). Reinforcer value moderates response magnitude and persistence during extinction: A randomized trial. *Journal of Applied Behavior Analysis, 57*(3), 615−634. https://doi.org/10.1002/jaba.1088

Levins, P., & Gilroy, S. P. (2024). Extending token economy systems with the operant demand framework. *Journal of Behavioral Education*. https://doi.org/10.1007/s10864-024-09556-6

Madden, G. J., Smethells, J. R., Ewan, E. E., & Hursh, S. R. (2007). Tests of behavioral-economic assessments of relative reinforcer efficacy II: Economic complements. *Journal of the Experimental Analysis of Behavior, 88*(3), 355. https://doi.org/10.1901/jeab.2007.88-355

Mangum, A., Roane, H., Fredrick, L., & Pabico, R. (2012). The role of context in the evaluation of reinforcer efficacy: Implications for the preference assessment outcomes. *Research in Autism Spectrum Disorders, 6*(1), 158. https://doi.org/10.1016/j.rasd.2011.04.001

Mason, S. A., McGee, G. G., Farmer-Dougan, V., & Risley, T. R. (1989). A practical strategy for ongoing reinforcer assessment. *Journal of Applied Behavior Analysis, 22*(2), 171. https://doi.org/10.1901/jaba.1989.22-171

Phillips, E. L. (1968). Achievement place: Token reinforcement procedures in a home-style rehabilitation setting for "predelinquent" boys. *Journal of Applied Behavior Analysis, 1*(3), 213−223. https://doi.org/10.1901/jaba.1968.1-213

Piazza, C. C., Fisher, W. W., Hagopian, L. P., Bowman, L. G., & Toole, L. (1996). Using a choice assessment to predict reinforcer effectiveness. *Journal of Applied Behavior Analysis, 29*(1), 1−9. https://doi.org/10.1901/jaba.1996.29-1

Poling, A. (2010). Progressive-ratio schedules and applied behavior analysis. *Journal of Applied Behavior Analysis, 43*(2), 347−349. https://doi.org/10.1901/jaba.2010.43-347

Reed, D. D., Niileksela, C. R., & Kaplan, B. A. (2013). Behavioral economics: A tutorial for behavior analysts in practice. *Behavior Analysis in Practice, 6*(1), 34−54. https://doi.org/10.1007/BF03391790

Reed, D. D., Reed, F. D. D., Chok, J., & Brozyna, G. A. (2011). The "tyranny of choice": Choice overload as a possible instance of effort discounting. *Psychological Record, 61*(4), 547−560. https://doi.org/10.1007/BF03395776

Roane, H. S., Call, N. A., & Falcomata, T. S. (2005). A preliminary analysis of adaptive responding under open and closed economies. *Journal of Applied Behavior Analysis, 38*(3), 335−348. https://doi.org/10.1901/jaba.2005.85-04

Roane, H. S., Falcomata, T. S., & Fisher, W. W. (2007). Applying the behavioral economics principle of unit price to DRO schedule thinning. *Journal of Applied Behavior Analysis, 40*(3), 529−534. https://doi.org/10.1901/jaba.2007.40-529

Roane, H. S., Lerman, D. C., & Vorndran, C. M. (2001). Assessing reinforcers under progressive schedule requirements. *Journal of Applied Behavior Analysis, 34*(2), 145−167. https://doi.org/10.1901/jaba.2001.34-145

Samuelson, P. A., & Nordhaus, W. D. (2009). *Economics* (19th ed.). McGraw Hill.

Trosclair-Lasserre, N. M., Lerman, D. C., Call, N. A., Addison, L. R., & Kodak, T. (2008). Reinforcement magnitude: An evaluation of preference and reinforcer efficacy. *Journal of Applied Behavior Analysis, 41*(2), 203−220. https://doi.org/10.1901/jaba.2008.41-203

Tullis, C. A., Cannella-Malone, H. I., Basbigill, A. R., Yeager, A., Fleming, C. V., Payne, D., & Wu, P.-F. (2011). Review of the choice and preference assessment literature for individuals with severe to profound disabilities. *Education and Training in Autism and Developmental Disabilities, 46*(4), 576−595.

Tustin, R. D. (1994). Preference for reinforcers under varying schedule arrangements: A behavioral economic analysis. *Journal of Applied Behavior Analysis, 27*(4), 597−606. https://doi.org/10.1901/jaba.1994.27-597

Wolf, M. M. (1978). Social validity: The case for subjective measurement or how applied behavior analysis is finding its heart 1. *Journal of Applied Behavior Analysis, 11*(2), 203−214.

An introduction to discounting

Mariah E. Willis-Moore, Kiernan T. Callister, David N. Legaspi, Daniel S. Da Silva and Amy L. Odum
Utah State University, Logan, UT, United States

An introduction to discounting

Each day, we are faced with a variety of choices. We decide what we eat, how we spend our time, and what we can or cannot accomplish. Although some choices have relatively little impact in the short term (e.g., today's snack option does not directly change overall health), repeated and frequent choices over time (e.g., recurrent choices to eat an apple in place of chips) do have long-term consequences (e.g., Rachlin, 1974). In many cases, however, people tend to overlook the impact of decisions that could have long-term benefits and instead favor outcomes with lesser but immediate outcomes. Choice of outcomes may also hinge on the certainty (i.e., probability) of experiencing and/or attaining those outcomes. For instance, individuals may prefer a reward that is smaller but more likely to occur over one that is larger but less likely. What the above examples share is that the outcome value is degraded as a function of the delay or probability of the outcome. This tendency is known as *discounting*.

A brief history of discounting

Discounting is a fundamental concept at the core of behavioral economics and psychology, with many wide-reaching implications and considerations for socially relevant behavior. For example, steep delay discounting is associated with substance abuse (see Amlung et al., 2017; Mackillop et al., 2011, for review), problem gambling (e.g., Alessi & Petry, 2003; Petry & Madden, 2010; Weinsztok et al., 2021), and various health-related behaviors such as risky sex (e.g., Johnson et al., 2015; for review see Johnson et al., 2021), and overeating (e.g., Bickel et al., 2021; Rodriguez et al., 2021). Similarly, the preference for probabilistic outcomes is also associated with problem gambling (see Kyonka & Schutte, 2018; Madden et al., 2009) and risky sexual behavior (e.g., Berry et al., 2019; Johnson et al., 2015).

Some of the earliest work in the study of discounting was pioneered in nonhuman animal research laboratories with roots in choice and matching research (e.g., Ainslie,

Author Note: All authors were supported in part during the preparation of this manuscript by R21 DA053818 Cutting Edge Basic Research (CEBRA) Award from the National Institute on Drug Abuse and Da Silva also in part by a Research Catalyst Award from the Alzheimer's Disease and Dementia Research Center of Utah State University.

1974; Chung & Herrnstein, 1967; Mazur & Logue, 1978; Navarick & Fantino, 1976; Rachlin & Green, 1972). For example, Chung and Herrnstein (1967) examined the impact of delay on choice in pigeons. Pigeons could peck one of two response keys: one that produced a smaller amount of food sooner and one that produced a larger amount of food later. First, the delays to both options were the same, and the pigeons preferred the larger amount. Next, the delay to the larger amount of grain systematically increased, and the choice for that amount decreased. That is, the pigeons preferred the smaller amount of grain at a shorter delay over the larger but more delayed option. This groundbreaking work provided early evidence that the value of outcomes is discounted as a function of delay to receipt. Today, nonhuman animal research remains a critical area in discounting, offering a variety of benefits to understanding the different relations, facets, and underlying mechanisms of discounting that cannot be investigated with humans.

Around the same time as the early nonhuman work, research on human discounting was underway (e.g., Ainslie, 1975; Mischel et al., 1969; Rachlin, 1974; Rotter, 1954). Mischel and colleagues, for example, examined choices in fourth and fifth graders as well as college students. In their study, participants made choices between hypothetical outcomes (e.g., 50¢) that were available immediately or after various delays (e.g., 1 week). Overall, Mischel et al. found that for both children and adults, "as the anticipated delay interval for attainment of a reward increases, the subjective value of the reward decreases" (p. 371). This early work also contributed to the foundation for the investigation of choice by delay in humans.

In the late 1990s and early 2000s, discounting by delay was extended in service of understanding human problems such as substance abuse (e.g., Madden et al., 1997; Mitchell, 1999; Petry, 2001), with many of these early studies relying on measurements of choices with hypothetical outcomes and delays (for discussion, see below). For example, Bickel et al. (1999) examined the discounting of delayed hypothetical monetary outcomes in three groups: current, never, and ex-smokers of cigarettes. Participants who currently smoked cigarettes had the greatest levels of hypothetical monetary discounting, followed by ex-smokers and never-smokers, who showed similar degrees of discounting. Current smokers also discounted cigarettes more steeply than money. In another study, Odum et al. (2000) examined discounting of delayed outcomes of hypothetical money or heroin in opioid-dependent individuals. A subset of the participants indicated in a scenario that they would be willing to share injection equipment with someone else to use heroin. In general, heroin was discounted more steeply than money, and people who indicated they would share needles discounted more steeply than those who did not. Importantly, these studies provided early evidence that discounting can offer insights into pressing societal issues. Along with other findings, this research cemented the foundational framework for examining discounting across different outcomes and subject populations and for practical applications to other societal problems. Following these developments, the number of experiments on discounting has grown at an accelerating pace.

There are various types of discounting, each with a distinctive focus. At the heart of discounting, however, is the common examination of how the valuation of outcomes decreases with changes in delay and probability of receipt, social distance from the person benefitting, or effort needed to earn the reward. We will first review the two most researched areas of discounting, delay and probability, before we turn to other discounting areas, including social, effort, and past discounting.

Delay discounting, the most extensively investigated area of discounting, refers to the decline in the value of an outcome with *delay* to its receipt (Mazur, 1987; Odum, 2011a). With steep delay discounting, organisms prefer smaller immediate outcomes over larger but delayed outcomes with positive outcomes (e.g., gaining money). When outcomes are negative, however, steep delay discounting can result in a choice of larger delayed punishers over smaller, more immediate ones (e.g., losing money; Green et al., 2014; Ostaszewski & Karzel, 2002; Rodriguez et al., 2018; Woolverton et al., 2012).

Probability discounting, however, refers to the decline in the value of an outcome with *uncertainty* in its receipt (see Green & Myerson, 2004; Rachlin et al., 1991). With steep probability discounting, organisms prefer larger riskier outcomes over smaller more certain outcomes with positive outcomes. When outcomes are negative, however, steep probability discounting can result in choices favoring smaller more certain outcomes over larger but riskier outcomes.

How do we measure discounting?

Various methods are employed to measure discounting (the breadth of which is expanded in Chapter 9, this volume). At their core, most delay and probability discounting tasks assess the choice between two outcomes: one that is smaller and immediately or certainly available and one that is larger and available after a delay or less likely to occur. Procedures for measuring delay and probability discounting are used to assess preference both in human and nonhuman animals.

Procedures with nonhuman animals

Several different procedures can measure delay and probability discounting with nonhuman animals. Some of the most used procedures for delay discounting include the adjusting-delay (Mazur, 1987), adjusting-amount (Richards et al., 1997), and increasing-delay (Evenden & Ryan, 1996) procedures. Overall, each procedure involves using operanda (e.g., keys, levers, nose pokes) that register responses for more or less of an outcome such as grain, food pellets, water, or drugs. In most of these methods, a center response starts the trial to ensure that the animal is equidistant between the two options on either side of the chamber before a choice is made. Subjects also typically are presented with single-option trials, in which only one outcome on one side is available, and choice trials, in which both outcomes on both sides are available. Single-option trials are included to ensure that the subjects sample both outcomes at least periodically so that behavior ideally would remain sensitive to the contingencies. Finally, an intertrial-interval (ITI) occurs after each trial to hold the times between trials constant. Intertrial intervals are used to prevent subjects from maximizing reward rates by repeatedly choosing the smaller option.

Mazur (1987) developed the first systematic procedure to measure delay discounting in nonhumans. In this adjusting-delay procedure, subjects are presented with two options: one that is larger and delivered after an adjusted delay, and one that is smaller and delivered after a fixed delay. Two single-option trials are presented in which only one outcome is available, followed by two choice trials in which both outcomes are available. The delay to the larger option adjusts based on choice behavior: If the larger option is chosen on both choice trials, the delay to the larger option increases by 1 second for the next block of trials, but if the smaller option is chosen on both choice trials, the delay to the larger option decreases by 1 second. If both options are chosen, however, the delay remains the same. These 4-trial blocks are repeated across each session. The adjusting-delay procedure identifies a delay that results in indifference between the two options. That is, the dependent variable is the delay to the larger reward, at which choice allocation is about 50% for the larger delayed option and about 50% for the smaller sooner option. This procedure repeats across several conditions in which the fixed delay to the smaller sooner outcome is varied.

Using similar logic, Richards et al. (1997) developed an adjusting-amount procedure in which the *amounts* of outcomes rather than the delays to them are titrated (see also Mazur, 1987). Specifically, two options are available to the subjects: a smaller immediate one that adjusts in size based on choice, and a larger delayed option (the standard) that remains constant. The smaller immediate option decreases by 10% if it was previously chosen on the last trial, and increases by 10% if the larger delayed option was chosen on the previous trial. If the rat chooses the same option on two consecutive trials, the next trial is a single-option trial which presents only the outcome not chosen in the previous two trials. This process continues across trials until the end of the experimental session, at which point the smaller adjusting and larger standard reward should be chosen with approximately equal frequency. Unlike the adjusting-delay procedure, in which the standard delay is in effect for many sessions, in the adjusting-amount procedure, the standard delay is different for each daily session.

The most used procedure to study delay discounting in nonhumans, developed by Evenden and Ryan (1996; see Mar & Robbins, 2007), however, does not adjust based on choice. In the *increasing*-delay procedure, as in adjusting procedures, the subject is presented with single-option trials to expose them to the alternatives and then presented with both options and can choose between them. However, the options on trials do not change based on behavior, but rather occur in blocks in which delays increase systematically across the session. In the first block, the delay to the larger outcome is 0 seconds to assess sensitivity to the amount of the outcomes (i.e., the choice of the larger amount of food should be near exclusive if the contingencies control behavior). Delays to the larger amount then increase across blocks within the session (e.g., 8, 12, & 24 seconds). The proportion of larger-later choices (number of larger-later choices made on choice trials out of total possible choices) is calculated at each delay and is the main dependent measure of interest. A similar procedure for probability discounting has been developed; instead of delay increasing across blocks, the probability decreases across blocks (e.g., Rojas et al., 2022; Yates et al., 2015) or sessions (e.g., Zoratto et al., 2016).

Delay and probability discounting can be measured using any one of these procedures, each with strengths and weaknesses. On one hand, each of the procedures is flexible and can be tailored to the experimental needs in terms of the duration of the delays, and probability and magnitude of the rewards. Each of these procedures has also been validated and produces consistent data. The adjusting delay (Mazur, 1987) and the within-session increasing delay (Evenden & Ryan, 1996) procedures both have good test-retest reliability (Peterson et al., 2015). One strength of the adjusting-delay and the adjusting-amount (Richards et al., 1997) procedures is that they generate multiple data points at which the choice is indifferent between the two options that can be used in theoretical quantitative analysis (e.g., Mazur, 1987). Experiments with the within-session increasing-delay or increasing-probability (e.g., Yates et al., 2015) procedure, however, have the advantage of being faster to conduct, given that each session produces data for a range of delays or probabilities. This advantage is especially powerful for studies on behavioral pharmacology, in which the effects of a range of drug doses are determined.

On the other hand, all discounting procedures have some limitations. One drawback of the original adjusting-amount procedure (Richards et al., 1997) is that the reinforcer size is adjusted in microliters (μL) of water, a level of precision that many laboratories cannot obtain with standard equipment. A difficulty with the adjusting-delay procedure (Mazur, 1987) is that it can be time-consuming to titrate multiple delays to the small reinforcer across sessions, particularly if it requires extensive time to develop a stable preference. Wahab et al. (2018) provided an updated adjusting-delay procedure which aims to achieve durable stability faster. Smethells and Carroll (2015) found that behavior maintained by the adjusting-delay procedure was insensitive to the effects of cocaine, whereas behavior maintained by the increasing delay procedure (Evenden & Ryan, 1996) was sensitive to the effects of cocaine, showing a decreased choice of the larger later reward. However, choice in the increasing-delay procedure can reflect the effects of prior delays due to the systematic increase in delay duration across blocks within the session, elevating the choice of the larger later reward at longer delays and raising concerns of response perseveration (e.g., Pitts & McKinney, 2005; Slezak & Anderson, 2009). Despite this limitation, however, the within-session increasing-delay procedure is the only one which allows assessment of amount discrimination (at the 0-second delay to the larger reinforcer), which can be impacted by bias or pharmacological manipulations, in each session.

Due to the variety of different procedures used, researchers have examined concordance across data generated by them. Green et al. (2007) compared data from the adjusting-amount (Richards et al., 1997) and adjusting-delay (Mazur, 1987) procedures and found that although the two procedures produced comparable measures of delay discounting, data from the adjusting-delay procedure were more systematic. Craig et al. (2014) found a positive correlation between data from the adjusting-delay and increasing-delay (Evenden & Ryan, 1996) procedures, suggesting these procedures may be representative of a similar discounting process. Finally, Peterson et al. (2015) found that data from systematic procedures, such as the increasing-delay procedure (Evenden & Ryan, 1996; see also Green & Estle, 2003), were strongly correlated, whereas data from the adjusting-delay procedure (Mazur, 1987) were not correlated with data from the systematic procedures. Overall, most studies use the within-session increasing-delay procedure because it is generally reliable, sensitive, and correlated with, yet faster than, other procedures.

Procedures with human participants

There are several procedures for examining discounting in humans (for a greater overview, see Chapter 9). For delay discounting, some of the most frequently used procedures are the Monetary Choice Questionnaire (MCQ; Kirby et al., 1999), the fixed sequence procedure (Odum et al., 2006; Rachlin et al., 1991), and the adjusting-amount procedure (Du et al., 2002; Richards et al., 1999). Similarly, the fixed-sequence (Rachlin et al., 1991) and adjusting-amount procedures (Du et al., 2002; Richards et al., 1999) are also used for probability discounting. Additionally, the MCQ has been adapted into the probability discounting questionnaire (PDQ; Madden et al., 2009).

What each of the above procedures shares is the measurement of preference between immediate/certain outcomes and delayed/uncertain outcomes, asking participants to choose with a variety of delays or probabilities. For example, in the fixed sequence procedure (Rachlin et al., 1991), choices typically start with the immediate and delayed amounts equal, and the amount of the immediate reward decreases across trials. Preference shifts at some point from the immediate amount (when it is the same as the delayed amount) to the delayed amount as the immediate amount decreases. In the adjusting-amount procedure (Du et al., 2002), participants make a series of choices across several increasing delays or increasing odds against receiving the larger outcome. Based on choices, the immediate or certain amount is adjusted up or down to titrate the amount to one equivalent to the larger, more delayed or less probable amount.

Each procedure is useful for measuring discounting and has different strengths. The MCQ and PDQ are the shortest and most easily administered tasks; however, data from these tasks are limited because the degree of discounting is inferred from the series of questions rather than directly assessed. The adjusting amount task (Du et al., 2002) requires the ability to calculate the choice options immediately after each trial, and so is administered via computer. The fixed-sequence procedure (Rachlin et al., 1991) is intermediate between the two tasks in terms of difficulty of administration and can be used as both a paper-and-pencil and computerized version. Furthermore, different ways of assessing discounting appear to produce similar results. For example, the fixed-sequence and adjusting-amount procedures produce similar estimates of delay discounting (Rodzon et al., 2011), as do the adjusting-delay and adjusting-amount procedures (Holt et al., 2012).

One less commonly used procedure for delay discounting, but widely used for measuring probability discounting, is the Visual Analog Scale (VAS; Johnson & Bruner, 2012). Typically, in this procedure, participants are first presented with a contextual prompt, phrase or vignette (e.g., pictures of people; Johnson & Bruner, 2012). They are then asked to indicate their preference for an outcome on a VAS from 0 to 100, across varying degrees of delay or probabilities to that outcome, by moving a slider on the VAS. In doing so, participants provide a value for the larger reward at each delay or probability (Rung et al., 2018). The VAS procedure has the advantage of being relatively quick and easy to use, but it produces a restricted range because participants tend to avoid the extreme values at the ends of the scale (Hayes et al., 2013; Jollant et al., 2019).

The order in which participants complete discounting assessments is an important factor to consider when conducting discounting research with human subjects in which multiple tasks are completed in a single experimental session (Robles et al., 2009; Rung et al., 2019; Willis-Moore et al., 2024). For example, Willis-Moore and colleagues found that the degree of discounting by delay in the second task of two differed depending on which task was completed first. In Experiment 1, Willis-Moore et al. found that the effect of date framing, in which delays expressed as specific dates have less impact on value, differed based on the order of task presentation. When delays were first expressed as dates (e.g., October 26th, 2025), reduced delay discounting continued into the typical condition with delays in calendar units (e.g., 1 year), and there was no difference between the degree of discounting in two conditions. When the typical condition was followed by delays expressed as dates, however, delay discounting was reduced by date framing. Willis-Moore and colleagues shed new light on the importance of research designs, as well as the potential mechanism of these effects and how they could be harnessed for interventions.

Research on discounting with people has been criticized for reliance on hypothetical outcomes and delays. Although questions on the use of hypothetical outcomes are indeed important (e.g., "Do studies with hypothetical outcomes represent what would be obtained with real outcomes?"), research with hypothetical outcomes and delays generally produces similar results to those conducted with real and experienced delays (e.g., Johnson & Bickel, 2002; Lagorio & Madden, 2005; Madden et al., 2004; see Miller et al., 2023 for review). Furthermore, hypothetical discounting tasks are useful frameworks for modeling decisions related to real-world issues that simply cannot be examined in the laboratory for practical or ethical reasons. For example, hypothetical outcomes and delays have been used to understand decisions related to hypothetical condom use and sexually transmitted infection (STI) risk (e.g., Johnson & Bruner, 2012). Generally, research using this task has uncovered that like with other outcomes, willingness or ability to wait for a condom decreases systematically as a function of delay. These findings, and others, underscore the possible research insights that can be uncovered with hypothetical outcomes and hypothetical delays. For instance, if individuals engage in risky sexual behavior because they are less willing or able to wait for delayed condom access, one solution would be to ensure they have readily accessible condoms. Research that continues to examine real versus hypothetical outcomes and delays and their impacts on choice could provide valuable insights for future applications of discounting research. Indeed, more research in this area should be conducted across various populations and contexts.

How do we analyze discounting data?

The shared goal of many of the procedures described above is to find the point at which outcomes are said to have equal value — referred to as the *indifference point*.

Indifference points are the main dependent variable in human-subject discounting research. Indifference points are considered to represent the *present value* of the delayed/probabilistic outcome, that is, how much the delayed reward is worth now, or what the probabilistic reward is worth if it were certain. Calculating indifference points varies depending on the discounting task. For example, in the Du et al. (2002) adjusting-amount procedure, indifference points are calculated as the midpoint between the last chosen smaller sooner or certain outcome and the last rejected smaller sooner or certain outcome. However, the indifference point with this procedure can also include the final adjustment to the smaller-sooner amount (e.g., DeHart et al., 2018; Rung & Madden, 2019). That is, once a participant completes the last trial of the respective delay block, a final adjustment can be made to the smaller-sooner amount. The amount of the last presented smaller-sooner option plus the final adjustment then serves as the indifference point. In the fixed-sequence discounting procedure, however, the indifference point is determined by the average amount of the immediate reward just before and after the preference reversal, or by the last immediate option chosen (see Rachlin et al., 1991; Odum et al., 2006 for details).

Once indifference points are obtained, they are often normalized to allow comparison across different reward magnitudes or outcomes. To normalize indifference points, each indifference point is divided by the amount of the larger-later or larger-probabilistic reward. In this way, all indifference points range from 1 (undiscounted) to 0 (completely discounted) regardless of reward magnitude. Normalized indifference points can be plotted as a function of each respective delay or probability to visualize discounting results (see Fig. 7.1 for an example). Note that indifference points are plotted as a function of odds against receiving the larger-probabilistic outcome for probability (p) discounting, where the odds against (Θ) are equivalent to $(1/p) - 1$ (Rachlin et al., 1991). For individual data, each obtained indifference point is plotted, whereas for indifference points summarized for groups of participants, median

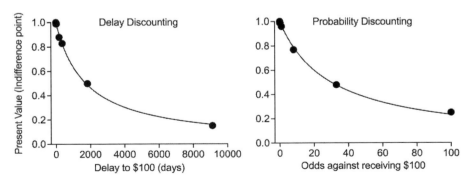

Figure 7.1 Hypothetical data representing present value (indifference point) as a function of delay to or odds against receiving $100. Hypothetical data showing delay discounting and model fit (left panel) and probability discounting and model fit (right panel). Curves through hypothetical indifference points represent model fits using (Eq. 7.1).

indifference points usually are plotted at each delay or probability (odds against) because the distributions are often not normal.

The degree to which outcomes are discounted: Steep versus shallow discounting

After indifference points are plotted as a function of delay or probability, discounting curves can be fitted to the data using nonlinear regression. One goal of curve fitting is to determine the degree to which outcomes are discounted, that is, to evaluate the steepness of discounting functions by delay or probability. Various quantitative models have been developed to describe the degree of discounting (see McKerchar et al., 2009; Gilroy et al., 2017, Chapter 10 of this volume for review). Here, we show one equation proposed by Mazur (1987):

$$V = \frac{A}{(1 + kD)} \quad (7.1)$$

V represents the present value of the outcome (the indifference point), A is the amount of the outcome, and D is the delay to receipt of the outcome; k is a free parameter that describes the degree of discounting. In probability discounting, D is replaced with the odds against the larger later outcome (Θ; Rachlin et al., 1991).

To determine which model best describes obtained discounting data, goodness of fit comparisons are calculated. Model fit comparisons can be conducted in several manners (Gelino et al., 2024). The Akaike Information Criterion (AIC) is one way that discounting models have been evaluated (e.g., DeHart et al., 2018). The AIC is a goodness of fit measure that compares model fit against the number of free parameters. The best model, indicated by a smaller AIC value, is the one that captures the most data with the least number of parameters. The Bayesian Information Criterion (BIC) is another goodness of fit measure for comparing model fits for discounting functions. Like AIC, BIC also relies on comparisons of model parameters; however, BIC is better suited for comparing more complex models (Gelino et al., 2024). Model comparison has also been conducted by comparing extra sums-of-squares F tests, which regress indifference points onto delay (see Berry et al., 2019; DeHart et al., 2018; Johnson et al., 2015, for examples and further discussion).

Area Under the Curve (AUC) is a model-free summary metric for delay and probability discounting (Myerson et al., 2001). To calculate AUC, lines are drawn from normalized indifference points at each respective delay, forming trapezoids. Next, the area of each trapezoid is found by using the following equation:

$$\sum (x_2 - x_1) \left[\frac{(y_1 + y_2)}{2} \right] \quad (7.2)$$

where x_1 and x_2 indicate successive delays and indifference points associated with those delays are represented by y_1 and y_2, respectively. Summing all trapezoidal areas produces AUC. The values of AUC range from 0.0, reflecting the steepest possible discounting, to 1.0, no discounting. That is, smaller AUC values reflect steeper discounting, whereas larger AUC values reflect shallow discounting. The AUC is inversely related to k in (Eq. 7.1); whereas larger AUC reflects shallow discounting, larger k reflects steep discounting.

Although AUC is a widely used and accepted summary measure, there are refinements to calculating it to reduce the disproportionate weighting of long delays or high probabilities (Borges et al., 2016). Logarithmic or ordinal transformations of the delays or probabilities can be performed prior to calculating AUC. For Log AUC, delays or probabilities are transformed into a log-10 base before normalization and application of Eq. (7.2). Similarly, Ordinal AUC is calculated by rank-ordering delays or probabilities prior to normalization and AUC calculation (e.g., 1 day = 1, 1 week = 2, 1 month = 3, and so on). Log AUC and Ordinal AUC often have better psychometric properties than the original AUC.

Robust findings in delay and probability discounting

One question posed in the discounting literature is whether discounting is a trait or state variable, and to be clear, the answer is both. Trait variables are stable, long-term characteristics of any one individual and are evident when there is relative endurance and stability of discounting across context, commodity, and time. State variables, however, are contextual or situational factors that change behavior in the short-term (i.e., relatively momentary shifts). Delay discounting, and to a lesser extent, probability discounting, appears to be influenced by both trait and state variables (Odum, 2011b; Odum & Baumann, 2010).

There are several forms of evidence that discounting can be considered a trait. For example, discounting for one commodity is often predictive of discounting for another commodity. Odum (2011b) found that AUCs for one commodity (e.g., money) were strongly and positively correlated with AUCs for several other commodities (e.g., cigarettes, heroin, food). Odum et al. (2020) reviewed the literature on the relation between discounting for different commodities and found that 97% of correlations were above 0. Thus, the discounting of one commodity generally predicts the degree of discounting for another. Although relatively little research has been conducted with nonhumans, the degree of discounting for food and water was positively related in rats (Haynes et al., 2021). Delay discounting also shows strong test-retest reliability in human and nonhuman animals over extended periods (e.g., Klein et al., 2022; Peterson et al., 2015). Furthermore, delay discounting is heritable. In humans, twin studies report higher positive correlations of degrees of delay discounting for identical (monozygotic) twins than for fraternal (dizygotic) twins (Anokhin et al., 2011, 2015). In rats, there are differences in the degree of delay discounting across different strains (e.g., Wilhelm & Mitchell, 2009).

Trait variables are also found in probability discounting. The relative stability of discounting by probability has been observed across different periods within individuals. For example, Escobar et al. (2023) found evidence for the relative stability of probability discounting within participants at three different periods over 1 month. Weatherly and Derenne (2013) found test-retest reliability in discounting by probability over 3 months (see also Peters & Büchel, 2009). Interestingly, Weatherly and Derenne found that although there is stability in probability discounting, it is less robust than the stability found in delay discounting.

When context or outcome characteristics are manipulated, state changes are produced in delay discounting. For example, Dixon et al. (2013) found that problem gamblers discounted to a higher degree in a gambling context relative to how they discounted in a nongambling context (e.g., coffee shop, restaurant). This short-term environmental change changed how an individual discounted (a state influence). Studies in nonhuman animals also demonstrate state influences. Haynes et al. (2021) found high variability in discounting from day-to-day sessions in rats, providing evidence for a large influence of short-term, state-related factors. These state influences were more impactful than trait influences in terms of variability between- and within-subjects.

The magnitude effect

One of the most prominent findings across delay discounting research with humans, and another example of a state effect is that larger outcomes are discounted less steeply than smaller outcomes, referred to as the *magnitude or amount effect* (e.g., Baker et al., 2003; Green et al., 2013; Willis-Moore et al., 2024). The magnitude effect is found across a wide array of hypothetical monetary amounts, including amounts as small as $30 and $85 (Kirby & Maraković, 1996), $10 and $100 (Baker et al., 2003), and larger amounts such as $100, $10,000, and $100,000 (Raineri & Rachlin, 1993). The magnitude effect is also found across a wide array of amounts ranging from $20 to $10 million (Green et al., 2013).

Although the magnitude effect is robust in humans, the extension and replication of the effect in different contexts are mixed. For example, the magnitude effect is found with real monetary outcomes (Johnson & Bickel, 2002) and nonmonetary commodities, including hypothetical health gains (Chapman, 1996), hypothetical vacations and rental cars (Raineri & Rachlin, 1993), and both hypothetical and real juice (Jimura et al., 2009). However, there are several circumstances in which the magnitude effect is not reliably found. For example, most nonhuman animal discounting studies have failed to find a magnitude effect (e.g., Calvert et al., 2010; Green et al., 2004; Holt & Wolf, 2019; Oliveria et al., 2014; Ong & White, 2004; Richards et al., 1997; but see Grace et al., 2012; Krebs et al., 2016). In addition, Odum et al. (2006) did not find the magnitude effect between-subjects with human participants when different participants experienced different magnitudes.

Other features impact the expression of the magnitude effect with humans as well. For example, Reyes-Huerta and Dos Santos (2016) explored how the representation of amount impacts the magnitude effect. Their results showed differential discounting by magnitude when the amount of the outcomes was represented symbolically (by numbers), but did not show differential discounting by magnitude when the amount of the outcomes was represented nonsymbolically (by dots). More recently, the expression of the magnitude effect was impacted by the order in which magnitudes were presented (Experiment 2, Willis-Moore et al., 2024; see also Dai et al., 2009). Willis-Moore et al. (2024) examined how $10 and $100 were discounted when the tasks were completed in different orders. Specifically, one group of participants first completed a discounting task in which the larger later amount was $10, and the other group first completed a task in which it was $100. Interestingly, when comparing between subjects, the groups discounted the first magnitude similarly. That is, $10 and $100 were discounted to similar degrees across subjects when they were the first magnitude encountered, replicating and extending the results of Odum et al. (2006). However, for discounting the second amounts across subjects, $100 was discounted less steeply than $10 (i.e., the typical magnitude effect). In addition, within-subjects, $10 was discounted more steeply when it followed $100, and $100 was discounted even less steeply following $10.

Together, the results of Reyes-Huerta and Dos Santos (2016) and Willis-Moore et al. (2024) demonstrate that the magnitude effect may be more nuanced than previously thought. Indeed, more research that uncovers mechanisms contributing to the magnitude effect is needed. For example, the results of Willis-Moore and colleagues are like those suggesting that contrast, in which previous experience influences current perceptions, may be one possible mechanism underlying the magnitude effect (see Dai et al., 2009; Grace et al., 2012; Smith et al., 2016, for further discussion). In Willis-Moore et al., the magnitude effect only appeared *after* participants had experienced a previous magnitude. Furthermore, *what* magnitude was encountered first also impacted the degree to which the second magnitude was discounted (i.e., $100 was discounted less steeply after $10, and $10 was discounted more steeply after $100), showing that the prior experience influenced the degree to which subsequent amounts were discounted.

The magnitude effect is also found in probability discounting research (Cox & Dallery, 2016; Estle et al., 2006; Green et al., 1999; Green & Myerson, 2010; Myerson et al., 2011); however, the observed finding is the inverse of that of delay discounting. Whereas for delay discounting, larger outcomes are discounted less steeply, for probability discounting, smaller certain outcomes are discounted less steeply compared to larger uncertain outcomes. For example, Cox and Dallery (2016) examined the magnitude effect where outcomes were either positive (gains) or negative (losses). Interestingly, they found the typical magnitude effect finding for probabilistic gains (i.e., smaller certain outcomes are discounted less steeply) as well as for probabilistic losses (see, however, Estle et al., 2006; Green et al., 2014). The inverse magnitude effect in probability discounting is also found in non-human animals. For example, Grace and McLean (2015) found that pigeons, like humans, discounted large probabilistic outcomes (i.e., 4 seconds access to food) more steeply than smaller ones (i.e., 2 seconds access to food). The inverse relationship in how magnitudes are discounted may imply that the underlying processes of delay and probability discounting are different. This distinction and others will be further discussed below.

The sign effect

Another robust phenomenon, as well as a state effect, in discounting research, is that the sign of the outcomes impacts the degree to which it is discounted. Specifically, positive outcomes (i.e., gains) are reliably discounted more steeply than negative outcomes (i.e., losses), a finding commonly referred to as *the sign effect* (e.g., Benzion et al., 1989; Cox et al., 2020; Estle et al., 2006; Johnson et al., 2007; Loewenstein & Thaler, 1989; Yeh et al., 2020). The sign effect has been replicated across a variety of studies. For example, Reyes-Huerta et al. (2023) recently found that delayed losses were discounted less steeply than delayed gains across different magnitudes and delay frames (i.e., date or calendar units). This finding is also true for probabilistic outcomes, as uncertain gains are discounted more than uncertain losses (Estle et al., 2006; Shead & Hodgins, 2009).

The outcome effect

Another common state influence in discounting is the outcome effect (sometimes referred to as the commodity effect; see Odum et al., 2020 for review). In the outcome effect, nonmonetary outcomes (e.g., substances of abuse) are discounted more steeply than monetary outcomes. To help characterize the robustness of this effect in delay discounting, Odum et al. (2020) surveyed the literature and reported the proportions found by dividing the discounting of nonmonetary outcomes by the sum of discounting for both nonmonetary and monetary outcomes. Proportions above 0.5 indicate a greater degree of discounting for nonmonetary outcomes relative to monetary ones. Mean proportions of 0.76 and 0.57 for k and AUC values were found, respectively, showing that nonmonetary outcomes were discounted to a greater extent. This finding was consistent across several types of commodities, including consumable outcomes (e.g., food, candy, juice), substances of abuse (e.g., alcohol, cigarettes, heroin, marijuana, cocaine), sex, entertainment, activities, exchangeables (e.g., vouchers, gift cards), freedom, and health-related outcomes (e.g., exercise, health, and temporary cures).

The outcome effect is also readily found for degrees of discounting in people with substance use issues. For example, Bickel et al. (1999) found that current smokers discounted delayed monetary outcomes more than controls (i.e., never-smokers) did and that cigarettes were more steeply discounted than money. Cigarette smokers have also shown steeper degrees of delay discounting than controls for other commodities, such as health-related gains or losses (Odum et al., 2020). This relatively steep discounting by tobacco users, including e-cigarette users (e.g., DeHart et al., 2020), is also found with people who use other substances such as opioids, stimulants, and alcohol (see Amlung et al., 2017; MacKillop et al., 2011).

Relatively little research has examined probability discounting across different outcomes, but the limited literature shows a mixed and less robust commodity effect. For example, Estle et al. (2007) compared discounting of monetary and directly consumable outcomes (i.e., food) for both probability and delay discounting. Although the well-established outcome effect for delay discounting (see above) was found, there was no difference between discounting of different commodities for probability discounting. Holt et al. (2014) also did not find a difference between discounting of probabilistic money and food but did find that sex was discounted significantly less steeply than money. In contrast, Rasmussen et al. (2010) found that mean AUC values were lower for probabilistic food than for probabilistic money. This finding is similar to the outcome effect in delay discounting, in which nonmonetary outcomes are discounted to a higher degree. These mixed results on the commodity effect and probability discounting should be addressed further.

Is two better than one? Comparing delay and probability discounting

Much research examines the characteristics of and the relationship between delay and probability discounting. One interesting aspect of these types of discounting is the debate on whether they are representative of the same processes. Some theories, termed single process theories, suggest that delay and probability discounting measure the same or similar behavioral processes (e.g., Benzion et al., 1989; Green & Myerson, 1996; Rachlin et al., 1986). Generally, these theories give two explanations for the processes involved in probability and delay discounting. First, it is argued that the risk involved in probability discounting incorporates the perception of time to receiving a probabilistic reward (risk-as-delay, e.g., Rachlin et al., 1986). More specifically, a risky choice usually involves multiple attempts and thus a period that elapses until a reward. Second, delayed rewards involve more risk in their receipt than an immediately given reward (delay-as-risk, e.g., Green & Myerson, 1996). That is, the longer the delay, the greater the chances that the reward may not be received due to intervening events. In this theoretical framework, it would be expected that both delay and probability discounting would be positively related. For example, Myerson et al. (2003) found a positive correlation between the degree of delay and probability discounting. That is, they found that individuals who steeply discounted delayed outcomes also steeply discounted probabilistic outcomes and vice versa.

However, although there is some evidence for a single underlying mechanism, many correlations between delay and probability discounting are variable and weak to moderate (see Johnson et al., 2020 for meta-analysis). Additionally, there are instances in which some variable differentially impacts delay and probability discounting. These inconclusive associations, as well as additional empirical evidence (e.g., Green & Myerson, 2004, 2013; Johnson et al., 2021; Weatherly et al., 2015) suggest the two types of discounting measure distinct but potentially related processes. For example, Green and Myerson (2004) reviewed the literature and found that, although both forms of discounting are described accurately by the same hyperbolic-like function, other variables impact one discounting type more or differently than the other. As an example, Ostaszewski et al. (1998) found that inflation increased the degree of delay discounting for monetary rewards, whereas probability discounting was unaffected. Additionally, Weatherly et al. (2015) found that although discounting of delayed outcomes was altered by incorporating a risky receipt, discounting of probabilistic outcomes was unaffected by incorporating a delay to those outcomes. Finally, the inverse magnitude effect between delay and probability discounting (see above) is additional evidence against single-process theories. Specifically, if the same process underlies both discounting types, outcome magnitude would be expected to have a similar, not inverse, effect. Therefore, these processes have been shown empirically to be at least somewhat distinctive.

Despite whether delay and probability discounting are one or two processes, events are often both delayed and probabilistic. Therefore, some studies have used discounting tasks that systematically combine both delay and probability (e.g., Yi, Piedad, & Bickel, 2006). Yi and colleagues explored the combination of delay and probability discounting in two tasks. In the first task, termed the delay-probability discounting (DPD) procedure, participants chose between options in which the probability of winning a lottery ticket was known, but the results were only revealed after a delay. In the second task, termed the probability–delay discounting procedure (PDD), the probability of the award was known. Still, the prize could only be collected after a delay (if the participant won). In both DPD and PDD procedures, a smaller immediate reward was available during choices. With these tasks, a magnitude effect was found (i.e., larger outcomes were discounted less steeply than smaller outcomes). Because the magnitude effect resembled the effect found in delay discounting and not the reverse magnitude effect found in probability discounting, Yi et al. suggested that delay overcomes probability for outcome magnitude in these combined tasks.

A few additional experiments have incorporated delay and probability. Vanderveldt et al. (2015) also examined the two types of discounting together. They found steep probability discounting at all delays and although delay discounting was observed at higher probabilities, it was much less at lower probabilities. This finding suggests that probability had a greater impact on delay discounting than delay had on probability discounting (see also Cox & Dallery, 2016). The combination of probability and delay discounting may be useful in understanding complex behaviors of social significance. Hayashi et al. (2018) used a combined task to study delay and probability discounting in hypothetical texting while driving. The likelihood of texting was influenced by both the delay until reaching the destination and the probability of a motor accident. Hayashi and colleagues found that delay discounting was influenced by probability, and probability discounting was affected by delay when a delayed reinforcer and a probabilistic punisher were present. The extent to which delay and probability influence the degree of discounting on a combined task may be a function of the scenario or context presented. More research combining delays and probabilities is needed to better understand the influence of either factor on the degree of discounting.

Other types of discounting

Social discounting examines the role of social distance on the value of outcomes. For example, an individual is asked to imagine they have ranked the individuals in their lives from one (the person closest to them) to 100 (a mere acquaintance). Next, they are asked if they would be willing to forgo a larger amount of money for themselves and instead have various smaller amounts given to the people at increasing social distances (i.e., person 1, 2, 5, 10, 20, 50, and 100; Jones & Rachlin, 2006; Rachlin & Jones, 2008). Jones and Rachlin (2006) found that willingness to forgo a larger amount of money was systematically related to the distance of the person. The closer in social distance, the greater the willingness to forgo money, whereas the further away the person, the less the willingness to forgo money.

Social discounting is theorized to measure altruism or a tendency to put others before oneself (Belisle et al., 2020). Social discounting has been applied to understand social cooperation with phenomena such as mask-wearing during the COVID-19 pandemic (Strickland et al., 2021). Specifically, Strickland and colleagues measured the hypothetical likelihood of wearing a mask around people who ranged in social distance given three hypothetical COVID-19 symptomologies: asymptomatic, symptomatic without a test confirmation, and symptomatic with a test confirmation. They found that in the hypothetical symptomatic scenarios, regardless of social distance and whether COVID-19 had been confirmed with a test, the likelihood of wearing a mask was high. However, when individuals were tasked with ranking their hypothetical likelihood of wearing a face mask around others by social distance when asymptomatic, the likelihood of wearing a mask increased as social distance increased. That is, individuals were likelier to wear a mask around those they were not close to. This work exemplifies how discounting research can apply to understanding a variety of socially relevant issues.

Effort discounting evaluates the devaluation of outcomes as a function of effort to attain them (Mitchell, 1999, 2004). For instance, the value of bodily health may decrease as a function of the effort needed to produce desired health outcomes (e.g., the number of steps to walk daily). Effort discounting has been examined in nonhuman animals (e.g., Floresco et al., 2008; Peck & Madden, 2021) as well as with humans (Escobar et al., 2023; Mitchell, 2004; Peck & Madden, 2023). In a study by Mitchell (2004), cigarette smokers made choices between an amount of money that required no effort and a larger amount of money that was effortful to obtain. Specifically, participants chose between a smaller amount of money that increased across trials and $10, which required them to expend different degrees of effort (squeeze a hand dynamometer with increasing forces). As the effort to obtain $10 increased (i.e., as the force increased), the value of that option decreased. This finding was true for both money and cigarettes, with steeper discounting of cigarettes by effort overall. More recently, effort discounting in humans has explored how to simulate effortful tasks. Macías-Navarrete and dos Santos (2023) examined hypothetical effort discounting in humans in which effort was measured as climbing steps or pedaling. Although both effortful tasks produced some discounting, climbing steps was discounted more steeply. Research in creating effortful tasks and applications of these tasks will be important next steps.

Past discounting describes the devaluation of an event or outcome as a function of time since it happened (Yi, Gatchalian, & Bickel, 2006). In other words, outcomes that happened further in the past are less valued than present outcomes, even if the present outcomes are of smaller magnitude. This phenomenon is like that of delay discounting, except outcomes in the past are compared to present outcomes, whereas in delay discounting, future outcomes are compared to present outcomes. Bickel et al. (2008) examined past and future delay discounting across cigarette smokers and nonsmoking controls. They found that discounting of past and future outcomes was steepest in the cigarette smoking group. Furthermore, the degree of discounting across the future and past discounting tasks was related. Participants who steeply discounted the past also steeply discounted the future, and vice versa. Further examinations of this area of work could be fruitful in understanding discounting processes.

Future applications of discounting research

Examining sustainability or environmental awareness within a discounting framework is a burgeoning area of research. For example, Kaplan et al. (2014) found that participant ratings of their concern and willingness to respond to hypothetical environmental loss were discounted as a function of delay, probability, and social distance. Participants rated their individual level of "action" or "concern" (e.g., How concerned are you about the effects of pollution on your farm?) on a VAS scale; scores ranged from 0 (Not concerned) to 100 (Extremely concerned) in response to an environmental disaster scenario. In three separate tasks, concern and action were discounted as a function of delay, probability, and social distance. On the topic of air quality, Berry et al. (2017) showed that improved air quality was discounted as a function of delay. Furthermore, different magnitudes of improved air quality (i.e., 100 days vs. 1000 days) were discounted to different degrees. In a follow-up experiment, Berry et al., 2019 showed that in the context of images of nature, delay discounting was shallower than in the context of images of built environments. Future research should determine if other interventions used to reduce steep discounting could impact decisions about the environment.

Several other contextual factors may affect the choices made by people across a variety of risky conditions. The delay and probability of consequences related to natural disasters or unsafe driving habits (e.g., texting while driving) may also contribute to decision-making. Gelino and Reed (2020) proposed a behavioral economic perspective to explain why people often ignore warnings: They tend to discount risks and delays. With respect to tornadoes, warnings are issued well before the events they predict, which may lead people to undervalue the urgency of seeking safety. Furthermore, tornado warnings are also not always followed by tornadoes. The high rate of false alarms could further reduce the likelihood of taking protective actions. Interventions that help participants make decisions by prompting them with potential future events, such as episodic future thinking (EFT; Brown & Stein, 2022), may be efficacious. The delay and likelihood of risky outcomes in the future, such as car accidents, impact how people discount decisions related to risky outcomes in the present (Hayashi et al., 2018). Future research could test existing and developing interventions on discounting across several contexts that occasion different experiences related to sustainability and risky outcomes.

Discounting and public health is another developing area of research and discussion. With pandemics such as COVID-19 appearing on societal landscapes, understanding the contextual variables that impact and influence human decision-making becomes more important. Regarding COVID-19, people were more willing to self-isolate when the perceived probability of their environment reaching epidemic levels was high and when there was a guarantee that other individuals within their community would self-isolate (Belisle et al., 2022). Lloyd et al. (2021) found that steeper degrees of hypothetical monetary discounting were associated with lower levels of adherence to social distancing measures during the COVID-19 pandemic, and Halilova et al. (2022) found that people who were unvaccinated against COVID-19 discounted hypothetical monetary rewards more steeply. Taken together, several factors impact how humans interact with public health decisions related to COVID-19. Discounting and public health remain a developing discounting research domain.

Another impactful research direction is the relation between healthcare-related behaviors, such as treatment adherence, and discounting. For example, Bruce et al. (2018) evaluated the relation between treatment adherence and probability discounting for those prescribed medications for multiple sclerosis (MS). People who discounted treatment to a greater degree as the function of the probability of side effects were found to have poor adherence to treatment and less knowledge regarding MS. Interestingly, increasing the amount of education a patient receives about their condition may change how they value certain treatment outcomes, such as efficacy and side effects (Bruce et al., 2018). In another study, Jarmolowicz et al. (2022) found that shallower delay discounting and higher medication demand were independently associated with greater adherence to the medical decision-making procedure in MS patients. Therefore, treatment adherence could potentially be promoted by identifying individuals with steeper delay/probability discounting, which is associated with nonadherence to treatment, to provide them with condition-specific education and resources.

Finally, future research could evaluate the relation between discounting and criminal behavior, as criminologists theorize that poor self-control contributes to deviant behavior (Gottfredson & Hirschi, 1990). More specifically, discounting methodologies could be used to further understand criminal offending. Little research has evaluated the relation between discounting and criminal behavior. However, the research that has been conducted uncovered relations between discounting and deviant behavior. For example, Lee et al. (2017) found that steep delay discounting in college students predicted subsequent self-reported endorsement of property crime years later. Additionally, people with a self-reported history of violent crime displayed steep discounting 1 year later. Interestingly, steep delay discounting did not predict subsequent violent crime. Criminal offenders in medium security prisons, which can include people convicted of violent and nonviolent crimes, also have steeper degrees of delay discounting when compared to nonoffenders, even when controlling for substance use (Arantes et al., 2013). Future research should continue to evaluate the relation between discounting and deviant behavior to identify those at risk for later criminal offending.

Interventions on discounting

Much research has examined ways to change discounting in nonhuman and human subjects (for review see Rung & Madden, 2018). In nonhumans, the techniques used to reduce steep discounting include delay exposure training (e.g., Peck et al., 2022; Renda et al., 2018; Stein et al., 2013), delay fading (e.g., Mazur & Logue, 1978), reward bundling (see Ashe & Wilson, 2020 for review), and training with different timing schedules (e.g., Bailey et al., 2018). In humans, additional interventions to reduce steep discounting include EFT (Atance & O'Neil, 2005; Brown & Stein, 2022), framing the delays as specific dates (e.g., DeHart & Odum, 2015; Reyes-Huerta et al., 2023; Willis-Moore et al., 2024), Acceptance and Commitment Therapy (ACT; Morrison et al., 2014; however, see Morrison et al., 2020), financial planning (DeHart et al., 2016), and exposure to nature (e.g., Berry et al., 2014).

Although much research has examined interventions on delay discounting, novel approaches are still being developed. For example, Madden et al. (2023) offer new insights on how Pavlovian conditioning can be harnessed to increase choices for larger later options, thereby reducing steep discounting. Specifically, they propose that steep delay discounting can be mitigated by altering the function of the delay-bridging stimuli present during the delay of the larger outcome through Pavlovian techniques. Indeed, in a recent preclinical study, Mahmoudi and Madden (2024) investigated the effects of appetitive Pavlovian sign-tracking, or lack thereof, in a delay discounting assessment in rats. In the Pavlovian training group, a conditioned stimulus (CS; a lever) predicted the availability of the unconditioned stimulus (US; food pellets); whereas, in the control group, the lever was not predictive of the US and did not acquire conditioned reinforcing properties. The lever from the training phase then served as the larger later option and remained inserted for the duration of the delay. Overall, Mahmoudi and Madden found that the Pavlovian training group made larger later choices compared to the control rats. These preliminary findings provide early evidence of the effects of Pavlovian training on discounting consistent with suggestions made by Madden et al. (2023). Furthermore, these results may improve interventions for self-control issues in clinical populations and real-world settings.

Although general ACT interventions on delay discounting have had mixed results (e.g., Morrison et al., 2014, 2020), it is still important to study the effect of ACT-based interventions on discounting. Specifically, processes related to ACT can help individuals make decisions in line with their values (see Gould et al., 2018; Paliiunas, 2021). Mindfulness is at the center of present-moment awareness and a component of ACT (Hayes et al., 2012). After engaging with a mindfulness video, participants had shallower degrees of delay discounting (Dixon et al., 2019). In another study focused on mindfulness, Adler and collaborators (2023) found that a small mindfulness-based guided meditation decreased the probability of discounting infidelity when the probability of getting caught varied. Although these two studies focused on mindfulness-based interventions, research may focus on present-moment awareness exercises as an intervention for steep discounting. Furthermore, Chastain and colleagues (2022) showed that a defusion intervention, a core process of ACT, reduced delay discounting. Therefore, further investigation into the processes of ACT to reduce steep delay discounting could be an important future direction. Indeed, continued exploration may explain the mixed results found when more general ACT practices are employed to reduce steep discounting.

Conclusion

From the early beginnings of studies that sought to understand how delaying impacts choice (e.g., Chung & Herrnstein, 1967) to uncovering the role of discounting in service of understanding issues faced today, the study of discounting has been a fruitful endeavor. Research in this area has revealed many relevant and important considerations for society, including shedding light on mechanisms that contribute to substance abuse, decisions related to food, the environment, condom use, and many more. Although the breadth of this work is wide-reaching, there is still more to learn from studying discounting. For example, recent work by Willis-Moore et al. (2024) and previous work by Reyes-Huerta and Dos Santos (2016) revealed interesting underlying mechanisms that may contribute to the magnitude effect (i.e., contrast or symbolic representation). Further research into understanding these phenomena is needed. Additionally, although the literature on interventions that seek to reduce steep delay discounting is expansive, developing and rigorously testing these interventions is widely needed (Brown & Stein, 2022; Madden et al., 2023). Such an endeavor will only uncover more information about discounting as a process and the possible driving mechanisms that lead to steep discounting. Furthermore, one developing area of research in the study of discounting that we see as a fruitful avenue of research is examining the relation between discounting and prosocial behaviors, such as concern for the environment. In conclusion, the future of discounting is bright! Discounting has been a successful cornerstone of behavioral economics, has revealed many important insights for socially relevant behaviors, and continues to provide a wealth of knowledge about decision-making.

References

Adler, M., Belisle, J., & Sickman, E. (2023). Evaluating the relationship between sexual arousal and mindfulness on probability discounting within infidelity. *The Psychological Record, 73*(4), 541–554. https://doi.org/10.1007/s40732-023-00563-z

Ainslie, G. W. (1974). Impulse control in pigeons. *Journal of the Experimental Analysis of Behavior, 21*(3), 485–489. https://doi.org/10.1901/jeab.1974.21-485

Ainslie, G. W. (1975). Specious reward: A behavioral theory of impulsiveness and impulse control. *Psychological Bulletin, 82*(4), 463. https://doi.org/10.1037/h0076860

Alessi, S. M., & Petry, N. M. (2003). Pathological gambling severity is associated with impulsivity in a delay discounting procedure. *Behavioural Processes, 64*(3), 345–354. https://doi.org/10.1016/s0376-6357(03)00150-5

Amlung, M., Vedelago, L., Acker, J., Balodis, I., & MacKillop, J. (2017). Steep delay discounting and addictive behavior: A meta-analysis of continuous associations. *Addiction, 112*(1), 51–62. https://doi.org/10.1111/add.13535

Anokhin, A. P., Golosheykin, S., Grant, J. D., & Heath, A. C. (2011). Heritability of delay discounting in adolescence: A longitudinal twin study. *Behavior Genetics, 41*, 175–183. https://doi.org/10.1007/s10519-010-9384-7

Anokhin, A. P., Grant, J. D., Mulligan, R. C., & Heath, A. C. (2015). The genetics of impulsivity: Evidence for the heritability of delay discounting. *Biological Psychiatry, 77*(10), 887–894. https://doi.org/10.1016/j.biopsych.2014.10.022

Arantes, J., Berg, M. E., Lawlor, D., & Grace, R. C. (2013). Offenders have higher delay-discounting rates than non-offenders after controlling for differences in drug and alcohol abuse. *Legal and Criminological Psychology, 18*(2), 240–253. https://doi.org/10.1111/j.2044-8333.2012.02052.x

Ashe, M. L., & Wilson, S. J. (2020). A brief review of choice bundling: A strategy to reduce delay discounting and bolster self-control. *Addictive Behaviors Reports, 11*, 100262. https://doi.org/10.1016/j.abrep.2020.100262

Atance, C. M., & O'Neill, D. K. (2005). The emergence of episodic future thinking in humans. *Learning and Motivation, 36*(2), 126–144. https://doi.org/10.1016/j.lmot.2005.02.003

Bailey, C., Peterson, J. R., Schnegelsiepen, A., Stuebing, S. L., & Kirkpatrick, K. (2018). Durability and generalizability of time-based intervention effects on impulsive choice in rats. *Behavioural Processes, 152*, 54–62. https://doi.org/10.1016/j.beproc.2018.03.003

Baker, F., Johnson, M. W., & Bickel, W. K. (2003). Delay discounting in current and never-before cigarette smokers: Similarities and differences across commodity, sign, and magnitude. *Journal of Abnormal Psychology, 112*(3), 382. https://doi.org/10.1037/0021-843x.112.3.382

Belisle, J., Paliliunas, D., Sickman, E., Janota, T., & Lauer, T. (2022). Probability discounting in college students' willingness to isolate during COVID-19: Implications for behavior analysis and public health. *Psychological Record, 72*(4), 713–725. https://doi.org/10.1007/s40732-022-00527-9

Belisle, J., Paliliunas, D., Vangsness, L., Dixon, M. R., & Stanley, C. R. (2020). Social distance and delay exert multiple control over altruistic choices. *Psychological Record, 70*, 445–457. https://doi.org/10.1007/s40732-020-00399-x

Benzion, U., Rapoport, A., & Yagil, J. (1989). Discount rates inferred from decisions: An experimental study. *Management Science, 35*(3), 270–284. https://doi.org/10.1287/mnsc.35.3.270

Berry, M. S., Johnson, P. S., Collado, A., Loya, J. M., Yi, R., & Johnson, M. W. (2019). Sexual probability discounting: A mechanism for sexually transmitted infection among undergraduate students. *Archives of Sexual Behavior, 48*, 495–505. https://doi.org/10.1007/s10508-018-1155-1

Berry, M. S., Nickerson, N. P., & Odum, A. L. (2017). Delay discounting as an index of sustainable behavior: Devaluation of future air quality and implications for public health. *Environmental Research and Public Health, 14*(9), 1–14. https://doi.org/10.3390/ijerph14090997

Berry, M. S., Repke, M. A., & Conway, I. I. I.,L. G. (2019). Visual exposure to natural environments decreases delay discounting of improved air quality. *Frontiers in Public Health, 7*, 308. https://doi.org/10.3389/fpubh.2019.00308

Berry, M. S., Sweeney, M. M., Morath, J., Odum, A. L., & Jordan, K. E. (2014). The nature of impulsivity: Visual exposure to natural environments decreases impulsive decision-making in a delay discounting task. *PLoS One, 9*(5), Article e97915. https://doi.org/10.1371/journal.pone.0097915

Bickel, W. K., Freitas-Lemos, R., Tomlinson, D. C., Craft, W. H., Keith, D. R., Athamneh, L. N., Basso, J. C., & Epstein, L. H. (2021). Temporal discounting as a candidate behavioral marker of obesity. *Neuroscience & Biobehavioral Reviews, 129*, 307−329. https://doi.org/10.1016/j.neubiorev.2021.07.035

Bickel, W. K., Odum, A. L., & Madden, G. J. (1999). Impulsivity and cigarette smoking: Delay discounting in current, never, and ex-smokers. *Psychopharmacology, 146*(4), 447−454. https://doi.org/10.1007/pl00005490

Bickel, W. K., Yi, R., Kowal, B. P., & Gatchalian, K. M. (2008). Cigarette smokers discount past and future rewards symmetrically and more than controls: Is discounting a measure of impulsivity? *Drug and Alcohol Dependence, 96*(3), 256−262. https://doi.org/10.1016/j.drugalcdep.2008.03.009

Borges, A. M., Kuang, J., Milhorn, H., & Yi, R. (2016). An alternative approach to calculating Area-Under-the-Curve (AUC) in delay discounting research. *Journal of the Experimental Analysis of Behavior, 106*(2), 145−155. https://doi.org/10.1002/jeab.219

Brown, J. M., & Stein, J. S. (2022). Putting prospection into practice: Methodological considerations in the use of episodic future thinking to reduce delay discounting and maladaptive health behaviors. *Frontiers in Public Health, 10*, 1020171. https://doi.org/10.3389/fpubh.2022.1020171

Bruce, J. M., Bruce, A. S., Lynch, S., Thelen, J., Lim, S. L., Smith, J., Catley, D., Reed, D. D., & Jarmolowicz, D. P. (2018). Probability discounting of treatment decisions in multiple sclerosis: Associations with disease knowledge, neuropsychiatric status, and adherence. *Psychopharmacology, 235*, 3303−3313. https://doi.org/10.1007/s00213-018-5037-y

Calvert, A. L., Green, L., & Myerson, J. (2010). Delay discounting of qualitatively different reinforcers in rats. *Journal of the Experimental Analysis of Behavior, 93*(2), 171−184. https://doi.org/10.1901/jeab.2010.93-171

Chapman, G. B. (1996). Temporal discounting and utility for health and money. *Journal of Experimental Psychology: Learning, Memory, and Cognition, 22*(3), 771. https://doi.org/10.1037/0278-7393.22.3.77

Chastain, A. N., Tarbox, J., Meshes, E., & Wang, Y. (2022). A pilot study: Evaluating the effectsof defusion on choice making under negative and positive reinforcement contingencies. *The Psychological Record, 72*(3), 449−463. https://doi.org/10.1007/s40732-022-00511-3

Chung, S. H., & Herrnstein, R. J. (1967). Choice and delay of reinforcement. *Journal of the Experimental Analysis of Behavior, 10*(1), 67−74. https://doi.org/10.1901/jeab.1967.10-67

Cox, D. J., & Dallery, J. (2016). Effects of delay and probability combinations on discounting in humans. *Behavioural Processes, 131*, 15−23. https://doi.org/10.1016/j.beproc.2016.08.002

Cox, D. J., Dolan, S. B., Johnson, P., & Johnson, M. W. (2020). Delay and probability discounting in cocaine use disorder: Comprehensive examination of money, cocaine, and health outcomes using gains and losses at multiple magnitudes. *Experimental and Clinical Psychopharmacology, 28*(6), 724. https://doi.org/10.1037/pha0000341

Craig, A. R., Maxfield, A. D., Stein, J. S., Renda, C. R., & Madden, G. J. (2014). Do the adjusting-delay and increasing-delay tasks measure the same construct: Delay discounting? *Behavioural Pharmacology, 25*(4), 306−315. https://doi.org/10.1097/FBP.0000000000000055

Dai, Z., Grace, R.,C., & Kemp, S. (2009). Reward contrast in delay and probability discounting. *Learning & Behavior, 37*(3), 281−288. https://doi.org/10.3758/LB.37.3.281

DeHart, W. B., Friedel, J. E., Berry, M., Frye, C. C., Galizio, A., & Odum, A. L. (2020). Comparison of delay discounting of different outcomes in cigarette smokers, smokeless tobacco users, e-cigarette users, and non-tobacco users. *Journal of the Experimental Analysis of Behavior, 114*(2), 203−215. https://doi.org/10.1002/jeab.623

DeHart, W. B., Friedel, J. E., Frye, C. C., Galizio, A., & Odum, A. L. (2018). The effects of outcome unit framing on delay discounting. *Journal of the Experimental Analysis of Behavior, 110*(3), 412−429. https://doi.org/10.1002/jeab.469

DeHart, W. B., Friedel, J. E., Lown, J. M., & Odum, A. L. (2016). The effects of financial education on impulsive decision making. *PLoS One, 11*(7), 412−429. https://doi.org/10.1371/journal.pone.0159561

DeHart, W. B., & Odum, A. L. (2015). The effects of the framing of time on delay discounting. *Journal of the Experimental Analysis of Behavior, 103*(1), 10−21. https://doi.org/10.1002/jeab.125

Dixon, M. R., Jacobs, E. A., & Sanders, S. (2013). Contextual control of delay discounting by pathological gamblers. *Journal of Applied Behavior Analysis, 39*(4), 413−422. https://doi.org/10.1901/jaba.2006.173-05

Dixon, M. R., Paliliunas, D., Belisle, J., Speelman, R. C., Gunnarsson, K. F., & Shaffer, J. L. (2019). The effect of brief mindfulness training on momentary impulsivity. *Journal of Contextual Behavioral Science, 11*, 15−20. https://doi.org/10.1016/j.jcbs.2018.11.003

Du, W., Green, L., & Myerson, J. (2002). Cross-cultural comparisons of discounting delayed and probabilistic rewards. *Psychological Record, 52*, 479−492. https://doi.org/10.1007/BF03395199

Escobar, G. G., Morales-Chainé, S., Haynes, J. M., Santoyo, C., & Mitchell, S. H. (2023). Moderate stability among delay, probability, and effort discounting in humans. *Psychological Record*, 1−14. https://doi.org/10.1007/s40732-023-00537-1

Estle, S. J., Green, L., Myerson, J., & Holt, D. D. (2006). Differential effects of amount on temporal and probability discounting of gains and losses. *Memory & Cognition, 34*(4), 914−928. https://doi.org/10.3758/bf03193437

Estle, S. J., Green, L., Myerson, J., & Holt, D. D. (2007). Discounting of monetary and directly consumable rewards. *Psychological Science, 18*(1), 58−63. https://doi.org/10.1111/j.1467-9280.2007.01849.x

Evenden, J. L., & Ryan, C. N. (1996). The pharmacology of impulsive behaviour in rats: The effects of drugs on response choice with varying delays of reinforcement. *Psychopharmacology, 128*(2), 161−170. https://doi.org/10.1007/s002130050121

Floresco, S. B., Tse, M. T., & Ghods-Sharifi, S. (2008). Dopaminergic and glutamatergic regulation of effort-and delay-based decision making. *Neuropsychopharmacology, 33*(8), 1966−1979. https://doi.org/10.1038/sj.npp.1301565

Gelino, B. W., Erath, T. G., Seniuk, H. A., Luke, M. M., Berry, M. S., Fuqua, R. W., & Reed, D. D. (2020). Global sustainability: A behavior analytic approach. *Behavior Science Perspectives on Culture and Community*, 257−281. https://doi.org/10.1007/978-3-030-45421-0_11

Gelino, B. W., Schlitzer, R. D., Reed, D. D., & Strickland, J. C. (2024). A systematic review and meta-analysis of test-retest reliability and stability of delay and probability discounting. *Journal of the Experimental Analysis of Behavior, 121*(3), 358−372. https://doi.org/10.1002/jeab.910

Gilroy, S. P., Franck, C. T., & Hantula, D. A. (2017). The discounting model selector: Statistical software for delay discounting applications. *Journal of the Experimental Analysis of Behavior, 107*(3), 388−401. https://doi.org/10.1002/jeab.257

Gottfredson, M. R., & Hirschi, T. (1990). *A general theory of crime.* Stanford University Press.

Gould, R. E., Trabox, J., & Coyne, L. (2018). Evaluating the effects of Acceptance and Commitment Training on the overt behavior of parents of children with autism. *Journal of Contextual Behavior Science, 7,* 81−88. https://doi.org/10.1016/j.jcbs.2017.06.003

Grace, R. C., & McLean, A. P. (2015). Evidence for a magnitude effect in probability discounting with pigeons. *Journal of Experimental Psychology: Animal Learning and Cognition, 41*(4), 406−418. https://doi.org/10.1037/xan0000077

Grace, R. C., Sargisson, R. J., & White, K. G. (2012). Evidence for a magnitude effect in temporal discounting with pigeons. *Journal of Experimental Psychology: Animal Behavior Processes, 38*(1), 102. https://doi.org/10.1037/a0026345

Green, L., & Estle, S. J. (2003). Preference reversals with food and water reinforcers in rats. *Journal of the Experimental Analysis of Behavior, 79*(2), 233−242. https://doi.org/10.1901/jeab.2003.79-233

Green, L., & Myerson, J. (1996). Exponential versus hyperbolic discounting of delayed outcomes: Risk and waiting time. *American Zoologist, 36*(4), 496−505. https://doi.org/10.1093/icb/36.4.496

Green, L., & Myerson, J. (2004). A discounting framework for choice with delayed and probabilistic rewards. *Psychological Bulletin, 130*(5), 769. https://psycnet.apa.org/doi/10.1037/0033-2909.130.5.769.

Green, L., & Myerson, J. (2010). Experimental and correlational analyses of delay and probability discounting. In G. J. Madden, & W. K. Bickel (Eds.), *Impulsivity: The behavioral and neurological science of discounting* (pp. 67−92). American Psychological Association. https://psycnet.apa.org/doi/10.1037/12069-003.

Green, L., & Myerson, J. (2013). How many impulsivities? A discounting perspective. *Journal of the Experimental Analysis of Behavior, 99*(1), 3−13. https://doi.org/10.1002/jeab.1

Green, L., Myerson, J., Holt, D. D., Slevin, J. R., & Estle, S. J. (2004). Discounting of delayed food rewards in pigeons and rats: Is there a magnitude effect? *Journal of the Experimental Analysis of Behavior, 81*(1), 39−50. https://doi.org/10.1901/jeab.2004.81-39

Green, L., Myerson, J., Oliveira, L., & Chang, S. E. (2013). Delay discounting of monetary rewards over a wide range of amounts. *Journal of the Experimental Analysis of Behavior, 100*(3), 269−281. https://doi.org/10.1002/jeab.45

Green, L., Myerson, J., Oliveira, L., & Chang, S. (2014). Discounting of delayed and probabilistic losses over a range of amounts. *Journal of the Experimental Analysis of Behavior, 101*(2), 186−200. https://doi.org/10.1002/jeab.56

Green, L., Myerson, J., & Ostaszewski, P. (1999). Amount of reward has opposite effects on the discounting of delayed and probabilistic outcomes. *Journal of Experimental Psychology. Learning, Memory, and Cognition, 25*(2), 418−427. https://doi.org/10.1037//0278-7393.25.2.418

Green, L., Myerson, J., Shah, A. K., Estle, S. J., & Holt, D. D. (2007). Do adjusting-amount and adjusting-delay procedures produce equivalent estimates of subjective value in pigeons? *Journal of the Experimental Analysis of Behavior, 87*(3), 337−347. https://doi.org/10.1901/jeab.2007.37-06

Halilova, J. G., Fynes-Clinton, S., Green, L., Myerson, J., Wu, J., Ruggeri, K., Addis, D. R., & Rosenbaum, R. S. (2022). Short-sighted decision-making by those not vaccinated against COVID-19. *Scientific Reports, 12*(1), 11906. https://doi.org/10.1038/s41598-022-15276-6

Hayashi, Y., Fessler, H. J., Friedel, J. E., Foreman, A. M., & Wirth, O. (2018). The roles of delay and probability discounting in texting while driving: Toward the development of a translational scientific program. *Journal of the Experimental Analysis of Behavior, 110*(2), 229−242. https://doi.org/10.1002/jeab.460

Hayes, J. E., Allen, A. L., & Bennett, S. M. (2013). Direct comparison of the generalized visual analog scale (gVAS) and general labeled magnitude scale (gLMS). *Food Quality and Preference, 28*(1), 36−44. https://doi.org/10.1016/j.foodqual.2012.07.012

Hayes, S. C., Strosahl, K. D., & Wilson, K. G. (2012). *Acceptance and commitment therapy: The process and practice of mindful change* (2nd ed.). Guilford Press.

Haynes, J. M., Galizio, A., Frye, C. C. J., Towse, C. C., Morrissey, K. N., Serang, S., & Odum, A. L. (2021). Discounting of food and water in rats shows trait- and state-like characteristics. *Journal of the Experimental Analysis of Behavior, 115*(2), 495−509. https://doi.org/10.1002/jeab.677

Holt, D. D., Green, L., & Myerson, J. (2012). Estimating the subjective value of future rewards: Comparison of adjusting-amount and adjusting-delay procedures. *Behavioural Processes, 90*(3), 302−310. https://doi.org/10.1016/j.beproc.2012.03.003

Holt, D. D., Newquist, M. H., Smits, R. R., & Tiry, A. M. (2014). Discounting of food, sex, and money. *Psychonomic Bulletin & Review, 21*, 794−802. https://doi.org/10.3758/s13423-013-0557-2

Holt, D. D., & Wolf, M. R. (2019). Delay discounting in the pigeon: In search of a magnitude effect. *Journal of the Experimental Analysis of Behavior, 111*(3), 436−448. https://doi.org/10.1002/jeab.515

Jarmolowicz, D. P.,, Schneider, T. D., Strickland, J. C., Bruce, A. S., Reed, D. D., & Bruce, J. M. (2022). Reinforcer pathology, probabilistic choice, and medication adherence in patients with multiple sclerosis. *Journal of the Experimental Analysis of Behavior, 119*(2), 275−285. https://doi.org/10.1002/jeab.830

Jimura, K., Myerson, J., Hilgard, J., Braver, T. S., & Green, L. (2009). Are people really more patient than other animals? Evidence from human discounting of real liquid rewards. *Psychonomic Bulletin & Review, 16*(6), 1071−1075. https://doi.org/10.3758/PBR.16.6.1071

Johnson, M. W., & Bickel, W. K. (2002). Within-subject comparison of real and hypothetical money rewards in delay discounting. *Journal of the Experimental Analysis of Behavior, 77*(2), 129−146. https://doi.org/10.1901/jeab.2002.77-129

Johnson, M. W., Bickel, W. K., & Baker, F. (2007). Moderate drug use and delay discounting: A comparison of heavy, light, and never smokers. *Experimental and Clinical Psychopharmacology, 15*(2), 187. https://doi.org/10.1037/1064-1297.15.2.187

Johnson, K. L., Bixter, M. T., & Luhmann, C. C. (2020). Delay discounting and risky choice: Meta-analytic evidence regarding single-process theories. *Judgment and Decision Making, 15*(3), 381−400. https://doi.org/10.1017/S193029750000718X

Johnson, M. W., & Bruner, N. R. (2012). The sexual discounting task: HIV risk behavior and the discounting of delayed sexual rewards in cocaine dependence. *Drug and Alcohol Dependence, 123*(1−3), 15−21. https://doi.org/10.1016/j.drugalcdep.2011.09.032

Johnson, M. W., Johnson, P. S., Herrmann, E. S., & Sweeney, M. M. (2015). Delay and probability discounting of sexual and monetary outcomes in individuals with cocaine use disorders and matched controls. *PLoS One, 10*(5), e0128641. https://doi.org/10.1371/journal.pone.0128641

Johnson, M. W., Strickland, J. C., Herrmann, E. S., Dolan, S. B., Cox, D. J., & Berry, M. S. (2021). Sexual discounting: A systematic review of discounting processes and sexual behavior. *Experimental and Clinical Psychopharmacology, 29*(6), 711. https://psycnet.apa.org/doi/10.1037/pha0000402.

Jollant, F., Voegeli, G., Kordsmeier, N.,C., Carbajal, J. M., Richard-Devantoy, S., Turecki, G., & Cáceda, R. (2019). A visual analog scale to measure psychological and physical pain: A preliminary validation of the PPP-VAS in two independent samples of depressed patients. *Progress Neuro-psychopharmacology & Biological Psychiatry, 2*(90), 55−61. https://doi.org/10.1016/j.pnpbp.2018.10.018

Jones, B., & Rachlin, H. (2006). Social discounting. *Psychological Science, 17*(4), 283−286. https://doi.org/10.1111/j.1467-9280.2006.01699.x

Kaplan, B. A., Reed, D. D., & McKerchar, T. L. (2014). Using a visual analogue scale to assess delay, social, and probability discounting of an environmental loss. *Psychological Record, 64*, 261−269. https://doi.org/10.1007/s40732-014-0041-z

Kirby, K. N., & Maraković, N. N. (1996). Delay-discounting probabilistic rewards: Rates decrease as amounts increase. *Psychonomic Bulletin & Review, 3*(1), 100−104. https://doi.org/10.3758/BF03210748

Kirby, K. N., Petry, N. M., & Bickel, W. K. (1999). Heroin addicts have higher discount rates for delayed rewards than non-drug-using controls. *Journal of Experimental Psychology: General, 128*(1), 78−87. https://doi.org/10.1037/0096-3445.128.1.78

Klein, S. D., Collins, P. F., & Luciana, M. (2022). Developmental trajectories of delay discounting from childhood to young adulthood: Longitudinal associations and test-retest reliability. *Cognitive Psychology, 139*, 101518. https://doi.org/10.1016/j.cogpsych.2022.101518

Krebs, C. A., Reilly, W. J., & Anderson, K. G. (2016). Reinforcer magnitude affects delay discounting and influences effects of *d*-amphetamine in rats. *Behavioural Processes, 130*, 39−45. https://doi.org/10.1016/j.beproc.2016.07.004

Kyonka, E. G. E., & Schutte, N. S. (2018). Probability discounting and gambling: A meta-analysis. *Addiction, 113*(12), 2173−2181. https://doi.org/10.1111/add.14397

Lagorio, C. H., & Madden, G. J. (2005). Delay discounting of real and hypothetical rewards III: Steady-state assessments, forced-choice trials, and all real rewards. *Behavioural Processes, 69*(2), 173−187. https://doi.org/10.1016/j.beproc.2005.02.003

Lee, C. A., Derefinko, K. J., Milich, R., Lynam, D. R., & DeWall, C. N. (2017). Longitudinal and reciprocal relations between delay discounting and crime. *Personality and Individual Differences, 111*, 193−198. https://doi.org/10.1016/j.paid.2017.02.023

Lloyd, A., McKay, R., Hartman, T. K., Vincent, B. T., Murphy, J., Gibson-Miller, J., Levita, L., Bennett, K., McBride, O., Martinez, A. P., Stocks, T. V. A., Vallières, F., Hyland, P., Karatzias, T., Butter, S., Shevlin, M., Bentall, R. P., & Mason, L. (2021). Delay discounting and under-valuing of recent information predict poorer adherence to social distancing measures during the COVID-19 pandemic. *Scientific Reports, 11*(1), 19237. https://doi.org/10.1038/s41598-021-98772-5

Loewenstein, G. F., & Thaler, R. H. (1989). Anomalies: Intertemporal choice. *The Journal of Economic Perspectives, 3*, 181−193. https://doi.org/10.1257/jep.3.4.181

Macías-Navarrete, R., & dos Santos, C. V. (2023). Effects of procedure and effort type on data systematicity and the rate of effort discounting. *Psychological Record, 73*(2), 253−262. https://psycnet.apa.org/doi/10.1007/s40732-023-00538-0.

MacKillop, J., Amlung, M. T., Few, L. R., Ray, L. A., Sweet, L. H., & Munafò, M. R. (2011). Delayed reward discounting and addictive behavior: A meta-analysis. *Psychopharmacology, 216*, 305−321. https://doi.org/10.1007/s00213-011-2229-0

Madden, G. J., Mahmoudi, S., & Brown, K. (2023). Pavlovian learning and conditioned reinforcement. *Journal of Applied Behavior Analysis, 56*(3), 498−519. https://doi.org/10.1002/jaba.1004

Madden, G. J., Petry, N. M., Badger, G. J., & Bickel, W. K. (1997). Impulsive and self-control choices in opioid-dependent patients and non-drug-using control participants: Drug and monetary rewards. *Experimental and Clinical Psychopharmacology, 5*(3), 256−262. https://doi.org/10.1037/1064-1297.5.3.256

Madden, G. J., Petry, N. M., & Johnson, P. S. (2009). Pathological gamblers discount probabilistic rewards less steeply than matched controls. *Experimental and Clinical Psychopharmacology, 17*(5), 283−290. https://doi.org/10.1037/a0016806

Madden, G. J., Raiff, B. R., Lagorio, C. H., Begotka, A. M., Mueller, A. M., Hehli, D. J., & Wegener, A. A. (2004). Delay discounting of potentially real and hypothetical rewards: II. Between-And within-subject comparisons. *Experimental and Clinical Psychopharmacology, 12*(4), 251. https://doi.org/10.1037/1064-1297.12.4.251

Mahmoudi, S., & Madden, G. J. (2024). Using sign tracking to experimentally increase self-control in rats. *Journal of the Experimental Analysis of Behavior*, 1−12. https://doi.org/10.1002/jeab.4211

Mar, A. C., & Robbins, T. W. (2007). Delay discounting and impulsive choice in the rat. *Current Protocols in Neuroscience.* https://doi.org/10.1002/0471142301.ns0822s39

Mazur, J. E. (1987). An adjusting procedure for studying delayed reinforcement. In M. L. Commons, J. E Mazur, J. A Nevin, & H. Rachlin (Eds.), *Quantitative analyses of behavior* (Vol 5, pp. 55−73). Hillsdale, NJ: Erlbaum.

Mazur, J. E., & Logue, A. W. (1978). Choice in a "self-control" paradigm: Effects of a fading procedure. *Journal of the Experimental Analysis of Behavior, 30*(1), 11−17. https://doi.org/10.1901/jeab.1978.30-11

McKerchar, T. L., Green, L., Myerson, J., Pickford, T. S., Hill, J. C., & Stout, S. C. (2009). A comparison of four models of delay discounting in humans. *Behavioural Processes, 81*(2), 256−259. https://doi.org/10.1016/j.beproc.2008.12.017

Miller, B. P., Reed, D. D., & Amlung, M. (2023). Reliability and validity of behavioral-economic measures: A review and synthesis of discounting and demand. *Journal of the Experimental Analysis of Behavior, 120*(2), 263−280. https://doi.org/10.1002/jeab.860

Mischel, W., Grusec, J., & Masters, J. C. (1969). Effects of expected delay time on the subjective value of rewards and punishments. *Journal of Personality and Social Psychology, 11*(4), 363−373. https://doi.org/10.1037/h0027265

Mitchell, S. H. (1999). Measures of impulsivity in cigarette smokers and non-smokers. *Psychopharmacology, 146*, 455−464. https://doi.org/10.1007/PL00005491

Mitchell, S. H. (2004). Measuring impulsivity and modeling its association with cigarette smoking. *Behavioral and Cognitive Neuroscience Reviews, 3*(4), 261−275. https://doi.org/10.1177/1534582305276838

Morrison, K. L., Madden, G. J., Odum, A. L., Friedel, J. E., & Twohig, M. P. (2014). Altering impulsive decision making with an acceptance-based procedure. *Behavior Therapy, 45*(5), 630−639. https://doi.org/10.1016/j.beth.2014.01.001

Morrison, K. L., Smith, B. M., Ong, C. W., Lee, E. B., Friedel, J. E., Odum, A., Madden, G. J., Ledermann, T., Rung, J., & Twohig, M. P. (2020). Effects of acceptance and commitment therapy on impulsive decision-making. *Behavior Modification, 44*(4), 600−623. https://doi.org/10.1177/0145445519833041

Myerson, J., Green, L., Hanson, J. S., Holt, D. D., & Estle, S. J. (2003). Discounting delayed and probabilistic rewards: Processes and traits. *Journal of Economic Psychology, 24*(5), 619−635. https://doi.org/10.1016/S0167-4870(03)00005-9

Myerson, J., Green, L., & Morris, J. (2011). Modeling the effect of reward amount on probability discounting. *Journal of the Experimental Analysis of Behavior, 95*(2), 175−187. https://doi.org/10.1901/jeab.2011.95-175

Myerson, J., Green, L., & Warusawitharana, M. (2001). Area under the curve as a measure of discounting. *Journal of the Experimental Analysis of Behavior, 76*(2), 235−243. https://doi.org/10.1901/jeab.2001.76-235

Navarick, D. J., & Fantino, E. (1976). Self-control and general models of choice. *Journal of Experimental Psychology: Animal Behavior Processes, 2*(1), 75−87. https://doi.org/10.1037/0097-7403.2.1.75

Odum, A. L. (2011a). Delay discounting: I'm a *k*, you're a *k*. *Journal of the Experimental Analysis of Behavior, 96*(3), 427−439. https://doi.org/10.1901/jeab.2011.96-423

Odum, A. L. (2011b). Delay discounting: Trait variable? *Behavioural Processes, 87*(1), 1−9. https://doi.org/10.1016/j.beproc.2011.02.007

Odum, A. L., & Baumann, A. A. L. (2010). Delay discounting: State and trait variable. In G. J. Madden, & W. K. Bickel (Eds.), *Impulsivity: The behavioral and neurological science of discounting* (pp. 39−65). American Psychological Association. https://doi.org/10.1037/12069-002

Odum, A. L., Baumann, A. A. L., & Rimington, D. D. (2006). Discounting of delayed hypothetical money and food: Effects of amount. *Behavioural Processes, 73*(3), 278−284. https://doi.org/10.1016/j.beproc.2006.06.008

Odum, A. L., Becker, R. J., Haynes, J. M., Galizio, A., Frye, C. C. J., Downey, H., Friedel, J. E., & Perez, D. M. (2020). Delay discounting of different outcomes: Review and theory. *Journal of the Experimental Analysis of Behavior, 113*(2), 657−679. https://doi.org/10.1002/jeab.589

Odum, A. L., Madden, G. J., Badger, G. J., & Bickel, W. K. (2000). Needle sharing in opioid-dependent outpatients: Psychological processes underlying risk. *Drug and Alcohol Dependence, 60*(3), 259−266. https://psycnet.apa.org/doi/10.1016/S0376-8716(00)00111-3.

Oliveira, L., Green, L., & Myerson, J. (2014). Pigeons' delay discounting functions established using a concurrent-chains procedure. *Journal of the Experimental Analysis of Behavior, 102*(2), 151−161. https://doi.org/10.1002/jeab.97

Ong, E. L., & White, K. G. (2004). Amount-dependent temporal discounting? *Behavioural Processes, 66*, 201−212. https://doi.org/10.1016/j.beproc.2004.03.005

Ostaszewski, P., Green, L., & Myerson, J. (1998). Effects of inflation on the subjective value of delayed and probabilistic rewards. *Psychonomic Bulletin & Review, 5*, 324−333. https://doi.org/10.3758/BF03212959

Ostaszewski, P., & Karzel, K. (2002). Discounting of delayed and probabilistic losses of different amounts. *European Psychologist, 7*(4), 295−301. https://doi.org/10.1027/1016-9040.7.4.295

Paliliunas, D. (2021). Values: A core guiding principle for behavior-analytic intervention and research. *Behavior Analysis in Practice, 15*(1), 115−125. https://doi.org/10.1007/s40617-021-00595-3

Peck, S., & Madden, G. J. (2021). Effects of effort training on effort-based impulsive choice. *Behavioural Processes, 189*, 104441. https://doi.org/10.1016/j.beproc.2021.104441

Peck, S., & Madden, G. J. (2023). Effects of episodic future thinking on delay and effort discounting. *Psychological Record, 73*(1), 139−145. https://doi.org/10.1007/s40732-022-00516-y

Peck, S., Preston, E., Smith, K. B., & Madden, G. J. (2022). Reducing impulsive choice: VIII. Effects of delay-exposure training in female rats. *Behavioural Processes, 197*, 104622. https://doi.org/10.1016/j.beproc.2022.104622

Peters, J., & Büchel, C. (2009). Overlapping and distinct neural systems code for subjective value during intertemporal and risky decision making. *Journal of Neuroscience, 29*(50), 15727−15734. https://doi.org/10.1523/JNEUROSCI.3489-09.2009

Peterson, J. R., Hill, C. C., & Kirkpatrick, K. (2015). Measurement of impulsive choice in rats: Same- and alternate-form test-retest reliability and temporal tracking. *Journal of the Experimental Analysis of Behavior, 103*(1), 166−179. https://doi.org/10.1002/jeab.124

Petry, N. M. (2001). Delay discounting of money and alcohol in actively using alcoholics, currently abstinent alcoholics, and controls. *Psychopharmacology, 154*(3), 243−250. https://doi.org/10.1007/s002130000638

Petry, N. M., & Madden, G. J. (2010). Discounting and pathological gambling. In G. J. Madden, & W. K. Bickel (Eds.), *Impulsivity: The behavioral and neurological science of discounting* (pp. 273−294). American Psychological Association. https://doi.org/10.1037/12069-010

Pitts, R. C., & McKinney, A. P. (2005). Effects of methylphenidate and morphine on delay-discount functions obtained within sessions. *Journal of the Experimental Analysis of Behavior, 83*(3), 297−314. https://doi.org/10.1901/jeab.2005.47-04

Rachlin, H. (1974). Self-control. *Behaviorism, 2*(1), 94−107. https://www.jstor.org/stable/27758811.

Rachlin, H., & Green, L. (1972). Commitment, choice and self-control. *Journal of the Experimental Analysis of Behavior, 17*(1), 15−22. https://doi.org/10.1901/jeab.1972.17-15

Rachlin, H., & Jones, B. A. (2008). Social discounting and delay discounting. *Journal of Behavioral Decision Making, 21*(1), 29−43. https://doi.org/10.1002/bdm.567

Rachlin, H., Logue, A. W., Gibbon, J., & Frankel, M. (1986). Cognition and behavior in studies of choice. *Psychological Review, 93*(1), 33−45. https://doi.org/10.1037/0033-295X.93.1.33

Rachlin, H., Raineri, A., & Cross, D. (1991). Subjective probability and delay. *Journal of the Experimental Analysis of Behavior, 55*(2), 233−244. https://doi.org/10.1901/jeab.1991.55-233

Raineri, A., & Rachlin, H. (1993). The effect of temporal constraints on the value of money and other commodities. *Journal of Behavioral Decision Making, 6*(2), 77−94. https://doi.org/10.1002/bdm.3960060202

Rasmussen, E. B., Lawyer, S. R., & Reilly, W. (2010). Percent body fat is related to delay and probability discounting for food in humans. *Behavioural Processes, 83*(1), 23−30. https://doi.org/10.1016/j.beproc.2009.09.001

Renda, C. R., Rung, J. M., Hinnenkamp, J. E., Lenzini, S. N., & Madden, G. J. (2018). Impulsive choice and pre-exposure to delays: IV. Effects of delay-and immediacy-exposure training relative to maturational changes in impulsivity. *Journal of the Experimental Analysis of Behavior, 109*(3), 587−599. https://doi.org/10.1002/jeab.432

Reyes-Huerta, H. E., & Dos Santos, C. V. (2016). The absence of numbers to express the amount may affect delay discounting with humans. *Journal of the Experimental Analysis of Behavior, 106*(2), 117−133. https://doi.org/10.1002/jeab.218

Reyes-Huerta, H. E., Robles, E., & Dos Santos, C. V. (2023). Valuing the future at different temporal points: The role of time framing on discounting. *Journal of the Experimental Analysis of Behavior, 120*(2), 214−227. https://doi.org/10.1002/jeab.871

Richards, J. B., Mitchell, S. H., De Wit, H., & Seiden, L. S. (1997). Determination of discount functions in rats with an adjusting-amount procedure. *Journal of the Experimental Analysis of Behavior, 67*(3), 353−366. https://doi.org/10.1901/jeab.1997.67-353

Richards, J. B., Zhang, L., Mitchell, S. H., & De Wit, H. (1999). Delay or probability discounting in a model of impulsive behavior: Effect of alcohol. *Journal of the Experimental Analysis of Behavior, 71*(2), 121−143. https://doi.org/10.1901/jeab.1999.71-121

Robles, E., Vargas, P. A., & Bejarano, R. (2009). Within-subject differences in degree of delay discounting as a function of order of presentation of hypothetical cash rewards. *Behavioural Processes, 81*(2), 260−263. https://doi.org/10.1016/j.beproc.2009.02.018

Rodríguez, W., Bouzas, A., & Orduña, V. (2018). Temporal discounting of aversive consequences in rats. *Learning & Behavior, 46*, 38−48. https://doi.org/10.3758/s13420-017-0279-9

Rodriguez, L. R., Rasmussen, E. B., Kyne-Rucker, D., Wong, M., & Martin, K. S. (2021). Delay discounting and obesity in food insecure and food secure women. *Health Psychology, 40*(4), 242. https://psycnet.apa.org/doi/10.1037/hea0001042.

Rodzon, K., Berry, M. S., & Odum, A. L. (2011). Within-subject comparison of degree of delay discounting using titrating and fixed sequence procedures. *Behavioural Processes, 86*(1), 164−167. https://doi.org/10.1016/j.beproc.2010.09.007

Rojas, G. R., Curry-Pochy, L. S., Chen, C. S., Heller, A. T., & Grissom, N. M. (2022). Sequential delay and probability discounting tasks in mice reveal anchoring effects partially attributable to decision noise. *Behavioural Brain Research, 5*, 1−39. https://doi.org/10.1016/j.bbr.2022.113951

Rotter, J. B. (1954). *Social learning and clinical psychology*. Prentice-Hall, Inc. https://doi.org/10.1037/10788-000

Rung, J. M., Argyle, T. M., Siri, J. L., & Madden, G. J. (2018). Choosing the right delay-discounting task: Completion times and rates of nonsystematic data. *Behavioural Processes, 151*, 119−125. https://doi.org/10.1016/j.beproc.2018.03.022

Rung, J. M., Frye, C. C., DeHart, W. B., & Odum, A. L. (2019). Evaluating the effect of delay spacing on delay discounting: Carry-over effects on steepness and the form of the discounting function. *Journal of the Experimental Analysis of Behavior, 112*(3), 254−272. https://doi.org/10.1002/jeab.556

Rung, J. M., & Madden, G. J. (2018). Experimental reductions of delay discounting and impulsive choice: A systematic review and meta-analysis. *Journal of Experimental Psychology: General, 147*(9), 1349−1381. https://doi.org/10.1037/xge0000462

Rung, J. M., & Madden, G. J. (2019). Demand characteristics in episodic future thinking II: The role of cues and cue content in changing delay discounting. *Experimental and Clinical Psychopharmacology, 27*(5), 482−495. https://doi.org/10.1037/pha0000260

Shead, N. W., & Hodgins, D. C. (2009). Probability discounting of gains and losses: Implications for risk attitudes and impulsivity. *Journal of the Experimental Analysis of Behavior, 92*(1), 1−16. https://doi.org/10.1901/jeab.2009.92-1

Slezak, J. M., & Anderson, K. G. (2009). Effects of variable training, signaled and unsignaled delays, and d-amphetamine on delay-discounting functions. *Behavioural Pharmacology, 20*(5−6), 424−436. https://doi.org/10.1097/fbp.0b013e3283305ef9

Smethells, J. R., & Carroll, M. E. (2015). Discrepant effects of acute cocaine on impulsive choice (delay discounting) in female rats during an increasing- and adjusting-delay procedure. *Psychopharmacology, 232*(14), 2455−2462. https://doi.org/10.1007/s00213-015-3874-5

Smith, A. P., Peterson, J. R., & Kirkpatrick, K. (2016). Reward contrast effects on impulsive choice and timing in rats. *Timing & Time Perception, 4*(2), 147–166. https://doi.org/10.1163/22134468-00002059

Stein, J. S., Johnson, P. S., Renda, C. R., Smits, R. R., Liston, K. J., Shahan, T. A., & Madden, G. J. (2013). Early and prolonged exposure to reward delay: Effects on impulsive choice and alcohol self-administration in male rats. *Experimental and Clinical Psychopharmacology, 21*(2), 172–180. https://psycnet.apa.org/doi/10.1037/a0031245.

Strickland, J. C., Reed, D. D., Hursh, S. R., Schwartz, L. P., Foster, R. N. S., Gelino, B. W., LeComte, R. S., Oda, F. S., Salzer, A. R., Schneider, T. D., Dayton, L., Latkin, C., & Johnson, M. W. (2021). Integrating operant and cognitive behavioral economics to inform infectious disease response: Prevention, testing, and vaccination in the COVID-19 pandemic. *PLoS One, 17*(1), Article e0258828. https://doi.org/10.1371/journal.pone.0258828

Vanderveldt, A., Green, L., & Myerson, J. (2015). Discounting of monetary rewards that are both delayed and probabilistic: Delay and probability combine multiplicatively, not additively. *Journal of Experimental Psychology: Learning, Memory, and Cognition, 41*(1), 148–162. https://doi.org/10.1037/xlm0000029

Wahab, M., Panlilio, L. V., & Solinas, M. (2018). An improved within-session self-adjusting delay discounting procedure for the study of choice impulsivity in rats. *Psychopharmacology, 235*, 2123–2135. https://doi.org/10.1007/s00213-018-4911-y

Weatherly, J. N., & Derenne, A. (2013). Testing the reliability of paper-pencil versions of the fill-in-the-blank and multiple-choice methods of measuring probability discounting for seven different outcomes. *Psychological Record, 63*, 835–862. https://link.springer.com/article/10.11133/j.tpr.2013.63.4.009#citeas.

Weatherly, J. N., Petros, T. V., Jónsdóttir, H. L., Derenne, A., & Miller, J. C. (2015). Probability alters delay discounting, but delay does not alter probability discounting. *Psychological Record, 65*, 267–275. https://doi.org/10.1007/s40732-014-0102-3

Weinsztok, S., Brassard, S., Balodis, I., Martin, L. E., & Amlung, M. (2021). Delay discounting in established and proposed behavioral addictions: A systematic review and meta-analysis. *Frontiers in Behavioral Neuroscience, 15*, 786358. https://doi.org/10.3389/fnbeh.2021.786358

Wilhelm, C. J., & Mitchell, S. H. (2009). Strain differences in delay discounting using inbred rats. *Genes, Brain and Behavior, 8*(4), 426–434. https://doi.org/10.1111/j.1601-183X.2009.00484.x

Willis-Moore, M. E., Haynes, J. M., Frye, C. C., Johnson, H. M., Cousins, D. J., Bamfo, H. D., & Odum, A. L. (2024). Recent experience affects delay discounting: Evidence across temporal framing, signs, and magnitudes. *Perspectives on Behavior Science*, 1–28. https://doi.org/10.1007/s40614-024-00412-6

Woolverton, W. L., Freeman, K. B., Myerson, J., & Green, L. (2012). Suppression of cocaine self-administration in monkeys: Effects of delayed punishment. *Psychopharmacology, 220*, 509–517. https://doi.org/10.1007/s00213-011-2501-3

Yates, J. R., Batten, S. R., Bardo, M. T., & Beckmann, J. S. (2015). Role of ionotropic glutamate receptors in delay and probability discounting in the rat. *Psychopharmacology, 232*(7), 1187–1196. https://doi.org/10.1007/s00213-014-3747-3

Yeh, Y. H., Myerson, J., Strube, M. J., & Green, L. (2020). Choice patterns reveal qualitative individual differences among discounting of delayed gains, delayed losses, and probabilistic losses. *Journal of the Experimental Analysis of Behavior, 113*(3), 609–625. https://doi.org/10.1002/jeab.597

Yi, R., Gatchalian, K. M., & Bickel, W. K. (2006). Discounting of past outcomes. *Experimental and Clinical Psychopharmacology, 14*(3), 311. https://doi.org/10.1037/1064-1297.14.3.311

Yi, R., Piedad, X., & Bickel, W. K. (2006). The combined effects of delay and probability in discounting. *Behavioural Processes, 73*(2), 149−155. https://doi.org/10.1016/j.beproc.2006.05.001

Zoratto, F., Laviola, G., & Adriani, W. (2016). The subjective value of probabilistic outcomes: Impact of reward magnitude on choice with uncertain rewards in rats. *Neuroscience Letters, 617*, 225−231. https://doi.org/10.1016/j.neulet.2016.02.026

Nonhuman research methods and procedures for studying delay discounting

Robert S. LeComte[1] and Erin B. Rasmussen[2]
[1]Department of Psychiatry & Behavioral Sciences, Behavioral Pharmacology Research Unit, Johns Hopkins University School of Medicine, Baltimore, MD, United States; [2]Department of Psychology, Idaho State University, Pocatello, ID, United States

The previous chapter(s) introduced the behavioral economic process of discounting. Recapitulating, discounting describes the subjective devaluation of reinforcers as a function of a change in some dimension of a reinforcer. To take one dimension, reinforcers can be devalued as a function of the delay to their receipt. Broadly speaking, we prefer access to reinforcers to occur now versus later. As the opportunity to receive a reinforcer becomes more temporally distant, its subjective value decreases. All organisms experience varying sensitivities to delays for valued reinforcers; some experience greater devaluation with delay, or "steeper" discounting, than others. Moreover, many studies point to such sensitivities as being highly adaptive and likely an integral part of many species' survival, including ours. Organisms with high metabolisms, such as pigeons and rats, for example, expend more energy and may be less likely to benefit from waiting for larger, delayed food reinforcers compared to those with lower metabolic rates (e.g., primates and humans) (Vanderveldt et al., 2016).

Despite its adaptive benefits, discounting of reinforcers can also take a more pathological turn. In such cases, higher rates of discounting are strongly correlated with problematic health behaviors such as substance use disorders (Amlung et al., 2017; Kollins, 2003), physical inactivity (Tate, 2015), overeating (Amlung et al., 2017; Rasmussen et al., 2016), and sexual risk taking (e.g., Lawyer & Mahoney, 2017). The role of discounting in health behaviors has led to the development of interventions that include discounting as an important target for research (Landes et al., 2012). Considering treatment strategies for substance use disorders, for example, pretreatment discounting rates have emerged as potentially meaningful predictors of treatment success (Washio et al., 2011). In adolescents, for example, Stanger et al. (2012) noted that lower pretreatment rates of delay discounting were predictive of greater success in achieving and maintaining drug abstinence. Like any course of behavior change treatment, effective intervention strategies require a thorough and ongoing understanding of the mechanisms, processes, and contextual variables affecting their expression. Fortunately, decades of research within basic operant laboratories, especially those using nonhuman animals, have laid a solid foundation on which these questions can be answered. The present chapter will detail the basic procedures used to study discounting in the nonhuman laboratory and review some of the outcomes and findings across various species. Finally, we include some animal research trends that identify neural structures that are involved in discounting and likely underlie behavioral processes that are described.

Nonhuman delay discounting procedures

Delay discounting tasks are often arranged as a series of choices between two options. In one option, often called the smaller, sooner (SS), an operant response (i.e., a lever-press with rats or a key peck with pigeons) results in a small amount of food or liquid immediately (0-second (s) delay). In a second option, called the larger, later (LL), a second response produces a larger amount of food, though after a delay greater than 0 s.

Adjusting-delay discounting procedure

The adjusting-delay procedure, developed by Mazur (1987), was the first to evaluate discounting in nonhumans (see Fig. 8.1). Here, behavior is allocated between a smaller-magnitude reinforcer delivered under a fixed delay (often beginning at 0 s) and a larger magnitude reinforcer delivered under an adjusting delay that is titrated based on the organism's response. Mazur's (1987) sessions comprised 64 reinforcement trials divided into 16 4-trial blocks. Within each four-trial block, the first two trials presented a forced choice, and the last two presented a free choice. Each trial was followed by an intertrial interval (ITI) so that all trial durations were held constant. During forced-choice trials, each key (e.g., red or green) and its associated contingency (e.g., SS for the red key; LL for the green key) were presented individually and sequentially, which served to maintain the organism's experience with the contingencies operating on each key (Mazur, 1987, p. 62). During free-choice trials, a trial began with the illumination of the center key, which darkened following a response. Next, both red and green side keys were lit, presenting both options simultaneously. If the green (adjusting delay) key was selected in both free-choice trials, its delay would increase by 1s in the next trial block. For instance, if it began at 3 s, the delay would increase to 4 s on the subsequent trial block. Alternatively, if the red (fixed delay) key was selected in both trials, the adjusted delay would decrease by 1s (i.e., to 2 s) for the subsequent trial block. If each reinforcement option was selected during both free choice trials (i.e., 50% allocation), no change was made to the adjusted delay in subsequent trial blocks. Once behavioral stability was met, the mean adjusted delay across trial blocks represented an estimation of the indifference point or the point at which SS and LL options were preferred equally.

Broadly, results showed that the adjusting-delay task produced orderly discounting data. As delays to the larger, delayed reinforcer increased, pigeons' choices were increasingly allocated to the smaller, fixed delayed reinforcer. Moreover, from a quantitative perspective, Mazur (1987) found that the rate at which the subjective value

Nonhuman research methods and procedures for studying delay discounting 183

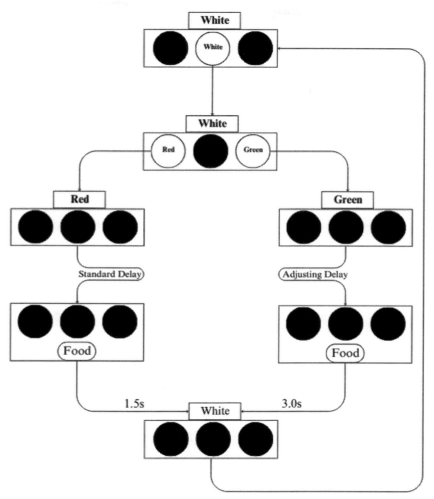

Figure 8.1 A schematic diagram of the adjusting-delay discounting procedure (Mazur, 1987).

(indifference points) decreased was hyperbolic—that is, shorter delays to food dramatically decreased its value.

Adjusting-amount discounting procedure

Building off the adjusting-delay procedure, Richards et al. (1997) developed an adjusting-amount paradigm to study discounting in nonhumans. As the name suggests, this approach differs in that the magnitude of reinforcement is adjusted rather than delays to accessing it. In this procedure, subjects are presented a choice between a large-magnitude reinforcer delivered after a delay and an adjusted magnitude reinforcer delivered immediately (see Fig. 8.2). Here, like the adjusting delay, magnitude

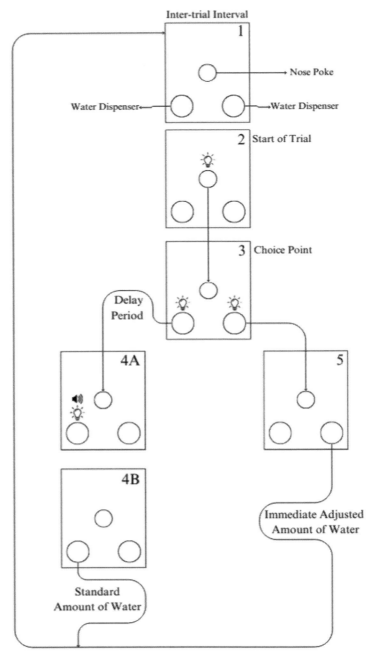

Figure 8.2 A schematic diagram of the adjusting-amount discounting procedure (Richards et al., 1997).

adjustments of the SS reinforcer are titrated based on the organism's choices. If the LL reinforcer is chosen, for example, the amount of the SS reinforcer is increased by a specific amount in the next trial. Conversely, if the SS reinforcer is chosen, its magnitude is decreased by the same specific amount in the following trial. An indifference point can be determined when the adjusting SS and LL reinforcers are chosen with approximately equal frequency across trials.

Richards et al. (1997) initially applied their procedure using rats and differential amounts of water. Testing chambers contained a front wall with a tone generator, stimulus lights, two infrared nose-poke receptacles with interior water dispensers as operants, and a centrally positioned infrared nose-poke receptacle. After a response in the central nose poke began a trial, subsequent head entries into the right receptacle resulted in immediate delivery of an adjusting amount of water, while head entries in the left receptacle initiated a delay, after which a standard amount of water was dispensed.

Individual sessions consisted of 60 free-choice trials and a varied number of forced-choice trials. Reinforcement trials were separated by an ITI and were signaled by illuminating a stimulus light above the central nose poke. After a center response, its stimulus light would turn off, followed by the illumination of lights above the left and right water receptacles. Head entries into the left receptacle resulted in the stimulus light above the right receptacle turning off, signaling the start of the delay period. At the end of the delay, 100 μL of water was dispensed into a dish at the bottom of the receptacle. Responses in the right receptacle resulted in both stimulus lights turning off, followed by immediate delivery of an adjusted amount of water. During each session, selecting the standard (left) option increased the adjusting (right) water amount by 10% in the next trial. Alternatively, if the adjusted option was selected, amounts delivered in the following trial would decrease by 10%. Choices for the standard 100 μL of water were assessed at delays of 0, 2, 4, 8, and 16 s. At each of these delays, the adjusted amounts of immediately delivered water began at 35 μL and 71 μL. In each session, the median droplet size (measured as μL of the immediate option) obtained from the last 30 choice trials represented the approximate indifference point between adjusting immediate and standard delayed alternatives.

Richards et al. (1997) found that the adjusting-amount procedure generated orderly patterns of water discounting in rats, which were adequately predicted by the hyperbolic discounting model (Mazur, 1987). Further, across three experiments, behavior during the discounting task stabilized quickly. This allowed researchers to efficiently determine discounting functions and readily manipulate experimental conditions such as the standard delay, presession satiation, and standard amount magnitude. Indeed, other orderly patterns emerged with these conditions.

Across-species research

Both adjusting-delay and adjusting-amount tasks have been adapted for a wide range of studies across species. Mazur (2000), for example, compared pigeons' responding between two keys: One containing a standard alternative delivering food under a variable time (VT) schedule (e.g., varied, 2s durations of grain access in a set time period) and another delivering food after an adjusting delay (e.g., 2 or 6s durations of grain access after a delay). Compared to the standard alternative, results showed that reinforcers maintaining responding in the adjusting alternative declined in effectiveness as delays increased. Mazur and Biondi (2009) determined the extent to which manipulation of both delays and amounts of reinforcers (e.g., one vs. two reinforcers per trial, one vs. three reinforcers per trial, and two vs. three reinforcers per trial) affected pigeons' discounting. They found that the slope of indifference points (i.e., mean adjusted delays) increased as the ratio of the two reinforcer magnitudes increased. For example, the slope of indifference points was highest for one versus three reinforcers compared to the other reinforcer ratio conditions.

In another study using pigeons, Green et al. (2007) explored whether both adjusting-amount and adjusting-delay procedures could yield comparable measures of discounting. This comparison involved a within-subject yoking technique wherein results from one procedure determined the parameters of the other. If the adjusting-amount procedure came first, for example, resulting indifference points would be used to set the standard reinforcer amount in the adjusting-delay procedure. Conversely, results from the adjusting-delay procedure would be used to determine delays to the LL reinforcer in the adjusting-amount procedure. Broadly, outcomes from each procedure were comparable in terms of orderliness and discounting rates, and were adequately described by the same quantitative models. From these results, Green et al. (2007) suggest that a common behavioral process underlies discounting in these procedures.

A number of studies have also examined discounting using rats. Logue et al. (1992), studying drug-behavior relations with the adjusting-delay procedure, found that food-deprived rats were more likely to choose the SS option following chronic injections of cocaine. Relatedly, Perry et al. (2005) observed that rats who showed a greater preference for SS food reinforcers in an adjusting-delay task more quickly acquired cocaine self-administration compared to rats preferring LL reinforcer outcomes. The adjusting-delay procedure also produces orderly indifference points in rats with non-tangible reinforcers. In Mazur (1987), for example, rats chose between low-frequency brain stimulation delivered after a fixed delay (SS reinforcer) and high-frequency brain stimulation (LL reinforcer) delivered after an adjusting delay. Results showed discounting curves for brain stimulation that were similar to those seen in studies of both rats and pigeons using food as reinforcers.

Studies of primates also reveal interesting interspecies differences in delay discounting using adjusting-delay procedures. For example, Stevens et al. (2005) observed that marmosets tolerated significantly longer delays for food than tamarins. Capuchins also showed a higher tolerance for delayed food rewards than tamarins and marmosets (Addessi et al., 2011). Interestingly, these discounting outcomes may be explained by evolutionary differences in feeding ecology across subspecies of primates. The diet of marmosets, for example, consists of saps and gums, which can take long periods of time to seep through trees. Conversely, species such as tamarins frequently feed on insects, which are more readily obtained through quick foraging behaviors (Stevens et al., 2005).

Studies using adjusting-amount procedures also note a similar diversity of findings across species. Like the approach by Richards et al. (1997), Reynolds et al. (2002) arranged choice contingencies between SS (adjusted) or LL (fixed) amounts of water in water-deprived rats (DD group). One key difference, however, involved using a delayed gratification condition (DG group). Here, rats made choices between the same alternatives. If the LL option was selected, however, rats could switch over to the adjusted alternative at any point during the delay period to receive the SS reinforcer. Results indicated similar discounting patterns in both DD and DG groups, but fewer switching responses occurred among rats during the DG condition.

Green et al. (2004) found that the adjusting-amount procedure for food pellets with rats generated outcomes like those observed with hypothetical rewards in human discounting (e.g., Rachlin et al., 1991). Specifically, subjective values of delayed food outcomes significantly decreased as a function of delay to receipt, an effect well accounted for by hyperbolic modeling. Interestingly, results differed from typical human studies (e.g., Hendrickson et al., 2015; Kirby & Marakovic, 1996) in that magnitude effects, or the phenomenon that discounting is inversely related to the amount of the delayed outcomes (i.e., lower magnitude outcomes are discounted more than those with higher magnitude), were not seen with rats. This may be because the magnitude differences with food were smaller with rats, as magnitude effects with humans are typically found in amounts that differ in terms of orders of magnitude. This study also found discounting outcomes with pigeons that were similar to the findings with rats, further adding to this area of literature.

Adjusting-amount discounting has also proved a useful tool for primate studies. In rhesus monkeys, for instance, an adjusting-amount task with differential concentrations of saccharin showed discounting functions that were consistent with findings from other primate research (Freeman et al., 2009). For example, Freeman et al. (2009) found that although rhesus monkeys preferred a 20% saccharin solution over a 10% solution, they did not discount these concentrations differently when made available as reinforcers in an adjusting-amount procedure. Similar to Green et al. (2004), these results differ from the magnitude effect seen in human subjects, wherein greater reinforcement magnitudes tend to be discounted less steeply.

Huskinson et al. (2015) also examined adjusting-amount discounting with rhesus monkeys but with food and cocaine as available reinforcers. In one condition, rhesus monkeys made choices between adjusted amounts of food and fixed amounts of food delivered after a delay. In another, choices were made between adjusting amounts of intravenous cocaine and a fixed amount of food after a delay. Results showed steeper discounting of delayed food when cocaine was the immediate alternative compared to the choices in which only food was offered for the choices. This suggests that the types of options that are offered in choices matter; immediate cocaine (compared to food) leads to steeper discounting when food is the delayed option.

Within-session adjusting-delay discounting (The Evenden and Ryan procedure)

One potential issue encountered in procedures such as the adjusting amount is that indifference points at only one delay can be assessed in a single session. This could pose a challenge to certain types of research, such as pharmacology, where observing a drug's acute effects on discounting may only be possible in a short span of time. The discounting procedure developed by Evenden and Ryan (1996) addresses this by gradually increasing delay magnitudes within session. In doing so, Evenden and Ryan (1996) argued the function between delay magnitudes and choices of SS versus LL rewards can be more completely characterized.

The original Evenden and Ryan procedure (see Fig. 8.3) consisted of individual sessions with 72 reinforcement trials. Each session began with the illumination of a house light and response-independent delivery of one food pellet. Following a 40 s ITI, a head entry response into the pellet magazine caused two response levers to be inserted on either side of the receptacle. Pressing one lever resulted in one food pellet being delivered immediately. Pressing the opposite lever produced a programmed delay, after which five pellets would be delivered successively in 1s intervals. Positioning of SS and LL reinforcement levers was counterbalanced across subjects and pressing either lever resulted in both being retracted to prevent further responding during reinforcer delivery. Of note, pressing either lever resulted in the onset of the programmed delay and ITI, which allowed the interval between each choice trial to be independent of whether the immediate or delayed options were selected. Delays (e.g., 0 s, 0.5 s, 1 s, 2 s, 3 s, 4 s, 6 s, 8 s, and 10 s) were increased progressively throughout each session, with eight reinforcement trials for each delay.

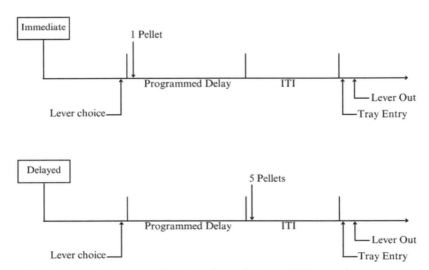

Figure 8.3 A schematic diagram of the Evenden and Ryan (1996) procedure.

This procedure also can be tailored for multiple measurement approaches. The number of delays assessed, delay step size, number of trials at each delay, as well as the number of days spent training at each level can be widely varied. In one testing arrangement, for example, choices were assessed across nine ascending delays from 0 to 10 s over 3 days with eight trials at each delay. The same procedure can operate with delays of 0, 10, 20, 40, and 60 s over 10 days with 12 trials at each delay.

By increasing delays to reinforcement within sessions and varying programmed delays between sessions, Evenden and Ryan (1996) found that sensitivities to delay could be more robustly maintained. Multiple groups of rats, for example, showed similar sensitivities to delay such that larger reinforcers would be chosen at the start of a session where delays were shorter—a stable effect seen across months of training. Further, their procedure allowed for within-session observations of drug-induced shifts between immediate and delayed outcomes, such as those seen after the administration of different psychoactive compounds. This may be valuable when studying drugs with a briefer time course of peak behavioral effects, such as short-acting stimulants.

Across-species research

As the literature stands, Evenden and Ryan's (1996) procedure has only been applied within strains of rats. Despite a lack of cross-species research, however, several publications note the procedure's utility in describing discounting in various experimental contexts. Examining the impacts of alcohol and serotonergic drugs on discounting, for example, Evenden and Ryan (1999) initially trained Sprague–Dawley rats to choose between SS and LL amounts of food (e.g., one vs. Five food pellets) before administering 1.0 g/kg doses of ethanol and three varieties of serotoninergic agonists. Post-administration, rats' preferences for the LL reinforcer were significantly reduced by both drugs, shifting choices to the SS reinforcer throughout sessions. In a similar study of drug effects, Cardinal et al. (2000) examined the impacts of amphetamines on discounting in Lister hooded rats. Their study involved two groups: One in which delays were signaled and another in which delays were unsignaled. Following amphetamine administration, rats showed decreased preferences for delayed outcomes in the unsignaled group and increased preference for delayed outcomes in the signaled group.

Evenden and Ryan's (1996) procedure has also been applied toward studying the effects of brain lesions on discounting. For example, Mobini et al. (2002) studied how lesions in the orbitofrontal cortex (OPFC) affected choices between SS and LL food in Wistar rats. Although both lesioned rats and controls (i.e., underwent shame surgery) showed decreased preferences for LL reinforcers as a function of delay, rats with impaired OPFC function discounted at a significantly steeper rate. Similar effects on discounting were noted by Mobini et al. (2000) following lesions to dorsal and medial raphe nuclei and by Cardinal et al. (2001), who induced lesions in the nucleus accumbens. Both brain areas are correlated with controlling impulsive behavior and are discussed in greater detail later in this chapter.

Concurrent chains discounting

An alternative approach to studying discounting in nonhumans comes from Grace (1999) with concurrent chains discounting. In this procedure, a choice phase (i.e., initial link) was followed by access to one of two reinforcement schedules (i.e., terminal link)—see Fig. 8.4. Sessions consisted of two components differentiated by key light color: Either red or green. Each color component contained a separate concurrent chain consisting of 36 initial and terminal link cycles. Each cycle began with the illumination of the side keys (red or green), which signaled the availability of concurrent variable interval (VI) 30 s initial link schedules. Once an initial link VI had elapsed and a response occurred, side keys changed from a steady to a blinking colored light, signaling the onset of terminal link schedules. Here, left and right keys operated on different VI schedules (e.g., VI 10 s and VI 20 s, respectively). In addition to key color, components also differed in terms of terminal link reinforcement magnitude (i.e., duration access to grain). In the red-light component, for example, both terminal links delivered brief access to grain (e.g., 1.7 s). In the green component, terminal link responses resulted in longer access to grain (e.g., 4.25 s). Therefore the terminal links set up delay discounting choices.

One of Grace's (1999) primary research questions was to assess the extent to which pigeons engaged in amount-dependent discounting. In the concurrent chains model, how responses are allocated during the initial link is interpreted as a choice preference

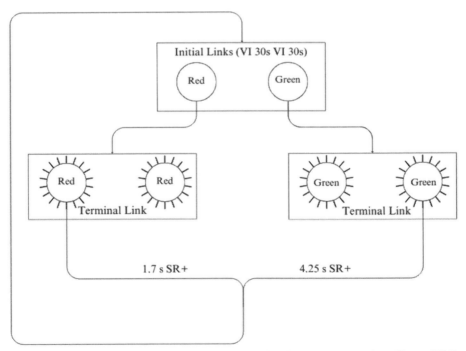

Figure 8.4 A schematic diagram of the concurrent chains discounting procedure (Grace, 1999).

for the terminal link. For example, a higher response rate in an initial link corresponding to a terminal link delivering SS reinforcers demonstrates a greater preference for immediate rewards (i.e., impulsivity) (Grace, 1999, p. 27). Pigeons in Grace's (1999) study showed a greater preference for the SS component as delay to the LL component increased. Grace (1999) notes, however, that although this was consistent with examples in human discounting literature, the overall effect was small and may not have represented a significant difference in sensitivity due to other variables (Grace, 1999, p. 39). Other studies (e.g., Grace et al., 2012) have sought to examine these variables more carefully.

Across-species research

The Grace (1999) study led to additional studies of discounting in pigeons using concurrent chains. For example, Ong and White (2004) made procedural variations to assess the generality of other methodological variations, including nonindependent initial link schedules, increased delay ratios, and fixed interval (FI) schedules during terminal links. Other procedural manipulations with pigeons were tested and reported by Oliveira et al. (2014), who developed a novel approach combining concurrent chains and adjusting-amount methods. In their procedure, if pigeons selected the initial link associated with an SS food amount, its magnitude would decrease across sessions. Conversely, selections of the delayed outcome initial link would increase the immediate magnitude across sessions. Results of their combined procedure showed that discounting was well-described by hyperbolic modeling—suggesting that both concurrent chains and adjusting-amount procedures have similar behavioral processes.

Concurrent chain discounting has also been extended into rodent research. For example, Orduña et al. (2013) observed greater sensitivities to delay during large-magnitude reinforcement components compared to smaller-magnitude conditions in rats. In another example, Aparicio et al. (2013) arranged a longitudinal concurrent chains procedure to compare discounting in two different strains of rats: Lewis and Fischer 344. Their study compared responding between SS (e.g., FI 5s) and LL terminal links (e.g., FI 5, 10, 20, 40, and 80 s, varied within session) across 115 days. Although Lewis rats showed greater sensitivity to terminal link delays early in training, differences between strains converged across sessions, and no significant differences in discounting were present at the end of training. These results suggest that differences in discounting between Lewis and Fischer 344 rats may be a function of learning histories more so than underlying neurobiological differences (Aparicio et al., 2015).

Identifying neural substrates in delay discounting

As seen with the previously discussed research, animal subjects are used to experimentally isolate variables that induce predictable variations in discounting, but they can also be used to identify underlying neural substrates. This is especially useful when modeling health-related disorders where impulse control is relevant (Rasmussen et al., 2016; Wilhelm & Mitchell, 2009). Such health conditions include, though are not limited to, attention deficit hyperactivity disorder (ADHD) (e.g., Fox et al., 2008; Sjoberg et al., 2023), substance use disorders (see Carroll et al., 2010; Mitchell, 2019), and obesity (see Rasmussen et al., 2016).

One area in which animal studies have been especially useful is characterizing specific neurotransmitter systems involved with discounting. For instance, lower serotonin signaling in structures involved with impulse control tends to increase delay discounting (e.g., Dalley et al., 2011; Darna et al., 2015; Miyazaki et al., 2012; see reviews by Hayes & Greenshaw, 2011; Homberg, 2012). These brain areas include the ventral tegmental area, substantia nigra, nucleus accumbens, hippocampus, amygdala, and prefrontal cortex. In addition, delay discounting is influenced by dopamine-rich neural areas (see Bickel et al., 2011). These structures include the striatum (e.g., Moreno et al., 2021; Tedford et al., 2015), ventral tegmental area (e.g., Bernowsky-Smith et al., 2018), nucleus accumbens (e.g., Moschak & Mitchell, 2014; Valencia-Torres et al., 2012), and prefrontal cortex (Feja & Koch, 2014). Not surprisingly, the serotonergic-dopaminergic overlap in a number of these structures, suggesting an interaction between these two neurotransmitter systems in terms of affecting delay discounting (e.g., Winstanley et al., 2003; Winstanley et al., 2005).

Some researchers use animal subjects to experimentally determine genetic variation in neurotransmitter systems that underlie discounting processes (e.g., Boomhower et al., 2013; Mitchell, 2019). For instance, glycoprotein M6-B has been identified as a candidate gene for human traits and disorders that involve impulsivity (Sanchez-Roige et al., 2018). The mutant *Gpm6B* mouse strain is one in which genes involved with this glycoprotein in serotonin signaling have been deleted. This strain also demonstrates steeper delay discounting compared to wild-type controls (Sanchez-Roige et al., 2022). Studies with genetic models, then, support human correlational research by experimentally determining the causal influence of specific genes on delay discounting.

Behavioral pharmacological studies with discounting

Behavioral pharmacological studies are also used to identify neural substrates involved in discounting. In a typical study, baseline discounting patterns are first determined, and differences in discounting between groups of animals with special genetic or environmental histories are often compared. Then, a range of drug doses that affect specific neurotransmitter systems (e.g., dopaminergic or perhaps a specific dopamine-receptor subtypes) are acutely administered before discounting sessions, and drug effects on discounting can be characterized. Drugs with consistent and systematic, i.e., dose-dependent, effects on discounting processes support the involvement of particular neurotransmitter systems of the drug on discounting; drugs with inconsistent or no effects on discounting suggest no or little involvement of the drug's underlying neurotransmitter systems. This process allows specificity (e.g., specific receptor subtypes) to be inferred. In addition, group comparisons in drug sensitivity may also support underlying neurological differences that indicate specific neural substrates. For instance, if one group of rodents, such as a genetic model, demonstrates a greater pharmacological sensitivity to a lower dose of a drug that is dopaminergic in nature, this would indicate an underlying dopaminergic neural difference in strain that manifests in behavior (e.g., Boomhower & Rasmussen, 2014; Boomhower et al., 2013).

Dopamine agonists

Behavioral pharmacological studies that describe the effects of acute drug administrations with monoaminergic compounds, especially those that involve dopamine, have predictable effects on discounting. Dopaminergic agonists, such as D-amphetamine, tend to reduce delay discounting (i.e., increase choice for the LL option) for food in rats (Huskinson et al., 2012; Maguire et al., 2014; Orsini et al., 2017; Slezak & Anderson, 2009, Tanno et al., 2014), though see Evenden and Ryan (1996) in which the opposite was found. Methylphenidate, a dopaminergic compound used to treat ADHD, also decreases discounting (Perry et al., 2008; Pitts & McKinney, 2005; Richards et al., 1999; van Gaalen et al., 2006). Amphetamine's effects on impulsive choice have also been shown in the B6 and the D2 mouse—strains that are more sensitive to drugs as reinforcers—which is also an implication for substance use disorders (Helms et al., 2006).

There is a procedural variant, however, that interacts with the trend of amphetamine-induced reductions in discounting. The ascending or descending nature of the delay sequence interacts with amphetamine effects in predictable ways. Tanno et al. (2014), for instance, showed that both amphetamine and methylphenidate increase choices for LL food options, but only when the delay sequences are ascending. When the delay sequence is descending, the opposite effect occurs—both drugs dose-dependently decrease choices for the LL food outcome (i.e., increased delay discounting). This sequence effect has also been shown when amphetamine is administered directly into the nucleus accumbens; rats will exhibit dose-dependent increases in the LL outcome when the delay is ascending, and dose-dependent decreases when the delay sequence is descending (Orsini et al., 2017). Another study showed that under an ascending delay sequence, amphetamine indeed decreases discounting, but with a descending sequence, no amphetamine-based effects were found (Maguire et al., 2014).

Strain differences may also matter. Huskinson et al. (2012), for instance, showed that amphetamine increased LL choices for Lewis rats but not Fischer 344 rats. Interestingly, Lewis and Fischer 344 rat strains both exhibit behavioral characteristics that are consistent with impulsivity when compared to other strains (see Wilhelm & Mitchell, 2009), including steeper delay discounting, though the Lewis strain tends to be especially prone to steeper discounting (Anderson & Diller, 2010; Anderson & Woolverton, 2005). The Lewis strain also has lower densities of dopamine D2 receptors and transporters in key brain reward areas, as well as extracellular dopamine in the nucleus accumbens (Flores et al., 1998; Mocsary & Bradberry, 1996). These differences in dopamine-rich areas may not only increase baseline levels of delay discounting relative to controls but may also heighten sensitivity to dopaminergic compounds, making them ideal animal models of substance use disorders as well as ADHD (see review by Cadoni, 2016).

It is also important to point out that amphetamine's reductive effects on delay discounting may also interact with environmental complexity. The default environment in most laboratory studies with rodents is an impoverished environment, in which basic needs (food, water, and bedding), but not much else, in terms of alternative reinforcement sources, are available. Consequently, in these environments, there is little diversity in operant behavior. To determine the extent to which environmental complexity affects discounting, Perry et al. (2008) compared methylphenidate and amphetamine's effects on delay discounting with rats reared in impoverished (singly housed with no toys) versus those that were enriched with pair-housing and a range of 14 plastic toys. Rats in impoverished environments demonstrated steeper delay discounting than those in enriched environments at baseline. Indeed, methylphenidate and amphetamine decreased impulsive choice, but *only with rats in the impoverished environment*. Those in the enriched environment showed amphetamine-induced *increases* in delay discounting, and no systematic effects were found with methylphenidate. These findings have substantial implications for the nature of factors such as poverty and the availability of alternative reinforcement in the development of impulsive choice. Moreover, these findings show that environmental complexity can also influence pharmacological effects on discounting.

Dopamine antagonists

Drugs that block dopamine receptors appear to have effects on discounting that are inverse to those of dopaminergic agonists; that is, antagonists *increase* choice for the smaller, sooner outcome (i.e., greater delay discounting). This mirrored process further supports that discounting is mediated by dopaminergic activity in the brain. For instance, flupentixol and SCH 23390, both dopamine D1 receptor subtype antagonists, increase impulsive choice (Stice et al., 2010; van Gaalen et al., 2006; Wade et al., 2000). Haloperidol, a D2 antagonist, has also been shown to dose-dependently induce steeper delay discounting (Boomhower & Rasmussen, 2014; Robertson & Rasmussen, 2017), though see Evenden and Ryan (1996) in which low-to-moderate doses of haloperidol and carbamazepine (also a D2 antagonist), had no consistent effect on discounting. In addition, amisulpride, haloperidol, and metoclopramide—all D2 antagonists—consistently increase delay discounting in humans (Arrando et al., 2015; Wagner et al., 2020; Weber et al., 2016).

Research on antagonism of D2 receptors is consistent with other studies in which impaired dopamine D2 signaling increases discounting. The deletion of D2 receptors in mice, for instance, also reduces dopamine-receptor interactions at the synapse and increases impulsive choice (Bernosky-Smith et al., 2018; Kim et al., 2018). Interestingly, individuals with methamphetamine substance use disorder have lower striatal D2 densities and exhibit higher delay discounting than controls (Ballard et al., 2015; Lee et al., 2009). While the direction of causation is not clear in these human studies, the relation further supports lower dopamine D2 involvement in steeper discounting. Indeed, the D2 receptor appears to be a critical neural mechanism of delay discounting (see review by Sarmiento et al., 2023).

Dopamine, discounting, and obesity

Delay discounting has also been used to model impulsive food choices related to obesity. Obese Zucker rats, for example, possess a single recessive gene allele combination that creates defective leptin signaling (Johnson et al., 1971; Zucker & Zucker, 1961). In a normally regulating organism, leptin is a satiety signal secreted by fat tissue that relays information about fat stores and also neuromodulates (i.e., reduces signaling of) several food-reward—based neurotransmitters, including dopamine and endocannabinoids (Di Marzo et al., 2001; Fulton et al., 2006; Opland et al., 2010). While obese Zucker rats have high amounts of leptin, the receptor is defective and fails to reduce dopamine and endocannabinoid signaling in food reward areas (e.g., Di Marzo et al., 2001; Opland et al., 2010). Consequently, food functions highly as a reinforcer (e.g., Rasmussen & Huskinson, 2008). Obese Zucker rats also exhibit altered dopaminergic D2 signaling in brain regions involved in food intake, such as the hypothalamus and striatum (Fetissov et al., 2002; Hamdi et al., 1992; Meguid et al., 2000).

Obese Zucker rats, compared to lean Zucker rats, also show steeper delay discounting for food (Boomhower et al., 2013). Moreover, they exhibit differential sensitivity to dopaminergic D2 drugs, such as haloperidol (Buckley & Rasmussen, 2014; Rasmussen & Hillman, 2011), as well as cannabinoid drugs, such as rimonabant, a CB1 receptor blocker (Huskinson et al., 2012; Rasmussen & Hillman, 2011; Smith & Rasmussen, 2010). These sensitivities support alterations at the neural level. Indeed, this sensitivity to both types of drugs is also shown with delay discounting tasks (Boomhower & Rasmussen, 2014).

While the obese Zucker rat is a genetic model of obesity, dietary models of obesity produce similar results. Behavioral pharmacological studies using dopaminergic compounds can "unmask" brain alterations caused by dietary manipulations. High-fat-high sugar diets, for instance, have been shown to alter dopaminergic (specifically D2) function in the brain, especially in areas involved in food reward. This has been demonstrated with imaging studies in both animals and humans (Stice et al., 2009, 2010; Val-Laillet et al., 2011) and with studies that directly examine specific changes in the brain, such as downregulation of dopamine D2 receptor densities in the striatum (Johnson & Kenny, 2010), reductions of dopamine in the nucleus accumbens shell (Geiger et al., 2009), and lower dopamine D2 receptor gene expression in the ventral tegmental area (Vucetic et al., 2012).

Haloperidol, a dopaminergic D2 antagonist, has been used as an agent to unmask dopaminergic alterations of high-fat-high-sugar diet with rats. Robertson and Rasmussen (2017) exposed rats to a standard chow or "cafeteria diet" comprising cheesecake, sausage, potato chips, frosting, and candy. Rats were then exposed to a delay discounting task in which they chose between SS versus LL sucrose pellets under an Evenden and Ryan (1996) procedure. Then varying acute doses of haloperidol were administered before some experimental sessions. Consistent with other research with D2 antagonists, haloperidol dose-dependently shifted preferences to the smaller-sooner sucrose option for both groups. However, those exposed to the cafeteria diet were more sensitive to the drug, i.e., less of a dose was required to reduce behavior.

Therefore, diet changes in sensitivity to haloperidol were shown using a DD procedure, implicating the D2 dopaminergic system.

In summary, animal studies, including those that are behavioral and pharmacological in nature, have contributed in meaningful ways to identifying neural substrates involved in discounting. Importantly, the dopaminergic and serotonergic neurotransmitter systems and corresponding brain areas related to impulse control have been identified as key neural areas involved in discounting. Animal studies also help characterize both genetic and environmental influences on discounting and how these variables may alter underlying neural substrates. Understanding these behavioral and neural mechanisms elucidates causes and has implications for treatments of disorders involving delay discounting, such as ADHD, substance abuse disorders, and obesity.

Conclusions

"I don't think Buddy Holly's much of a waiter" ((Tarantino, 1994, 00:46:00), often quoted by the first author's mentor, David Jarmolowicz, PhD (1976−2022), in reference to slower-to-learn rats). Whether counting down the days to vacation, opening a gift, or eyeing that beautiful slice of cake in the bakery window, it is sometimes difficult to wait for the things we value most. Although occasionally failing to wait and making impulsive choices is natural, it can often manifest into patterns of behavior that might require treatment. Thankfully, our knowledge of delay discounting, its underlying mechanisms, and its relations to health behavior has been greatly informed by decades of work in the nonhuman operant laboratory. Moreover, continued research using the procedures outlined above maintains strong foundations at multiple levels of analysis (i.e., behavioral and neurological) from which applied treatment strategies for substance use, obesity, ADHD, and more can continue to be developed and refined.

References

Addessi, E., Paglieri, F., & Focaroli, V. (2011). The ecological rationality of delay tolerance: Insights from capuchin monkeys. *Cognition, 119*(1), 142−147. https://doi.org/10.1016/j.cognition.2010.10.021

Amlung, M., Vedelago, L., Acker, J., Balodis, I., & MacKillop, J. (2017). Steep delay discounting and addictive behavior: A meta-analysis of continuous associations. *Addiction, 112*(1), 51−62. https://doi.org/10.1111/add.13535

Anderson, K. G., & Diller, J. W. (2010). Effects of acute and repeated nicotine administration on delay discounting in Lewis and Fischer 344 rats. *Behavioural Pharmacology, 21*(8), 754−764. https://doi.org/10.1097/FBP.0b013e328340a050

Anderson, K. G., & Woolverton, W. L. (2005). Effects of clomipramine on self-control choice in Lewis and Fischer 344 rats. *Pharmacology Biochemistry and Behavior, 80*(3), 387−393. https://doi.org/10.1016/j.pbb.2004.11.015

Aparicio, C. F., Elcoro, M., & Alonso-Alvarez, B. (2015). A long-term study of the impulsive choices of Lewis and Fischer 344 rats. *Learning & Behavior, 43*(3), 251−271. https://doi.org/10.3758/s13420-015-0177-y

Aparicio, C. F., Hughes, C. E., & Pitts, R. C. (2013). Impulsive choice in Lewis and fischer 344 rats. *Conductual, 1*(3), 22−46. https://doi.org/10.1016/j.bbr.2017.09.040

Arrondo, G., Aznárez-Sanado, M., Fernández-Seara, M. A., Goñi, J., Loayza, F. R., Salamon-Klobu, T. E., Heukamp, F. H., & Pastor, M. A. (2015). Dopaminergic modulation of the trade-off between probability and time in economic decision-making. *European Neuropsychopharmacology, 25*(6), 817−827. https://doi.org/10.1016/j.euroneuro.2015.02.011

Ballard, M. E., Mandelkern, M. A., Monterosso, J. R., Hsu, E., Robertson, C. L., Ishibashi, K., Dean, A. C., & London, E. D. (2015). Low dopamine D2/D3 receptor availability is associated with steep discounting of delayed rewards in methamphetamine dependence. *International Journal of Neuropsychopharmacology, 18*(7), Article pyu119. https://doi.org/10.1093/ijnp/pyu119

Bernosky-Smith, K. A., Qiu, Y. Y., Feja, M., Lee, Y. B., Loughlin, B., Li, J. X., & Bass, C. E. (2018). Ventral tegmental area D2 receptor knockdown enhances choice impulsivity in a delay-discounting task in rats. *Behavioural Brain Research, 341*, 129−134. https://doi.org/10.1016/j.bbr.2017.12.029

Bickel, W. K., Jarmolowicz, D. P., Mueller, E. T., & Gatchalian, K. M. (2011). The behavioral economics and neuroeconomics of reinforcer pathologies: Implications for etiology and treatment of addiction. *Current Psychiatry Reports, 13*(5), 406−415. https://doi.org/10.1007/s11920-011-0215-1

Boomhower, S., & Rasmussen, E. B. (2014). Haloperidol and rimonabant enhance impulsive choice in rats exposed to high-fat diets. *Behavioural Pharmacology, 25*(8), 705−716. https://doi.org/10.1097/FBP.0000000000000058

Boomhower, S., Rasmussen, E. B., & Doherty, T. S. (2013). Impulsive choice in the obese Zucker rat. *Behavioural Brain Research, 241*(15), 214−221. https://doi.org/10.1016/j.bbr.2012.12.013

Buckley, J., & Rasmussen, E. B. (2014). Rimonabant reduces relative amount of food intake not palatability in a choice procedure with obese and lean Zucker rats. *Psychopharmacology, 231*(10), 2159−2170. https://doi.org/10.1007/s00213-013-3366-4

Cadoni, C. (2016). Fischer 344 and Lewis rat strains as a model of genetic vulnerability to drug addiction. *Frontiers in Neuroscience, 10*(13). https://doi.org/10.3389/fnins.2016.00013

Cardinal, R. N., Pennicott, D. R., Sugathapala, C. L., Robbins, T. W., & Everitt, B. J. (2001). Impulsive choice induced in rats by lesions of the nucleus accumbens core. *Science, 292*(5526), 2499−2501. https://doi.org/10.1126/science.1060818

Cardinal, R. N., Robbins, T. W., & Everitt, B. J. (2000). The effects of d-amphetamine, chlordiazepoxide, α-flupenthixol, and behavioral manipulations on choice of signaled and unsignaled delayed reinforcement in rats. *Psychopharmacology, 152*, 362−375. https://doi.org/10.1007/s002130000536

Carroll, M. E., Anker, J. J., Mach, J. L., Newman, J. L., & Perry, J. L. (2010). Delay discounting as a predictor of drug abuse. In G. J. Madden, & W. K. Bickel (Eds.), *Impulsivity: The behavioral and neurological science of discounting* (pp. 243−271). American Psychological Association. https://doi.org/10.1037/12069-009

Dalley, J. W., Everitt, B. J., & Robbins, T. W. (2011). Impulsivity, compulsivity, and top-down cognitive control. *Neuron, 69*(4), 680−694. https://doi.org/10.1016/j.neuron.2011.01.020

Darna, M., Chow, J. J., Yates, J. R., Charnigo, R. J., Beckmann, J. S., Bardo, M. T., & Dwoskin, L. P. (2015). Role of serotonin transporter function in rat orbitofrontal cortex in impulsive choice. *Behavioural Brain Research, 293*, 134−142. https://doi.org/10.1016/j.bbr.2015.07.025

Di Marzo, V., Goparaju, S. K., Wang, L., Liu, J., Bátkai, S., Járai, Z., ... Kunos, G. (2001). Leptin-regulated endocannabinoids are involved in maintaining food intake. *Nature, 410*(6830), 822−825. https://doi.org/10.1038/35071088

Evenden, J. L., & Ryan, C. N. (1996). The pharmacology of impulsive behaviour in rats: The effects of drugs on response choice with varying delays of reinforcement. *Psychopharmacology, 128*(2), 161−170. https://doi.org/10.1007/s002130050121

Evenden, J. L., & Ryan, C. N. (1999). The pharmacology of impulsive behaviour in rats VI: The effects of ethanol and selective serotonergic drugs on response choice with varying delays of reinforcement. *Psychopharmacology, 146*(4), 413−421. https://doi.org/10.1007/s002130050121

Feja, M., & Koch, M. (2014). Ventral medial prefrontal cortex inactivation impairs impulse control but does not affect delay-discounting in rats. *Behavioural Brain Research, 264*, 230−239. https://doi.org/10.1016/j.bbr.2014.02.013

Fetissov, S. O., Meguid, M. M., Sato, T., & Zhang, L. H. (2002). Expression of dopaminergic receptors in the hypothalamus of lean and obese Zucker rats and food intake. *American Journal of Physiology - Regulatory, Integrative and Comparative Physiology, 283*(4), R905−R910. https://doi.org/10.1152/ajpregu.00092.2002

Flores, G., Wood, G. K., Barbeau, D., Quirion, R., & Srivastava, L. K. (1998). Lewis and fischer rats: A comparison of dopamine transporter and receptors levels. *Brain Research, 814*(1−2), 34−40. https://doi.org/10.1002/syn.20463

Fox, A. T., Hand, D. J., & Reilly, M. P. (2008). Impulsive choice in a rodent model of attention-deficit/hyperactivity disorder. *Behavioural Brain Research, 187*(1), 146−152. https://doi.org/10.1016/j.bbr.2007.09.008

Freeman, K. B., Green, L., Myerson, J., & Woolverton, W. L. (2009). Delay discounting of saccharin in rhesus monkeys. *Behavioural Processes, 82*(2), 214−218. https://doi.org/10.1016/j.beproc.2009.06.002

Fulton, S., Pissios, P., Manchon, R. P., Stiles, L., Frank, L., Pothos, E. N., Maratos-Flier, E., & Flier, J. S. (2006). Leptin regulation of the mesoaccumbens dopamine pathway. *Neuron, 51*(6), 811−822. https://doi.org/10.1016/j.neuron.2006.09.006

Geiger, B. M., Haburcak, M., Avena, N. M., Moyer, M. C., Hoebel, B. G., & Pothos, E. (2009). Deficits of mesolimbic dopamine neurotransmission in rat dietary obesity. *Neuroscience, 159*(4), 1193−1199. https://doi.org/10.1016/j.neuroscience.2009.02.007

Grace, R. C. (1999). The matching law and amount-dependent exponential discounting as accounts of self-control choice. *Journal of the Experimental Analysis of Behavior, 71*(1), 27−44. https://doi.org/10.1901/jeab.1999.71-27

Grace, R. C., Sargisson, R. J., & White, K. G. (2012). Evidence for a magnitude effect in temporal discounting with pigeons. *Journal of Experimental Psychology: Animal Behavior Processes, 38*(1), 102. https://doi.org/10.1037/a0026439

Green, L., Myerson, J., Holt, D. D., Slevin, J. R., & Estle, S. J. (2004). Discounting of delayed food rewards in pigeons and rats: Is there a magnitude effect? *Journal of the Experimental Analysis of Behavior, 81*(1), 39−50. https://doi.org/10.1901/jeab.2004.81-39

Green, L., Myerson, J., Shah, A. K., Estle, S. J., & Holt, D. D. (2007). Do adjusting-amount and adjusting-delay procedures produce equivalent estimates of subjective value in pigeons? *Journal of the Experimental Analysis of Behavior, 87*(3), 337−347. https://doi.org/10.1901/jeab.2007.87-337

Hamdi, A., Porter, J., & Chandan, P. (1992). Decreased striatal D2 dopamine receptors in obese Zucker rats: Changes during aging. *Brain Research, 589*(2), 338−340. https://doi.org/10.1016/0006-8993(92)91296-Q

Hayes, D. J., & Greenshaw, A. J. (2011). 5-HT receptors and reward-related behaviour: A review. *Neuroscience & Biobehavioral Reviews, 35*(6), 1419−1449. https://doi.org/10.1016/j.neubiorev.2011.03.005

Helms, C. M., Reeves, J. M., & Mitchell, S. H. (2006). Impact of strain and D-amphetamine on impulsivity (delay discounting) in inbred mice. *Psychopharmacology, 188*(1), 144−151. https://doi.org/10.1007/s00213-006-0478-0

Hendrickson, K. L., Rasmussen, E. B., & Lawyer, S. R. (2015). Measurement and validation of measures for impulsive food choice across obese and healthy-weight individuals. *Appetite, 90*(1), 254−263. https://doi.org/10.1016/j.appet.2015.03.015

Homberg, J. R. (2012). Serotonin and decision-making processes. *Neuroscience & Biobehavioral Reviews, 36*(1), 218−236. https://doi.org/10.1016/j.neubiorev.2011.06.001

Huskinson, S. L., Krebs, C. A., & Anderson, K. G. (2012). Strain differences in delay discounting between Lewis and Fischer 344 rats at baseline and following acute and chronic administration of d-amphetamine. *Pharmacology Biochemistry and Behavior, 101*(3), 403−416. https://doi.org/10.1016/j.pbb.2012.02.005

Huskinson, S. L., Woolverton, W. L., Green, L., Myerson, J., & Freeman, K. B. (2015). Delay discounting of food by rhesus monkeys: Cocaine and food choice in isomorphic and allomorphic situations. *Experimental and Clinical Psychopharmacology, 23*(3), 184−193. https://doi.org/10.1037/pha0000018

Johnson, P. M., & Kenny, P. J. (2010). Dopamine D2 receptors in addiction-like reward dysfunction and compulsive eating in obese rats. *Nature Neuroscience, 13*(5), 635−641. https://doi.org/10.1038/nn.2519

Johnson, P. R., Zucker, L. M., Cruce, J. A. F., & Hirsch, J. (1971). Cellularity of adipose depots in the genetically obese Zucker rat. *Journal of Lipid Research, 12*(6), 706−714. https://doi.org/10.1016/S0022-2275(20)39459-1

Kim, B., Yoon, S., Nakajima, R., Lee, H. J., Lim, H. J., Lee, Y. K., … Baik, J. H. (2018). Dopamine D2 receptor-mediated circuit from the central amygdala to the bed nucleus of the stria terminalis regulates impulsive behavior. *Proceedings of the National Academy of Sciences of the United States of America, 115*(45), E10730−E10739. https://doi.org/10.1073/pnas.1811664115

Kirby, K. N., & Marakovic, N. N. (1996). Delay-discounting probabilistic rewards: Rates decrease as amounts increase. *Psychonomic Bulletin & Review, 33*(1), 100−104. https://doi.org/10.3758/BF03212320

Kollins, S. H. (2003). Delay discounting is associated with substance use in college students. *Addictive Behaviors, 28*(6), 1167−1173. https://doi.org/10.1016/S0306-4603(02)00220-4

Landes, R. D., Christensen, D. R., & Bickel, W. K. (2012). Delay discounting decreases in those completing treatment for opioid dependence. *Experimental and Clinical Psychopharmacology, 20*(3), 184−193. https://doi.org/10.1037/a0027391

Lawyer, S. R., & Mahoney, C. T. (2017). Delay discounting and probability discounting, but not response inhibition, are associated with sexual risk-taking in adults. *The Journal of Sex Research, 55*(2), 1−10. https://doi.org/10.1080/00224499.2017.1350627

Lee, B., London, E. D., Poldrack, R. A., Farahi, J., Nacca, A., Monterosso, J. R., … Mandelkern, M. A. (2009). Striatal dopamine D2/D3 receptor availability is reduced in methamphetamine dependence and is linked to impulsivity. *Journal of Neuroscience, 29*(47), 14734−14740. https://doi.org/10.1523/JNEUROSCI.3765-09.2009

Logue, A. W., Tobin, H., Chelonis, J. J., Wang, R. Y., Geary, N., & Schachter, S. (1992). Cocaine decreases self-control in rats: A preliminary report. *Psychopharmacology, 109*(2), 245−247. https://doi.org/10.1007/BF02245509

Maguire, D. R., Henson, C., & France, C. P. (2014). Effects of amphetamine on delay discounting in rats depend upon the manner in which delay is varied. *Neuropharmacology, 87*, 173−179. https://doi.org/10.1016/j.neuropharm.2014.04.012

Mazur, J. E. (1987). An adjusting procedure for studying delayed reinforcement. In M. L. Commons, J. E. Mazur, J. A. Nevin, & H. Rachlin (Eds.), *Quantitative analyses of behavior: Vol. 5. The effect of delay and of intervening events on reinforcement value* (pp. 55−73). Lawrence Erlbaum Associates.

Mazur, J. E. (2000). Tradeoffs among delay, rate, and amount of reinforcement. *Behavioural Processes, 49*(1), 1−10. https://doi.org/10.1016/s0376-6357(00)00070-x

Mazur, J. E., & Biondi, D. R. (2009). Delay-amount tradeoffs in choices by pigeons and rats: Hyperbolic versus exponential discounting. *Journal of the Experimental Analysis of Behavior, 91*(2), 197−211. https://doi.org/10.1901/jeab.2009.91-197

Meguid, M., Fetissov, S., Blaha, V., & Yang, J. (2000). Dopamine and serotonin VMN release is related to feeding status in obese and lean Zucker rats. *NeuroReport, 11*(9), 2069−2072.

Mitchell, S. H. (2019). Linking delay discounting and substance use disorders: Genotypes and phenotypes. *Perspectives on Behavior Science, 42*(3), 419−432. https://doi.org/10.1007/s40614-019-00218-x

Miyazaki, K., Miyazaki, K. W., & Doya, K. (2012). The role of serotonin in the regulation of patience and impulsivity. *Molecular Neurobiology, 45*(2), 213−224. https://doi.org/10.1007/s12035-012-8232-6

Mobini, S., Body, S., Ho, M.-Y., Bradshaw, C. M., Szabadi, E., Deakin, J. F. W., & Anderson, I. M. (2002). Effects of lesions of the orbitofrontal cortex on sensitivity to delayed and probabilistic reinforcement. *Psychopharmacology, 160*(3), 290−298. https://doi.org/10.1007/s00213-001-0983-0

Mobini, S., Chiang, T.-J., Ho, M.-Y., Bradshaw, C. M., & Szabadi, E. (2000). Effects of central 5-hydroxytryptamine depletion on sensitivity to delayed and probabilistic reinforcement. *Psychopharmacology, 152*(4), 390−397. https://doi.org/10.1007/s002130000532

Mocsary, Z., & Bradberry, C. W. (1996). Effect of ethanol on extracellular dopamine in nucleus accumbens: Comparison between Lewis and Fischer 344 rat strains. *Brain Research, 706*(2), 194−198. https://doi.org/10.1016/0006-8993(95)01200-1

Moreno, M., Azocar, V., Vergés, A., & Fuentealba, J. A. (2021). High impulsive choice is accompanied by an increase in dopamine release in rat dorsolateral striatum. *Behavioural Brain Research, 405*, Article 113199. https://doi.org/10.1016/j.bbr.2021.113199

Moschak, T. M., & Mitchell, S. H. (2014). Partial inactivation of nucleus accumbens core decreases delay discounting in rats without affecting sensitivity to delay or magnitude. *Behavioural Brain Research, 268*, 159−168. https://doi.org/10.1016/j.bbr.2014.03.044

Oliveira, L., Green, L., & Myerson, J. (2014). Pigeons' delay discounting functions established using a concurrent-chains procedure. *Journal of the Experimental Analysis of Behavior, 102*(2), 151−161. https://doi.org/10.1002/jeab.97

Ong, E. L., & White, K. G. (2004). Amount-dependent temporal discounting? *Behavioural Processes, 66*(3), 201−212. https://doi.org/10.1016/j.beproc.2004.03.007

Opland, D. M., Leinninger, G. M., & Myers, M. G. (2010). Modulation of the mesolimbic dopamine system by leptin. *Brain Research, 1350*, 65−70. https://doi.org/10.1016/j.brainres.2010.04.028

Orduña, V., Valencia-Torres, L., Cruz, G., & Bouzas, A. (2013). Sensitivity to delay is affected by magnitude of reinforcement in rats. *Behavioural Processes, 98*, 18−24. https://doi.org/10.1016/j.beproc.2013.05.010

Orsini, C. A., Mitchell, M. R., Heshmati, S. C., Shimp, K. G., Spurrell, M. S., Bizon, J. L., & Setlow, B. (2017). Effects of nucleus accumbens amphetamine administration on performance in a delay discounting task. *Behavioural Brain Research, 321*, 130−136. https://doi.org/10.1016/j.bbr.2017.01.001

Perry, J. L., Larson, E. B., German, J. P., Madden, G. J., & Carroll, M. E. (2005). Impulsivity (delay discounting) as a predictor of acquisition of IV cocaine self-administration in female rats. *Psychopharmacology, 178*(2−3), 193−201. https://doi.org/10.1007/s00213-004-1994-4

Perry, J. L., Stairs, D. J., & Bardo, M. T. (2008). Impulsive choice and environmental enrichment: Effects of d-amphetamine and methylphenidate. *Behavioural Brain Research, 193*(1), 48−54. https://doi.org/10.1016/j.bbr.2008.04.019

Pitts, R. C., & McKinney, A. P. (2005). Effects of methylphenidate and morphine on delay-discount functions obtained within sessions. *Journal of the Experimental Analysis of Behavior, 83*(3), 297−314. https://doi.org/10.1901/jeab.2005.47-04

Rachlin, H., Raineri, A., & Cross, D. (1991). Subjective probability and delay. *Journal of the Experimental Analysis of Behavior, 55*(2), 233−244. https://doi.org/10.1901/jeab.1991.55-233

Rasmussen, E. B., & Hillman, C. (2011). Rimonabant and naloxone attenuate the reinforcing properties of exercise. *Experimental and Clinical Psychopharmacology, 19*(5), 389−400. https://doi.org/10.1037/a0024142

Rasmussen, E. B., & Huskinson, S. (2008). Effects of rimonabant on behavior maintained by progressive ratio schedules of sucrose reinforcement in obese Zucker (fa/fa) rats. *Behavioural Pharmacology, 19*(8), 735−742. https://doi.org/10.1097/FBP.0b013e3283123cc2

Rasmussen, E. B., Robertson, S., & Rodriguez, L. (2016). The utility of behavioral economics: Expanding the free-feed model of obesity. *Behavioural Processes, 127*, 25−34. https://doi.org/10.1016/j.beproc.2016.02.014

Reynolds, B., De Wit, H., & Richards, J. B. (2002). Delay of gratification and delay discounting in rats. *Behavioural Processes, 59*(3), 157−168. https://doi.org/10.1016/S0376-6357(02)00096-3

Richards, J. B., Mitchell, S. H., de Wit, H., & Seiden, L. S. (1997). Determination of discount functions in rats with an adjusting-amount procedure. *Journal of the Experimental Analysis of Behavior, 67*(3), 353−366. https://doi.org/10.1901/jeab.1997.67-353

Richards, J. B., Sabol, K. E., & de Wit, H. (1999). Effects of methamphetamine on the adjusting amount procedure, a model of impulsive behavior in rats. *Psychopharmacology, 146*(4), 432−439. https://doi.org/10.1007/PL00005488

Robertson, S., & Rasmussen, E. B. (2017). Effects of a cafeteria diet and age of onset on delay discounting and dopaminergic sensitivity. *Journal of Psychopharmacology, 31*(11), 1419−1429. https://doi.org/10.1177/0269881117735750

Sanchez-Roige, S., Barnes, S. A., Mallari, J., Wood, R., Polesskaya, O., & Palmer, A. A. (2022). A mutant allele of glycoprotein M6-B (Gpm6b) facilitates behavioral flexibility but increases delay discounting. *Genes, Brain and Behavior, 21*(4), Article e12800. https://doi.org/10.1111/gbb.12800

Sanchez-Roige, S., Fontanillas, P., Elson, S. L., et al. (2018). Genome-wide association study of delay discounting in 23,217 adult research participants of European ancestry. *Nature Neuroscience, 21*(1), 16−18. https://doi.org/10.1038/s41593-017-0032-x

Sarmiento, L. F., Ríos-Flórez, J. A., Paez-Ardila, H. A., Lima de Sousa, P. S., Olivera-La Rosa, A., Oliveira da Silva, A. M. H., & Gouveia, A., Jr. (2023). Pharmacological modulation of temporal discounting: A systematic review. *Healthcare, 11*(7), 1046. https://doi.org/10.3390/healthcare11071046

Sjoberg, E., Ottåsen, H. M., Wilner, R. G., & Johansen, E. B. (2023). Previous experience with delays affects delay discounting in an animal model of ADHD. *Behavioral and Brain Functions, 19*(1), 1−10. https://doi.org/10.1186/s12993-022-00199-z

Slezak, J. M., & Anderson, K. G. (2009). Effects of variable training, signaled and unsignaled delays, and d-amphetamine on delay-discounting functions. *Behavioural Pharmacology, 20*(5−6), 424−436. https://doi.org/10.1097/FBP.0b013e3283305ef9

Smith, S., & Rasmussen, E. B. (2010). Effects of 2-AG on the reinforcing properties of exercise in lean and obese Zucker rats. *Behavioural Pharmacology, 21*(3), 292−300. https://doi.org/10.1097/FBP.0b013e32833aec4d

Stanger, C., Ryan, S. R., Fu, H., Landes, R. D., & Jones, B. A. (2012). Delay discounting predicts adolescent substance abuse treatment outcome. *Experimental and Clinical Psychopharmacology, 20*(3), 205−212. https://doi.org/10.1037/a0027352

Stevens, J. R., Hallinan, E. V., & Hauser, M. D. (2005). The ecology and evolution of patience in two New World monkeys. *Biology Letters, 1*(2), 223−226. https://doi.org/10.1098/rsbl.2004.0285

Stice, E., Spoor, S., Ng, J., & Zald, D. H. (2009). Relation of obesity to consummatory and anticipatory food reward. *Physiology & Behavior, 97*(5), 551−560. https://doi.org/10.1016/j.physbeh.2009.03.020

Stice, E., Yokum, S., Blum, K., & Bohon, C. (2010). Weight gain is associated with reduced striatal response to palatable food. *Journal of Neuroscience, 30*(39), 13105−13109. https://doi.org/10.1523/JNEUROSCI.2105-10.2010

Tanno, T., Maguire, D. R., Henson, C., & France, C. P. (2014). Effects of amphetamine and methylphenidate on delay discounting in rats: Interactions with order of delay presentation. *Psychopharmacology, 231*(1), 85−95. https://doi.org/10.1007/s00213-013-3209-3

Tarantino, Q. (1994). Pulp fiction [film]. *Miramax Films*.

Tate, L. M. (2015). Temporal discounting rates and their relation to exercise behavior in older adults. *Physiology & Behavior, 152*, 295−299. https://doi.org/10.1016/j.physbeh.2015.10.026

Tedford, S. E., Persons, A. L., & Napier, T. C. (2015). Dopaminergic lesions of the dorsolateral striatum in rats increase delay discounting in an impulsive choice task. *PLoS One, 10*(4), Article e0122063. https://doi.org/10.1371/journal.pone.0122063

Val-Laillet, D., Layec, S., Guérin, S., Meurice, P., & Malbert, C. H. (2011). Changes in brain activity after a diet-induced obesity. *Obesity, 19*(4), 749−756. https://doi.org/10.1038/oby.2010.292

Valencia-Torres, L., Olarte-Sánchez, C. M., da Costa Araújo, S., Body, S., Bradshaw, C. M., & Szabadi, E. (2012). Nucleus accumbens and delay discounting in rats: Evidence from a new quantitative protocol for analysing inter-temporal choice. *Psychopharmacology, 219*(1), 271−283. https://doi.org/10.1007/s00213-011-2459-1

van Gaalen, M. M., van Koten, R., Schoffelmeer, A. N., & Vanderschuren, L. J. (2006). Critical involvement of dopaminergic neurotransmission in impulsive decision making. *Biological Psychiatry, 60*(1), 66−73. https://doi.org/10.1016/j.biopsych.2005.06.005

Vanderveldt, A., Oliveira, L., & Green, L. (2016). Delay discounting: Pigeon, rat, human—does it matter? *Journal of Experimental Psychology: Animal Learning and Cognition, 42*(2), 141−162. https://doi.org/10.1037/xan0000097

Vucetic, Z., Carlin, J. L., Totoki, K., & Reyes, T. M. (2012). Epigenetic dysregulation of the dopamine system in diet-induced obesity. *Journal of Neurochemistry, 120*(6), 891−898. https://doi.org/10.1111/j.1471-4159.2012.07649.x

Wade, T. R., de Wit, H., & Richards, J. B. (2000). Effects of dopaminergic drugs on delayed reward as a measure of impulsive behavior in rats. *Psychopharmacology, 150*(1), 90−101. https://doi.org/10.1007/s002130000402

Wagner, B., Clos, M., Sommer, T., & Peters, J. (2020). Dopaminergic modulation of human intertemporal choice: A diffusion model analysis using the D2-receptor antagonist haloperidol. *Journal of Neuroscience, 40*(41), 7936−7948. https://doi.org/10.1523/JNEUROSCI.0592-20.2020

Washio, Y., Higgins, S. T., Heil, S. H., McKerchar, T. L., Badger, G. J., Skelly, J. M., & Dantona, R. L. (2011). Delay discounting is associated with treatment response among cocaine-dependent outpatients. *Experimental and Clinical Psychopharmacology, 19*(3), 205−212. https://doi.org/10.1037/a0023664

Weber, S. C., Beck-Schimmer, B., Kajdi, M. E., Müller, D., Tobler, P. N., & Quednow, B. B. (2016). Dopamine D2/3- and μ-opioid receptor antagonists reduce cue-induced responding and reward impulsivity in humans. *Translational Psychiatry, 6*(7), e850. https://doi.org/10.1038/tp.2016.113

Wilhelm, C. J., & Mitchell, S. H. (2009). Strain differences in delay discounting using inbred rats. *Genes, Brain and Behavior, 8*(4), 426−434. https://doi.org/10.1111/j.1601-183X.2009.00484.x

Winstanley, C. A., Dalley, J. W., Theobald, D. E., & Robbins, T. W. (2003). Global 5-HT depletion attenuates the ability of amphetamine to decrease impulsive choice on a delay-discounting task in rats. *Psychopharmacology, 170*(3), 320−331. https://doi.org/10.1007/s00213-003-1546-3

Winstanley, C. A., Theobald, D. E., Dalley, J. W., & Robbins, T. W. (2005). Interactions between serotonin and dopamine in the control of impulsive choice in rats: Therapeutic implications for impulse control disorders. *Neuropsychopharmacology, 30*(4), 669−682. https://doi.org/10.1038/sj.npp.1300610

Zucker, L. M., & Zucker, T. F. (1961). Fatty, a new mutation in the rat. *Journal of Heredity, 52*(6), 275−278. https://doi.org/10.1093/oxfordjournals.jhered.a107093

Further reading

Green, L., Fry, A. F., & Myerson, J. (1994). Discounting of delayed rewards: A life-span comparison. *Psychological Science, 5*(1), 33−36. https://doi.org/10.1111/j.1467-9280.1994.tb00610.x

Green, L., & Myerson, J. (1996). Exponential versus hyperbolic discounting of delayed outcomes: Risk and waiting time. *American Zoologist, 36*(4), 496−505. https://doi.org/10.1093/icb/36.4.496

Herrnstein, R. J. (1961). Relative and absolute strength of response as a function of frequency of reinforcement. *Journal of the Experimental Analysis of Behavior, 4*, 267−272.

Holt, D. D., Green, L., & Myerson, J. (2003). Is discounting impulsive? Evidence from temporal and probability discounting in gambling and non-gambling college students. *Behavioural Processes, 64*(3), 355−367. https://doi.org/10.1016/S0376-6357(03)00141-4

Koffarnus, M. N., Newman, A. H., Grundt, P., Rice, K. C., & Woods, J. H. (2011). Effects of selective dopaminergic compounds on a delay discounting task. *Behavioural Pharmacology, 22*(4), 300–309. https://doi.org/10.1097/FBP.0b013e3283473bcb

Madden, G. J., & Johnson, P. S. (2010). A discounting primer. In G. J. Madden, & W. K. Bickel (Eds.), *Impulsivity: The behavioral and neurological science of discounting* (pp. 11–37). American Psychological Association. https://doi.org/10.1037/12069-001

McKerchar, T. L., & Renda, C. R. (2012). Delay and probability discounting in humans: An overview. *Psychological Record, 62*(4), 817–834. https://doi.org/10.1007/BF03395837

Mitchell, S. H. (2011). The genetic basis of delay discounting and its genetic relationship to alcohol dependence. *Behavioural Processes, 87*(1), 10–17. https://doi.org/10.1016/j.beproc.2011.02.008

Reynolds, B., Richards, J. B., Horn, K., & Karraker, K. (2004). Delay discounting and probability discounting as related to cigarette smoking status in adults. *Behavioural Processes, 65*(1), 35–42. https://doi.org/10.1016/S0376-6357(03)00109-8

Robertson, S., Boomhower, S. R., & Rasmussen, E. B. (2017). High-fat diet alters weight, caloric intake, and haloperidol sensitivity in the context of effort-based responding. *Behavioural Pharmacology, 28*(5), 323–333. https://doi.org/10.1097/FBP.0000000000000295

Schneider, T. D., Gunville, J. A., Papa, V. B., Brucks, M. G., Daley, C. M., Martin, L. E., & Jarmolowicz, D. P. (2022). Differential probability discounting rates of gamblers in an American Indian population. *Frontiers in Behavioral Neuroscience, 16*, Article 809963. https://doi.org/10.3389/fnbeh.2022.809963

Yates, J. R., Gunkel, B. T., Rogers, K. K., Breitenstein, K. A., Hughes, M. N., Johnson, A. B., & Sharpe, S. M. (2018). Effects of N-methyl-D-aspartate receptor (NMDAr) uncompetitive antagonists in a delay discounting paradigm using a concurrent-chains procedure. *Behavioural Brain Research, 349*, 125–129. https://doi.org/10.1016/j.bbr.2018.04.038

Human research methods for studying discounting

Mikhail N. Koffarnus[1], Mark J. Rzeszutek[1], Haily K. Traxler[2] and Sarah E. Iglehart[1]
[1]Department of Family and Community Medicine, University of Kentucky, Lexington, KY, United States; [2]Department of Behavioral Science, University of Kentucky, Lexington, KY, United States

Discounting processes have seen a very large growth in interest by the research community in recent decades. In response to this growth in interest, discounting tasks have been iterated upon and modified to specific contexts, resulting in a large diversity of tasks. While most discounting tasks share the goal of obtaining a discounting rate, the specific parameters and choice algorithms among tasks vary widely. In this chapter, we describe some of the more common discounting task types and considerations for specific contexts. We end the chapter by providing some general recommendations on choosing among the task types and making analysis choices.

Examples of discounting studied in humans

Multiple processes can affect the reinforcing value of a commodity, and many of these have been modeled in a discounting framework. To help provide some examples and context, we describe some popular areas of discounting research prior to focusing on specific methods used to obtain discounting data.

Delay discounting

Delay discounting assesses the devaluation of future rewards as a function of delay to obtain them. To measure delay discounting, individuals are typically presented with a series of dichotomous choices that measure preference for smaller, sooner (SS) rewards compared to larger, later (LL) rewards. This produces a measure of the rate of devaluation of the LL reward over time. Delay discounting tasks are most commonly administered using an adjusting time or an adjusting-amount procedure (Reynolds, 2006). In the adjusting-time task, participants are offered a choice between a small amount of an immediately available reward and a larger amount of a delayed reward. The delay to obtain the LL reward is manipulated. For example, an individual may be asked to choose between $10 available now versus $100 available across various timepoints (e.g., 1 day, 7 days, and 30 days). In the adjusting-amount task, participants choose between the SS reward and the LL reward, but the magnitude of the SS reward offered is manipulated and the LL reward and delay are held constant. For example, an individual may be asked to choose between various amounts of money available now versus $100 available after a specified timepoint, held constant. The goal of delay discounting tasks is to find the indifference point between the SS and LL rewards, where the SS outcome is equivalent to the LL outcome (Odum & Rainaud, 2003).

Probability discounting

Probability discounting differs from delay discounting in that rewards are devalued due to their delivery being probabilistic instead of certain. In a probability discounting task, participants are presented with a choice between a smaller, certain reward and a larger, uncertain reward (McKercher & Renda, 2012). To find the indifference point between smaller, certain, and larger, uncertain rewards, the magnitude of the certain reward, and the probability of the uncertain reward are manipulated. For example, one set of tasks may involve manipulating the size of the certain reward, such that the certain reward decreases in size while the larger, uncertain reward stays constant (e.g., 100% chance of $50 vs. 50% chance of $100; 100% chance of $30 vs. 50% chance of $100). A different approach to probability discounting involves manipulating the probability of the uncertain reward while holding the certain reward constant (e.g., 100% chance of $50 vs. 95% chance of $100; 100% chance of $50 vs. 75% chance of $100).

Effort discounting

Effort-discounting tasks measure the devaluation of rewards relative to the effort required to obtain them (Białaszek et al., 2019). Effort-discounting tasks often involve participants making decisions based on two outcomes requiring differing efforts. Measuring effort discounting is more complex than measuring delay or probability discounting, as effort is multi-dimensional (Pinkston & Libman, 2017). When developing effort-discounting tasks, one must consider variations in intensity and duration, for example. Additionally, tasks can vary based on the type of effort (i.e., physical or cognitive) (Ostazewski et al., 2013). Effort-discounting tasks may be implemented by manipulating the type of effort exerted, the amount of effort required, and the size of the reward (Ostazewski et al., 2013). For example, participants may be presented with a choice between an outcome (e.g., $10) available with no effort and an outcome (e.g., $50) available after engaging in a physical task (e.g., walking 5 miles) or a cognitive task (e.g., reading 50 pages). The goal of effort discounting tasks is to identify the point at which an effortless reward and the effort required to obtain a larger reward are equal.

Social discounting

Social discounting is often conceptualized as a measure of altruistic decision making based on the social closeness to a participant (Buddiga & Locey, 2021). In social discounting, individuals decide between rewards for themselves and rewards for others based on social distance. Participants are asked to imagine a rank order of people in their life, with Person 1 being the person who they are most close to (e.g., spouse, parent, and child) and each additional person on the list being slightly further in social distance. Then, participants are asked to imagine a scenario in which they have the choice to keep money or give money to another person. Typically, the reward for the other person is kept constant (e.g., $75) while the reward for the participant is varied. The task is repeated by manipulating the social distance of the other person to the participant. The goal of this procedure is to determine the point at which keeping the money is equivalent in value to giving away money for each listed person who varies based on their social distance.

Multiple dimensions

Occasionally, researchers utilize multiple discounting processes within a single task. For example, delay and probability discounting are sometimes combined (e.g., Cox & Dallery, 2016; Yi et al., 2006). In combined delay and probability discounting procedures, participants are given the choice between a smaller immediate, certain reward and a larger reward that is both delayed and probabilistic (e.g., Vanderveldt et al., 2015). Research has shown that combining delay and probability discounting leads to greater changes in discounting rates, such that steeper discounting is observed when outcomes are delayed and probabilistic (Vanderveldt et al., 2015).

In addition to probability, delay discounting has also been combined with social discounting. Combinations of delay and social discounting include asking participants to choose between a reward for themselves after a delay or a reward for another person of varying social distances immediately (Rachlin & Jones, 2008; Belisle et al., 2020) or a reward for themselves immediately or for another person of varying social distances after a delay (Belisle et al., 2020). Other tasks have involved the choice between an immediate reward for themselves or a shared reward after a delay in people who drink alcohol and smoke cigarettes (Bickel et al., 2012), and the choice to send a text to somebody while driving immediately or after a delay relative to social distance (Foreman et al., 2019). Other combinations of delay, probability, social, and effort discounting are possible, though there has been limited research in these areas.

Discounting of monetary versus nonmonetary commodities

Researchers have investigated discounting for a variety of commodities. For example, delay discounting procedures have been used to study the devaluation of money (e.g., Johnson & Bickel, 2002), drugs (e.g., MacKillop et al., 2011), food (e.g., Epstein et al., 2010; Skrynka & Vincent, 2019), and risky sexual behavior (e.g., Berry et al., 2022; Johnson & Bruner, 2012; Koffarnus et al., 2016). In general, the procedures and structure of a discounting task differ by whether the outcome is monetary (including close monetary equivalents such as gift cards) or nonmonetary. Discounting with monetary outcomes is straightforward, as money is nearly universally valued and has a known and easily quantifiable value. For example, researchers can assume that $100 is worth twice as much as $50. Researchers can also assume that both $50 and $100 will function as reinforcers because this money can be exchanged for a wide range of goods and services.

Researchers studying nonmonetary outcomes are sometimes faced with additional challenges compared to monetary outcomes because nonmonetary outcomes may not function as a reinforcer for all participants, and even if they are a reinforcer, may be valued differently by different participants. Many outcomes studied by researchers only serve as reinforcers to a subset of participants. A drug of abuse, for example, may be highly valued to someone who uses that drug regularly but may not be valued to someone who would not use that drug if offered to them for free. Receipt of the drug may even be considered aversive if the person would not be willing to consume it, and also views the prospect of being caught with the drug and/or disposing of it as an undesirable outcome. Most discounting procedures rely on the outcome having value to the participant, so nonsensical outcomes can sometimes be obtained when some portion of participants do not value the outcome of the study. For example, when participants with and without a history of stimulant use completed cocaine delay discounting tasks, the nonusers' data indicated that they did not value cocaine regardless of delay (Wesley et al., 2014). Therefore the calculation of a discounting rate was not possible, as a rate of devaluation from zero (no value) is not calculable.

Comparing discounting rates for nonmonetary rewards to other commodities can also be a challenge when the value of a nonmonetary reward can differ dramatically from person to person. This is because discounting rates are systematically associated with the amount of the commodity being discounted (Green et al., 2013). If a researcher would like to know if discounting rates for delayed candy differ from rates for delayed money, they will first need to know how much candy is worth when not delayed to control for the overall amount of reward being offered. If both the amount of reward and reward type differ at the same time, it will not be knowable which factor is associated with the effect on discounting rate. The value of nonmonetary rewards is often obtained by asking participants how much a given amount of that commodity is worth to them as money (e.g., Odum et al., 2006), although one must also be aware that values of nonmonetary commodities may not be scalable as money. For example, nonfungible or perishable commodities (see Holt et al., 2016) may only hold their value in small amounts, with large amounts that cannot be reasonably consumed holding little incremental value.

Hypothetical outcomes versus real outcomes

Tasks that are used in discounting research can be categorized by whether participants imagine the outcomes (i.e., hypothetical tasks) or experience the outcomes (i.e., operant or "real" tasks) of each choice. Hypothetical tasks measure imaginary rewards or outcomes through question-based measures (Robertson & Rasmussen, 2018). Hypothetical tasks involve presenting questions with imaginary scenarios involving choice preference to a participant (Reynolds, 2006). Like in the examples of different forms of discounting described earlier, these are typically questions that assess an individual's preference between monetary, food, and drug choices across delayed amounts of time. An example of a hypothetical task involving monetary rewards would be: "Would you prefer: $100 in 30 days or $20 now?" Another tool researchers use to study discounting is an operant task. In operant tasks, also referred to as real-reward and real-time tasks, participants are able to receive actual rewards and experience real-time delays (Steele et al., 2019). The rewards received and delays experienced in operant tasks are chosen by participants based on preference questions presented to each individual before the task begins.

Hypothetical and operant tasks both have advantages and disadvantages. Hypothetical tasks are often used for ethical or practical reasons (Hinvest & Anderson, 2010). For example, ethical reasons, such as when preferences for large amounts of money or drugs are assessed. Hypothetical tasks can also be more cost-efficient when researchers are studying discounting with larger monetary amounts. Another advantage of researchers utilizing hypothetical tasks is that questions asked to assess discounting typically test differences between longer and shorter delays of time, therefore making discounting studies time-consuming (Green & Lawyer, 2014). With the use of hypothetical tasks, researchers can substantially decrease the amount of time discounting studies take because the amounts of delayed time are hypothetical scenarios instead of real scenarios. Research has also shown that results of tasks with real and hypothetical outcomes generally have high correspondence (Madden et al., 2003), which can cause researchers to determine that the advantages of hypothetical tasks outweigh the disadvantages.

Delay discounting tasks are administered in a variety of formats, including hypothetical, real-world, and real-time tasks (Reynolds, 2006). Hypothetical delay discounting tasks require participants to imagine their preferred choice between SS and LL rewards, but choices do not result in actual rewards. Hypothetical delay discounting tasks allow for the analysis of behaviors that are typically difficult to study for practical or ethical reasons. "Real" discounting tasks were developed to improve the face validity of hypothetical discounting tasks (Reynolds, 2006). In real discounting, the delay and outcomes are actually experienced. Participants make choices between SS and LL rewards, and one randomly selected choice is honored. Therefore the participant receives one of their selections either immediately or after a delay. Real-time procedures involve participants experiencing the conditions in real time and with real rewards while completing the assessment.

Real and hypothetical outcomes take on different forms depending on the discounting process being studied. Realized delays require participants waiting for the outcome in accordance with the delay specified in the task (Madden et al., 2003). Probability discounting tasks with real outcomes have been used to study behaviors such as gambling (e.g., Kyonka & Schutte, 2018), legal and nonlegal outcomes (e.g., Weatherly et al., 2012), sexual behavior (e.g., Lawyer, 2008; Lawyer et al., 2010), and substance use (e.g., Acuff et al., 2023). For effort discounting, hypothetical tasks require participants to predict their choices as if effort were required to obtain the reward. Real-effort tasks require participants to engage in the specified effort to obtain the reward. This is often achieved by randomly selecting one of the participant's choices on the task and requiring them to engage in the task to obtain the reward (e.g., Malesza, 2019). Effort discounting has been studied under a range of motivating conditions, including sleep deprivation (e.g., Boland et al., 2022; Libedinsky et al., 2013), hunger (e.g., Brassard & Balodis, 2021), nicotine withdrawal (e.g., Mitchell, 2004), or following a gain or loss (e.g., Massar et al., 2020). Real and hypothetical tasks may also be used to study social discounting. Real tasks often involve laboratory-based procedures and involve collaboration between participants (e.g., Locey et al., 2013). However, hypothetical tasks allow researchers to study altruistic behaviors under a wide range of conditions, including difficult to study behaviors like giving and receiving pain (Story et al., 2020) or helping in a cyberbullying situation (Hayashi & Tahmasbi, 2020).

Methods of obtaining indifference points

While not a complete list of every task used to obtain indifference points, the following is a brief overview of studies that either introduced or popularized different categories of discounting methods and how they arrive at indifference points used in behavior analytic research in discounting processes. Most of these tasks have been developed with monetary discounting, although most of the procedures described have been or could be extended to other commodities. Because most of the research on discounting in humans has used hypothetical outcomes rather than real outcomes, most of the methods overviewed are hypothetical discounting tasks.

Fixed ascending/descending procedure

Rachlin et al. (1991) was one of the first to develop a task to assess discount rates via indifference points using an ascending/descending binary-choice procedure. See Fig. 9.1 for a depiction of a delay discounting scenario and a probability discounting scenario for this task. In this task, participants are presented with a series of options in either an ascending or descending order; in the case of Rachlin et al. (1991) 30 monetary options ($1,000, $990, $980, $960, $940, $920, $900, $850, $800, $750, $700, $650, $600, $550, $500, $450, $400, $350, $300, $250, $200, $150, $100, $80, $60,

Human research methods for studying discounting 211

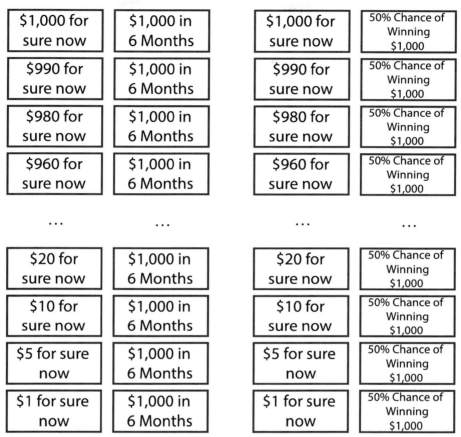

Figure 9.1 Example of how options might be presented to participants based on methods from Rachlin et al. (1991). Each pair of options of either delay (left pairs) or probability (right pairs) would be presented in either an ascending or descending order. Participants would then select the option of the pair they preferred and then presented with the next smaller sooner/certain amount in the sequence. The ellipses indicate pairs in the sequence between the higher and lower values.

$40, $20, $10, $5, or $1), available immediately or for certain, while having a fixed option of $1000 at either some delay (1 month, 6 months, 1 year, 5 years, 10 years, 25 years, and 50 years) or at some probability (95%, 90%, 70%, 50%, 30%, 10%, and 5%). Participants would always start with the larger option at the lowest delay or highest probability, and complete options in sequence to the highest delay or lowest probability after an indifference point was determined at each delay or probability. Each immediate/certain option was presented to participants on cards, and they would point to their preferred option between the immediate/relative monetary outcome to the delayed/uncertain monetary outcome.

The indifference point was determined by the switch point in preference between the immediate/certain outcome relative to the delayed/uncertain outcome. For Rachlin et al. (1991), switching was defined as selecting the non-preferred alternative for two choices in a row. The average value before and the value after a participant switched was their indifference point. For example, if a participant was completing the 1-month delay condition and selected the immediate $1,000, $990, $980, $940, $920, and $900, then selected the larger delayed option ($1000 in 1 month) at $850, their indifference point for the 1-month delay condition would be $875, the average between $900 and $850. In this procedure, participants are expected to complete all options for each delay/probability/factor. In the case of Rachlin et al. (1991), this results in 60 binary choices, 30 up and 30 down, for each of the seven delays/probabilities, resulting in 420 choices to produce seven indifference points for each factor. Variants of this procedure have been used to identify differences in discount rates in individuals with opioid dependence between monetary rewards and opioid rewards (Madden et al., 1999), and similarities between discount rates of real and hypothetical monetary rewards (Madden et al., 2003). Of all methods discussed in this section, this procedure is typically the most time-consuming hypothetical task as it requires the highest number of trials to obtain indifference points.

Adjusting amount

Du et al. (2002) created an algorithm to determine indifference points based on adjusting the amount of the smaller sooner outcome relative to a fixed, delayed outcome. Du et al. (2002) conducted a procedure for both delay and probability discounting where seven delays to (1 month, 3 months, 9 months, 2 years, 5 years, 10 years, and 20 years) and seven probabilities of (95%, 90%, 70%, 50%, 30%, 10%, and 5%) were assessed at magnitudes of $200 and $10,000. To determine indifference points for each delay or probability, participants would be initially presented with a choice between, for example, $5000 now or $10,000 in 2 years. Depending on the participant's choice, the smaller amount would increase by half the difference between it and the larger option if the larger option was selected or decrease by half the difference between the smaller and larger option. After the first choice, the remaining increases and decreases were half the amount of the last increase/decrease. For example, if during the first choice the participant chose the fixed, larger option in the $10,000 condition, the immediate choice would increase to $7500. If the participant then chose the smaller immediate option, the smaller option would decrease to $6,250, half of the original difference between options (i.e., $1,250, half of $2500). The next choice would either decrease the smaller amount to $5,925, or increase it to $6,875 (i.e., $625, half of $1250). This process would continue so that participants would make a total of six choices. This adjustment to the smaller immediate amount would then be made for a seventh time, which results in the indifference point for that condition. This decreased the number of choices a participant would be required to make relative to the ascending/descending procedure (Rachlin et al., 1991) from 60 choices per delay to 6.

Johnson and Bickel (2002) also created an algorithm for determining indifference points for both real and hypothetical rewards based on adjusting the smaller sooner value but was based on a system of inner and outer upper and lower limits based on participant responding. Fig. 9.2 depicts a schematic of this task. The larger delay amount was at a fixed value ($10, $25, $100, and $250 for possible real rewards and $1000 and $2500 for additional hypothetical rewards) and delay (1 day, 1 week, 2 weeks, 1 month, and 6 months). The initial value of the smaller immediate amount reward was determined by a computer as a multiple of 2% of the larger value that was between the inner and outer upper limits (set at the undiscounted value) and the inner and outer-lower limits (initially set at $0). Briefly, a choice for the smaller reward would set the outer upper limit to the inner lower limit, and then the inner lower limit would be set to the smaller reward's value. If the inner lower limit was greater than the smaller reward, then the inner lower limit was also set to the smaller reward's value, and the outer-lower limit was set to 0. If the smaller reward was not lower than the inner lower limit, then the outer and lower limits would remain the same. The same logic was applied if the larger reward was chosen. Once the outer limits converged to where the difference between the outer lower and outer upper limits was within a difference of 2% or less of the larger reward, that value was considered the indifference point for that delay.

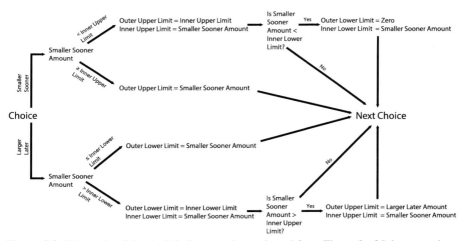

Figure 9.2 Schematic of the dual-limits procedure, adapted from Figure 9 of Johnson and Bickel (2002). Based on a choice of the smaller sooner (top half) or of the larger later (bottom half), the limits will change based on this algorithm. This algorithm continues until both outer limits (lower and upper) are within 2% of the larger later amount. The smaller sooner amount for the next choice is a random value that is within the range of the outer limits. The " = " can be read as "set to."

Adjusting delay

Green et al. (1994) used a binary choice procedure to determine preference reversals that would adjust the delays to the smaller outcome and/or larger outcome depending on participant choice. Contrasted to the ascending/descending procedure, participants were presented with binary choices between $20 and $50, $100 and $250, and $500 and $1250. The smaller reward was available either immediately or after 1 week, 2 weeks, 1 month, 3 months, 6 months, 1 year, 2 years, 3 years, 5 years, 7 years, 10 years, 12 years, 15 years, 17 years, or 20 years. The larger reward was available at the delay of the smaller reward and an additional delay of 1 week, 1 month, 3 months, 6 months, 1 year, 3 years, 5 years, 7 years, 10 years, 15 years, or 20 years. The experimenter would begin by presenting choices between the smaller more immediate reward and increasing the larger later reward until the participant chose the smaller sooner reward. At this point, the delay to the smaller reward increased, while the delay to the larger reward increased to its previous delay plus the delay to the smaller reward. For example, if a participant switched their choice to the smaller monetary amount once the larger amount was delayed by 6 months, both the smaller and larger rewards would increase by 1 week (larger delay is now 6 months and 1 week), then 2 weeks (larger delay is now 6 months and 2 weeks), 1 month (larger delay is now 7 months), and continue until the participant switched back to the larger amount for two consecutive selections. After this, the delay to the smaller reward would reset to immediate, while the larger reward would be delayed to the next longer delay based on what was previously achieved.

Koffarnus and Bickel (2014) designed a 5-trial adjusting delay task that was meant to identify the delay that corresponded with the larger later reward being discounted by 50% of its original value, otherwise referred to as Effective Delay 50 (ED50, Yoon & Higgins, 2008). Mathematically, the ED50 is simply the inverse of k (i.e., $1/k$) when using Mazur's hyperbolic equation (Mazur, 1987). In the task, participants make five choices between a smaller immediate reward and an adjusting delayed reward, where the smaller reward is always 50% of the amount of the larger reward. In the Koffarnus and Bickel (2014) task, there are 31 indexes, which correspond to approximately 31 evenly spaced delays in logarithmic units between 1 hour and 25 years that the later reward can delayed by. If a participant selected the delayed option on the first trial, its delay would increase by eight delay increments. Conversely, if a participant selected the immediate option, the delay to the larger option would decrease in the same manner. In subsequent trials, the delay increment adjustment decreases by half each trial, from 8 to 4, to 2 to 1 on the fifth and final trial. This is a conceptually similar algorithm to Du et al. (2002) but indexes are halved between bounded delays rather than amounts. Participants begin at index 16 (the center index, of which there are 15 indexes above and below with approximately evenly spaced logarithmic delays), which is associated with a delay of 3 weeks. If a participant chose the delayed option, on the next trial the larger outcome's delay would be the one at index 24, which is 2 years. If the participant then selected the immediate option, the next trial would have a larger outcome delay at index 20. If the participant then selected the larger option, the next trial would be at the index. If the next choice is the smaller option, the participant would be presented with the final options at index 21, and their last choice at this index determines their ED50 value, which is the geometric mean of the delay values at the last choice and one above or one below depending on the final choice. This task is correlated with adjusting-amount tasks (e.g., Du et al., 2002) but takes about 1/6th of the time to complete. Other versions of the task exist for probability discounting as well as a 6-trial version to allow for more precision (Koffarnus et al., 2021), both of which follow the same logic as the task described previously.

Single-question indifference procedures

Equivalence procedures (e.g., Johnson et al., 2015; Weatherly & Derenne, 2011) are meant to quickly obtain an indifference point by simply asking participants what immediate (or certain) smaller monetary value would be equal to a delayed (or probabilistic) larger monetary value. A question might be framed in this way: "Receiving $1000 after 1 year makes me feel JUST AS GOOD as": where the participant is then able to write in a response (Weatherly & Derenne, 2011), select an option via multiple choice (Weatherly & Derenne, 2011), or using a visual analog scale (VAS; e.g., Johnson et al., 2015). Briefly, a VAS is a bounded scale (e.g., $1 − $1000), where one side of the scale represents the lower bound, and the other side represents the upper bound. Participants then identify on the scale what their equivalent value of the smaller option would be on the scale. This is repeated for each delay (e.g., once at 1 week, 1 month, and 1 year) for the desired number of indifference points. While these procedures are associated with a high amount of nonsystematic data (Rung et al., 2018), they are relatively quick to complete.

The Kirby Monetary Choice Questionnaire

Kirby and Maraković (1995) and Kirby et al. (1999) developed a 21- and 27-item questionnaire, often referred to as the Monetary Choice Questionnaire (MCQ). This task is meant to obtain a series of discount rates by asking a series of questions requiring participants to choose between a smaller immediate (or certain reward) and a larger delayed (or probabilistic) reward at a variety of different delays (or probabilities) and values of small ($25 to $35), medium ($50 to $60), and large ($75 to $85) rewards for the monetary outcomes. There are an equal number of delays for the larger reward ranging from 7 to 186 days. The MCQ then produces three discount rate values, one for each magnitude of reward. Administration of the MCQ is relatively straightforward, as participants simply indicate their choice between two options (e.g., "$34 today" or "$35 186 days from now"). Rather than a single indifference point or set of indifference points being derived, scoring requires associating a single k value to each amount series based on the consistency of participant responding relative to instances of switching on the survey. However, automated scoring systems exist (Kaplan et al., 2016) that can calculate k values and other measures of interest. Each choice itself represents an indifference point, and overall discount rates for each magnitude are determined by the consistency in choices prior to and after switches from the smaller reward to the larger reward.

Single-question discount rates procedures

One of the first empirical studies on temporal discounting was Thaler (1981). In this study, participants were told they won (or were fined) from a lottery and their winnings (or losses) were either able to be withdrawn or fined immediately or could be delayed until later. Participants were then asked what amount the delayed winnings and/or losses would be equivalent to compared to their immediate counterparts. There were four forms used, three of which focused on gains and one assessed losses. Each form was assessed with three different immediate amounts and three different delays, yielding nine questions for each form. Discount rate was determined by the compounded discount rates based on their responses. Chapman and Elstein (1995) conducted a similar procedure, asking what the equivalent value of a delayed (6 months, 1 year, 2 years, and 4 years) amount of money would be, relative to varying magnitudes ($200, $1000, $5000, and $25,000). Discount rates were calculated by determining the annual discount rate based on the equivalent value reported and its delay. Procedurally, these are similar to the single-question indifference procedures described earlier.

Three-choice discount rate

Yoon and Chapman (2016) created a three-option adaptive discount rate measure (ToAD), which is a three-choice algorithm that extends upon two-choice adjusting algorithms. This task does not identify individual indifference points but instead converges on a discounting rate by responses to three different choices across 10 questions: A smaller immediate value, a medium delayed value, and a larger more delayed value. An example would be $100 today for the immediate choice, $110 in a year as the first larger delayed choice, and $115 in 2 years as the second larger delayed choice. Each choice represents a range of possible discount rates. The algorithm in the ToAD narrows the range of possible discount rates presented based on participant responses. Monetary values and delays are dynamically adjusted across the 10 questions to yield a discount rate. Conceptually, the algorithm is similar to the limit procedure described by Johnson and Bickel (2002). However, rather than using both inner- and outer-lower and upper limits, the ToAD just uses a lower and upper limit. Responses for the immediate options increases the limit of presented discounting rates, while responses for the second larger delayed option decreases the limits of presented discounting rates. Responses for the first larger delayed option shrink the range of the limits as these responses indicate that the correct discounting rate is within the

Table 9.1 Logic of next question options for the three-option adaptive discount rare measure (Yoon & Chapman, 2016).

			Previous selection		
			Option 1	Option 2	Option 3
Current selection	Option 1	Next k	Increase	Increase	Increase
		Next r	Expand	Maintain	Shrink
	Option 2	Next k	Maintain	Maintain	Maintain
		Next r	Shrink	Shrink	Shrink
	Option 3	Next k	Decrease	Decrease	Decrease
		Next r	Shrink	Maintain	Expand

General schematic of the logic of how the options of the next three-option choice are presented based off the response to the previous selection (columns) and the current select (rows). Next k indicates what happens to the estimated discount rate (increases, maintains, or decreases), and next r indicates the change to the resolution (i.e., upper and lower boundaries) of the options.
Adapted from Table 9.1 in Yoon, H., & Chapman, G. B. (2016). A closer look at the yardstick: A new discount rate measure with precision and range. *Journal of Behavioral Decision Making*, 29(5), 470–480.

bounds. Table 9.1 presents the general logic of how discount rate and resolution of the questions are changed based on different participant responding in the ToAD task.

Multiple dimensions

Further extensions of the abovementioned methods have been used to study combinations of multiple factors, such as how individuals might discount outcomes that are both delayed and probabilistic. Methods to do so are essentially extensions of studying single factors but with some extra considerations. Vanderveldt et al. (2015) used the adjusting amount procedure of Du et al. (2002) to determine indifference points across combinations of five delays (none, 1 month, 6 months, 2 years, and 5 years) and five probabilities (10%, 25%, 40%, 80%, and 100%) across two magnitudes ($800 and $40,000). Much like in Du et al. (2002), in Vanderveldt et al. (2015) participants were presented with two options, an immediate/certain option at 50% of the value of the larger, fixed delayed/uncertain option. Delay and probability values were adjusted according to the Du et al. (2002) algorithm. Delay and probability combinations were presented in random order. Cox and Dallery (2016) replicated this experiment by extending the 5-trial adjusting delay task (Koffarnus & Bickel, 2014) to a 10-trial variant of the task that combined delay and probability discounting. The logic of the task used in Cox and Dallery (2016) follows the same logic as above but includes both a delay to and probability of the larger outcome. First, participants completed either an adjusting delay or adjusting probability for 5 trials where the alternate factor was fixed. For example, if delay adjusted first, probability would remain fixed at 100%, if probability adjusted first, delay remained fixed at 3 weeks. After these first five trials, the delay/probability selected from the fifth trial was fixed and the other factor was adjusted for the remainder of trials.

A variant of the VAS single-question task was introduced in Rzeszutek et al. (2022) to examine multiple dimensions of discounting. For this task, participants indicated their relative likelihood of selecting between a fixed 99% chance of gaining/losing $500 in 1 week and an X% chance of gaining/losing $1000 in Y delay. On the VAS, the fixed option was always on the left side of the scale, whereas the changing delay and probability were always on the right side. Delay values were 1 week, 6 months, 2 years, 5 years, and 15 years. Probability values were 99%, 80%, 50%, 20%, and 1%. Participants were presented with five questions at a fixed delay, with the probability of the larger outcome decreasing from top to bottom. Delays increased across probability sets. This procedure does not produce indifference points per se, but instead relative likelihoods between the two options presented.

Experiential discounting

Reynolds and Schiffbauer (2004) created an experiential discounting task. It is referred to as experiential since participants will actually experience delays in reward and receive real outcomes in contrast to hypothetical rewards and outcomes. This differs from procedures that compared hypothetical and real rewards (e.g., Johnson & Bickel, 2002; Madden et al., 2003) as those only resulted in a single choice being rewarded rather than every choice. In Reynolds and Schiffbauer (2004), participants completed blocks of choices between $0.30 and an adjusting amount, both of which had a 35% chance of being awarded. The larger amount was delayed by 0, 15, 30, or 60 seconds. Participants began a choice phase by picking either a fixed or an adjusting option. If they chose the fixed option, participants would then be required to wait for the delay, and when given the reward they could "bank" the money. Following banking, the next trial would begin. If they were not awarded the money following the delay, the next trial would begin automatically. After a minimum of 16 choices, participants were required to wait during an inter-block interval to normalize the length of blocks so they could not complete the session sooner based on the choices they made. The smaller, adjusting option would always begin at 50% (i.e., $0.15) of the larger option (i.e., $0.30). If a choice was made on the fixed option, the value of the adjusting option would increase. If a choice was made on the adjusting option, the value of the adjusting option would decrease. The first increase/decrease was 15% of the starting adjusting value rounded to the nearest cent, and each subsequent choice was a 2% less of an increase or decrease from that 15%. That is, the first adjustment was 15% of $0.15, then 13% of $0.15, 11% of 0.15, and so on such that the smallest increase/decrease was 2% of the original 15% of $0.15. Indifference points for this task were determined by choice patterns that held the relative adjusting option value stable over time, a result of a participant alternating between the fixed and adjusting option over six choice trials. The indifference point was then determined by averaging the value of the adjusting amount over those last six choice trials. Similar procedures have also been used comparing discounting between experiential and hypothetical discounting tasks (Smits et al., 2013), and for both real and hypothetical M&Ms with both real and hypothetical delays (Steele et al., 2019).

Discounting tasks for neuroscience research

Delay discounting tasks have become popular in neuroscience research, especially within functional Magnetic Resonance Imaging (fMRI) paradigms. While discounting tasks for behavioral research tend to be primarily concerned with accurately determining a discounting rate, fMRI discounting tasks are typically designed to assess aspects of decision making in an experimentally balanced manner. For example, while individual participants will have differing proportions of choices of immediate and delayed options in a behavioral discounting task, an fMRI discounting task may be structured to try to balance the number of immediate and delayed choices across participants. This is because the fMRI researcher may be interested in comparing neural correlates of immediate and delayed choices, and therefore a task with a balanced number of those choice types will provide more data from each choice type to sample. Furthermore, fMRI researchers are often interested in the neural response to simply seeing choice options separately from making a choice response. Therefore fMRI tasks may temporally separate the choice presentation from the choice response to individually measure both. We have summarized the literature in this area, and presented a novel task designed for fMRI research that attempts to balance the many use cases of fMRI discounting tasks in a time-efficient package (Koffarnus et al., 2017). This task is designed to balance the contribution of different choice trials and likely response types such that researchers have a high degree of flexibility when designing and analyzing fMRI discounting data.

General recommendations

Choosing task type

When choosing a discounting type, one must select the discounting process (e.g., delay and probability) and specific task variant (e.g., adjusting amount and adjusting delay). The discounting process often follows naturally from the research question at hand. However, sometimes researchers are more interested in nonspecific concepts such as "risk" or "impulsivity," which could conceivably relate to more than one type of discounting task. In these cases, researchers should review the literature to see if (1) there are specific discounting processes known to be associated with the conditions under study in the proposed experiment, or (2) there are discounting processes that are known to be associated with the types of behaviors of interest in the proposed experiment, especially if those processes are understudied in the context of interest. In addition, as some task types are brief and can be conducted with little participant burden, choosing more than one discounting process to study can facilitate the exploration of novel associations that were previously unknown.

Choosing a specific task variant often comes down to a tradeoff between administration time and data specificity. In general, longer tasks will generate more data that can sometimes provide more specificity in determining a discounting rate. Some tasks have fallen out of favor among researchers (e.g., Rachlin et al., 1991) as subsequent tasks have been developed that are quicker to administer without sacrificing data quality. When choosing between longer tasks that generate a series of indifference points (e.g., adjusting-amount tasks) and brief tasks that are focused on estimating a discounting rate directly (e.g., 5-trial adjusting delay task, MCQ), one must consider whether obtaining individual indifference points are important to the research question. For example, is the researcher interested in data modeling and assessing the *shape* of discounting, or is the researcher interested in collecting enough data to determine if an individual's responses are logically consistent with one another? If so, then a task that generates indifference points will facilitate the research goals. If there is less interest in these properties, then a brief task may provide a more efficient way of estimating discounting rates.

Choosing task parameters

Once a task type is chosen, some tasks require additional parameters to be chosen by the researcher. These can include the amount of the commodity to be discounted and the increments of the discounting process (e.g., delays and probabilities) that should be evaluated. When choosing an amount, the researcher should take care to choose an amount that is valued by the participant, and that is familiar enough to the participant such that they can make informed decisions in the task. Amounts that are very small may not be valued by the participant enough for the discounting process to be studied accurately. Similarly, participants may be unfamiliar with making decisions about very large amounts of money or may be unwilling or unable to consume very large amounts of consumable goods that they otherwise like (e.g., two strawberries could be a nice treat, while 2000 strawberries could not be consumed before most of them spoiled). Research has corroborated this idea that amounts that are high enough to be meaningful are more likely to reveal a discounting rate that correlates with other known correlates of discounting. Mellis et al. (2017) found that monetary delay discounting did not distinguish between substance users and controls at small amounts (i.e., $0.10 and $1.00). Above those amounts, significant associations were observed, with effect sizes increasing with amounts up to $1000.

The choice of specific increments of the discounting process is sometimes predetermined by the task protocol (e.g., Koffarnus & Bickel, 2014). For some task types such as the popular adjusting-amount task, however, the research can specify any delays or probabilities they would like to study. The choice of this range of delays or probabilities can be informed by previous discounting research with that population, if available. Ideally, one would choose a range of delays that encompasses the ED50 values (ED50 = 1/k) of all or nearly all participants. For a participant population with very high discounting rates, this may require adding shorter delays to the task. Once the range of delays is determined, intermediate delays can be added so that the total number of delays is at least 4, but ideally at least 6. Discounting rates tend to be normally distributed in a population when log-transformed, and for that reason, delays evenly distributed on a logarithmic scale provide the ability to resolve discounting rates better than delays that are poorly distributed on a logarithmic scale (Koffarnus & Kaplan, 2018).

Choosing task reward

Researchers interested in discounting processes are also often faced with the choice between assessing a generalized monetary reward or a nonmonetary reward that is more specific to the population or disease process under study. For example, in a study of adults with alcohol use disorder, is it "better" to include a monetary discounting task or an alcohol discounting task? While often correlated, discounting on general monetary rewards and specific nonmonetary rewards often provide unique associations with other study parameters. Monetary discounting may also provide a discounting rate that is easier to compare across studies and across populations, as it is commonly used and money serves as a reinforcer to most populations. If time allows, one can often learn more about their population by conducting both monetary and a population-specific nonmonetary reward. If time does not allow, the researcher should decide if they are more interested in a general discounting rate (monetary) or population-specific discounting rate (nonmonetary).

Handling nonsystematic responding

Procedures have been proposed to identify nonsystematic responding in discounting tasks. The most common of these is described in Johnson and Bickel (2008). The goal of procedures such as these is to identify a series of choices that is logically inconsistent, thereby indicating that the participant may not understand the instructions of the task or was not answering thoughtfully. Algorithms like that described in Johnson and Bickel (2008) have been used to remove data from an experiment, with only the consistent data retained for analysis and conclusions. While identifying inconsistent data can reveal whether participants understood the task and answered in a way consistent with the researcher's hypotheses, eliminating data based on consistency should be done with caution. Removing inconsistent data will likely serve to increase any effect sizes observed and increase the likelihood of declaring an experimental manipulation statistically significant. The assumptions of statistical inference rely on the inclusion of all participants in a sample who meet inclusion criteria. Eliminating those participants that are most likely to respond counter to a hypothesis may violate those assumptions and artificially increase the likelihood of declaring a null effect statistically significant.

Conclusions

Discounting has seen a large growth in interest in the research community in the past few decades. With this increase in use, researchers have adapted discounting procedures to fit a wide variety of contexts and experimental questions. With this variety comes a great deal of flexibility for researchers interested in novel applications of discounting methods. With carefully chosen task types and parameters, discounting methods should continue being a fruitful source of insight into participants' choice behavior for decades to come.

References

Acuff, S. F., Boness, C. L., McDowell, Y., Murphy, J. G., & Sher, K. J. (2023). Contextual decision-making and Alcohol Use Disorder criteria: Delayed reward, delayed loss, and probabilistic reward discounting. *Psychology of Addictive Behaviors, 37*(1), 121–131. https://doi.org/10.1037/adb0000867

Belisle, J., Paliliunas, D., Vangsness, L., Dixon, M. R., & Stanley, C. R. (2020). Social distance and delay exert multiple control over altruistic choices. *Psychological Record, 70*(3), 445–457. https://doi.org/10.1007/s40732-020-00399-x

Berry, M. S., Bruner, N. R., Herrmann, E. S., Johnson, P. S., & Johnson, M. W. (2022). Methamphetamine administration dose effects on sexual desire, sexual decision making, and delay discounting. *Experimental and Clinical Psychopharmacology, 30*(2), 180–193. https://doi.org/10.1037/pha0000398

Białaszek, W., Ostaszewski, P., Green, L., & Myerson, J. (2019). On four types of devaluation of outcomes due to their costs: Delay, probability, effort, and social discounting. *Psychological Record, 69*, 415–424. https://doi.org/10.1007/s40732-019-00340-x

Bickel, W. K., Jarmolowicz, D. P., Mueller, E. T., Franck, C. T., Carrin, C., & Gatchalian, K. M. (2012). Altruism in time: Social temporal discounting differentiates smokers from problem drinkers. *Psychopharmacology, 224*(1), 109–120. https://doi.org/10.1007/s00213-01202745-6

Boland, E. M., Kelley, N. J., Chat, I. K. Y., Zinarg, R., Craske, M. G., Bookheimer, S., & Nusslock, R. (2022). Poor sleep quality is significantly associated with effort but not temporal discounting of monetary rewards. *Motivational Science, 8*(1), 70–76. https://doi.org/10.1037/mot0000258

Brassard, S., & Baladis, I. (2021). A review of effort-based decision-making in eating and weight disorders. *Progress in Neuro-Psychopharmacology and Biological Psychiatry, 110*(110333). https://doi.org/10.1016/j.pnpbp.2021.110333

Buddiga, N. R., & Locey, M. L. (2021). Social discounting towards relatives and nonrelatives. *Psychological Record, 72*, 487–495. https://doi.org/10.1007/s40732-021-00479-6

Chapman, G. B., & Elstein, A. S. (1995). Valuing the future: Temporal discounting of health and money. *Medical Decision Making, 15*(4), 373–386. https://doi.org/10.1177/0272989X9501500408

Cox, D. J., & Dallery, J. (2016). Effects of delay and probability combinations on discounting in humans. *Behavioural Processes, 131*, 15–23. https://doi.org/10.1016/j.beproc.2016.08.002

Du, W., Green, L., & Myerson, J. (2002). Cross-cultural comparisons of discounting delayed and probabilistic rewards. *Psychological Record, 52*(4), 479−492. https://doi.org/10.1007/BF03395199

Epstein, L. H., Salvy, S. J., Carr, K. A., Dearing, K. K., & Bickel, W. K. (2010). Food reinforcement, delay discounting and obesity. *Physiology & Behavior, 100*(5), 438−445. https://doi.org/10.1016/j.physbeh.2010.04.029

Foreman, A. M., Hayashi, Y., Friedel, J. E., & Wirth, O. (2019). Social distance and texting while driving: A behavioral economic analysis of social discounting. *Traffic Injury Prevention, 20*(7), 702−707. https://doi.org/10.1080/15389588.2019.1636233

Green, L., Fristoe, N., & Myerson, J. (1994). Temporal discounting and preference reversals in choice between delayed outcomes. *Psychonomic Bulletin & Review, 1*(3), 383−389. https://doi.org/10.3758/BF03213979

Green, R. M., & Lawyer, S. R. (2014). Steeper delay and probability discounting of potentially real versus hypothetical cigarettes (but not money) among smokers. *Behavioural Processes, 108*, 50−56. https://doi.org/10.1016/j.beproc.2014.09.008

Green, L., Myerson, J., Oliveira, L., & Chang, S. E. (2013). Delay discounting of monetary rewards over a wide range of amounts. *Journal of the Experimental Analysis of Behavior, 100*(3), 269−281. https://doi.org/10.1002/jeab.45

Hayashi, Y., & Tahmasbi, N. (2020). Decision-making underlying bystanders' helping cyberbullying victims: A behavioral economic analysis of role of social discounting. *Computers in Human Behavior, 104*, 106157. https://doi.org/10.1016/j.chb.2019.106157

Hinvest, N. S., & Anderson, I. M. (2010). The effects of real versus hypothetical reward on delay and probability discounting. *Quarterly Journal of Experimental Psychology, 63*(6), 1072−1084. https://doi.org/10.1080/17470210903276350

Holt, D. D., Glodowski, K., Smits-Seemann, R. R., & Tiry, A. M. (2016). The domain effect in delay discounting: The roles of fungibility and perishability. *Behavioural Processes, 131*, 46−52. https://doi.org/10.1016/j.beproc.2016.08.006

Johnson, M. W., & Bickel, W. K. (2002). Within-subject comparison of real and hypothetical money rewards in delay discounting. *Journal of the Experimental Analysis of Behavior, 77*(2), 129−146. https://doi.org/10.1901/jeab.2002.77-129

Johnson, M. W., & Bickel, W. K. (2008). An algorithm for identifying nonsystematic delay discounting data. *Experimental and Clinical Psychopharmacology, 16*, 264−274. https://doi.org/10.1037/1064-1297.16.3.264

Johnson, M. W., & Bruner, N. R. (2012). The sexual discounting task: HIV risk behavior at the discounting of delayed sexual rewards in cocaine dependence. *Drug and Alcohol Dependence, 123*(1−3), 15−21. https://doi.org/10.1016/j.drugalcdep.2011.09.031

Johnson, P. S., Herrmann, E. S., & Johnson, M. W. (2015). Opportunity costs of reward delays and the discounting of hypothetical money and cigarettes. *Journal of the Experimental Analysis of Behavior, 103*(1), 87−107. https://doi.org/10.1002/jeab.110

Kaplan, B. A., Amlung, M., Reed, D. D., Jarmolowicz, D. P., McKerchar, T. L., & Lemley, S. M. (2016). Automating scoring of delay discounting for the 21- and 27-item monetary choice questionnaires. *The Behavior Analyst, 39*(2), 293−304. https://doi.org/10.1007/s40614-016-0070-9

Kirby, K. N., & Marakovič, N. N. (1995). Modeling myopic decisions: Evidence for hyperbolic delay-discounting within subjects and amounts. *Organizational Behavior and Human Decision Processes, 64*(1), 22−30. https://doi.org/10.1006/obhd.1995.1086

Kirby, K. N., Petry, N. M., & Bickel, W. K. (1999). Heroin addicts have higher discount rates for delayed rewards than non-drug-using controls. *Journal of Experimental Psychology: General, 128*(1), 78−87. https://doi.org/10.1037/0096-3445.128.1.78

Koffarnus, M. N., & Bickel, W. K. (2014). A 5-trial adjusting delay discounting task: Accurate discount rates in less than 60 seconds. *Experimental and Clinical Psychopharmacology, 22*(3), 222−228. https://doi.org/10.1037/a0035973

Koffarnus, M. N., Deshpande, H. U., Lisinski, J. M., Eklund, A., Bickel, W. K., & LaConte, S. M. (2017). An adaptive, individualized fMRI delay discounting procedure to increase flexibility and optimize scanner time. *NeuroImage, 161*, 56−66. https://doi.org/10.1016/j.neuroimage.2017.08.024

Koffarnus, M. N., Johnson, M. W., Thompson-Lake, D. G. Y., Wesley, M. J., Lohrenz, T., Montague, P. R., & Bickel, W. K. (2016). Cocaine-dependent adults and recreational cocaine users are more likely than controls to choose immediate unsafe sex over delayed safer sex. *Experimental and Clinical Psychopharmacology, 24*(4), 297−304. https://doi.org/10.1037/pha0000080

Koffarnus, M. N., & Kaplan, B. A. (2018). Clinical models of decision making in addiction. *Psychopharmacology, Biochemistry, and Behavior, 164*, 71−83. https://doi.org/10.1016/j.pbb.2017.08.010

Koffarnus, M. N., Rzeszutek, M. J., & Kaplan, B. A. (2021). *Additional discounting rates in less than one minute: Task variants for probability and a wider range of delays.* https://doi.org/10.13140/RG.2.2.31281.92000

Kyonka, E. G. E., & Schutte, N. S. (2018). Probability discounting and gambling: A meta-analysis. *Addiction, 113*(12), 2173−2181. https://doi.org/10.1111/add.14397

Lawyer, S. R. (2008). Probability and delay discounting of erotic stimuli. *Behavioural Processes, 79*(1), 36−42. https://doi.org/10.1016/j.beproc.2008.04.009

Lawyer, S. R., Williams, S. A., Prihodova, T., Rollins, J. D., & Lester, A. C. (2010). Probability and delay discounting of hypothetical sexual outcomes. *Behavioural Processes, 84*(3), 687−692. https://doi.org/10.1016/j.beproc.2010.04.002

Libedinsky, C., Massar, S. A. A., Ling, A. Q., Chee, W., Huettel, S. A., & Chee, M. W. L. (2013). Sleep deprivation alters effort discounting but not delay discounting of monetary rewards. *Sleep, 36*(6), 899−904. https://doi.org/10.5665/sleep.2720

Locey, M. L., Safin, V., & Rachlin, H. (2013). Social discounting and the prisoner's dilemma game. *Journal of the Experimental Analysis of Behavior, 99*(1), 85−97. https://doi.org/10.1002/jeab.3

MacKillop, J., Amlung, M. T., Few, L. R., Ray, L. A., Sweet, L. H., & Munafò, M. R. (2011). Delayed reward discounting and addictive behavior: A meta-analysis. *Psychopharmacology, 216*(3), 305−321. https://doi.org/10.1007/s00213-011-2229-0

Madden, G. J., Begotka, A. M., Raiff, B. R., & Kastern, L. L. (2003). Delay discounting of real and hypothetical rewards. *Experimental and Clinical Psychopharmacology, 11*(2), 139−145. https://doi.org/10.1037/1064-1297.11.2.139

Madden, G. J., Bickel, W. K., & Jacobs, E. A. (1999). Discounting of delayed rewards in opioid-dependent outpatients: Exponential or hyperbolic discounting functions? *Experimental and Clinical Psychopharmacology, 7*(3), 284−293. https://doi.org/10.1037/1064-1297.7.3.284

Malesza, M. (2019). The effects of potentially real and hypothetical rewards on effort discounting in a student sample. *Personality and Individual Differences, 151*(108807). https://doi.org/10.1016/j.paid.2018.03.030

Massar, S. A. A., Pu, Z. H., Chen, C., & Chee, M. W. L. (2020). Losses motivate cognitive effort more than gains in effort-based decision making and performance. *Frontiers in Human Neuroscience, 14*. https://doi.org/10.3389/fnhum.2020.00287

Mazur, J. E. (1987). An adjusting procedure for studying delayed reinforcement. In *The effect of delay and of intervening events on reinforcement value* (pp. 55–73). Lawrence Erlbaum Associates, Inc.

McKercher, T. L., & Renda, C. R. (2012). Delay and probability discounting in humans: An overview. *Psychological Record, 62*, 817–834. https://doi.org/10.1007/BF03395837

Mellis, A. M., Woodford, A. E., Stein, J. S., & Bickel, W. K. (2017). A second type of amount effect: Reinforcer magnitude differentiates delay discounting between substance users and controls. *Journal of the Experimental Analysis of Behavior, 107*(1), 151–160. https://doi.org/10.1002/jeab.235

Mitchell, S. H. (2004). Effects of short-term nicotine deprivation on decision-making: Delay, uncertainty, and effort discounting. *Nicotine & Tobacco Research, 6*(5), 819–828. https://doi.org/10.1080/14622200412331296002

Odum, A. L., Baumann, A. A. L., & Rimington, D. D. (2006). Discounting of delayed hypothetical money and food: Effects of amount. *Behavioural Processes, 73*(3), 278–284. https://doi.org/10.1016/j.beproc.2006.06.008

Odum, A. L., & Rainaud, C. P. (2003). Discounting of delayed hypothetical money, alcohol, and food. *Behavioural Processes, 64*(3), 305–313. https://doi.org/10.1016/S0376-6357(03)00145-1

Ostazewski, P., Bąbel, P., & Swebodsiński, B. (2013). Physical and cognitive effort discounting of hypothetical monetary rewards. *Japanese Psychological Research, 55*(4), 329–337. https://doi.org/10.1111/jpr.12019

Pinkston, J. W., & Libman, B. M. (2017). Aversive functions of response effort: Fact or artifact? *Journal of the Experimental Analysis of Behavior, 108*(1), 73–96. https://doi.org/10.1002/jeab.264

Rachlin, H., & Jones, B. A. (2008). Social discounting and delay discounting. *Journal of Behavioral Decision Making, 21*, 29–43. https://doi.org/10.1002/bdm.567

Rachlin, H., Raineri, A., & Cross, D. (1991). Subjective probability and delay. *Journal of the Experimental Analysis of Behavior, 55*(2), 233–244. https://doi.org/10.1901/jeab.1991.55-233

Reynolds, B. (2006). A review of delay-discounting research with humans: Relations to drug use and gambling. *Behavioural Pharmacology, 17*(8), 651–667. https://doi.org/10.1097/FBP.0b013e3280115f99

Reynolds, B., & Schiffbauer, R. (2004). Measuring state changes in human delay discounting: An experiential discounting task. *Behavioural Processes, 67*(3), 343–356. https://doi.org/10.1016/j.beproc.2004.06.003

Robertson, S. H., & Rasmussen, E. B. (2018). Comparison of potentially real versus hypothetical food outcomes in delay and probability discounting tasks. *Behavioural Processes, 149*, 8–15. https://doi.org/10.1016/j.beproc.2018.01.014

Rung, J. M., Argyle, T. M., Siri, J. L., & Madden, G. J. (2018). Choosing the right delay-discounting task: Completion times and rates of nonsystematic data. *Behavioural Processes, 151*, 119–125. https://doi.org/10.1016/j.beproc.2018.03.022

Rzeszutek, M. J., DeFulio, A., & Brown, H. D. (2022). Risk of cancer and cost of surgery outweigh urgency and messaging in hypothetical decisions to remove tumors. *Psychological Record, 72*(3), 331–352. https://doi.org/10.1007/s40732-021-00489-4

Skrynka, J., & Vincent, B. T. (2019). Hunger increases delay discounting of food and non-food rewards. *Psychonomic Bulletin & Review, 26,* 1729−1737. https://doi.org/10.3758/s13423-019-01655-0

Smits, R. R., Stein, J. S., Johnson, P. S., Odum, A. L., & Madden, G. J. (2013). Test−retest reliability and construct validity of the Experiential Discounting Task. *Experimental and Clinical Psychopharmacology, 21*(2), 155−163. https://doi.org/10.1037/a0031725

Steele, C. C., Gwinner, M., Smith, T., Young, M. E., & Kirkpatrick, K. (2019). Experience matters: The effects of hypothetical versus experiential delays and magnitudes on impulsive choice in delay discounting tasks. *Brain Sciences, 9*(12), 12. https://doi.org/10.3390/brainsci9120379

Story, G. W., Kurth-Nelson, Z., Crockett, M., Vlaev, I., Darzi, A., & Dolan, R. J. (2020). Social discounting of pain. *Journal of the Experimental Analysis of Behavior, 114*(3), 308−325. https://doi.org/10.1002/jeab.631

Thaler, R. (1981). Some empirical evidence on dynamic inconsistency. *Economics Letters, 8*(3), 201−207. https://doi.org/10.1016/0165-1765(81)90067-7

Vanderveldt, A., Green, L., & Myerson, J. (2015). Discounting of monetary rewards that are both delayed and probabilistic: Delay and probability combine multiplicatively, not additively. *Journal of Experimental Psychology − Learning Memory and Cognition, 41*(1), 148−162. https://doi.org/10.1037/xlm0000029

Weatherly, J. N., & Derenne, A. (2011). Comparing delay discounting rates when using the fill-in-the-blank and multiple-choice methods. *The Journal of General Psychology, 138*(4), 300−318. https://doi.org/10.1080/00221309.2011.606442

Weatherly, J. N., Wise, R. A., & Derenne, A. (2012). Probability discounting of legal and non-legal outcomes. *Behavior and Social Issues, 21,* 165−187. https://doi.org/10.5210/bsi.v.2110.4183

Wesley, M. J., Lohrenz, T., Koffarnus, M. N., McClure, S. M., De La Garza II, R., Salas, R., Thompson-Lake, D. G. Y., Newton, T. F., Bickel, W. K., & Montague, P. R. (2014). Choosing money of drugs: The neural underpinnings of difficult choice in chronic cocaine users. *Journal of Addiction, 2014,* Article 189853. https://doi.org/10.1155/2014/189853

Yi, R., de la Piedad, X., & Bickel, W. K. (2006). The combined effects of delay and probability in discounting. *Behavioural Processes, 73*(2), 149−155. https://doi.org/10.1016/j.beproc.2006.05.001

Yoon, H., & Chapman, G. B. (2016). A closer look at the yardstick: A new discount rate measure with precision and range. *Journal of Behavioral Decision Making, 29*(5), 470−480. https://doi.org/10.1002/bdm.1890

Yoon, J. H., & Higgins, S. T. (2008). Turning k on its head: Comments on use of an ED50 in delay discounting research. *Drug and Alcohol Dependence, 95*(1), 169−172. https://doi.org/10.1016/j.drugalcdep.2007.12.011

Further reading

Koot, S., Bos, R., Adriani, W., & Laviola, G. (2009). Gender differences in delay- discounting under mild food restriction. *Behavioural Brain Research, 200*(1), 134−143. https://doi.org/10.1016/j.bbr.2009.01.00

Madden, G. J., Raiff, B. R., Lagorio, C. H., Begotka, A. M., Mueller, A. M., Hehli, D. J., & Wegener, A. A. (2004). Delay discounting of potentially real and hypothetical rewards. *Experimental and Clinical Psychopharmacology, 12*(4), 251−261.

Matusiewicz, A. K., Carter, A. E., Landes, R. D., & Yi, R. (2004). Statistical equivalence and test—retest reliability of delay and probability discounting using real and hypothetical rewards. *Behavioural Processes, 100*, 116—122. https://doi.org/10.1016/j.beproc.2013.07.019

Quantitative models of discounting

10

Christopher T. Franck
Department of Statistics, Virginia Tech, Blacksburg, VA, United States

Overview of the chapter

The ability to confidently fit models to indifference point data requires expertise in behavioral analytic concepts and statistical modeling. Since many readers of this book may have more primary training on the behavioral side of things, the purpose of this chapter is to demystify the process of fitting discounting models to observed data. There will be a special emphasis on fully reproducible code that allows the reader to execute the analyses described herein. The chapter features instructive prose, a real-world dataset, and snippets of R code which will enable the interested reader to practice analyzing data.

This chapter provides a tutorial that the reader can follow toward analyzing discounting data. Previous work has already described the breadth of outcomes associated with discounting (Odum et al., 2020) and other background information (Odum, 2011). We focus on delay discounting, where indifference points describe the value of a delayed reward that a participant would be willing to accept to have the reward immediately for a variety of delays. This chapter describes the two-stage approach to analyzing discounting data, as this is the simplest approach that is also statistically defensible. The two-stage approach first quantifies the discounting rate of each participant individually, and the second stage analyzes these rates as a function of relevant variables (e.g., between smokers and nonsmokers).

We use the R software (R Core Team, 2024) to illustrate the analyses presented in this chapter. While several software choices are available, we choose R because it is a free and robust statistical modeling package. Especially compared to point-and-click menu-driven software, R's programmatic approach to data analysis enables more control and creativity, and it naturally facilitates reproducibility and transparency since the code that conducts an analysis can be archived and re-run later and/or by different users. Despite this chapter's commitment to R, do not conflate the data-analytic approach with the tools used to execute the analysis. Other software packages exist that are just as capable of organizing and visualizing data, fitting models, and conducting other statistical analyses.

Several approaches have been used to analyze multi-subject behavioral economic data. An overview of these approaches in the context of demand can be found here (Kaplan et al., 2021). Much of the terminology in this chapter (especially the terms defined in Table 1 of Kaplan et al. (2021)) is extremely relevant for the analysis of discounting data. In addition, if the reader is interested in learning about quantifying behavioral economic demand data, please see Chapter 5—Quantitative models of demand in this book.

The study of discounting is vast and no single chapter can cover everything. Once the skills in this chapter are familiar, the reader may wish to next consider: Additional models for delay discounting (McKerchar et al., 2009) and model selection, including the tension between the model fit and theoretical appeal of models (Franck et al., 2015), probability discounting (Killeen, 2023; Rachlin et al., 1986, 1991), hierarchical modeling (Young, 2017; Chávez et al., 2017), useful cross-model metrics of delay discounting (e.g., Effective delay 50 (Franck et al., 2015; Yoon & Higgins, 2008), area under the fitted curve (Gilroy & Hantula, 2018)), and Bayesian statistical approaches for delay discounting (Franck et al., 2019).

How to use this chapter

The remainder of the chapter is a tutorial. The next step is to download R (https://www.r-project.org/) and the free interface program RStudio (https://posit.co/downloads/). You can easily find a 3 minute video on the internet that explains how to download and install R and RStudio for either PC or Mac. Once that is complete, come along on the journey by running the embedded code as you encounter it in the chapter.

We alternate among descriptive prose, lines of R code that run statistical analyses, the results of those analyses, and a description of those results. We reserve **bold** font for terms that, if unfamiliar, can be Googled by the reader to better understand the context of what is being presented. This chapter is designed to be a pathway, but on your journey, stopping to read more about related concepts is the equivalent of sight-seeing. We conclude the chapter with a series of exercises to give the reader the opportunity to flex their new knowledge. Treating these exercises like homework might even make you feel like a kid again.

Please note that this chapter is a broad overview of many topics and is not organized to reflect a typical research analysis pipeline. Many planning steps and other considerations must take place before responsible data analysis, and these issues are described further later in the chapter in the *Contemporary issues in statistical practice* and *The role of planning in scientific investigation* Sections.

R and RStudio

R is a free programming language, and RStudio (https://posit.co/) is a convenient graphical user interface for R with a free individual-use license. Once R and RStudio are installed on your machine, you open RStudio and it automatically connects with R. All R programming, running of code, and other analysis happens within RStudio.

Quantitative models of discounting 231

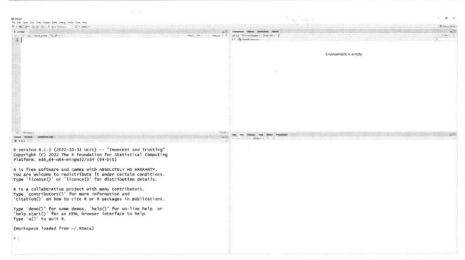

RStudio interface. Top left pane is the script, bottom left pane is the console, top right pane shows the (currently empty) environment and bottom right pane can show help files and data visualizations.

The above figure depicts the RStudio interface. The top left pane, which is blank, is the **script**. This is where the user (you) writes R code. A good way to follow along with the demos below is to copy and paste the code from this chapter into the R script, modify it as necessary (e.g., change file paths), and then run the code. On PC, the line of code with the cursor can be run by pressing "Ctrl + Enter." On Mac, press "command + return" to run the current line of code. On both platforms, you can run multiple lines of code by highlighting those lines you wish to run before using the run commands just described. R is case sensitive.

The bottom left panel is the **console**. When lines of code are run from the script, those lines appear in the console followed by R's reaction to those lines. To familiarize yourself with this, first treat the console as a simple calculator. Type "2 + 2" directly into the console, press "Enter" ("return" on Mac), and note that R comes back with "4." Now write "2 + 2" in the script, press "Ctrl + Enter" ("command + return" on Mac), and you will see the same results appear in the console. You will frequently find yourself in a workflow loop in which you enter commands into the script, submit them to the console, and then assess the outcome of those commands by checking the console for results and any warning or error messages (which you should Google to help you understand and resolve).

The top right panel of RStudio shows the **environment** by default. The environment lists each **object** the user has defined along with some basic information about those objects. Objects include data the user may have imported, any functions they have written, and any variables that are stored. The bottom right panel can be used to show graphical output and help files. Keep your eyes on the top right and bottom right panels as you run the code below to get a feel for the role these panels play.

We could fill the rest of the chapter describing R and RStudio and not run out of things to talk about. But the purpose of this chapter is to describe the analysis of discounting data. The reader is encouraged to liberally use other available R resources alongside this chapter as necessary, but for now, we turn our attention toward the analysis of discounting data.

Use R to import and examine data

Let us now import the study data. The data analyzed in this chapter were gathered as part of a larger study (Traxler et al., 2022). These data and code are available from https://osf.io/f62h3. Before replicating the analysis below, be sure you have downloaded the data and stored it in the folder of your choice on your computer. The first line of code below indicates to R which folder stores the data. You will need to modify this line to reflect the data file's location on your own machine. The second line defines an object called *dat*, which contains the full set of data used in this chapter. Copy paste the following code into an R script, change the "setwd" directory to reflect the location of the data on your own machine, and run the code.

```
setwd("C:/Dropbox/Discounting book chapter/Rmarkdown") #set working directory
dat<-read.csv('Traxler 2022.csv') #define an object "dat" that is the data
```

The pound sign "#" is used in R to denote **comments**. Comments are not evaluated by R, which makes them useful for humans to write messages to each other within the code (as seen earlier), and also to indicate to R if you wish to omit certain lines of code from being evaluated. This second use is important for **debugging**. Essentially all computer programming languages include the ability to write comments, and thus commenting is a general programming concept.

It is important to examine the data post-import to make sure that the file is read correctly. You can examine the full set of data by clicking the "dat" entry in the environment pane (top right), or running the following command in the console:View(dat). This will create a tab in the top left pane that shows the study data in a spreadsheet.

Click the "dat" entry in the environment pane now, and confirm you are able to observe the following. This data set includes columns id number, Age (years), gender ("Male" or "Female"), and smoking status as "smoke_cigs" ("Yes" or "No"). The data set also includes indifference points gathered at six delays using a hypothetical delay discounting titrating questionnaire. The delays are 1 day, 1 week, 1 month, 3 months, 1 year, and 5 years. These indifference points are labeled y1, y7, y30, y90, y365, and y1825, respectively. Note that these indifference points are expressed on a scale between zero and one, as the raw indifference points have already been dived by the larger later amount in the production of this dataset. An attention check question "ddattend" was asked to determine which participants would choose "$0.00 now" versus "$100.00 in 1 day". Choosing no money over 100 dollars tomorrow reflects a participant who did not understand the task, was not being attentive to their answers, or for other reasons is exhibiting irrational patterns of valuation. The data also include indifference points that violate the Johnson & Bickel criteria (Johnson & Bickel, 2008), and the presence of these violations is included in the "Jbviol" column. Additional description of attention checks and non-systematic discounting patterns appears in the next subsection on first-stage analyses. Each row in this spreadsheet contains the data from a single research participant.

There are two lines of code below that offer additional information about the data. The first line uses the "class" function to indicate that the data object is stored as a **data frame**. Data frames are the typical data format for rectangular data objects in R. Data frames store variables in the columns and data records (i.e., participant data) in the rows. Data frames can include both numeric or character variables, e.g., our data has the character variable "gender" which takes the values "Male" or "Female", and numeric data for age and many others. The *class* function is used on R objects in general to reveal the **type** of object. R is able to recognize different object types, including **character variables, numeric variables, vectors of numbers, matrices, data frames**, lists of different types of objects, models, and many more. A good first debugging step when faced with warnings and error messages is to check the type of objects being used.

The second line uses the "dim" function to reveal that there are 106 rows (participants) and 13 columns (variables) in the dataset.

```
class(dat)
## [1] "data.frame"
dim(dat)
## [1] 106  13
```

These data are considered to be in **wide** format since the identifier for participant id does not repeat in different rows. Each row corresponds to the full data available for a single participant. The first row, for example, tells us the age, gender, smoking status, indifference points, and attention and data quality checks for the first participant. Data in which the same participant ID occurs on multiple lines (e.g., if each participant completes assessments multiple times) are said to be in a **long** format. Choice of wide versus long format is frequently made based on the software tools the analyst plans to use, and R functions exist to readily switch between formats. Recognizing the data format is an important early step since it enables the researcher to know how to write the code to conduct the analysis.

Stage 1 analyses

The first stage of a two-stage analysis involves quantifying the rate of discounting for each participant on the basis of their indifference points. To accomplish this, we first analyze a single participant's indifference point data. This includes graphically plotting their indifference points by delay, then fitting a discounting model, adding the model fit to the plot, and finally extracting the discounting rate for subsequent analysis in stage two. Do not worry about the fact that we have to do this 106 times. Once we have the first subject's Stage 1 analysis complete, we will show how to tweak and embed that code in a **loop** that automatically and near-instantaneously conducts the same analysis for the remaining 105 participants and stores the results in a format convenient for Stage 2 analysis.

Now we plot the first participant's data. Note the "<-" is an assignment statement used to define new objects (see how it looks like a little arrow). So the first line creates a new object called "i" which takes the value "1".

```
i<-1 #Set an index number to 1 for the first subject
y.frame<-dat[i,5:11,drop=FALSE] #ith row, columns 5 through 11
y.frame #Check indifference points

##          y1     y7    y30    y90   y365  y1825  y9125
## 1    0.4922 0.9922 0.9454 0.8984 0.8984 0.3984 0.1016

y<-as.vector(as.matrix(t(y.frame))) #Make y a vector
D<-c(1,7,30,90,365,1825,9125) #Define the delays D
plot(D,y, #scatter plot. First argument is horizontal axis, second is
vertical axis
     xlab='Delay (days)',ylab='Indifference point') # Label axes
```

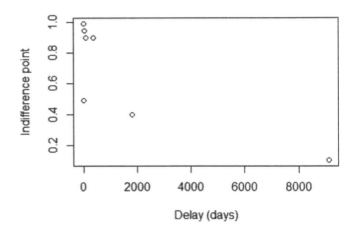

Our plot for the indifference points and delays of the first participant reveal that generally, as delay increases, the indifference point decreases. However, there is a notable jump between 1 day and 1 week delay. One might expect that indifference points would get lower and lower as the delay increases (reflecting the reduced utility a larger later reward has at longer delays). In practice, not all observed discounting data follow this trend. Unusual or unexpected discounting patterns might emerge due to lack of attention on the part of the participant, a single mistaken response early in a sequence of a titrating questionnaire, the participant has failed to understand the task's directions, or due to other considerations that a participant has that the experimenter cannot be aware of (e.g., an unexpectedly high indifference point might be due to an upcoming event like a medical bill the participant is thinking about).

Visualizing discounting on the log-delay scale

If you are anything like me, your first algebra teacher tried to tell you how important the logarithm function is. You ignored them since you figured you would never use this abstract information on a daily basis. If you are reading this sentence, then the day has arrived when you will be using the logarithm function on a daily basis.

The logarithmic function (which is the inverse function of the exponential function) is central to modern data-analytic practices. It simplifies mathematical optimization, computationally stabilizes numbers extremely close to zero, and aids in visualization for many types of analyses in many fields, including visualizing delay discounting data by log-transforming delay. In the present case, we have a troublesome vertical jump among the indifference points early in the delay sequence that is incredibly difficult to appreciate visually in the scatter plot above. Let us consider the same scatter plot but put the natural log of delay on the horizontal axis.

```
plot(log(D),y,
     xlab='ln(Delay)',ylab='Indifference point') # Label axes
```

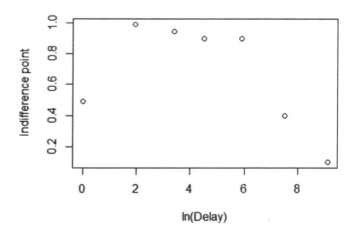

(Brief note: In R syntax, "log( )" is the natural log function (frequently denoted "ln( )" mathematically), while the "log10( )" function is log base 10 in R).

The logarithm function spreads out numbers that are closer to zero and compresses numbers that are further from zero. Thus very short distances between delays early on (such as 1 day and 1 week) get spread out while more remote distances (e.g., five years and 25 years to the right side of the panel) are compressed when the log is taken. Thus, the reader can see that on the natural log scale, delays are more equally spaced and we can assess patterns of indifference points among the shorter delays with much greater ease. (Further information and exercises to review the logarithm function can be found at the end of this chapter.)

Specifically, we can now easily see that the first participant's jump in indifference point between a day and a week is very large, indicating the apparent contradiction. This participant reports quickly devaluing a reward for a delay of 1 day but exhibiting essentially no discounting of a reward in a week. This is not the idealized behavior we expect for delay discounting, and this jump violates one of the Johnson & Bickel criteria (Johnson & Bickel, 2008).

The purpose of the Johnson & Bickel criteria is to give researchers a simple method to identify patterns of indifference points that may be inconsistent with the expected behavior of delay discounting. Quoting that paper, the Johnson & Bickel criteria would flag a data set if: "Either or both of the two following criterion were met: (1) if any indifference point (starting with the second delay) was greater than the preceding indifference point by a magnitude greater than 20% of the larger later reward" and "(2) if the last (i.e., 25-year) indifference point was not less than the first (1 day or 1 week, depending on the study) indifference point by at least a magnitude equal to 10% of the larger later reward."

As with any other data-analytic exercise focusing on unusual data points, outliers, etc., the decision about how to proceed with analysis in the face of unexpected, unusual, or atypical data is ultimately subjective but should be considered prior to conducting analysis. Going forward, we will analyze the full set of data without excluding participants who violate the Johnson & Bickel criteria or attention checks. This is meant to illustrate overall analyses without being overly prescriptive about how to handle non-systematic data. Note that there are exercises at the end of the chapter that guide the motivated reader to reconduct the presented analyses with various exclusion criteria in place and to determine to what extent changing exclusion criteria can alter the analysis conclusions. Inclusion criteria are set prior to analysis in a typical study and not second-guessed midstream. In research practice, one does not simply change things at will and try every combination of analyses until a preconceived conclusion is reached. This is called "p-hacking," and more information can be found in the **Contemporary issues in statistical practice** Section.

We should not automatically delete any data that is unusual because it is still valid if collected according to the research protocols. However, being mindful about situations in which a small number of data points yield an out-sized influence on study conclusions is also not ideal. The point of statistical analysis is to aggregate information from many subjects to make broader conclusions about the population as a whole, and if a few individual data points change or obscure our view of the entire picture, have we really focused on the broader population or just a handful of unusual points? Perhaps unsurprisingly, decisions about how to handle participant data that does not follow expected discounting patterns can impact the final conclusions of a study.

We next turn our attention to fitting discounting models. Several models have been proposed. We first illustrate the widely used hyperbolic discounting model, sometimes referred to as the "Mazur model" (Mazur, 1987), which is

$$E(y) = \frac{A}{1 + k * D},$$

where $E(y)$ is the expected value of the indifference point y, i.e., the regression line value at delay D. The value A is the amount of the delayed reward, and k is the discounting rate. Note that the hyperbolic model fits the data in terms of unlogged delay, not ln(Delay) as was previously visualized. If $k = 0$ then the participant does not devalue the reward as a function of delay. The data we analyze in this chapter has been scaled by A already, so our indifference points are between zero and one and A is replaced by 1 subsequently.

The hyperbolic discounting function is just one example of a functional form that describes delay discounting. Exercise (2) at the end of this chapter explores another popular discounting function. For more information on other discounting functions, see McKerchar et al. (2009).

When interpreting the output of data analyses and drawing inferences about populations larger than the sample that was collected, it is vitally important to clearly distinguish between unknown population parameters and sample statistics that estimate those parameters. The parameter k is unknown and must be estimated on the basis of delay data D and indifference point data y. We follow the convention in most statistical texts by denoting data-based estimates of unknown parameters with a hat. Thus we use the symbol $\hat{k}$ to denote the data-based statistic that estimates the true (but unknown) parameter k. We follow this convention for statistics and parameters throughout this chapter.

To begin to make some of the above statistical concepts more concrete, we now fit the Mazur model to the first participants' data using nonlinear regression via the "nls" (which stands for "nonlinear least squares") function. We will fit the model, plot the fit alongside indifference points, and extract the estimated discounting rate $\hat{k}$.

```
mod<-nls(y~1/(1+k*D),start=list(k=.1)) #Fit the Mazur model to these data
mod #View the estimated value of k

## Nonlinear regression model
##   model: y ~ 1/(1 + k * D)
##    data: parent.frame()
##        k
## 0.0007053
##  residual sum-of-squares: 0.2733
##
## Number of iterations to convergence: 8
## Achieved convergence tolerance: 2.113e-06

#Verify computation of residual sum-of-squares
sum(((y-predict(mod))^2))

## [1] 0.2732825
```

The above code creates an object called "mod" (short for "model") that stores the results of a nonlinear regression. The R syntax $y \sim 1/(1 + k * D)$ indicates that we want to fit indifference points y as the outcome variable with the model form following the Mazur model. By running the object "mod," we see a reminder of the form of the model we chose (useful when several models are being considered), an estimate $\hat{k} = 0.0007053$, residual sum of squares (which quantify the sum of squared residuals, i.e., the vertical distance between each point and a regression line squared and added up), and some information about model convergence. We say more about least squares and the model fitting that is happening "under-the-hood" in a few paragraphs.

Speaking candidly, I have always had difficulty intuitively understanding the discount rate k. For this participant, the estimate $\hat{k} = 0.0007$. The discounting rate k is higher among individuals who discount rapidly, and lower among individuals who do not. Beyond that, k is not particularly interpretable for most people. A related metric, called the *Effective delay 50* (ED50) describes the length of delay for which the participant would forfeit half of the larger later reward to have the reward immediately (Yoon & Higgins, 2008). Conveniently, ED50 $= 1/k$ when the Mazur model is in use. Thus, a data-based estimator for ED50 is $\widehat{ED50} = 1/\hat{k}$. Effective delay 50 is important due to its interpretability, the fact that its interpretation is the same among competing discounting models (Franck et al., 2015), and its role and implementation in the development of a very brief but effective discounting questionnaire (Koffarnus & Bickel, 2014) that titrates to ED50 then infers $\hat{k}$ based on the form of Mazur's model rather than by obtaining indifference points directly.

Now let us have a look at the line of best fit for these data and also visualize and compute ED50. For longer code chunks like this one, feel free to run the code one line at a time to learn how each command works.

```
D.s<-seq(0,9500,1) #Create a fine grid across delays. Used later to plot the
regression line.
preds<-predict(mod,newdata=data.frame(D=D.s)) #Obtain predicted values for
each grid point
plot(D,y,xlab='Delay (days)',ylab='Indifference point',
     main="Indifference points, model fit, and ED50") #Scatter plot
lines(D.s,preds,col='red') #Add the regression line to the plot

##Add a Legend
legend(x=4500,y=.8,legend=c("Indifference point","Regression
line"),col=c("black","red"),
       pch=c(1,NA),lty=c(NA,1))



k.hat<-summary(mod)$coef[1,1] #Store k.hat
ED50=1/k.hat #Store ED50
k.hat

## [1] 0.0007052959

ED50

## [1] 1417.845

#Add lines and text to illustrate ED50
lines(x=c(ED50,ED50),y=c(0,0.5),lty=3)
lines(x=c(-2000,ED50),y=c(0.5,0.5),lty=3)
text(2700,0.54,paste('ED50 =',round(ED50),'days'))
```

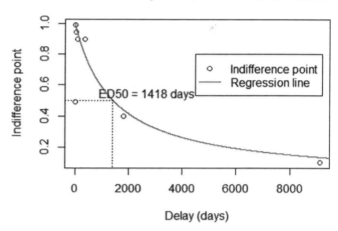

We estimate $\widehat{ED50} = \frac{1}{k} = 1418$ days. The plot includes the indifference points, the nonlinear regression line, and a visual depiction of the ED50 value, which corresponds to the point on the regression line where the indifference point is 0.5.

Before we proceed with similar analyses for the remaining study participants' data, we describe a few more statistical concepts that are under the hood. The above plot cogently shows that the goal is to determine which value of k provides the "best fitting line" to the data. For basic analyses, this is frequently accomplished by **least squares**. We will focus initially on explaining this approach. Other methods to estimate parameters include **maximum likelihood estimation** and **Bayesian** methods, which have been described in the context of discounting here Franck et al. (2023) and here Franck et al. (2019), respectively.

In order to place a regression line "close" to observed data points, we must have some notion of collective distance between the set of data points and the line. Our nonlinear **least squares** approach uses **residual sum-of-squares** (RSS) as a notion of distance. RSS is calculated by (i) taking the difference between each data point and the corresponding point on the regression line with the same delay D, (2) squaring those individual differences (so everything is positive and points below the line do not "cancel out" points above the line), and finally (3) adding up these squared differences.

Mathematically,

$$\text{RSS} = \sum_{i=1}^{n} (y_i - \widehat{y}_i)^2$$

where n is the sample size, y_i is the ith indifference point, and $\widehat{y}_i$ is the value of the regression line corresponding to the ith indifference point. The large sample operator $\sum_{i=1}^{n}$ indicates the summation of all squared differences for the data set.

RSS describes how far a given regression line is from the observed data in the least squares sense. To find the least squares line, one must search the space of all possible parameter values (k in this problem) in order to find the value $\hat{k}$ that produces a line with the smallest possible RSS. The field of mathematics that studies strategies to determine optimal values of criterion as a function of the criterion's inputs is called **optimization**. The good news is that (i) least squares approaches are easy to implement for the Mazur model, and (ii) we have already shown how to use R to obtain optimal $\hat{k}$ values for discounting data (using the "nls" function above).

For those who would like a more concrete demonstration that we indeed have the best possible line and who would also like to see some more R code, see the code below.

```
#define a function that computes RSS on basis of provided k for observed data
RSS<-function(k){
    yhat<-1/(1+k*D)
    resid<-y-yhat
    rss<-sum((y-yhat)^2)
    return(rss)
}

k.seq<-seq(0,.01,.0001) #sequence of k values
RSS.seq<-sapply(k.seq,RSS) #sequence of RSS values at each k in sequence
plot(k.seq,RSS.seq,type='l',ylab='RSS',xlab='k',
    main="Lowest RSS occurs at estimated k value")
abline(v=k.hat,col='red',lty=3)
optimize(RSS,interval=c(0,100))

## $minimum
## [1] 0.0007296753
##
## $objective
## [1] 0.2734153

#add a legend
legend(x=.002,y=.2,legend=c("RSS as a function of k", "k.hat from previous analysis"),
        col=c("black","red"),lty=c(1,3))
```

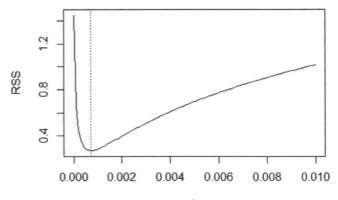

Area under the curve as a measure of discounting

Thus far, we have quantified discounting using the value k from the Mazur equation and ED50. Another approach that does not assume a specific functional form involves computing area under the discounting curve (AUC) (Myerson et al., 2001). The idea is to join up the indifference points with line segments, and then calculate the area of the region below this curve. Using the data from subject 1:

```
plot(D,y, #scatter plot. First argument is horizontal axis, second is
vertical axis
     xlab='Delay (days)',ylab='Indifference point') # Label axes
lines(D,y)
lines(D,y,type='h',lty=2,col='lightgray')
```

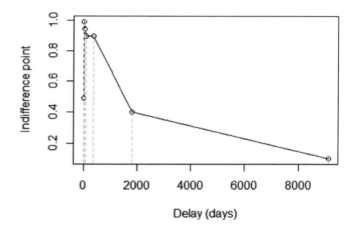

It is clear from the abovementioned picture that the region under the adjoined line segments consists of adjoined trapezoids. Computing the area of trapezoids and adding them up is easy, which is why this strategy for computing area under connect-the-dots style curves is called the *trapezoidal rule*. (Note that in calculus, the trapezoidal rule produces close approximations to the area under smooth functions by evaluating the function on a dense grid, connecting the dots, and adding up the area of the trapezoids). This can be conveniently obtained in R using the *trapz* function in the *pracma* package.

While base R comes with many capabilities, there are also a great number of add-on libraries that can be accessed free of charge that further extend R's capabilities. Many available packages are stored on the Comprehensive R Archive Network (CRAN). If you are connected to the internet, you can access the CRAN repository by clicking

"Tools —> Install Packages ..." menu through RStudio, and then using the menu options to choose among available packages. Alternatively, one can use the install.packages ("package_name") command in the console to access available packages. If you have a goal in mind but do not know the name of an R package that meets that goal, then it is usually a good idea to do some Google searching to determine whether a suitable package is available. In the present case, the *pracma* package should be obtained and installed before running the following code.

```
library(pracma)
trapz(D,y)
## [1] 3100.774
```

The AUC for these data is 3100.774.

AUC has some pros and some cons. For pros, it is easy to compute. AUC is directly associated with discounting since more devaluation of rewards across delays leads to shorter trapezoids, which in turn leads to lower AUC.

AUC is unlike a typical statistical regression approach because AUC does not attempt to describe an underlying function and quantify the departure of observed outcome data (indifference points in this case) from that function. Thus the AUC metric is not tied to any specific theoretical framework (a quote from authors' abstract). Whether this nontheoretical take on discounting is a pro or con, the availability of AUC is at minimum a useful empirical benchmark to compare other theoretical models' quantification of discounting. There is a practice problem at the end of the chapter that tasks the reader with evaluating the association among various discounting metrics including AUC.

In terms of cons, AUC alone does not enforce or even evaluate whether rewards are devalued as a function of delay. A participant whose indifference points are increasing as a function of delay could end up with an AUC value very similar to a participant who discounts sensibly. A valid straight-line pattern of indifference points decreasing from top left to bottom right would have the same AUC as an invalid increasing line from bottom left to top right, for example.

Another downside of AUC is that, as a nontheoretical approach, it is difficult to definitively resolve best practices on theoretical grounds. For example, an analyst may be concerned that the shorter delays form trapezoids that are much smaller than the longer delays, and thus relatively short delays may be severely underweighted when computing AUC. This provides useful information in the delay range where rewards are being devalued rapidly. But this also produces very narrow trapezoid bases, thus arguably the most important delays play a much smaller role in AUC than the subsequent delays which are spaced out more. A natural approach to increase the emphasis on early delays might be to compute an area under the curve metric on the basis of logged delays (Borges et al., 2016), as presented in the code below.

```
plot(log(D),y, #scatter plot. First argument is horizontal axis, second is
vertical axis
     xlab='ln(Delay)',ylab='Indifference point') # Label axes
lines(log(D),y)
lines(log(D),y,type='h',lty=2,col='lightgray')
```

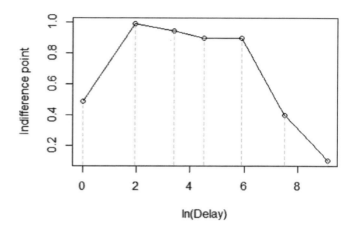

```
trapz(log(D),y)
## [1] 6.570705
```

The analyst who computed AUC on the basis of unlogged delays got 3100.774 in unlogged delay space. The analyst who was concerned this gave too small weight to the short delays got 6.57 but in logged delay space. Who is right and who is wrong? I have no idea, and since there is no underlying theory for AUC, decisions such as these have no definitive resolution. We can just argue about best practices.

Another potential downside is the inability of AUC to quantify error variance in the Stage 1 fit. A hallmark of statistical reasoning is the notion that observed data are a noisy realization arising from some underlying data-generating model. Deliberately characterizing observed data with a model with an unrealistically low estimate of error variance (zero in fact) might be viewed as inelegant.

How do we easily complete the above analyses for the remaining 105 participants' data?

Stage 1 has been focused on obtaining discounting metrics for a participant based on their indifference point data. Stage 2 will analyze these metrics as a function of other predictors (e.g., determine whether smokers discount faster than nonsmokers on average). Thus we must automate the Stage 1 analyses so we can quickly obtain discounting metrics for all participants in the sample before we move on to Stage 2.

Rather than copy-pasting similar commands to those above for each of the 106 participants' data, we will instead embed our code in a **for loop**. A for loop is a general programming technique that allows the user to repeat a set of user-specified commands for a prespecified number of iterations. We will see that once the analysis plan is in place for a single subject, repeating that same analysis a great number of times is actually easy.

The for loops typically used in analyzing discounting data typically involve defining an index value that increments at each iteration of the loop. We use the letter i. The index i is typically set to the value one initially, and then it ticks up each iteration. Commands are written to operate on, e.g., the *ith* individual's data (currently the first participant), results are stored for a later-on analysis, the value of i increments to 2, the same commands are applied to the second participant's data, and so on until each participant's data are analyzed and results stored.

Below find the syntax to make a for loop that captures all participants' estimated $\widehat{k}$ values. We create an empty vector called "K.vec". The shorthand "vec" stands for "vector." In R, a vector is a list of either numeric or character variables where the order of the entries is important. In our code, K.vec is initially empty. The for loop will store the first participant's estimated $\widehat{k}$ value in the first position of K.vec, the second participant's $\widehat{k}$ goes in the second position of K.vec, and so on.

```
K.vec<-c() #initialize K.vec as an empty vector
for(i in 1:106){ #begin at i=1, do everything in curly brackets, increment i, repeat
  y.frame<-dat[i,5:11,drop=FALSE] #pull indifference points for ith participant
  y<-as.vector(as.matrix(t(y.frame))) #turn data frame y.frame into vector y
  K.vec[i]<-summary(nls(y~(1+K*D)^(-1),start=list(K=.1)))$coef[1,1] #fit Mazur model
                                                                    #store k estimate
}
```

With each participant's value of $\widehat{k}$ stored in the corresponding element of the vector K.vec, let us examine these values and confirm that there are indeed 106 of them stored.

```
#print the k.hat values inside K.vec to the console
K.vec
##   [1] 7.052959e-04 1.952525e-02 6.279889e-03 3.106513e+00 9.443459e-04
##   [6] 1.183173e-02 7.792405e-03 4.121380e-02 2.166866e-03 1.851430e-03
##  [11] 1.835216e-02 6.848412e-02 1.253200e-02 5.644911e-05 3.917017e-03
##  [16] 2.750789e-02 9.416390e-03 2.706837e-03 1.158562e-01 2.339159e-04
##  [21] 5.654420e-02 1.924157e-02 7.786736e-04 2.225344e-03 1.238148e-02
##  [26] 1.737184e-03 1.006645e-02 6.653795e-02 4.119001e-04 4.115331e-04
##  [31] 2.122284e-02 8.613770e-02 1.438784e+00 2.457380e-02 1.087262e-03
##  [36] 4.645629e-03 4.105892e-02 9.843393e-03 2.102845e-03 3.947858e-01
##  [41] 4.392440e-03 1.043863e-02 5.207565e-03 2.480165e-03 2.890474e-01
##  [46] 7.969068e-03 1.041180e-06 1.111135e-02 1.334191e-03 4.690139e-02
##  [51] 1.541998e-02 2.656261e-03 2.676365e-03 1.582058e-01 2.288003e-03
##  [56] 1.606234e-02 1.598051e-02 5.757535e-02 1.524680e-02 5.524457e-01
##  [61] 1.029969e-03 4.620361e-01 1.040897e-02 3.163147e-04 5.727909e-03
##  [66] 1.660060e-01 1.531857e-02 5.343197e-01 3.719899e-02 1.558544e-01
##  [71] 1.345135e-03 3.329768e-04 4.723153e-05 3.592244e-02 8.398586e-01
##  [76] 3.267308e+00 1.283517e-03 2.957418e-02 5.499067e-03 1.423051e-01
##  [81] 2.190507e-03 3.898910e-03 6.109505e-04 5.744756e-04 1.192669e-02
##  [86] 3.503430e-04 5.695165e-02 1.393875e-02 1.192544e-01 1.404184e-04
##  [91] 4.431371e-04 1.813248e-02 3.385442e-03 4.639068e-03 1.151348e-02
##  [96] 1.204211e-02 1.318007e-03 5.991004e-03 1.141583e-02 6.315233e-04
## [101] 1.683690e-02 4.873263e-04 4.684650e-03 1.041180e-06 1.500254e-03
## [106] 6.310517e-03

#confirm there are n=106 observations in K.vec
length(K.vec)

## [1] 106

#Add the k.hat values to the data set
dat$k<-K.vec
```

R uses a specific format for scientific notation to express numbers that are very small or very large. For example, 7.05e-04 = 7.05×10^{-4} = 0.000705.

Once the above code has been run, the loop is complete and the vector "K.vec" is a length 106 vector where each element corresponds to that participant number's $\widehat{k}$ value. Now that $\widehat{k}$ values have been obtained for all participant data we move on the second stage of analysis.

Probability discounting

We have focused most of our attention on the analysis of delay discounting data, where we quantify the rate of devaluation of a reward as a function of delay to that reward. *Probability discounting* instead quantifies the rate of devaluation of a reward as a function of the probability of not receiving the reward. For example, in Rachlin et al. (1991), study participants were asked to choose between hypothetical smaller but certain cash rewards and larger uncertain rewards. For example, $500 for sure or a 50% chance of receiving $1000. Such prompts vary the probability of winning, express this probability in terms of odds against, and use discounting functions to quantify discounting rates. As with delay discounting, a one-parameter hyperbolic equation has been proposed. In addition, like delay discounting, several models for probability discounting have been proposed. The extent to which probability and delay discounting are comparable phenomena is also a topic of discussion in the literature. See Killeen (2023) and the references therein for more discussion.

Stage 2

In Stage 2, we analyze the collection of estimated discounting rates (the $\widehat{k}$ values) for the participants, including as a function of potential predictors. These estimated discounting rates are considered as data for the second stage of analysis. For this illustration we will compare discounting rates (i) between males and females, (ii) between smokers and nonsmokers, and (iii) as a function of age. With these goals in mind, we begin with an **exploratory data analysis**. Exploratory data analysis typically begins by plotting data. We consider both univariate plots and also multivariate plots.

A good first rule for exploratory data analysis is to establish which scale of measurement the data are measured on. There are frequently many potential variables that could be collected with respect to a research question. For example, in these data, smoking status was measured as a binary yes/no variable. However, researchers could instead ask how many cigarettes participants smoke in a given week. This latter question would be measured using a numeric variable that would be a whole number greater than or equal to zero. Analyzing data appropriately on the scale they are measured is a core tenet of a properly conducted analysis. In this study, we have variables that were measured on a binary scale (smoking status and gender) and two variables measured on a numeric scale (age in years and discounting rate $\widehat{k}$).

Univariate analyses

We will begin our overview of exploratory data analysis by illustrating **univariate** summaries and graphics. Univariate approaches focus on understanding each variables' data alone without any assessment of association with other variables. We may be interested in, for example, determining the number of participants who are smokers, how many are male and female, what the distribution of observed ages is, and also the distribution of observed $\widehat{k}$ values.

We may wish to tabulate the number of participants in each category of our categorical variables.

Note that in R, the dollar sign notation allows the user to specify an object inside another object. In this case, "dat$gender" reads the "gender" variable out of the "dat" object.

```
table(dat$gender) #make a table of gender data from the dat object

##
## Female   Male
##     27     79

table(dat$smoke_cigs) #make a table of smoking status from the dat object

##
##  No Yes
##  52  54
```

There are 27 females and 79 males in this sample. There are 54 smokers and 52 non-smokers in this sample.

Now let us consider the distribution of age. **Histograms** are a useful graphic to show features of a distribution of numeric data. Histograms organize the range of observed data into bins, then a bar is constructed for each bin to reflect the number of participants in that bin. We can also compute summary statistics for age.

```
hist(dat$age,main="Histogram of age",xlab="Age")
```

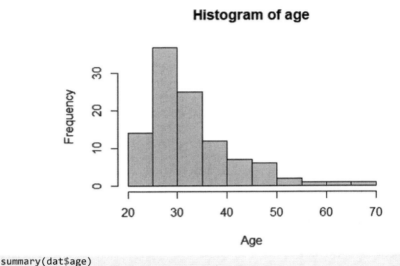

```
summary(dat$age)
##    Min. 1st Qu.  Median    Mean 3rd Qu.    Max.
##   21.00   28.00   31.00   33.49   36.00   67.00
```

We can see that ages range from 21 to 67 years with a mean age of 33.49 years, etc. The histogram reveals that the distribution of age is not symmetric. It has a heavier right tail, i.e., it is skewed to the right. The bars can be interpreted to indicate (for example) that about 14 individuals have an age between 20 and 25.

Let us next consider the distribution of $\widehat{k}$ obtained in Stage 1.

```
hist(K.vec,main="Estimated k values from n=106 participants",
     xlab='k',breaks=20) #make a histogram
```

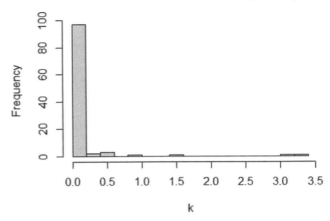

The above histogram shows the 106 estimated $\widehat{k}$ values. It is visually apparent that the distribution of these $\widehat{k}$ values is skewed right and bounded below by zero. For these reasons, it is customary to analyze k values on the natural log scale. The R code below also superimposes a normal distribution density function on to the $\widehat{k}$ values. This density curve is centered at the sample mean with sample standard deviation also obtained from the data.

```
hist(log(K.vec),main="Estimated ln(k) values from the n=106 participants",
     xlab='ln(k)',breaks=20,freq=FALSE)
xbar<-mean (log(K.vec));s<-sqrt(var(log(K.vec)))
ks<-seq(-15,5,.1)
lines(ks,dnorm(ks,mean=xbar,s),col='red')
```

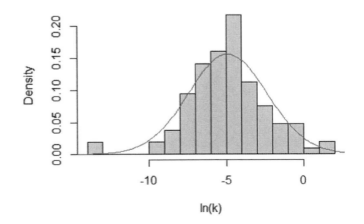

The above histogram of ln(k) is more symmetric and bell-shaped than the original version, and thus more suitable for typical statistical analyses which assume data are normally distributed. Analytic approaches that assume normality include t-tests and corresponding confidence intervals, analysis of variance (ANOVA), and typical regression approaches. These rudimentary analyses are presented in most intro textbooks, but rest assured more sophisticated statistical techniques have been developed and continue to be developed to model data of every sort no matter the distribution.

A subtle but very important statistical point: The appearance of a bell-shaped curve is typically assumed for **residuals** (i.e., the difference between a data point and an average or regression line) rather than the raw data themselves. To elaborate, the normality assumption requires slightly more than for us to look for a plausible normal distribution in a univariate histogram. For two-sample t-tests and ANOVA-based approaches, we presume the outcome variable $\ln(\widehat{k})$ is distributed normally within each group. Ordinary regression problems model the outcome variable $\ln(\widehat{k})$ as a function of (potentially several) predictor variables, and the extent to which individual data points depart from the line (i.e., residuals) are assumed to be normally distributed with constant variance. We will explore these techniques in more depth subsequently, including an assessment of whether the appropriate normality conditions hold in an end-of-chapter exercise. It is generally true that $\ln(\widehat{k})$ usually satisfies normality assumptions adequately and certainly more than the $\widehat{k}$ values, and so we can proceed with these sorts of techniques and models.

Many statistical techniques exist for settings where data are not normally distributed, but many of the most well-known techniques do assume a normal distribution. For the sake of brevity, we will not consider alternative techniques in depth. These include nonparametric rank-based procedures, quantile regression, and other techniques specifically developed to handle non-normal data, such as logistic regression for binary outcomes. Simple two-group comparisons, such as the rank-based Mann–Whitney test are available that do not assume normally distributed data. However, rank-based tests do not scale up well for multiple predictors. In these data, a researcher may be interested in modeling delay discounting as a function of smoking status, gender, and age simultaneously. Rank-based inference is not readily available, even for a small problem like this.

Multivariate analyses

Examining the association among variables is central to scientific and statistical practice. While the above univariate analyses helped familiarize us with the data and anticipate potential challenges with subsequent analysis (e.g., needing to log transform the $\widehat{k}$ data), we are centrally interested in the association among the variables. To proceed, let us consider each pairwise association in these data. With four variables, there are six pairwise associations.

As with univariate associations, the scales of measurement for each variable imply which graphical approaches may be sensible. When both variables are numeric, a scatter plot is typically a good choice. When there is one categorical variable and one numeric variable, we might consider producing a box plot. When both variables are categorical, mosaic plots are a viable choice. There are a variety of other viable choices as well, but these three graphics are fundamental.

```
lnk<-log(dat$k)
plot(dat$age,lnk,xlab="Age")
```

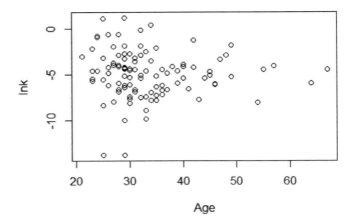

```
cor(dat$age,lnk)
## [1] -0.04820072
```

The scatter plot does not appear to show a particularly strong relationship between age and $\ln(\widehat{k})$. The cor( ) function computes the **correlation coefficient** between two variables, which measures the strength and direction of the linear relationship and is always between -1 and 1. Negative values show an inverse relationship and positive values show a direct relationship between the variables. The closer further the correlation is from zero, the stronger the relationship. Here, we see the correlation is $r = -0.048$, indicating a slight negative association in these data.

```
par(mfrow=c(2,2)) #Make a 2X2 figure
boxplot(dat$age~dat$gender,xlab="Gender",ylab="Age")
boxplot(dat$age~dat$smoke_cigs,xlab="Smoker",ylab="Age")

boxplot(lnk~dat$gender,xlab="Gender")
boxplot(lnk~dat$smoke_cigs,xlab="Smoker")
```

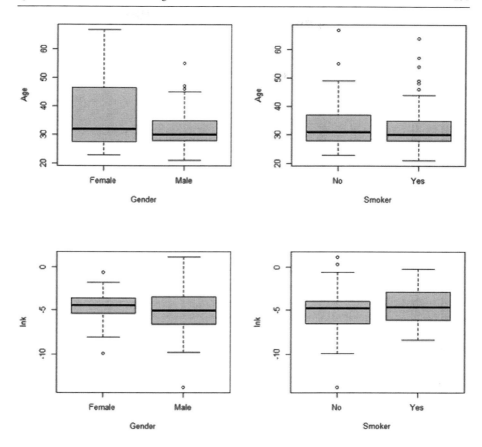

The age box plots indicate that females tended to be older than males in this study, but there was no substantive difference in age between smokers and nonsmokers. The $\ln(\widehat{k})$ box plots show a very slight difference in logged discounting rates, with females in this study slightly higher than males, and smokers slightly higher than nonsmokers.

Mosaic plots can be a useful graphic when multiple categorical variables' are being considered. A mosaic plot consists of a series of rectangular regions organized to show the relative size of all combinations of the levels of the categorical variables (female smokers, female nonsmokers, male smokers, and male nonsmokers in this case). The code below shows this. An upside of the mosaic plot is that it is easy to visually interpret the areas of rectangles compared for example with the pie-slice regions of a pie chart.

```
tab<-table(dat$gender,dat$smoke_cigs)
mosaicplot(tab,main='Mosaic plot',xlab='Gender',ylab='Smoker')
```

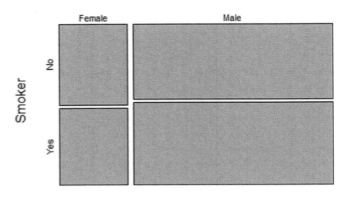

The above mosaic plot reexpresses that smokers and nonsmokers are roughly evenly split in these data and that there are more males than females. The gender split among smokers resembles that among nonsmokers (and the overall split), and similarly, the smoking status split is similar for both genders, suggesting that these variables do not share much of an association. If, for example, almost all of the smokers were male and the nonsmokers were female, this would be reflected in the plot with very large rectangles in one diagonal, and small rectangles in the other, and would indicate a strong association.

A note about plots

For our demonstration, we will load the "ggplot2" package and the "GGally" package. Both of these packages provide the user with sophisticated graphical options. The analysis code we are adapting for this example and related discussion appears here (https://ggobi.github.io/ggally/reference/ggpairs.html). Once those have been acquired and installed as described above, the following code will enable their use within R.

```
library(ggplot2)
library(GGally)

## Registered S3 method overwritten by 'GGally':
##   method from
##   +.gg   ggplot2
```

The function we will use is called "ggpairs." To read the help file documentation, run the following code, first removing the comment symbol.

```
#?ggpairs
```

Next, we pass a data frame that includes age, gender, smoker, and $\ln(\widehat{k})$ to the "ggpairs" function

```
plot.frame<-
data.frame(age=dat$age,gender=dat$gender,smoker=dat$smoke_cigs,lnk=log(dat$k)
)

plot.ob <- ggpairs(
  plot.frame,
  upper = list(continuous = "density", combo = "box_no_facet"),
  lower = list(continuous = "points", combo = "dot_no_facet")
)
plot.ob
```

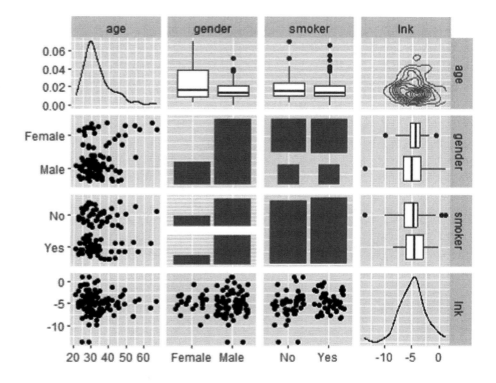

The above plot summarizes all two-way associations and uses a variety of graphical plotting techniques. It is rife with visual information. This is a sophisticated example of a **pairs plot**. In a pairs plot, variables (age, gender, and smoking status, $\ln(\widehat{k})$ in this case) indicates the position of a variable is summarized in both rows and columns. The diagonal panels from the top left to bottom right are univariate summaries of each variable. All other panels are bivariate associations, where the reader looks "left-to-right" to learn what is plotted on the vertical axis and "up-and-down" to determine what is on the horizontal axis.

Starting from the top left and moving across rows, the first panel is a density plot of age. The second and third panels in the first row are box plots of gender by age and smoking status by age, respectively. The fourth panel in the first row is a contour plot of $\ln(\widehat{k})$ by age.

The first panel in the second row is a jitter plot showing individual data points for age by gender. A small amount of random noise (i.e., jitter) is added to points on the vertical axis here to help unstack points within gender groups. The second row second column panel is a bar plot of gender. Next is a mosaic plot of smoking status by gender, then an $\ln(\widehat{k})$ by gender box plot.

The third row includes a jitter plot of age by smoking status, bar plots of gender by smoking status, bar plots of smoking status, a bar plot of smoking status, and a box plot of $\ln(\widehat{k})$ by smoking status.

The fourth row includes a scatter plot of age by $\ln(\widehat{k})$, jitter plots of gender by $\ln(\widehat{k})$ and smoking status by $\ln(\widehat{k})$, and a univariate density plot of $\ln(\widehat{k})$.

Creating useful and beautiful graphics is both a science and an art. The initial plots we made convey core data-analytic insight but are not especially visually appealing and are arguably not a judicious use of space for most publication venues. (We commonly agonize over attempts to perfect plots for publication). By contrast, the "GGally" pairs plot looks sleeker (with many additional plotting options available— see documentation), but is potentially dense to the point of being hard to digest. Details such as axis labels for the inner bar plots must be minimized or omitted to fit other information. When making plots we recommend organizing the core plots to emphasize and add clarity to the core points of the writing, and relegate other potentially useful plots (e.g., the pairs plot above) to an appendix to satisfy extra-curious readers. For the purpose of teaching the basics, we have opted to include code for fairly simple plots in this chapter. These plots adequately convey data-analytic insight but are probably not appealing enough to be publication quality in general.

Descriptive versus inferential statistical approaches

Broadly speaking, statistical statements are *Descriptive* or *Inferential*. **Descriptive statistics** describe sample data only.

```
mean(lnk)
## [1] -4.904101
```

In the above example code, we compute the sample mean of $-4.90$$. A *descriptive* interpretation of this number is "Among the 106 participants in our research study, the average $\ln(\hat{k})$" value is -4.90." We simply summarize what we see in the data, with no suggestion that this statistic is being extended in its interpretation beyond the sample. While making descriptive statements about the sample is always defensible, the true goal is usually to try and learn something more fundamental to a larger setting than merely the research participants at hand.

The true goal of discovering and/or describing fundamental truths underlying data generation involves the use of **inferential statistics**. Inferential statistics aim to extend observations from a sample and generalize to the broader **population** from which the sample was drawn. For example, if we are studying associations between smoking and delay discounting, it is not particularly impactful to merely summarize this association in 106 research participants. Instead, we hope we have learned something that extends to the broader population of smokers. A **Statistical Inference** is a statement made about the broader population on the basis of data analyzed from a sample, accompanied by an appropriate probability statement that quantifies uncertainty.

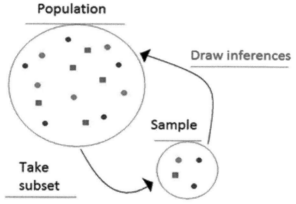

Statistical inference occurs when probability-based conclusions are drawn about the population on the basis of a carefully drawn and analyzed set of sample data.

The above schema shows that there is an overall population of interest. It is impractical or impossible to measure every unit in the population. The major innovation of statistical reasoning is that, when a **representative sample** is drawn from the population, statistical methods (derived on the basis of probability theory) enable analysts to generalize findings from the sample to the broader population with accompanying statements of uncertainty. Uncertainty is explained using the language of probability.

We will discuss three widely used inferential approaches here: Point estimation, confidence intervals, and hypothesis testing.

Point estimation occurs when the analyst purports that a summary statistic is a "good guess" for the corresponding population value. Using the above example, the sample mean for $\ln(k)$ among smokers is -4.90. This is a summary statistic based on the sample. However, the moment we say something like "Our best guess for the true population mean $\ln(k)$ is -4.90" we engage in *point estimation* as a statistical inference exercise. The notion that a sample statistic is "close to" or "a good guess for" the true but unknown value in the population (of all smokers in this example) is intuitively appealing and also mathematically justified. Upper-level and graduate courses in statistics use calculus and probability theory to justify formally, for example, that the sample mean is a good guess for the population mean.

Confidence intervals are derived to ensure that true but unknown population parameters are contained within the interval with a user-controlled long-run rate of success (e.g., we expect 95 out of 100 95% confidence intervals to contain the true but unknown parameter). Hypothesis tests are derived to have user-controlled rates of obtaining a false positive finding (i.e., type I error), traditionally set to 5% (i.e., $\alpha = 0.05$). A good book that develops ideas of statistical inference using calculus while teaching probability theory is Wackerly et al. (2014).

Of course, not just any sample is **representative** of the broader population. The gold standard approach for obtaining a representative sample is to obtain a **random sample**. The term "random" has a specific technical meaning in this context. We do not mean "haphazard," "chaotic," or any other colloquial use of the term "random."

Instead, random sampling occurs when each element of the population has a chance of being included in the sample, and a probability-based mechanism is in charge of drawing the sample. You could think about drawing names out of a really big hat. A **Simple random sample** is the most conceptually straightforward design, as it gives every subset of a fixed size the same chance of being selected, thus every member of the population has the same chance of being included in the sample.

It is easy to discuss drawing a sample completely randomly from a larger population and admiring the simple elegance and amazing theoretical properties of statistical approaches when this is the case. Reality is messier than this. It is not easy to obtain a representative sample. It might not be possible to even list every element in the population (such a list is called the **sampling frame**), let alone locate all individuals sampled from that list and ensure every individual selected by the researcher actually enrolls in and completes the study.

I am quite fond of the following "Fundamental Rule for using data for inference," as it comments on the viability of applying statistical methods to data even in situations where sampling is not perfect (Utts & Heckard, 2014). This rule is written as follows:

"The fundamental rule for using data for inference is that available data can be used to make inferences about a much larger group if the data can be considered to be representative with regard to the questions of interest."

Samples that are not drawn representatively from a population are broadly known as **convenience samples**. Convenience samples can be valuable (e.g., when studying an extremely rare disease, researchers may consider themselves lucky to obtain data from anyone with the disease regardless of sampling design). However, when convenience samples are drawn and their data analyzed, we do have a certain level of skepticism in the statistical results owing to the potential for unquantifiable bias to manifest in the results.

Another key point is that representativeness is a function of the sampling mechanism, not the sample size. An ideally drawn random sample is representative of the population even if the sample size is not large. By contrast, if a flawed sampling design specifically excludes certain segments of the population (e.g., affluent recreational cocaine users are unlikely to enroll in a discounting study on cocaine users because the compensation is likely too low to induce them to participate), then merely increasing the sample size will not overcome the bias introduced by the flawed sampling approach. Sampling theory is its own field within statistics. A good introductory textbook on sampling is Lohr (2021).

The notion of randomization as a method to ensure valid inference is also ubiquitous within the study of the design of experiments. Unlike in an observational study, in an **experiment**, the researcher assigns experimental units to different treatments. Sophisticated experimental designs can randomize in a way to account for known confounds (e.g., ensure that members of each socioeconomic stratum are present in all experimental groups so socioeconomic effects do not mask experimental effects). Even if many known confounding variables are accounted for in this way, randomization remains essential. *Random assignment of units to treatments is ingenious because randomization makes treatment groups the same on average, both with respect to known and also with respect to unknown potential confounding variables.* A good book for further reasoning design of experiments is Montgomery (2008).

Executing Stage 2 analysis using inferential statistics

The exploratory data analysis above is descriptive in nature. We have not (yet) made any assertions that the patterns in these data extend to a broader population. Next, we will do just this for the three comparisons of discounting rates (i) between males and females, (ii) between smokers and nonsmokers, and (iii) as a function of age. We will assume our sample data are representative of a relevant larger population. We will illustrate hypothesis tests and confidence intervals for parameters for each comparison. Like many topics in this chapter, we provide a brief overview of common techniques appropriate for analysis in this setting. We assume the reader has been exposed to the basic idea of statistical hypothesis testing and confidence intervals. For those who may wish to review these concepts, an excellent book to further study the applied statistical techniques presented here is Utts and Heckard (2014).

Comparing discounting between males and females

Recall the box plot of estimated $\ln(\widehat{k})$ values as a function of sex.

```
boxplot(lnk~dat$gender,xlab="Gender")
```

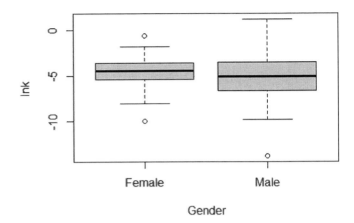

```
t.test(lnk~dat$gender)

## 
##  Welch Two Sample t-test
## 
## data:  lnk by dat$gender
## t = 0.66633, df = 64.897, p-value = 0.5076
## alternative hypothesis: true difference in means between group Female and
group Male is not equal to 0
## 95 percent confidence interval:
##  -0.6400484  1.2809534
## sample estimates:
## mean in group Female    mean in group Male
##            -4.665273             -4.985726
```

The above code compares males and females in terms of discounting rates. The box plot shows little shift between the genders, although it visually appears that males are generating more variability in their discounting rates. We estimate the average discounting $\ln(\hat{k})$ among females and males to be -4.67 and -4.99, respectively. The t.test( ) code conducts a statistical comparison between these groups. The "Welch Two Sample t-test" phrase indicates that the testing procedure does not assume a common variance between the groups. For the test with null hypothesis of no difference in $\ln(k)$ between the groups, the P-value is 0.508. We fail to reject the null hypothesis, as results or more extreme against the null would arise half the time if the null hypothesis is true. (i.e., If there truly is no underlying difference between groups, results such as those we see here are not particularly improbable). A 95% confidence interval for the difference in means is $(-0.64, 1.28)$. Since this interval contains zero, it is plausible that there is no underlying difference between males and females on the basis of these data.

Using the data in this chapter as an example, we might study the association between smoking status and delay discounting as measured by $\ln(\widehat{k})$ within this sample, which contains 52 nonsmokers and 54 smokers. We can accomplish this graphically with box plots and in tabular format with summary statistics.

Comparing discounting between smokers and nonsmokers

Recall the box plot of estimated $\ln(\widehat{k})$ values as a function of smoking status.

```
boxplot(lnk~dat$smoke_cigs,xlab="Smoking status")
```

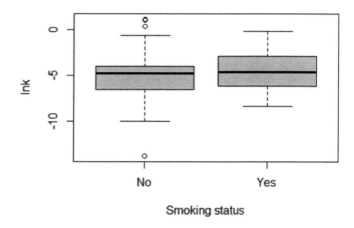

```
t.test(lnk~dat$smoke_cigs)

## 
##  Welch Two Sample t-test
## 
## data:  lnk by dat$smoke_cigs
## t = -0.96964, df = 95.021, p-value = 0.3347
## alternative hypothesis: true difference in means between group No and
group Yes is not equal to 0
## 95 percent confidence interval:
##  -1.4765590  0.5074968
## sample estimates:
##  mean in group No mean in group Yes
##         -5.150938         -4.666407
```

The box plot above suggests that smokers may have higher discounting rates on average than nonsmokers. We estimate the average discounting $\ln(\widehat{k})$ among nonsmokers is -5.15 and among smokers the average discounting $\ln(\widehat{k})$ is estimated to be $-4:67$ among nonsmokers. For the test with null hypothesis of no difference in $\ln(k)$ between the groups, the *P*-value is 0.334. We fail to reject the null hypothesis, as results as or more extreme against the null would arise one-third of the time if the null hypothesis is true. A 95% confidence interval for the difference in means is $(-1.48, 0.51)$. Since this interval contains zero, it is plausible that there is no underlying difference in discount rate between smokers and nonsmokers on the basis of these data.

Assessing discounting as a function of age

Recall the scatter plot with $\ln(\widehat{k})$ on the vertical axis and age on the horizontal axis. The following code fits a *simple linear regression model* to these data. Simple linear regression proceeds by identifying the straight line that is "closest" to the data in the least squares sense. We have already seen the idea of least squares with the nonlinear regression approach we used to fit the Mazur function to indifference point data. As before, the least squares approach identifies regression lines for which the sum of squared residuals is minimized. In this simple linear model, the parameters are the slope and y-intercept of the regression line.

```
plot(dat$age,lnk)
mod<-lm(lnk~dat$age)
abline(mod,col='red',xlab="age",lwd=2)
```

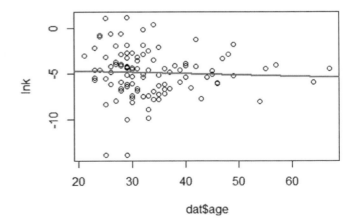

```
summary(mod)

## 
## Call:
## lm(formula = lnk ~ dat$age)
## 
## Residuals:
##     Min      1Q  Median      3Q     Max
## -8.9914 -1.4603  0.1821  1.3617  6.0244
## 
## Coefficients:
##              Estimate Std. Error t value Pr(>|t|)
## (Intercept) -4.42937    0.99637  -4.446  2.2e-05 ***
## dat$age     -0.01418    0.02880  -0.492    0.624
## ---
## Signif. codes:  0 '***' 0.001 '**' 0.01 '*' 0.05 '.' 0.1 ' ' 1
## 
## Residual standard error: 2.567 on 104 degrees of freedom
## Multiple R-squared:  0.002323,   Adjusted R-squared:  -0.00727
## F-statistic: 0.2422 on 1 and 104 DF,  p-value: 0.6237

confint(mod)

##                   2.5 %      97.5 %
## (Intercept) -6.40520520 -2.45353056
## dat$age     -0.07129443  0.04294416
```

The estimated slope and intercept are -0.014 and -4.429, respectively. This means that for a 1 year increase in age, we estimate the average $\ln(k)$ *decreases* (due to a negative sign) by 0.014. The mathematical interpretation of the y-intercept is that individuals with age $= 0$ have an average $\ln(k)$ of -4.43. In this case, it is not meaningful to consider a zero-year-old's discounting, so direct interpretation of the y-intercept is basically meaningless. Nonetheless, the y-intercept is important because it governs the overall height of the line. Do not omit the y-intercept from the model unless you have compelling scientific information that at $x = 0$ the outcome $y = 0$ (e.g., x is fuel burned and y is exhaust emitted).

As before, we may be interested in confidence intervals and hypothesis tests for the parameters of interest. Since the y-intercept is not meaningful in this analysis, we focus our statistical inference on the slope parameter. The summary( ) function provides estimates, standard errors, test statistics, and *P*-values for the null hypothesis that the true parameter value is zero. In this case, for the age effect, the *P*-value is 0.624. We fail to reject the null hypothesis because a slope value of zero is plausible on the basis of these observed data. This corresponds to the visual evidence in the scatter plot where these data do not appear to show much of a linear relationship. A 95% confidence interval for the slope is $(-0.071, 0.043)$.

Ordinary regression, such as the analysis we have conducted here, assumes that residuals have a normal distribution with constant variance. Some of the exercises at the end of this chapter will guide you through a way to assess the plausibility of these assumptions.

Regression is one of the most flexible and important classes of statistical techniques. Regression can be tailored to suit a vast collection of problems. Further topics include multiple regression (i.e., what to do when multiple predictors are available), model selection (i.e., which predictors should be included and what function of these best describe the response), regression for outcomes that do not have normally distributed residuals (i.e., *generalized linear models* are useful for outcomes with categorical or count outcomes). A good book to learn more about regression is Montgomery et al. (2015).

Contemporary issues in statistical practice

There are a number of interesting issues and controversies related to contemporary statistical practice. The largest-looming of these is the *replication crisis*. If the goal of science is to uncover and understand observable truths in the universe, then similar studies should produce similar results. If a well-executed replication study fails to produce the same conclusions as the original study, then arguably the original study fell short of finding the correct answer to the research question. Readers are hopefully aware of the replication crisis in general (Ioannidis, 2005) and in psychology specifically (Collaboration 2015). Many factors can contribute to the failure of a study to replicate, including choices made during experimental design, data collection and processing, initial exploratory data analysis, and modeling. Certainly, a lot of scrutiny has been given to issues of classical hypothesis testing, including the use of P-values and surrounding practices (Leek & Peng, 2015; Young & Karr, 2011) describes the situation of scientific publishing based on statistical significance and P-values as an out-of-control process. In response to these concerns, the American Statistical Association issued a statement with clarifications and a few suggestions to clarify definitions and best practices related to P-values (Wasserstein & Lazar, 2016). The literature review in Franck et al. (2022) describes some of the conversations about statistical hypothesis testing and P-values that have been tied to the replication crisis. An entire chapter or possibly even a textbook could be filled with this discussion. The goal here is to outline some issues broadly and describe statistical workflows that are transparent and responsible.

The previous analyses in this chapter are not a blueprint for a reasonable analytic strategy in a research project. Our goal has been to demonstrate a wide variety of relevant methods for analyzing discounting data. With this focus, we have not articulated a primary analysis strategy. We have not guarded against problems of multiple comparisons, i.e., *multiplicity*. We have not decided in advance how to handle participants who fail attention checks or commit Johnson & Bickel violations. Instead, we have conducted a collection of individual analyses to illustrate each concept in a safe sandbox using data without particularly strong associations between discounting and other measures. We make no claims about research conclusions on the basis of the analyses in this chapter. This has been a training ground, and the next exercise is to think more about how a reasonable analytic pipeline will look for a research project.

Behavior analysts know well that organisms tend to behave in a manner for which they are rewarded. This extends to scientific publishing as well, where the rewards to publish novel, "statistically significant" research are compelling. These include rising notoriety, competitive advantage in the pursuit of extramural funding, and the chance to continue participating in science. The consequences for failing to publish novel research are punishing and involve either a quick or prolonged exit from a scientific career.

Mix this reward/punishment structure with the historical but controversial bright line rule of declaring any scientific finding to be "statistically significant" so long as the data analysis yields a P-value below 0.05, and there is an inherent conflict of interest that incentivizes analysts to select analyses that achieve "statistical significance" and portraying these results in a manner that failed to acknowledge uncertainty in conclusions. This process of repeatedly conducting analyses and/or gathering more data, then stopping once an analysis has a P-value below $\alpha = 0.05$ is known as p-hacking, and it is problematic because it fundamentally violates the statistical error rates that come with hypothesis testing.

By way of review, classical hypothesis testing works by controlling the rate at which a false positive finding occurs. This false positive error rate, also known as the Type I error rate, is set in advance and has traditionally been $\alpha = 0.05$. This means that even in the case where every other aspect of the study is done correctly, we would reject the null hypothesis in 5% of the cases where it is actually true, i.e., make a false positive error. Note that this traditional threshold has recently been challenged and there are reasonable arguments for setting $\alpha = 0.005$ for new discoveries (Benjamin et al., 2018). Thus, the Type I error rate α is the rate at which an analyst is willing to incorrectly reject a true null hypothesis (which is commonly a hypothesis of no association although specific null values of parameters can be stipulated).

The idea is that hypothesis testing protects the broader scientific effort from a preponderance of false positive findings. But if an unscrupulous analyst decides to continually try various analysis plans until a single analysis yields a P-value below 0.05, then obviously this procedure leads to much higher than a 5% false positive rate.

This conflict of interest can be insidious. Imagine your primary analysis plan calls for using Mazur's $\ln(k)$ as a discounting metric and examining its association with a key predictor. The statistical analysis reveals a small association between your predictor and discounting, with a P-value of 0.13. According to this primary analysis (and a traditional error rate of $\alpha = 0.05$), the true association is plausibly null, your chances of publishing in a high-impact journal are low, you have no compelling pilot data for a grant application, and the clock is ticking on the remaining time in your graduate school/post-doc/faculty position.

Imagine you decide to mess around a little more to get a lower P-value. Suppose switching to a different metric (e.g., AUC) and eliminating two outliers makes the same analysis yield a P-value of 0.03. Now, the actual false positive error rate of your procedure is MUCH higher than 5%. You must choose between fundamentally violating the error rate and publishing your work in a less-than-honest manner (presenting the results as ironclad), or possibly risking your future in academia if you publish nothing.

The term "p-hacking" refers to deliberately choosing specific analyses that reveal "statistically significant" associations while deliberately failing to acknowledge that a greater number of statistical tests were conducted whose results were nonsignificant, and the choice of which analysis to report was based only on finding an analysis with a significant *P*-value. The incentive to p-hack is that by illegitimately obtaining low *P*-values, research findings are presented as though they are more "statistically significant" than the data suggest, more journals are more likely to look favorably on the findings, and the researcher is able to reap the rewards of successful publication, albeit at the cost of polluting the literature with findings that are unlikely to replicate, potentially sending other researchers down faulty lines of inquiry.

One idea to combat this incentive structure is to pursue the idea of preregistered journal articles. The basic idea with preregistered articles is that a researcher will draft the introduction and methods section (which fully details the primary analysis plan) for a paper, and then submit these to a journal for publication *before* collecting and analyzing the data. The journal accepts or rejects the paper based on scientific novelty and methodological soundness. Then the researcher completes the study and is guaranteed publication regardless of the results of the statistical analysis. If an investigation is deemed scientifically sound but does not yield strong evidence of association for a reasonably powered study, then that should be reported.

Here are three pieces of advice we would offer to aspiring statistical analysts in the world of behavior analysis:

(1) Preplan your primary analysis. Describe everything from data collection, articulation of inclusion/exclusion criteria, how to handle outliers, how missing data will be handled, which models will be fit, how associations between discounting will be quantified, and which multiplicity adjustments will be used BEFORE data collection begins. Execute that plan and report the results.

(2) Transparently report all comparisons and secondary analyses you conduct. Of course, data may provide value and insights beyond what the analyst anticipated with their primary analysis plan. (Imagine if Alexander Fleming threw away the contaminated Petri dish that led to the discovery of antibiotics!) By clearly demarcating primary analyses and secondary analyses, and reporting on all analyses attempted, you acknowledge multiplicity and protect against perceptions of p-hacking. (Relegate low-impact analysis results to an appendix or online supplement).

(3) Report and discuss interpretable effect sizes and graphical displays of data. Help the audience understand the *strength of the associations* among key variables in your data. Do not merely report *P*-values and declare "statistical significance." A good reference is Cohen (1992).

Let us also briefly distinguish between replication and reproducibility. A study is *replicable* if another research group can redo your study by following your study protocol and obtaining the same results and conclusions as your study. *Reproducibility* refers to the ability of an analyst with access to your data and code to reproduce the same results you published on the basis of your data. It is important for analysts to be impeccably organized in data collection and store all analysis codes for posterity. Increasingly, journals urge authors to make raw data and analysis scripts public where possible so that claims in articles can be reproduced by other researchers.

Finally, we note that the list of things "not-to-do" is infinitely large. Once upon a time at Virginia Tech, the consulting director asked the design of experiments teacher why nobody had written a book of common mistakes in study design. To this, the professor responded that such a book could never be completed!

The role of planning in scientific investigation

We have meandered through a number of different topics related to the analysis of delay discounting data. For this chapter to be maximally informative, we have introduced a topic, illustrated it on our example dataset, and then explained the outcome of that investigation. We have had little regard for what topic is next, how many (i.e., the **multiplicity** of) statistical comparisons were conducted, or establishing a concrete primary analysis plan. We believe this is the way to maximize the educational value of the chapter.

In many ways, this is the *opposite* of what should be done when conducting a formal research study. Before one begins analyzing data, we remind the reader that *this has been an instructional textbook chapter not intended to resemble a typical research analysis*. This distinction is important because when designing a research study, the analyst must consider many study design issues *before data analysis begins*. Some of the specific statistical and data-analytic issues are:

(i) Missing data. The reason for the patterns of missing data guides best practices for subsequent analysis (Allison, 2001; Little & Rubin, 2014).
(ii) Whether and how to prescreen participant data and how to handle data patterns that diverge sharply from model form (e.g., we expect a decreasing trend between valuation and delay but sometimes see a flat, wildly variable, or increasing trend which seems irrational).
(iii) How to handle outliers and other unusual data points. Even a small number of extreme data points can greatly influence analysis results. Why are there unusual points and how should they be handled?
(iv) Which models to fit and which methods to fit them? Many competing models have been proposed.
(v) How many comparisons will we make and how to make them (e.g. smokers vs. nonsmokers; number of cigarettes smoked daily)? Failure to account for the effects of multiple testing (i.e., multiplicity) leads to greatly increased chances of false positive findings. Deliberately exploiting this practice is known as "p-hacking." More discussion of some of these issues and other contemporary issues and controversies related to statistical analysis can be found in the **Contemporary issues in statistical practice** Section above.

To summarize the point, this textbook chapter is designed to impart skills and knowledge one item at a time. By contrast, research studies are proactively planned by research teams with combined experience in statistical, behavioral analysis, and other relevant research skills and knowledge.

Continuing your statistical training

This chapter is intended to be an on-ramp for behavior analysts who wish to move toward greater statistical knowledge. So unfortunately, if we were successful you may feel you are suddenly on a highway with little idea of what to do next! The machinery here is powerful enough to be dangerous, and we share the statistical highway with hobbyists, professionals, fools, and charlatans. What we have covered here is just a tiny introductory piece of the broader statistical field.

To continue the driving example, the best rule is to move carefully and safely at the speed you are comfortable. If you aren't sure what to do next, read! Ask! Like any road trip, the more knowledge you have about the route ahead, the better. Consider the value of finding trusted traveling companions who can help navigate and drive through challenging parts of the landscape. The biggest surprise about statistics, to me, is how subtle the field is. I think this is mostly due to the fact humans are not naturally good at understanding uncertainty, and statistics is all about finding a few crude signals in a world dominated by uncertainty. We wish the reader the best of luck on this journey, and do not hesitate to reach out.

Exercises

General questions:

(1) Let us review the logarithm function more thoroughly. Do you know what the logarithm function looks like? Take a pen and paper and try to draw the function $y = \ln(x)$. Now, write an R program to graph this function. In what ways is your drawing similar to the R plot? Are there any differences or things you learned from this activity?

Stage 1 questions:

(2) Consider again the first stage of analysis. We used the Mazur model but another discounting model that has two parameters was popularized by Rachlin, (2006):

$$E(y) = \frac{A}{1 + k * D^s},$$

where k and s are unknown parameters that must be estimated. Adjust the code that fits the Mazur model to instead fit the Rachlin model to the first participant's data. Report the estimated $\hat{k}$ and $\hat{s}$ values from the Rachlin model, and plot indifference points by delay including regression lines for both Mauzr's and Rachlin's model.

(3) Recall that Effective Delay 50 (ED50) is the delay at which a future reward is devalued by half of the larger later amount. Use algebra to show that the ED50 for the Rachlin model is

$$\left(\frac{1}{k}\right)^{1/s}.$$

Hint—set right hand size of Rachlin equation in the first problem to $A/2$, then solve for D.

(4) Estimate ED50 for the first participant's data using both the Mazur model and also the Rachlin model. Do these estimates agree to a reasonable extent? Does this corroborate what you see in the plot from the previous problem? Do you think the agreement between models would be as similar for ED90 (i.e., the delay at which 90% of the larger later reward is devalued)? Justify your explanation using the plot from problem (2).

Stage 2 questions

(5) Report the number of participants who violated one or both Johnson & Bickel criteria (i.e., they have a value of JBviol = 1 in the original data). Report the number of participants who

failed the attention check (i.e., they have a value of ddattend = "$0.00 now" in the original data). Make a two-way table of these variables and comment on the extent to which those who failed the attention check are also Johnson & Bickel criteria violators.

(6) Consider an analysis in which violators of the Johnson & Bickel criteria are not analyzed with the full group in the broader statistical analysis. Subset the data to include only individuals who do not violate the criteria (i.e., they have a value of JBviol = 0 in the original data). Redo the two-stage analyses presented in the chapter to determine whether our results comparing discounting between smokers and nonsmokers, females and males change and whether the association between discounting and age changes if Johnson & Bickel criteria violators are omitted from the main analysis.

(7) Write a loop that computes and stores AUC for all subject participants. Make a histogram of these AUC values. Take the natural log of each AUC value and make a second histogram of these lnAUC values. Which of AUC and logAUC do you think more closely resembles a normal distribution and why?

(8) Create a pairs plot that includes Mazur lnk, Mazur ED50, AUC, and ln(AUC). Interpret the plot. Does this plot alone definitively determine which discounting metric is best?

(9) Ordinary regression assumes residuals (i.e., the difference between data points and the corresponding values on the regression line at the same x values) are normally distributed, and that variance in these residuals is constant. For the regression problem with $\ln(\hat{k})$ as the outcome and age as the predictor, use the skills in this book plus a few Google searches to (i) Obtain the predicted values and residuals from this analysis, (ii) make a histogram of the residuals, and (iii) a scatter plot with predicted values on the horizontal axis and residuals on the vertical axis. Does it appear that the assumptions are reasonably satisfied?

Hints for exercises

Unless otherwise stated, objects in the code below are as defined in the chapter.

(1)
```
#Log is defined on positive number line
#Make a dense grid of points there
x<-seq(.001,4,.001)
lnx<-log(x)
plot(x,lnx,type='l')
abline(v=1,col='lightgrey',lty=3)
abline(h=0,col='lightgrey',lty=3)
```

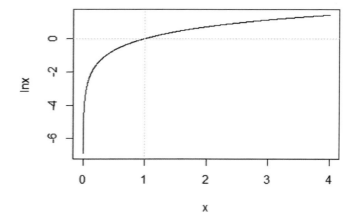

```
#log of 1 is zero
#log of zero not defined
#vertical range of log function as x increases is unbounded
#smooth, monotone increasing function
#not defined for negative numbers

(2)
i<-1 #Set an index number to 1 for the first subject
y.frame<-dat[i,5:11,drop=FALSE] #ith row, columns 5 through 11
y<-as.vector(as.matrix(t(y.frame))) #Make y a vector
D<-c(1,7,30,90,365,1825,9125) #Define the delays D

#Fit the Rachlin model
Rachlin.mod<-nls(y~1/(1+k*D^s),start=list(k=.1,s=.1)) #Fit the Mazur model to
these data
summary(mod) #Summary of the fitted model

##
## Call:
## lm(formula = lnk ~ dat$age)
##
## Residuals:
##     Min      1Q  Median      3Q     Max
## -8.9914 -1.4603  0.1821  1.3617  6.0244
##
## Coefficients:
##             Estimate Std. Error t value Pr(>|t|)
## (Intercept) -4.42937    0.99637  -4.446 2.2e-05 ***
## dat$age     -0.01418    0.02880  -0.492   0.624
## ---
## Signif. codes:  0 '***' 0.001 '**' 0.01 '*' 0.05 '.' 0.1 ' ' 1
##
## Residual standard error: 2.567 on 104 degrees of freedom
## Multiple R-squared:  0.002323,   Adjusted R-squared:  -0.00727
## F-statistic: 0.2422 on 1 and 104 DF,  p-value: 0.6237

k.hat<-summary(Rachlin.mod)$coef[1,1]
s.hat<-summary(Rachlin.mod)$coef[2,1]
print("k.hat and s.hat")

## [1] "k.hat and s.hat"

k.hat; s.hat

## [1] 9.418203e-05

## [1] 1.277788

D.s<-seq(0,9500,1) #Create a fine grid across delays. Used later to plot the
regression line.
preds.Rachlin<-predict(Rachlin.mod,newdata=data.frame(D=D.s)) #Obtain
predicted values
plot(D,y,xlab='Delay (days)',ylab='Indifference point',
     main="Indifference points, model fit, and ED50") #Scatter plot
lines(D.s,preds.Rachlin,col='blue') #Add the regression line to the plot
lines(D.s,preds,col='red',lty=2) #Add the regression line to the plot
legend(6000,0.8,legend=c("Mazur","Rachlin"),col=c("red","blue"),lty=c(2,1))
```

Quantitative models of discounting

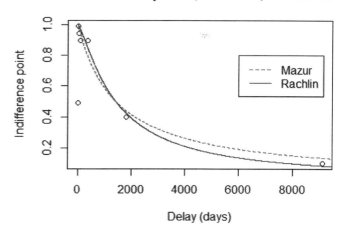

Indifference points, model fit, and ED50

The parameter estimates are $\hat{k} = 9.4 \times 10^{-5} = .000094$ and $\hat{s} = 1.277788$. The scatter plot shows the Mazur fit in a red dashed line and the Rachlin fit in a solid blue line.

(3)

$$\frac{A}{2} = \frac{A}{1 + kD^s}, \text{divide both sides by A, then cross multiply}$$

$$2 = 1 + kD^s, \text{subtract 1 from both sides}$$

$$1 = kD^s, \text{divide both sides by k, then exponentiate both sides to the } 1/s \text{ power}$$

$$\left(\frac{1}{k}\right)^{1/s} = D$$

Thus, the delay D at which the regression line is half the larger later value is $\left(\frac{1}{k}\right)^{1/s}$. This is the general process for obtaining analytical solutions for ED50, see Franck et al. (2015) for more details about ED50 for different discounting models.

(4)
```
ED50.Rachlin=(1/k.hat)^(1/s.hat)
ED50.Rachlin
```
```
## [1] 1415.088
```

For the Mazur model, the estimated ED50 value is $\frac{1}{k} = 1418$ days (from earlier in the chapter). For the Rachlin model, the estimated ED50 is $\left(\frac{1}{k}\right)^{1/\hat{s}} = 1415$ days. It is unsurprising that these values are close because as the above plot shows, the lines happen to be very close to each other when indifference point $= 0.5$. We do not expect ED90 values to agree very much, because at an indifference point value of 0.1, these curves are further apart.

(5)
```
table(dat$JBviol)
```
```
## 
##  0  1
## 82 24
```
```
table(dat$ddattend)
```
```
## 
##   $0.00 now $100.00 in 1 day
##       6                  100
```
```
table(dat$JBviol,dat$ddattend)
```
```
##     
##      $0.00 now $100.00 in 1 day
##   0      1                   81
##   1      5                   19
```

Twenty four participants violate the Johnson & Bickel criteria. Six individuals failed the attention check by answering they would rather have zero dollars now instead of 100 dollars in a day. Five of the six individuals who failed the attention check also violated Johnson & Bickel criteria.

(6)
```
dat.noJB<-dat[dat$JBviol==0,]
```

Quantitative models of discounting

The above code creates a data set called dat.noJB which starts as the original dat set, then (using square bracket notation), only rows with JBbiol = 0 are retained (since this condition is before the comma in the square brackets). Since there is no condition after the comma, this indicates that all columns from dat remain in dat.noJB. Complete the analysis by using the new data object to perform similar steps to what we saw in the chapter.

(7)
```
library(pracma)
AUC.vec<-c() #initialize AUC.vec as an empty vector
for(i in 1:106){ #begin at i=1, do everything in curly brackets, increment i, repeat
  y.frame<-dat[i,5:11,drop=FALSE] #pull indifference points for ith participant
  y<-as.vector(as.matrix(t(y.frame)))   #turn data frame y.frame into vector y
  AUC.vec[i]<-trapz(D,y)
}
ln.AUC.vec<-log(AUC.vec)
hist(AUC.vec)
```

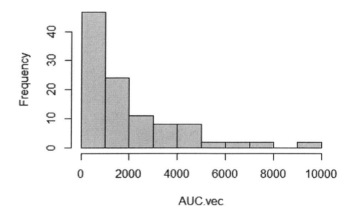

```
hist(ln.AUC.vec)
```

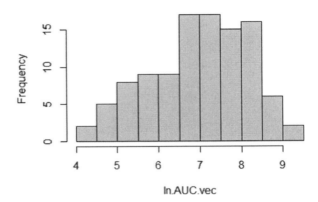

Histogram of ln.AUC.vec

Neither really looks like a normal distribution.

```
(8)
library(ggplot2)
library(GGally)
ED50.Mazur<-1/K.vec
plot.frame<-data.frame(lnk=lnk,ED50=ED50.Mazur,AUC=AUC.vec,ln.AUC=ln.AUC.vec)
plot.ob <- ggpairs(
  plot.frame,
  upper = list(continuous = "density", combo = "box_no_facet"),
  lower = list(continuous = "points", combo = "dot_no_facet")
)
plot.ob
```

Quantitative models of discounting

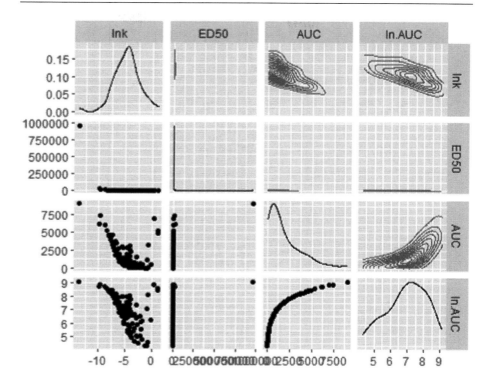

The above plot visualizes the distributions of and associations among four discounting metrics but does not definitively recommend any as intrinsically better than the others. We note an outlier in lnk, and we might consider log-transforming ED50 in a revision of this plot.

(9)
```
mod<-lm(lnk~dat$age)
preds<-predict(mod)
resids<-resid(mod)
hist(resids) #Eh good enough
```

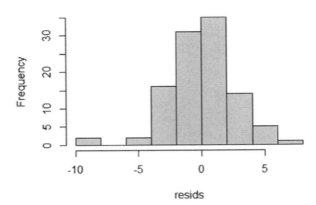

Histogram of resids

```
plot(preds, resids) #*Maybe* some non constant variance
```

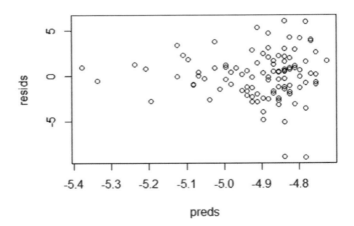

```
#probably ok
```

Both assumptions seem to be reasonably well met, though neither is perfect. I would personally be comfortable analyzing the data with the proposed model.

References

Allison, P. D. (2001). Missing data. In *Quantitative applications in the social sciences*. SAGE Publications. https://books.google.com/books?id=LJB2AwAAQBAJ.

Benjamin, D. J., Berger, J. O., Johannesson, M., Nosek, B. A., Wagenmakers, E.-J., Berk, R., Bollen, K. A., et al. (2018). Redefine statistical significance. *Nature Human Behaviour, 2*(1), 6−10. https://doi.org/10.1038/s41562-017-0189-z

Borges, A. M., Jinyi, K., Milhorn, H., & Yi, R. (2016). An alternative approach to calculating area-under-the-curve (AUC) in delay discounting research. *Journal of the Experimental Analysis of Behavior, 106*(2), 145−155. https://doi.org/10.1002/jeab.219

Chávez, M. E., Villalobos, E., Baroja, J. L., & Bouzas, A. (2017). Hierarchical bayesian modeling of intertemporal choice. *Judgment and Decision Making, 12*(1), 19−28.

Cohen, J. (1992). A power primer. *Psychological Bulletin, 112*(1), 155−159. https://doi.org/10.1037//0033-2909.112.1.155. PMID: 19565683.

Collaboration, Open Science. (2015). Estimating the reproducibility of psychological science. *Science, 349*(6251), Article aac4716.

Franck, C. T., Koffarnus, M. N., House, L. L., & Bickel, W. K. (2015). Accurate characterization of delay discounting: A multiple model approach using approximate bayesian model selection and a unified discounting measure. *Journal of the Experimental Analysis of Behavior, 103*(1), 218−233. https://doi.org/10.1002/jeab.128

Franck, C. T., Koffarnus, M. N., McKerchar, T. L., & Bickel, W. K. (2019). An overview of bayesian reasoning in the analysis of delay-discounting data. *Journal of the Experimental Analysis of Behavior, 111*(2), 239−251. https://doi.org/10.1002/jeab.504

Franck, C. T., Madigan, M. L., & Lazar, N. A. (2022). How to write about alternatives to classical hypothesis testing outside of the statistical literature: Approximate bayesian model selection applied to a biomechanics study. *Stat, 11*(1), e508. https://doi.org/10.1002/sta4.508

Franck, C. T., Traxler, H. K., Kaplan, B. A., Koffarnus, M. N., & Rzeszutek, M. J. (2023). A tribute to howard Rachlin and his two-parameter discounting model: Reliable and flexible model fitting. *Journal of the Experimental Analysis of Behavior, 119*(1), 156−168. https://doi.org/10.1002/jeab.820

Gilroy, S. P., & Hantula, D. A. (2018). Discounting model selection with area-based measures: A case for numerical integration. *Journal of the Experimental Analysis of Behavior, 109*(2), 433−449. https://doi.org/10.1002/jeab.318

Ioannidis, J. P. A. (2005). Why most published research findings are false. *PLoS Medicine, 2*(8), e124. https://doi.org/10.1371/journal.pmed.0020124

Johnson, M. W., & Bickel, W. K. (2008). An algorithm for identifying nonsystematic delay-discounting data. *Experimental and Clinical Psychopharmacology, 16*(3), 264−274. https://doi.org/10.1037/1064-1297.16.3.264

Kaplan, B. A., Franck, C. T., McKee, K., Gilroy, S. P., & Koffarnus, M. N. (2021). Applying mixed-effects modeling to behavioral economic demand: An introduction. *Perspectives on Behavior Science, 44*(2), 333−358. https://doi.org/10.1007/s40614-021-00299-7

Killeen, P. R. (2023). Variations on a theme by Rachlin: Probability discounting. *Journal of the Experimental Analysis of Behavior, 119*(1), 140−155. https://doi.org/10.1002/jeab.817

Koffarnus, M. N., & Bickel, W. K. (2014). A 5-trial adjusting delay discounting task: Accurate discount rates in less than one minute. *Experimental and Clinical Psychopharmacology, 22*(3), 222−228. https://doi.org/10.1037/a0035973

Leek, J. T., & Peng, R. D. (2015). Statistics: P values are just the tip of the iceberg. *Nature, 520*(7549). https://doi.org/10.1038/520612a

Little, R. J. A., & Rubin, D. B. (2014). *Statistical analysis with missing data. Wiley series in probability and statistics*. Wiley. https://books.google.com/books?id=AyVeBAAAQBAJ.

Lohr, S. L. (2021). *Sampling: Design and analysis. Chapman & Hall/CRC texts in statistical science*. CRC Press. https://books.google.com/books?id=DahGEAAAQBAJ.

Mazur, J. E. (1987). An adjusting procedure for studying delayed reinforcement. In , *Quantitative analyses of behavior: Vol 5. The effect of delay and of intervening events on reinforcement value* (pp. 55–73). Hillsdale, NJ, US: Lawrence Erlbaum Associates, Inc.

McKerchar, T., Green, L., Myerson, J., Pickford, T., Hill, J., & Stout, S. (2009). A comparison of four models of delay discounting in humans. *Behavioural Processes, 81*(June), 256–259. https://doi.org/10.1016/j.beproc.2008.12.017

Montgomery, D. C. (2008). *Design and analysis of experiments*. John Wiley & Sons. Design and Analysis of Experiments https://books.google.com/books?id=kMMJAm5bD34C.

Montgomery, D. C., Peck, E. A., & Vining, G. G. (2015). *Introduction to linear regression analysis. Wiley series in probability and statistics*. Wiley. https://books.google.ca/books?id=27kOCgAAQBAJ.

Myerson, J., Green, L., & Warusawitharana, M. (2001). Area under the curve as a measure of discounting. *Journal of the Experimental Analysis of Behavior, 76*(2), 235–243. https://doi.org/10.1901/jeab.2001.76-235

Odum, A. L. (2011). Delay discounting: I'm a k, YOU'RE a k. *Journal of the Experimental Analysis of Behavior, 96*(3), 427–439. https://doi.org/10.1901/jeab.2011.96-423

Odum, A. L., Becker, R. J., Haynes, J. M., Galizio, A., Frye, C. C. J., Downey, H., Friedel, J. E., & Perez, D. M. (2020). Delay discounting of different outcomes: Review and theory. *Journal of the Experimental Analysis of Behavior, 113*(3), 657–679. https://doi.org/10.1002/jeab.589

R Core Team. (2024). *R: A language and environment for statistical computing*. Vienna, Austria: R Foundation for Statistical Computing. https://www.R-project.org/.

Rachlin, H. (2006). Notes on discounting. *Journal of the Experimental Analysis of Behavior, 85*(June), 425–435. https://doi.org/10.1901/jeab.2006.85-05

Rachlin, H., Logue, A., Gibbon, J., & Frankel, M. (1986). Cognition and behavior in studies of choice. *Psychological Review, 93*(January), 33–45. https://doi.org/10.1037/0033-295X.93.1.33

Rachlin, H., Raineri, A., & Cross, D. (1991). Subjective probability and delay. *Journal of the Experimental Analysis of Behavior, 55*(2), 233–244. https://doi.org/10.1901/jeab.1991.55-233

Traxler, H. K., Kaplan, B. A., Rzeszutek, M. J., Franck, C. T., & Koffarnus, M. N. (2022). Interest in and perceived effectiveness of contingency management among alcohol drinkers using behavioral economic purchase tasks. *Experimental and Clinical Psychopharmacology*. https://doi.org/10.1037/pha0000580

Utts, J. M., & Heckard, R. F. (2014). *Mind on statistics*. Cengage Learning. https://books.google.com/books?id=PuLKAgAAQBAJ.

Wackerly, D., Mendenhall, W., & Scheaffer, R. L. (2014). *Mathematical statistics with applications*. Cengage Learning. https://books.google.ca/books?id=lTgGAAAAQBAJ.

Wasserstein, R. L., & Lazar, N. A. (2016). The ASA statement on p-values: Context, process, and purpose. *The American Statistician, 70*(2), 129–133. https://doi.org/10.1080/00031305.2016.1154108

Yoon, J. H., & Higgins, S. T. (2008). Turning k on its head: Comments on use of an ED50 in delay discounting research. *Drug and Alcohol Dependence, 95*(1–2), 169–172. https://doi.org/10.1016/j.drugalcdep.2007.12.011

Young, M. E. (2017). Discounting: A practical guide to multilevel analysis of indifference data. *Journal of the Experimental Analysis of Behavior, 108*(1), 97–112. https://doi.org/10.1002/jeab.265

Young, S. S., & Karr, A. (2011). Deming, data and observational studies: A process out of control and needing fixing. *Significance, 8*(3), 116–120.

Practical applications of discounting

Maribel Rodriguez Perez[1], Shahar Almog[1], Andrea Vásquez Ferreiro[1] and Meredith S. Berry[1,2]
[1]Department of Health Education and Behavior and Center for Behavioral Economic Health Research (CBEHR), University of Florida, Gainesville, FL, United States; [2]Department of Psychology, University of Florida, Gainesville, FL, United States

Practical applications of discounting

A major theme that has emerged in discounting theory and research is the potential for meaningful discounting applications toward improving human and environmental health. As discussed in other chapters in this volume, discounting is a behavioral economic approach with origins in the matching law (e.g., Herrnstein, 1961), and is associated with behaviors outside of laboratory settings. To this end, this chapter summarizes several key practical themes and subsequent implications for decision-making and policy that have emerged from the discounting literature. This synthesis is selective, with a primary focus on the applicability and utility of delay discounting (Mazur, 1987)—the decrease in the subjective value of an outcome with delay to its receipt—although other forms of discounting are also discussed (e.g., probability discounting).

The utility of delay discounting across diverse applications: Select examples

Historically, a key focus of human delay discounting research in the behavior analytic tradition was monetary discounting, potential underlying processes, and associations with real-world behaviors (e.g., substance use). For example, a wealth of research has shown that rapid discounting of delayed monetary outcomes (whether the outcomes are hypothetical or real) is associated with heavier use of substances, including alcohol, stimulants, nicotine and tobacco, and opioids (Bickel & Johnson, 2003; de Wit & Mitchell, 2010; Friedel et al., 2014; Johnson et al., 2007; Madden et al., 1997; Yi et al., 2010). This research formed the basis for increased applicability, such as extending delay discounting for use as a transdiagnostic process (a process that occurs across a range of disorders), and tool for mental health and addictive-related behaviors with a focus on comorbidities (Amlung et al., 2019; Bickel et al., 2012). Such early research also gave rise to applications to clinically relevant behaviors such as sexual risk behavior and food choices framed as immediate or delayed outcomes to facilitate understanding the influence of delay on choices other than money.

Yet another applied area of delay discounting research that has emerged across both psychological and economic disciplines is discounting of environmental outcomes (e.g., improved air quality), with implications for environmental decision-making.

Here, we focus on several select but diverse areas noted previously to demonstrate the breadth of delay and other discounting applications, including the use of delay discounting as a transdiagnostic tool, and various applications to clinically relevant individual behaviors (e.g., sexual risk behaviors and food choice). We also touch on environmentally relevant applications of discounting with broader societal implications (e.g., discounting of air quality valuation). We outline individual and societal implications throughout the chapter and conclude with a discussion of the research covered, the potential to alter delay discounting, future directions, and conclusions.

Delay discounting as a transdiagnostic tool

One example of an application of delay discounting is its suggested use as a transdiagnostic tool. Given the substantial evidence regarding associations between the degree of delay discounting and drug misuse, researchers have proposed delay discounting as a behavioral marker of addiction (Bickel et al., 2014). That is, delay discounting has been shown to predict the course and severity of addiction, and has been proposed to identify those at risk for developing addiction (Bickel et al., 2014). In addition, it has been shown to predict treatment outcomes in relation to abstinence, cessation, and relapse. Bickel and colleagues have suggested that delay discounting could be used as a screening tool to identify those with substance dependence and those at risk of developing substance dependence, as well as an intervention target (e.g., personalized intervention and treatment). Delay discounting has also been proposed as a transdiagnostic tool for psychiatric conditions (e.g., depression, see Amlung et al., 2019 for a meta-analysis), that often share comorbidities with substance use (Bickel & Mueller, 2009), and discussed in more detail later.

As a result of the potential utility of delay discounting in clinical applications researchers have investigated whether delay discounting has its own etiology or whether it is a shared process across different mental conditions. Bickel and Mueller (2009) proposed delay discounting as a transdisease process for a novel approach to understanding processes that operate in more than one condition. That is, understanding the commonalities among different conditions that share the same processes such as excessive delay discounting rates might make findings of one condition relevant to other conditions. For example, delay discounting as a transdisease process appears to be a promising approach in our understanding of the processes operating in comorbidity, exemplified by the excessive discounting rates observed in smoking and schizophrenia (Bickel & Mueller, 2009). This more comprehensive approach might be beneficial in the diagnosis and treatment of different disorders.

To understand delay discounting as a transdisease process, researchers have investigated whether elevated rates of delay discounting are present across different maladies. Excessive rates of discounting have been found in a multitude of disorders or resulting from unhealthy lifestyle choices such as substance use disorders (SUDs), pathological gambling, poor health, and overeating (Bickel et al., 2012), suggesting a common underlying process that occurs in a range of behavioral, psychological, and psychiatric disorders. Evidence of delay discounting as a transdisease process has not only been found between individuals across different disorders but also within individuals. Snider et al. (2016) found that among cigarette smokers delay discounting was predictive of engagement of other maladaptive behaviors such as lack of exercise and unhealthy eating (for other examples, see Bickel et al., 2019).

Excessive delay discounting rates have also been observed in other health and psychiatric conditions. For example, Amlung et al. (2019) found that excessive discounting has been related to major depressive disorder, schizophrenia, borderline, bipolar, and bulimia nervosa. Interestingly, anorexia nervosa was found to encompass shallower discounting compared to bulimia nervosa (Amlung et al., 2019), which may be related to common characteristics of anorexia nervosa related to forgoing immediate outcomes for longer-term goals (Decker et al., 2015). Beauchaine et al. (2017) have also examined the associations between attention deficit hyperactivity disorder (ADHD) symptoms, temporal discounting of monetary rewards, and financial outcomes. Results indicated that ADHD symptoms were related to excessive discounting, late credit card payments, credit card balances, personal debt, and other negative financial outcomes. Taken together, these and other studies might suggest that delay discounting is not universally applied to all psychiatric disorders rather it may fall on a continuum. The suggestion of delay discounting falling onto a continuum may have important implications in the diagnosis of psychological and psychiatric disorders that have typically been classified under general categories (Amlung et al., 2019).

Delay discounting as a transdisease process may represent a promising approach to our understanding of different clinical disorders. Some, however, have cautioned regarding the use of delay discounting in clinical applications. Bailey et al. (2021) discussed the need for additional research in terms of convergent and divergent validity of delay discounting measures and also noted that steep discounting has been observed in a variety of clinical samples, thus indicating that there is not a specific relationship between delay discounting rates to any specific psychological phenomena, and it may lack ecological validity. Here, we simply suggest its potential utility as part of a larger battery of diagnostic tools with a focus on comorbidities, not as a replacement.

Clinically relevant applications of sexual discounting and implications for individual risk behavior

Sexual discounting: An overview of methods, applications, and implications

Moving forward in this chapter, we focus on discounting tasks using outcomes other than money that provide enhanced ecological validity (e.g., discounting clinically relevant measures, such as the likelihood of condom use) and may represent the next phase of delay discounting research. Another clinically relevant application of discounting that has gained traction in recent years has been the use of sexual discounting tasks. Some examples of sexual discounting tasks include tasks based on probabilistic outcomes (e.g., Berry, Repke, & Conway, 2019; Lawyer et al., 2010), delay discounting for sex acts (Jarmolowicz et al., 2013), sexual partners delay discounting (e.g., more vs. less preferred partners, Jarmolowicz et al., 2015), sexual arousal discounting (Wongsomboon & Cox, 2021), and delay discounting of condom-protected sex (Johnson & Bruner, 2012). Two recent reviews have been published on this topic (Gebru et al., 2022; Johnson et al., 2021). Johnson et al. (2021) reviewed and evaluated different methods used to determine discounting in the context of sexual decision-making, and Gebru et al. (2022) focused specifically on the Sexual Delay Discounting Task (SDDT).

The Sexual Delay Discounting Task: General methods

To date, the most widely used application of delay discounting for clinically relevant sexual behavior is the SDDT, and thus we focus on this example here. Although condom use is one of the most effective ways to prevent HIV and other sexually transmitted infections (STIs), many sexually active individuals do not use condoms consistently. The SDDT evaluates the likelihood of condom use in a casual sex scenario if a condom is available immediately and after various delays. The SDDT allows researchers to study the impact of delay to condom availability (e.g., 1 hour, 1 day) on the likelihood of condom use using hypothetical vignettes that describe casual sex scenarios. Participants are instructed to imagine they are not in a committed relationship and there is zero chance of pregnancy. After participants select a number of pictures of individuals they would be willing to have sex with, a visual analog scale is used to assess the likelihood of condom use across a range of delays to condom availability and with various partners selected (e.g., most want to have sex with, most likely to have an STI). Research has shown that condom-use likelihood decreases systematically with increased delay to condom availability, and can vary based on sex, partner selection, and acute intoxication.

The Sexual Delay Discounting Task among various populations

The SDDT has been evaluated among different populations including college students, men who have sex with men (MSM), and individuals with SUDs. Several general findings have emerged from this literature, including sexual delay discounting is more strongly associated with self-reported sexual risk behavior compared to money discounting (Johnson & Bruner, 2012), and the SDDT appears to have good test-retest reliability (Johnson & Bruner, 2013). Individuals tend to discount more steeply (i.e., decreased likelihood of condom use) as delays increased for partners they "most want to have sex with" (compared to those they would "least want to have sex with") and those who the participant perceived as "least likely to have an STI" (compared to those they perceive as "most likely to have an STI"; Dariotis & Johnson, 2015; Herrmann et al., 2015). An important finding highlighting the contribution of delay to condom availability in sexual risk decisions was noted by Herrmann et al. (2015). Specifically, *24% of the MSM sample reported unprotected anal intercourse in the last 6 months in situations where they would have used a condom, but did not because one was not immediately available* (Herrmann et al., 2015). These data suggest the role of delay in condom availability as a fundamental driver of lack of condom use and risky sex for some individuals and highlight the importance of immediate access to condoms. Further, individuals with SUDs discounted condom-protected sex more steeply compared to controls in all partner conditions related to "most/least want to have sex with" and "most/least likely to have an STI" (e.g., Herrmann et al., 2014; Koffarnus et al., 2016).

Several studies have also evaluated the effects of drug administration on the SDDT to better understand how sexual behavior might be influenced by substances (e.g., Berry et al., 2022; Bolin et al., 2016; Johnson et al., 2016; Strickland et al., 2017). This research is particularly important given higher rates of STIs reported among individuals who may misuse substances that cannot be attributed to other potential explanations (e.g., needle sharing). Some substances (e.g., alcohol and cocaine) can increase sexual delay discounting. In other words, individuals engage in riskier decisions (report less likelihood of condom use) while under the influence of alcohol compared to placebo or cocaine compared to placebo (Johnson et al., 2016, 2017) when a delay to condom availability is involved. Importantly, in these studies (Johnson et al., 2016, 2017), no differences were found in the effects of alcohol or cocaine administration on condom use likelihood when a condom was immediately available, suggesting a major role of delay to condom availability as a vector for risk, particularly while intoxicated.

Clinical implications for sexual discounting and future research

Sexual discounting tasks may provide increased specificity compared to monetary discounting tasks when examining risky sexual behavior and prevention of HIV and STIs (Johnson & Bruner, 2012; Jones, Guest, Sullivan, Kramer et al., 2018; Jones, Guest, Sullivan, Sales et al., 2018). The SDDT has been shown to be effective in measuring sexual decision-making among different populations, is systematic, and demonstrates good test-retest reliability. Therefore this task may be a useful tool among people who are more vulnerable to HIV/STIs and other understudied populations such as transgender individuals or to pose hypothetical scenarios such as infidelity or the probability of losing an erection (Gebru et al., 2022; Johnson et al., 2021). Importantly, most studies to date have examined conditions under which sexual delay discounting *increases*. Future research may examine conditions under which sexual delay discounting is *decreased* (e.g., Strickland et al., 2017) allowing for additional implications for individual interventions and public health measures. Sexual discounting tasks might be helpful to indicate those who might benefit from educational and behavioral interventions to increase their condom use and could point to tailored interventions (e.g., visualizations of condom carrying; Gebru et al., 2022).

Future research might also examine if interventions designed to reduce sexual discounting in laboratory settings translate to changing sexual decision-making in real-world experiences (Gebru et al., 2022; Johnson et al., 2021). Moreover, educational programs to explain how to make safer decisions and explain misperceptions about STIs appear critical (i.e., attractive partners are not synonymous with STI-free; Dariotis & Johnson, 2015; Collado et al., 2017; Gebru et al., 2022). One major implication of this work is the importance of access to immediately available condoms in convenient locations. Dariotis and Johnson (2015) suggested that condoms should be freely accessible in schools, bathrooms, employment training centers, rehabilitation centers, community health clinics, and similar locations.

Clinically relevant applications of food discounting and implications for individual eating behavior

Food discounting: An overview of methods, applications, and implications

Demonstrating the further utility of delay discounting, applications of food discounting have been explored. Understanding decision-making underlying food-related choices and learning about food reinforcement will be important for increasing healthy food choices and minimizing unhealthy food choices that can lead to lifestyle morbidities (e.g., obesity). Food delay discounting may inform treatment and prevention for obesity (e.g., Manwaring et al., 2011) or other behaviors related to unhealthy eating. Food discounting has also been suggested in the study of clinical populations paralleling the concepts of immediate gratification (e.g., eating) and future goals (e.g., weight loss or weight gain; McClelland et al., 2016).

Food discounting: General methods

Researchers have used different measures to quantify food discounting such as the Food Choice Questionnaire (FCQ), adjusting amount procedure for food (AA-F), delayed gratification tasks, and some variations adapted from monetary discounting tasks. The AA-F asks participants to imagine that a small white cube in front of them is a bite of their favorite food, and adjusts based on their choices. During the AA-F task, participants can have 10 bites of their favorite food at different delays (e.g., 1, 5, or 20 hours) or a smaller amount (i.e., 7 bites) to be available promptly. This task has been used in several studies (Hendrickson et al., 2015; Hendrickson & Rasmussen, 2013; Rasmussen et al., 2010). Another popular task is the FCQ, which is modified from the Monetary Choice Questionnaire (MCQ). Similar to the AA-F, participants are shown a cube to imagine to be a bite of their favorite food followed by 27 fixed-set choices between a smaller sooner reward now (less number of bites) or a larger later amount (larger number of bites). The delays range from 0.5 to 24 hours. The AA-F and FCQ are highly correlated (Hendrickson et al., 2015). Studies have used this task to measure the outcome of mindful eating interventions (e.g., Hendrickson & Rasmussen, 2013). Other variations of these measures have also been used (e.g., Dassen et al., 2015; Privitera et al., 2015).

Food discounting among healthy and clinical populations

Food discounting research has been conducted among both healthy-weight individuals and populations with obesity and eating disorders (EDs). Across generally healthy populations and some studies, including healthy-weight and obese individuals, individuals who have higher percent body fat (PBF) tend to more steeply discount delayed and probabilistic food rewards than those individuals who have a lower PBF (e.g., Rasmussen et al., 2010). PBF, however, did not predict monetary discounting. This finding provides evidence that PBF is a significant and robust predictor of food discounting, but not necessarily money (see Rasmussen et al., 2010; Hendrickson & Rasmussen, 2013; Hendrickson et al., 2015 for food discounting examples). In addition, a study conducted among healthy participants found that individuals with a higher body mass index (BMI) and who reported depressive symptoms discounted more steeply for "comfort foods" such as cake and chicken wings compared to individuals who did not have these conditions (Privitera et al., 2015). Moreover, food discounting may vary with age (see Lee & Rasmussen, 2022).

Studies conducted among people with obesity (classified with a BMI ≥ 30 kg/m^2) tend to discount food more steeply (i.e., more "impulsively") compared to people who do not have obesity (Schiff et al., 2016). In addition, high-calorie foods (e.g., pizza) lead to more behavioral steeper discounting among individuals with a BMI ≥ 30 kg/m^2 and no cardiovascular conditions or individuals with a cardiovascular condition and a BMI ≥ 27 kg/m^2 (Weygandt et al., 2013). Steeper discounting also predicted less weight loss in a subsequent diet intervention (Weygandt et al., 2013). See also Manwaring et al. (2011) and Hagan et al. (2021) for discounting studies among women with binge eating disorder (BED) and bulimia nervosa, respectively.

Intervention studies in food discounting

Several studies have also conducted interventions and used food discounting as an outcome measure (Hendrickson & Rasmussen, 2013, 2017; Rasmussen et al., 2022). These studies conducted experiments determining the effects of a mindfulness intervention versus control condition(s) on food discounting. Hendrickson and Rasmussen (2013) randomized participants to either the mindful eating or control group. Those in the mindful eating condition attended a 50-minute workshop on mindful eating (e.g., chewing slowly) and the control group watched a 50-minute video called "Learn Nutrition" explaining the food pyramid and nutrition. Individuals who attended the mindful eating workshop discounted food less steeply when compared to their baseline discounting rates, and there was no change detected for the control group who watched the general nutrition video (Hendrickson & Rasmussen, 2013). This general effect was consistent across both adolescents and adults in food-secure populations and appears to be specific to food (e.g., monetary discounting was not altered following the mindful food intervention; Hendrickson & Rasmussen, 2017). On the contrary, women with food insecurity who were part of the mindful eating group had a steeper food and monetary delay discounting compared to their baseline and higher risk aversion for food (i.e., they were prone to choosing a certain food choice despite it being a smaller portion; Rasmussen et al., 2022). Food and monetary discounting were not affected in the control conditions (see also Dassen et al., 2016 for episodic future thinking manipulations testing food intake and monetary discounting). These studies show the potential to use delay discounting as an applied measure of the effectiveness of an intervention for changing food choices, and results may vary across food security and food insecurity. These results highlight the interplay between individual discounting and broader food systems.

Clinical implications of food discounting and future research

Given successful initial applications of food discounting to clinical populations as noted earlier, increased use of food discounting tasks in this area would be beneficial for translation and enhanced application (Amlung et al., 2016). Decision-making tools resulting from food delay discounting can serve as indicators for those potentially at risk for gaining excessive weight and developing an ED (Stojek & MacKillop, 2017). Indeed, it may be possible to decrease the reinforcing value of food (e.g., Buscemi et al., 2014; Stojek & MacKillop, 2017), and increase the reinforcing value of nonfood alternatives. Early interventions using food delay discounting as an indicator could facilitate prevention efforts in this regard. Intervention studies of mindfulness and episodic future thinking have shown that food delay discounting may be manipulable, indicating the possibility for changing food delay discounting and related food choice, and potentially global decision-making processes (Odum, 2011). For example, future interventions can focus on unhealthy eating to think more about their future health when making food-related decisions (Dassen et al., 2015).

In addition, as food delay discounting is more strongly related to relevant metrics such as body fat percentage than monetary discounting (Hendrickson & Rasmussen, 2013; Rasmussen et al., 2010), these results further highlight the need for clinically relevant measures of discounting, beyond the standard monetary discounting tasks. Food discounting measures can be used to test the effectiveness of an intervention such as mindful eating (e.g., Hendrickson & Rasmussen, 2013) or changing an individual's food choices and food-related decision-making (Stojek & MacKillop, 2017). A meta-analysis evaluating discounting of delayed food and monetary outcomes in obesity suggested the need for increased use of food discounting and potential clinical applications (Amlung et al., 2016).

Environmentally relevant discounting applications

Environmentally relevant discounting: An overview of methods, applications, and implications

In this chapter, we have primarily focused on discounting immediately relevant to the individual and individual decision-making processes. These applications have broad relevance for public health. Similar to sexual and food discounting, environmentally relevant discounting (e.g., discounting of air quality and water quality) is often assessed among individuals; however, with implications for societal resource exploitation as well as individual behaviors (e.g., consuming meat/diary/animal products or driving a personal car). This area of research holds important implications for how we might alter human behavior for improved conservation of resources and sustainability.

Discounting future outcomes is also applicable to areas of environmental research and sustainable behaviors as those partly depend on how much the individual discounts future environmental outcomes. In fact, to directly address environmental issues, including climate change, some economists and policy makers have stressed adopting a degree of "zero discounting" (or the lowest possible) to promote more sustainable use of resources and avoid environmental catastrophe (Weitzman, 1998). With the acceleration of climate change, species extinction, and resource exploitation, understanding the decision-making processes and behavioral aspects of discounting environmental outcomes has become of interest to both economists and psychologists (Hirsh et al., 2015). Understanding how people discount environmental outcomes specifically, and why, beyond monetary rewards or self-reported measures, may inform future educational and behavioral interventions. Moreover, in some western countries, including the U.S., climate change has been politicized (McCright et al., 2014), and governmental reports are often interpreted by the lay public with a confirmation bias (i.e., the information is used to support existing values and opinions (Budescu et al., 2012)). Thus, research on behavioral decision-making in general and discounting processes in particular can inform the framing and communication of environmental policies that would gain public support.

Environmentally relevant discounting: General methods

The environmental discounting literature presents a variety of discounting tasks. While monetary discounting may indicate environmental discounting processes, as both may share underlying processes, the two outcomes are substantially different. Monetary rewards are personal and are easy to quantify. In contrast, environmental outcomes are harder to quantify (e.g., the effects of climate change on a particular area), and although might directly affect the individual's life, are considered societal, affecting many more people, possibly distant in space and/or time from the individual's local choice. In contrast to the simple choice between two monetary outcomes, environmental tasks usually involve a vignette, where participants are asked to imagine themselves in a situation where an environmental event is impacting their life.

Beyond the temporal distance (i.e., when will an environmental event occur?), other factors influence perception and decision-making. For example, where will the environmental event take place, how certain is it to happen, and who will be affected by it—the answers to these questions will affect the individual's rate of discounting across differing tasks. To account for these processes, environmental discounting research uses spatial discounting tasks, where the environmental event happens across different distances from the participant, probability discounting tasks across different odds that the event will happen, and social discounting tasks, where the event will affect people who are in different social proximity with the participant. All of these contextual factors were found relevant to environmental decision-making. Participants tend to discount events that are far, uncertain, and affect people that are not in one's social circles (Hanley et al., 2003; Kaplan et al., 2014; Sargisson & Schöner, 2020). Similarly, in a recent study, using a combined choice procedure, Sparkman et al. (2021) investigated the patterns of temporal and spatial discounting of support for different environmental policies. The authors found that policies gained increased support when they occurred locally and within 10 years.

Environmental events might impact air (e.g., Hardisty & Weber, 2009), water (e.g., Meyer, 2013), or soil quality (Kaplan et al., 2014), as well as other outcomes including health-related outcomes (Berry, Nickerson, et al., 2017) or environmental policy (Sparkman et al., 2021). Like the monetary delay discounting tasks, the participant is asked for his/her preferred choice of, for example, different amounts of the same outcome, across different delays. The outcomes can be framed as gains or losses (e.g., shorter durations of improved or poor air quality now, or longer durations later (Berry, Friedel, et al., 2017)), and in different magnitudes (Berry, Friedel, et al., 2017; Berry, Nickerson, et al., 2017). Because some of the environmental outcomes may only affect future generations, maximal delays vary from 5 years (Meyer, 2013), and up to 80 years (Sargisson & Schöner, 2020). Similar to monetary discounting tasks, the tasks result in a series of indifference points (or similar) where the immediate outcome and the delayed one are subjectively equal, which are used to estimate a single discounting index.

As discussed previously, other discounting tasks ask the participants to rate their level of concern or willingness to take action, when the environmental outcome will take place across different delays (or spatial distance, or probability of occurring, some of which are discussed later in this chapter (e.g., Kaplan et al., 2014; Sargisson & Schöner, 2020)). These tasks use a visual analog scale (VAS) of 0—100, which the participant is asked to respond by moving the slider to his/her subjective value. Similar to indifference points, the ratings are then used to graph and assess the degree of discounting. Lastly, another type of task utilizes a different model of choice where the individual is asked to select between choices that involve a combination of options. For example, rather than assessing the discounting rate per se (i.e., decay in value), Viscusi et al. (2008a) assessed the participants' valuation of water quality in lakes and rivers as a function of cost of living. The participants were asked about their preference between two regions with different costs of living and percentage of water bodies with good quality water (e.g., Region A with $100 cost and 40% of water bodies in good quality, or Region B with $300% and 60%). In these combined choice tasks, the discounting/valuation is analyzed with different procedures (for different methods see (Meyer, 2013; Sparkman et al., 2021; Viscusi et al., 2008)).

Environmentally relevant and monetary discounting, environmental concern, and sustainable behaviors

To learn whether temporal discounting is similar across domains (i.e., environmental outcomes and money), in a series of experiments, Berry, Friedel, et al. (2017); Berry, Nickerson, et al. (2017) (replicating similar findings from Hardisty and Weber (2009)) found that environmental discounting and monetary discounting were positively correlated. Individuals who steeply discount future monetary rewards also tend to discount environmental outcomes in a similar manner, results that support the proposition that discounting has trait-like characteristics (state-like characteristics have also been shown within discounting of environmental outcomes with framing and cognitive manipulations, e.g., Berry, Repke, and Conway (2019)). Moreover, in one study (experiment 2 in Berry, Friedel, et al., 2017), similar to monetary discounting, longer durations of improved air quality were discounted less than shorter durations (the magnitude effect). In contrast, some inconsistencies between the domains were found. In one experiment (Experiment 1 Berry, Friedel, et al., 2017), college students discounted improved air quality more steeply than money, while in the second experiment (Experiment 2) with MTurk Workers, money was discounted more steeply. In Berry et al. (2017b), MTurk Workers discounted money gains more steeply than environmental gains, but not losses. Hardisty and Weber (2009) also collected qualitative data on the thought process of their participants, which revealed different reasons for discounting money (e.g., financial investment) versus environmental outcomes (e.g., will to experience the improvement in air quality immediately). Taken together, these results suggest that environmental discounting shares common processes with monetary discounting, however, there might also be unique elements underlying the two processes, warranting more research involving both, to learn on the similarities and differences between the processes among different populations.

Research on discounting relations with real pro-environmental outcomes or personal characteristics has revealed several interesting relations or lack thereof. For example, Viscusi and colleagues found that visitors to water bodies discounted water quality less than non-visitors (Viscusi et al., 2008). However, using different experimental tasks, Berry, Nickerson, et al. (2017) found that the importance of air quality and related health, and nature connectedness were correlated with one another (i.e., people who were more connected to nature also valued air quality and health-related outcomes more) but they were not correlated with any of the discounting outcomes (i.e., money, air quality, and respiratory health). Kaplan et al. (2014) found that environmental disaster involving soil and water pollution was discounted as a function of time, social distance, and probability; however, willingness to act was discounted more steeply than concern. In other words, while individuals may be highly concerned, they are not as willing to devote their time to act against the environmental disaster (see also Sargisson & Schöner, 2020). These results suggest that self-perceived pro-environmental characteristics are not necessarily aligned with environmental discounting measures, emphasizing the value of environmental discounting as a potential objective index of sustainable behavior.

Delay, probability, social, and other forms of discounting provide specific frameworks for understanding environmentally relevant and sustainable behaviors and systems. Other behavior analytic and multidisciplinary frameworks combined with discounting might serve to increase the translational relevance of proposed discounting questions and study designs, and enhance behavioral approaches to addressing sustainability (please see Gelino, Erath & Reed, 2021 for a pertinent review and discussion of pro-environmental behavior analytic research). Additional research regarding the relations between delay discounting and attitudes toward "green purchasing," delay discounting, gratitude, and sustainable product choice, differences in monetary and environmental discounting, and discounting and green agricultural technology adoption has also been conducted (Farias et al., 2021; Liang & Guo, 2021; Mao et al., 2021; Richards & Green, 2015).

Implications of environmentally relevant discounting and future research

Another research question, also parallel to the monetary discounting literature, is whether environmental discounting is manipulable. Berry, Repke, & Conway (2019) examined whether visual exposure to natural environment (vs. built environment) can reduce discounting of improved air quality across different delays, similar to how it reduced monetary delay discounting (Berry et al., 2015). As hypothesized, after viewing natural (vs. built) environment images, participants showed reduced discounting (i.e., increased preference for longer-later durations of improved air quality). These results suggest that like monetary discounting, environmental discounting is manipulable, which holds implications for future interventions. Nevertheless, more research is needed to examine whether any shift in discounting will lead to changes in behavior with real-world sustainable relevance (e.g., eliminating animal and animal product consumption).

Environmental research in the behavioral economic framework has some limitations. The task choices are sometimes framed in an artificial choice structure (pollution now or pollution later), whereas real-world complexities between cost now (in money or effort) or disaster later may be more informative. These choices may be considered as cross-commodity tasks which may offer enhanced translational relevance to real-world decision-making including in other domains (Pritschmann et al., 2021). For example, future studies can assess how different environmental outcomes are discounted as a function of green goods consumption and prices, as sustainable industries might mean greater effort or cost for the consumer. Moreover, environmental discounting still mostly exists in laboratory settings, and thus there is still much to learn. While it is a useful tool, the system and the context play a role in environmental behaviors regardless of the individual's discounting rates. For example, independent of the discount rate, an individual may hope to eliminate meat/diary consumption, a leading contributor to environmental degradation, but lives in a food desert or food swamp, making this change difficult or unattainable. Similarly, a reduction in private car use may be impossible if public transit does not exist in the area.

Further, while individual behavior is a measurable contributor to environmental degradation, larger industries and systems must also fundamentally shift for the major impact needed to address climate and land use change and resource exploitation. To the extent that individual behavior does influence environmental outcomes, identifying individuals and the reasons behind their decision-making processes, as well as investigating more ways to change environmental discounting (e.g., framing and episodic future thinking), may help develop targeted education programs. In summary, derived from the monetary discounting research, environmental discounting tasks appear to be an objective tool that could inform both governmental legislation and education efforts; however, more research is warranted, as environmental outcomes are more complex, with many contextual factors impacting decision-making.

The utility of discounting applications: Implications and conclusions

Summary and implications

In this chapter, we discussed several key applications of delay discounting. To summarize, delay discounting as a transdiagnostic tool, sexual discounting, food discounting, and environmental discounting each holds overlapping but distinct implications for individual and societal application and policy. The research reviewed suggests that delay and other forms of discounting processes (e.g., probability and spatial) play a fundamental role in both health and environmental and resource use decisions, and may be targeted for individual interventions and policy for improved human health and ecosystem function. The discounting assessments summarized here have sound measurement properties and have been tested among a range of individuals with direct relevance to clinically (e.g., sexual risk-taking and food consumption behaviors) and environmentally relevant behaviors (e.g., sustainable and proenvironmental behaviors), and are firmly grounded in behavioral economic theory and research. Please also see Reed et al. (2022) for a discussion of policy implications of behavioral economic findings, including discounting, particularly in the context of emerging events or crises (e.g., severe weather events and COVID-19), as well as in other chapters in this volume.

The immediate implications of this body of discounting work point to guiding clinical practice and individual decision-making. For example, monetary delay discounting as a transdisease process may represent a promising approach to our understanding of different clinical disorders. Delay discounting may have potential utility as part of a larger battery of diagnostic tools for various mental health conditions particularly substance use and associated comorbidities (Bickel et al., 2014; Bickel & Mueller, 2009). Future research in this area may inform the specificity of the use of discounting in this context.

Clinically relevant discounting with outcomes other than money (e.g., sex discounting and food discounting) may further increase ecological validity and enhance significance and has been shown to be more strongly associated with specific real-world behaviors (sexual risk and body fat percentage) than monetary discounting. Based on this research highlighting the reduction in the likelihood of condom use even with a small delay to obtaining a condom, public health policy makers might consider the importance of access to immediately and freely available condoms in convenient locations such as schools, bathrooms, employment training centers, rehabilitation centers, and community health clinics. Sexual discounting tasks might be helpful to indicate those who might benefit from educational and behavioral interventions to increase their condom use and could point to tailored interventions (e.g., visualizations of condom carrying; Gebru et al., 2022; Johnson et al., 2021). In addition, many studies have examined conditions under which sexual delay discounting *increases*. Future research may examine conditions under which sexual delay discounting is *decreased* (e.g., Strickland et al., 2017) allowing for additional implications for individual interventions and public health measures.

Similarly, decision-making tools resulting from food delay discounting can serve as indicators for those potentially at risk for gaining excessive weight or developing an ED (Stojek & MacKillop, 2017). Early interventions using food delay discounting as an indicator could facilitate prevention efforts in this regard. Intervention studies of mindfulness and episodic future thinking have shown that food delay discounting may be manipulable, indicating the possibility for changing food delay discounting and related food choice, and potentially global decision-making processes (Odum, 2011). For example, future interventions might focus on populations with unhealthy eating habits to think more about their future health when making food-related decisions (Dassen et al., 2015). We recognize, however, that some areas lack access to nutritive foods (e.g., food deserts and food swamps). In such cases targeting individual discounting processes without systemic change for access to healthy foods may only be marginally useful.

Environmentally relevant discounting may hold implications for corporate and societal resource exploitation as well as individual behaviors (e.g., consuming meat/diary/animal products and driving a personal car). This area of research points to how we might alter human behavior for improved conservation of resources and sustainability. As discussed previously, to directly address environmental issues including climate change, some economists and policy makers have stressed adopting a rate of "zero discounting" (or the lowest possible) to promote more sustainable use of resources and avoid environmental catastrophe (Weitzman, 1998). Environmental discounting tasks appear to be an objective tool that could inform both governmental legislation and education efforts. However, more research is warranted, as environmental outcomes are more complex than monetary outcomes, with many contextual factors that can impact decision-making. In general, environmental discounting in combination with other areas of sustainability research suggests increased state and federal regulation of industries will be required (e.g., augmented restrictions on emissions, pollutants, water usage, and forest degradation). Environmentally relevant discounting also points to the increased need for willingness to act (e.g., Kaplan et al., 2014), with individual contributions required to reduce resource usage including immediate plant-based diet changes and energy usage on a grassroots scale to push sustainability efforts forward. The selected research covered in this chapter (i.e., societal and individual environmental discounting rates are not zero, and tend to be high), highlights these changes, regulations, and precommitments are needed *immediately*, as delaying action will further reduce resource availability given discounting processes discussed herein (Weitzman, 1998). Continued research on behavioral decision-making in general and discounting processes in particular can inform the framing and communication of environmental policies that might gain public support (Berry, Friedel, et al., 2017).

Potential to alter discounting and associated behaviors

One area of research that has emerged may have implications for each of the applications discussed in this chapter—the potential to *change* discounting. In other words, are there experimental manipulations or clinical interventions that reduce the degree of discounting, and if so, what implications may these findings have on associated real-world behavior (e.g., substance use, sexual risk-taking, and sustainable behavior)? Discounting appears to have both state and trait-like properties, and as noted by Odum (2011), delay discounting shares features of a personality trait with epigenetic bases. In other words, delay discounting can be influenced by its interaction with the environment, suggesting that changes in discounting in one domain could influence changes in other domains. As a result of the potential malleability of delay and other forms of discounting that may also produce global changes in behaviors, researchers have investigated whether delay discounting is susceptible to change and whether this alteration extends to other behaviors. Various manipulations have been successful in decreasing the rate/degree of delay discounting in different populations and behaviors, and more research is needed on delay and other forms of discounting.

For example, contingency management interventions, learning-based manipulations, and fading procedures among others have also been shown to decrease delay discounting (for a review on manipulations altering delay discounting see, Rung & Madden, 2018a, 2018b). Episodic future thinking (EFT) is another manipulation that has been used to alter delay discounting. This manipulation asks participants to vividly imagine and describe future events they may engage in at different points in time (Stein et al., 2018). This intervention has been shown to be effective at reducing monetary discounting and cigarette self-administration among cigarette smokers not only in controlled laboratory settings but also in online samples of cigarette smokers (Stein et al., 2016, 2018; although see Naudé et al., 2021). In addition, EFT has shown some efficacy in reducing delay discounting and hypothetical alcohol consumption (Snider et al., 2016; see also Mellis et al., 2019; Daniel et al., 2013; Sze et al., 2017 for EFT and eating-related behaviors). Memory, incorporation of personal goals, valence, and vividness of the events used in EFT might moderate the relationship between delay discounting and the effectiveness of EFT. Although the mechanisms driving these effects are not well understood, EFT could produce a shift-in-time perspective that favors the valuation of future outcomes, and could also be related to demand characteristics (see Rung & Madden, 2018a, 2018b). These results demonstrate the relevance of EFT as an intervention approach to reduce "impulsive" decision-making or as a complementary component to treatment or lifestyle changes (e.g., reducing substance use and reducing unhealthy eating). Future research can continue to explore the utility of EFT in applied settings.

Other manipulations have shown evidence of potentially reducing delay discounting. Mindfulness meditation has also been shown to alter delay discounting. Ashe et al. (2015) explored the differences between mindfulness-based and distraction techniques used to alter delay discounting in treatments for addiction. Results suggested that distraction-based interventions might be more effective for individuals that are experiencing acute cravings while mindfulness-based interventions might be more effective in the long term. Mindfulness-based interventions have been effective at reducing discounting rates of hypothetical monetary rewards and hypothetical food rewards (Hendrickson & Rasmussen, 2013), and might help to shift attention to relevant stimuli, prompting more controlled choices (Dixon et al., 2019). Nature exposure (visual or actual) has also been shown to alter delay discounting. Across three experiments Van der Wal et al. (2013) found that nature compared to built environment exposure was associated with lower discounting rates for hypothetical monetary rewards in both laboratory settings and actual immersion into nature (see also Berry et al., 2014; Berry et al., 2015; Kao et al., 2019; Repke et al., 2018). Repke et al. (2018) extended these results showing that nature accessibility predicted a decrease in delay discounting, and this decrease was associated with improved health outcomes. Kao et al. (2019) found that participants exposed to nature scenes had lower discounting rates and preferred drinks with smaller amounts of sugar compared to participants exposed to built/urban and control scenes. Various potential mechanisms have been suggested for nature-based changes in delay discounting including evolutionary processes (Van der Wal et al., 2013), and expanded time and space perception with nature-viewing (Berry et al., 2014, 2015, 2019). These studies provide initial insight into the application of nature and nature stimuli as a potential approach for interventions to reduce delay discounting and unhealthy behaviors in different domains.

Taken together these results show that delay discounting rates are susceptible to change. However, as suggested by Amlung et al. (2019) future research on altering delay discounting should consider the bidirectionality of rates of delay discounting. That is, research should focus on both, techniques to decrease and increase discounting to better understand under what conditions these shifts occur, and to further explore mechanistic drivers. Much of this research has occurred within delay discounting and individual consumption (substances and food), and future research might address shifting other forms of discounting, other real-world behaviors, and subsequent implications. Further, limited research exists on how these experimental manipulations scale-up to efficacious longer-term real-world interventions. However, this body of research represents a distinct step in the field toward meaningful application of laboratory findings that are ripe for testing in longer-term interventions. Shifts in societal practice in early childhood (e.g., teaching mindfulness, connection to nature, and focus on empathy for others and self) may also influence longer-term and sustainable discounting decreases across the life span with far-reaching implications, and remains an area of potential future research.

Conclusions

In summary, the behavioral economic discounting research presented in this chapter has promise to continue to advance an expanded view of discounting applications with real-world behavioral and societal implications. Discounting factors should be considered at least as vital in understanding and assessing behavior patterns as common self-report assessments (e.g., self-reported substance use, self-reported risky sexual practices, and sustainable behavior questionnaires). Delay and other forms of discounting should be an integral feature used to understand and target behavioral and societal change for individual, collective, and ecosystem health promotion (e.g., substance use, risky sex, sustainable behavior, and resource management).

References

Amlung, M., Marsden, E., Holshausen, K., Morris, V., Patel, H., Vedelago, L., & McCabe, R. E. (2019). Delay discounting as a transdiagnostic process in psychiatric disorders: A meta-analysis. *JAMA Psychiatry, 76*(11), 1176−1186. https://doi.org/10.1001/jamapsychiatry.2019.2102

Amlung, M., Marsden, E., Holshausen, K., Morris, V., Patel, H., Vedelago, L., Naish, K. R., Reed, D. D., & McCabe, R. E. (2019). Delay discounting as a transdiagnostic process in psychiatric disorders: A meta-analysis. *JAMA Psychiatry, 76*(11), 1176−1186. https://doi.org/10.1001/jamapsychiatry.2019.2102

Amlung, M., Petker, T., Jackson, J., Balodis, I., & MacKillop, J. (2016). Steep discounting of delayed monetary and food rewards in obesity: A meta-analysis. *Psychological Medicine, 46*(11), 2423−2434.

Ashe, M. L., Newman, M. G., & Wilson, S. J. (2015). Delay discounting and the use of mindful attention versus distraction in the treatment of drug addiction: A conceptual review. *Journal of the Experimental Analysis of Behavior, 103*(1), 234−248. https://doi.org/10.1002/jeab.122

Bailey, A. J., Romeu, R. J., & Finn, P. R. (2021). The problems with delay discounting: A critical review of current practices and clinical applications. *Psychological Medicine*, 1−8. https://doi.org/10.1017/s0033291721002282

Beauchaine, T. P., Ben-David, I., & Sela, A. (2017). Attention-deficit/hyperactivity disorder, delay discounting, and risky financial behaviors: A preliminary analysis of self-report data. *PLoS One, 12*(5), Article e0176933. https://doi.org/10.1371/journal.pone.0176933

Berry, M. S., Bruner, N. R., Herrmann, E. S., Johnson, P. S., & Johnson, M. W. (2022). Methamphetamine administration dose effects on sexual desire, sexual decision making, and delay discounting. *Experimental and Clinical Psychopharmacology, 30*(2), 180.

Berry, M. S., Friedel, J., DeHart, W., Mahamane, S., Jordan, K., & Odum, A. (2017). The value of clean air: Comparing discounting of delayed air quality and money across magnitudes. *Psychological Record, 67*(2), 137−148. https://doi.org/10.1007/s40732-017-0233-4

Berry, M. S., Johnson, P. S., Collado, A., Loya, J. M., Yi, R., & Johnson, M. W. (2019). Sexual probability discounting: A mechanism for sexually transmitted infection among undergraduate students. *Archives of Sexual Behavior, 48*(2), 495−505.

Berry, M. S., Nickerson, N. P., & Odum, A. L. (2017). Delay discounting as an index of sustainable behavior: Devaluation of future air quality and implications for public health. *International Journal of Environmental Research and Public Health, 14*(9), Article 9. https://doi.org/10.3390/ijerph14090997

Berry, M. S., Repke, M., & Conway, L. (2019). Visual exposure to natural environments decreases delay discounting of improved air quality. *Frontiers in Public Health, 7*. https://doi.org/10.3389/fpubh.2019.00308

Berry, M. S., Repke, M. A., Nickerson, N. P., Conway, L. G., Odum, A. L., & Jordan, K. E. (2015). Making time for nature: Visual exposure to natural environments lengthens subjective time perception and reduces impulsivity. *PLoS One, 10*(11), Article e0141030. https://doi.org/10.1371/journal.pone.0141030

Berry, M. S., Sweeney, M. M., Morath, J., Odum, A. L., & Jordan, K. E. (2014). The nature of impulsivity: Visual exposure to natural environments decreases impulsive decision-making in a delay discounting task. *PLoS One, 9*(5), Article e97915.

Bickel, W. K., Athamneh, L. N., Basso, J. C., Mellis, A. M., DeHart, W. B., Craft, W. H., & Pope, D. (2019). Excessive discounting of delayed reinforcers as a trans-disease process: Update on the state of the science. *Current Opinion in Psychology, 30*, 59–64. https://doi.org/10.1016/j.copsyc.2019.01.005

Bickel, W. K., Jarmolowicz, D. P., Mueller, E. T., Koffarnus, M. N., & Gatchalian, K. M. (2012). Excessive discounting of delayed reinforcers as a trans-disease process contributing to addiction and other disease-related vulnerabilities: Emerging evidence. *Pharmacology & Therapeutics, 134*(3), 287–297. https://doi.org/10.1016/j.pharmthera.2012.02.004

Bickel, W. K., & Johnson, M. W. (2003). *Delay discounting: A fundamental behavioral process of drug dependence*.

Bickel, W. K., Koffarnus, M. N., Moody, L., & Wilson, A. G. (2014). The behavioral-and neuroeconomic process of temporal discounting: A candidate behavioral marker of addiction. *Neuropharmacology, 76*, 518–527. https://doi.org/10.1016/j.neuropharm.2013.06.013

Bickel, W. K., & Mueller, E. T. (2009). Toward the study of trans-disease processes: A novel approach with special reference to the study of co-morbidity. *Journal of Dual Diagnosis, 5*(2), 131–138. https://doi.org/10.1080/15504260902869147

Bolin, B. L., Lile, J. A., Marks, K. R., Beckmann, J. S., Rush, C. R., & Stoops, W. W. (2016). Buspirone reduces sexual risk-taking intent but not cocaine self-administration. *Experimental and Clinical Psychopharmacology, 24*(3), 162.

Budescu, D. V., Por, H.-H., & Broomell, S. B. (2012). Effective communication of uncertainty in the IPCC reports. *Climatic Change, 113*(2), 181–200. https://doi.org/10.1007/s10584-011-0330-3

Buscemi, J., Murphy, J. G., Berlin, K. S., & Raynor, H. A. (2014). A behavioral economic analysis of changes in food-related and food-free reinforcement during weight loss treatment. *Journal of Consulting and Clinical Psychology, 82*(4), 659. https://doi.org/10.1037/a0036376

Collado, A., Johnson, P. S., Loya, J. M., Johnson, M. W., & Yi, R. (2017). Discounting of condom-protected sex as a measure of high risk for sexually transmitted infection among college students. *Archives of Sexual Behavior, 46*(7), 2187–2195.

Daniel, T. O., Stanton, C. M., & Epstein, L. H. (2013). The future is now: Comparing the effect of episodic future thinking on impulsivity in lean and obese individuals. *Appetite, 71*, 120–125. https://doi.org/10.1016/j.appet.2013.07.010

Dariotis, J. K., & Johnson, M. W. (2015). Sexual discounting among high-risk youth ages 18–24: Implications for sexual and substance use risk behaviors. *Experimental and Clinical Psychopharmacology, 23*(1), 49.

Dassen, F. C., Houben, K., & Jansen, A. (2015). Time orientation and eating behavior: Unhealthy eaters consider immediate consequences, while healthy eaters focus on future health. *Appetite, 91*, 13–19.

Dassen, F. C. M., Jansen, A., Nederkoorn, C., & Houben, K. (2016). Focus on the future: Episodic future thinking reduces discount rate and snacking. *Appetite, 96*, 327–332. https://doi.org/10.1016/j.appet.2015.09.032

de Wit, H., & Mitchell, S. H. (2010). *Drug effects on delay discounting*.

Decker, J. H., Figner, B., & Steinglass, J. E. (2015). On weight and waiting: Delay discounting in anorexia nervosa pretreatment and posttreatment. *Biological Psychiatry, 78*(9), 606−614. https://doi.org/10.1016/j.biopsych.2014.12.016

Dixon, M. R., Paliliunas, D., Belisle, J., Speelman, R. C., Gunnarsson, K. F., & Shaffer, J. L. (2019). The effect of brief mindfulness training on momentary impulsivity. *Journal of Contextual Behavioral Science, 11*, 15−20. https://doi.org/10.1016/j.jcbs.2018.11.003

Farias, A. R., Coruk, S., & Simão, C. (2021). The effects of temporal discounting on perceived seriousness of environmental behavior: Exploring the moderator role of consumer attitudes regarding green purchasing. *Sustainability, 13*(13), 7130.

Friedel, J. E., DeHart, W. B., Madden, G. J., & Odum, A. L. (2014). Impulsivity and cigarette smoking: Discounting of monetary and consumable outcomes in current and non-smokers. *Psychopharmacology, 231*, 4517−4526. https://doi.org/10.1007/s00213-014-3597-z

Gebru, N. M., Kalkat, M., Strickland, J. C., Ansell, M., Leeman, R. F., & Berry, M. S. (2022). Measuring sexual risk-taking: A systematic review of the sexual delay discounting task. *Archives of Sexual Behavior*, 1−22.

Gelino, B. W., Erath, T. G., & Reed, D. D. (2021). Going green: A systematic review of pro-environmental empirical research in behavior analysis. *Behavior and Social Issues,* (30), 587−611. https://doi.org/10.1007/s42822-020-00043-x

Hagan, K. E., Jarmolowicz, D. P., & Forbush, K. T. (2021). Reconsidering delay discounting in bulimia nervosa. *Eating Behaviors, 41*, Article 101506.

Hanley, N., Schläpfer, F., & Spurgeon, J. (2003). Aggregating the benefits of environmental improvements: Distance-decay functions for use and non-use values. *Journal of Environmental Management, 68*(3), 297−304. https://doi.org/10.1016/S0301-4797(03)00084-7

Hardisty, D., & Weber, E. (2009). Discounting future green: Money versus the environment. *Journal of Experimental Psychology: General, 138*(3), 329−340. https://doi.org/10.1037/a0016433

Hendrickson, K. L., & Rasmussen, E. B. (2013). Effects of mindful eating training on delay and probability discounting for food and money in obese and healthy-weight individuals. *Behaviour Research and Therapy, 51*(7), 399−409. https://doi.org/10.1016/j.brat.2013.04.002

Hendrickson, K. L., & Rasmussen, E. B. (2017). Mindful eating reduces impulsive food choice in adolescents and adults. *Health Psychology, 36*(3), 226.

Hendrickson, K. L., Rasmussen, E. B., & Lawyer, S. R. (2015). Measurement and validation of measures for impulsive food choice across obese and healthy-weight individuals. *Appetite, 90*, 254−263.

Herrmann, E. S., Hand, D. J., Johnson, M. W., Badger, G. J., & Heil, S. H. (2014). Examining delay discounting of condom-protected sex among opioid-dependent women and non-drug-using control women. *Drug and Alcohol Dependence, 144*, 53−60.

Herrmann, E. S., Johnson, P. S., & Johnson, M. W. (2015). Examining delay discounting of condom-protected sex among men who have sex with men using crowdsourcing technology. *AIDS and Behavior, 19*(9), 1655−1665.

Herrnstein, R. J. (1961). Relative and absolute strength of response as a function of frequency of reinforcement. *Journal of the Experimental Analysis of Behavior, 4*, 267−272.

Hirsh, J. L., Costello, M. S., & Fuqua, R. W. (2015). Analysis of delay discounting as a psychological measure of sustainable behavior. *Behavior and Social Issues, 24*(1), 187−202. https://doi.org/10.5210/bsi.v24i0.5906

Jarmolowicz, D. P., Bickel, W. K., & Gatchalian, K. M. (2013). Alcohol-dependent individuals discount sex at higher rates than controls. *Drug and Alcohol Dependence, 131*(3), 320−323.

Jarmolowicz, D. P., Lemley, S. M., Asmussen, L., & Reed, D. D. (2015). Mr. right versus Mr. right now: A discounting-based approach to promiscuity. *Behavioural Processes, 115*, 117−122.

Johnson, M. W., Bickel, W. K., & Baker, F. (2007). Moderate drug use and delay discounting: A comparison of heavy, light, and never smokers. *Experimental and Clinical Psychopharmacology, 15*(2), 187.

Johnson, M. W., & Bruner, N. R. (2012). The sexual discounting task: HIV risk behavior and the discounting of delayed sexual rewards in cocaine dependence. *Drug and Alcohol Dependence, 123*(1−3), 15−21.

Johnson, M. W., & Bruner, N. R. (2013). Test−retest reliability and gender differences in the sexual discounting task among cocaine-dependent individuals. *Experimental and Clinical Psychopharmacology, 21*(4), 277−286. https://doi.org/10.1037/a0033071

Johnson, M. W., Herrmann, E. S., Sweeney, M. M., LeComte, R. S., & Johnson, P. S. (2017). Cocaine administration dose-dependently increases sexual desire and decreases condom use likelihood: The role of delay and probability discounting in connecting cocaine with HIV. *Psychopharmacology, 234*(4), 599−612.

Johnson, M. W., Strickland, J. C., Herrmann, E. S., Dolan, S. B., Cox, D. J., & Berry, M. S. (2021). Sexual discounting: A systematic review of discounting processes and sexual behavior. *Experimental and Clinical Psychopharmacology, 29*(6), 711.

Johnson, P. S., Sweeney, M. M., Herrmann, E. S., & Johnson, M. W. (2016). Alcohol increases delay and probability discounting of condom-protected sex: A novel vector for alcohol-related HIV transmission. *Alcoholism: Clinical and Experimental Research, 40*(6), 1339−1350.

Jones, J., Guest, J. L., Sullivan, P. S., Kramer, M. R., Jenness, S. M., & Sales, J. M. (2018). Concordance between monetary and sexual delay discounting in men who have sex with men. *Sexual Health, 15*(3), 214−222.

Jones, J., Guest, J. L., Sullivan, P. S., Sales, J. M., Jenness, S. M., & Kramer, M. R. (2018). The association between monetary and sexual delay discounting and risky sexual behavior in an online sample of men who have sex with men. *AIDS Care, 30*(7), 844−852.

Kao, C. C., Wu, W. H., & Chiou, W. B. (2019). Exposure to nature may induce lower discounting and lead to healthier dietary choices. *Journal of Environmental Psychology, 65*, Article 101333. https://doi.org/10.1016/j.jenvp.2019.101333

Kaplan, B. A., Reed, D. D., & McKerchar, T. L. (2014). Using a visual Analogue scale to assess delay, social, and probability discounting of an environmental loss. *Psychological Record, 64*(2), 261−269. https://doi.org/10.1007/s40732-014-0041-z

Koffarnus, M. N., Johnson, M. W., Thompson-Lake, D. G., Wesley, M. J., Lohrenz, T., Montague, P. R., & Bickel, W. K. (2016). Cocaine-dependent adults and recreational cocaine users are more likely than controls to choose immediate unsafe sex over delayed safer sex. *Experimental and Clinical Psychopharmacology, 24*(4), 297.

Lawyer, S. R., Williams, S. A., Prihodova, T., Rollins, J. D., & Lester, A. C. (2010). Probability and delay discounting of hypothetical sexual outcomes. *Behavioural Processes, 84*(3), 687−692.

Lee, Y. J., & Rasmussen, E. B. (2022). Age-related effects in delay discounting for food. *Appetite, 168*, Article 105783.

Liang, J., & Guo, L. (2021). Gratitude and sustainable consumer behavior: A moderated mediation model of time discounting and connectedness to the future self. *Psychology & Marketing, 38*(8), 1238–1249. https://doi.org/10.1002/mar.21502

Madden, G. J., Petry, N. M., Badger, G. J., & Bickel, W. K. (1997). Impulsive and self-control choices in opioid-dependent patients and non-drug-using control patients: Drug and monetary rewards. *Experimental and Clinical Psychopharmacology, 5*, 256–262. https://doi.org/10.1037/1064-1297.5.3

Manwaring, J. L., Green, L., Myerson, J., Strube, M. J., & Wilfley, D. E. (2011). Discounting of various types of rewards by women with and without binge eating disorder: Evidence for general rather than specific differences. *Psychological Record, 61*(4), 561–582.

Mao, H., Zhou, L., Ying, R., & Pan, D. (2021). Time preferences and green agricultural technology adoption: Field evidence from rice farmers in China. *Land Use Policy, 109*, Article 105627.

Mazur, J. E. (1987). An adjusting procedure for studying delayed reinforcement. In M. L. Commons, J. E. Mazur, J. A. Nevin, & H. Rachlin (Eds.), *Quantitative analyses of behavior: The effect of delay and of intervening events on reinforcement value* (Vol 5, pp. 55–73). Hillsdale, NJ: Erlbaum.

McClelland, J., Dalton, B., Kekic, M., Bartholdy, S., Campbell, I. C., & Schmidt, U. (2016). A systematic review of temporal discounting in eating disorders and obesity: Behavioural and neuroimaging findings. *Neuroscience & Biobehavioral Reviews, 71*, 506–528.

McCright, A. M., Dunlap, R. E., & Xiao, C. (2014). Increasing influence of party identification on perceived scientific agreement and support for government action on climate change in the United States, 2006–12. *Weather, Climate, and Society, 6*(2), 194–201. https://doi.org/10.1175/WCAS-D-13-00058.1

Mellis, A. M., Snider, S. E., Deshpande, H. U., LaConte, S. M., & Bickel, W. K. (2019). Practicing prospection promotes patience: Repeated episodic future thinking cumulatively reduces delay discounting. *Drug and Alcohol Dependence, 204*, Article 107507. https://doi.org/10.1016/j.drugalcdep.2019.06.010

Meyer, A. (2013). Intertemporal valuation of river restoration. *Environmental and Resource Economics, 54*(1), 41–61. https://doi.org/10.1007/s10640-012-9580-4

Naudé, G. P., Dolan, S. B., Strickland, J. C., Berry, M. S., Cox, D. J., & Johnson, M. W. (2021). The influence of episodic future thinking and graphic warning labels on delay discounting and cigarette demand. *International Journal of Environmental Research and Public Health, 18*(23), Article 12637.

Odum, A. L. (2011). Delay discounting: Trait variable? *Behavioural Processes, 87*(1), 1–9. https://doi.org/10.1016/j.beproc.2011.02.007

Pritschmann, R. K., Yurasek, A. M., & Yi, R. (2021). A review of cross-commodity delay discounting research with relevance to addiction. *Behavioural Processes, 186*, Article 104339. https://doi.org/10.1016/j.beproc.2021.104339

Privitera, G. J., McGrath, H. K., Windus, B. A., & Doraiswamy, P. M. (2015). Eat now or later: Self-control as an overlapping cognitive mechanism of depression and obesity. *PLoS One, 10*(3), Article e0123136.

Rasmussen, E. B., Lawyer, S. R., & Reilly, W. (2010). Percent body fat is related to delay and probability discounting for food in humans. *Behavioural Processes, 83*(1), 23–30.

Rasmussen, E. B., Rodriguez, L. R., & Pemberton, S. (2022). Acute and enduring effects of mindful eating on delay and probability discounting for food and money in food-insecure women. *Mindfulness, 13*(3), 712–729.

Reed, D. D., Strickland, J. C., Gelino, B. W., Hursh, S. R., Jarmolowicz, D. P., Kaplan, B. A., & Amlung, M. (2022). Applied behavioral economics and public health policies: Historical precedence and translational promise. *Behavioural Processes, 198*, Article 104640.

Repke, M. A., Berry, M. S., Conway III, L. G., Metcalf, A., Hensen, R. M., & Phelan, C. (2018). How does nature exposure make people healthier?: Evidence for the role of impulsivity and expanded space perception. *PLoS One, 13*(8), Article e0202246. https://doi.org/10.1371/journal.pone.0202246

Richards, T. J., & Green, G. P. (2015). Environmental choices and hyperbolic discounting: An experimental analysis. *Environmental and Resource Economics, 62*, 83–103.

Rung, J. M., & Madden, G. J. (2018a). Experimental reductions of delay discounting and impulsive choice: A systematic review and meta-analysis. *Journal of Experimental Psychology: General, 147*(9), 1349. https://doi.org/10.1037/xge0000462

Rung, J. M., & Madden, G. J. (2018b). Demand characteristics in episodic future thinking: Delay discounting and healthy eating. *Experimental and Clinical Psychopharmacology, 26*(1), 77–84. https://doi.org/10.1037/pha0000171

Sargisson, R. J., & Schöner, B. V. (2020). Hyperbolic discounting with environmental outcomes across time, space, and probability. *Psychological Record, 70*, 515–527. https://doi.org/10.1007/s40732-019-00368-z

Schiff, S., Amodio, P., Testa, G., Nardi, M., Montagnese, S., Caregaro, L., ... Sellitto, M. (2016). Impulsivity toward food reward is related to BMI: Evidence from intertemporal choice in obese and normal-weight individuals. *Brain and Cognition, 110*, 112–119.

Snider, S. E., LaConte, S. M., & Bickel, W. K. (2016). Episodic future thinking: Expansion of the temporal window in individuals with alcohol dependence. *Alcoholism: Clinical and Experimental Research, 40*(7), 1558–1566. https://doi.org/10.1111/acer.13112

Sparkman, G., Lee, N. R., & Macdonald, B. N. J. (2021). Discounting environmental policy: The effects of psychological distance over time and space. *Journal of Environmental Psychology, 73*, Article 101529. https://doi.org/10.1016/j.jenvp.2020.101529

Stein, J. S., Tegge, A. N., Turner, J. K., & Bickel, W. K. (2018). Episodic future thinking reduces delay discounting and cigarette demand: An investigation of the good-subject effect. *Journal of Behavioral Medicine, 41*(2), 269–276. https://doi.org/10.1007/s10865-017-9908-1

Stein, J. S., Wilson, A. G., Koffarnus, M. N., Daniel, T. O., Epstein, L. H., & Bickel, W. K. (2016). Unstuck in time: Episodic future thinking reduces delay discounting and cigarette smoking. *Psychopharmacology, 233*(21–22), 3771–3778. https://doi.org/10.1007/s00213-016-4410-y

Stojek, M. M., & MacKillop, J. (2017). Relative reinforcing value of food and delayed reward discounting in obesity and disordered eating: A systematic review. *Clinical Psychology Review, 55*, 1–11.

Strickland, J. C., Bolin, B. L., Romanelli, M. R., Rush, C. R., & Stoops, W. W. (2017). Effects of acute buspirone administration on inhibitory control and sexual discounting in cocaine users. *Human Psychopharmacology: Clinical and Experimental, 32*(1), Article e2567.

Sze, Y. Y., Stein, J. S., Bickel, W. K., Paluch, R. A., & Epstein, L. H. (2017). Bleak present, bright future: Online episodic future thinking, scarcity, delay discounting, and food demand. *Clinical Psychological Science*. https://doi.org/10.1177/2167702617696511

Van der Wal, A. J., Schade, H. M., Krabbendam, L., & Van Vugt, M. (2013). Do natural landscapes reduce future discounting in humans? *Proceedings of the Royal Society B: Biological Sciences, 280*(1773), Article 20132295. https://doi.org/10.1098/rspb.2013.2295

Viscusi, W. K., Huber, J., & Bell, J. (2008). The economic value of water quality. *Environmental and Resource Economics, 41*(2), 169–187. https://doi.org/10.1007/s10640-007-9186-4

Weitzman, M. L. (1998). Why the far-distant future should be discounted at its lowest possible rate. *Journal of Environmental Economics and Management, 36*, 201.

Weygandt, M., Mai, K., Dommes, E., Leupelt, V., Hackmack, K., Kahnt, T., ... Haynes, J. D. (2013). The role of neural impulse control mechanisms for dietary success in obesity. *NeuroImage, 83*, 669−678.

Wongsomboon, V., & Cox, D. J. (2021). Sexual arousal discounting: Devaluing condom-protected sex as a function of reduced arousal. *Archives of Sexual Behavior, 50*(6), 2717−2728.

Yi, R., Mitchell, S. H., & Bickel, W. K. (2010). *Delay discounting and substance abuse-dependence.*

Further reading

Epstein, L. H., Leddy, J. J., Temple, J. L., & Faith, M. S. (2007). Food reinforcement and eating: A multilevel analysis. *Psychological Bulletin, 133*(5), 884.

Epstein, L. H., Salvy, S. J., Carr, K. A., Dearing, K. K., & Bickel, W. K. (2010). Food reinforcement, delay discounting and obesity. *Physiology & Behavior, 100*(5), 438−445.

Hahn, H., Kalnitsky, S., Haines, N., Thamotharan, S., Beauchaine, T. P., & Ahn, W. Y. (2019). Delay discounting of protected sex: Relationship type and sexual orientation influence sexual risk behavior. *Archives of Sexual Behavior, 48*(7), 2089−2102.

Johnson, M. W., Johnson, P. S., Herrmann, E. S., & Sweeney, M. M. (2015). Delay and probability discounting of sexual and monetary outcomes in individuals with cocaine use disorders and matched controls. *PLoS One, 10*(5), Article e0128641.

Johnson, A. E., & Saunders, D. K. (2014). Time preferences and the management of coral reef fisheries. *Ecological Economics, 100*, 130−139. https://doi.org/10.1016/j.ecolecon.2014.01.004

Lilienthal, K. R., & Weatherly, J. N. (2013). Decision-making impulsivity in disordered eating: Outcomes from a discounting task. *Advances in Eating Disorders, 1*(2), 148−160.

Odum, A. L., & Rainaud, C. P. (2003). Discounting of delayed hypothetical money, alcohol, and food. *Behavioural Processes, 64*(3), 305−313.

Stoltman, J. J. (2019). *Differences in sexual delay discounting among in-treatment adults with opioid use disorder.* West Virginia University.

Policy implications of applied behavioral economics

Brett W. Gelino and Justin C. Strickland
Department of Psychiatry and Behavioral Sciences, Johns Hopkins University School of Medicine, Baltimore, MD, United States

Policy implications for applied behavioral economics

In 2018, the World Health Organization (WHO) launched the "SAFER" initiative with the goal of reducing the global public health threat of alcohol and alcohol-related harms (World Health Organization, 2024). As part of this initiative, WHO called for bans on discounts or other cost-saving mechanisms that might substantially reduce the cost of or otherwise incentivize alcohol consumption. The inflated alcohol demand that can result from these policies, WHO argued, can lead to episodes of heavy drinking that exacerbate the tendency for alcohol-related risks. At approximately the time WHO brought this initiative public, Kaplan and Reed (2018) published findings that corroborated concerns over the marketing of alcoholic drink specials. In their research, participants completed simulated measures of operant demand for alcohol in which prices either modeled those observed in a typical market or modeled happy hour specials such as "half price" or "buy one get one (BOGO)" advertising. Just as the WHO initiative foretold, participants in Kaplan and Reed (2018) study exhibited a statistically significant increase in alcohol consumption when prices were halved, and particularly when per-drink prices were already low (i.e., < $4 USD). This is largely consistent with the premise of demand—a reduction in cost should result in a corresponding increase in consumption. Interestingly, however, participants reported disproportionately greater increases in alcoholic drinks consumed when prices were framed specifically as "buy one get one," far more so than in the "half price" condition, suggesting that these happy hour advertising methods may not be exacting the same influence over consumer behavior. This substantial and relatively disjoined shift in alcohol demand based on contextual factors offers broad empirical support for WHO's call to prohibit alcohol discounts.

In a world where global public health concerns abound, public policy offers vetted solutions for community-scale intervention. The behavioral economic framework is poised to support and inform the development of new public policy initiatives. As a rule, public policy should prove most efficacious when it is empirical, meaning a reliable scientific conclusion serves as a foundation for action. Still, as Kaplan and Reed (2018) data demonstrate, behavioral economic research findings may also sufficiently vet ongoing initiatives to offer retroactive support for or evidence against policy effectiveness or provide precise information about where, when, how, and for whom public policy is most effective. This chapter will discuss policy implications for applied behavioral economics, beginning with an overview of public policy and policymaker action. We will then discuss the specific goals of behavioral economic models of choice as extended to policy-relevant contexts, describe methods for gathering policy-relevant choice data, and conclude by outlining crucial next steps for applied behavioral economics and policy outcomes.

What is public policy?

The SAFER initiative launched by WHO, a global enterprise focused on improving international health outcomes, is a call for domestic public policy changes that would restrict alcohol access toward reducing alcohol-imposed health risks. So, what is public policy? When government officials or their respective committee and subcommittee members implement or modify laws, create new industry standards, or otherwise set an expectation for behavioral outcomes that impact a wide array of individuals, they are engaging in policy making. Thus, public policy might be best viewed as a mechanism by which elected or appointed officials can influence behavior toward a certain goal (Critchfield, 2024).

A defining feature of public policy is that it extends to the public—policymakers are working to address the concerns of persons under their jurisdiction (Gerson, 2014). Often these individuals are constituents, meaning said policymaker was appointed or elected to represent their community as a government official. Public policy can be enacted at any level of government and so can vary widely in the scope of influence from city-level urban policy to international policies on health standards, human rights, trade, and conflict negotiation. Some topics will span all levels of policy enactment. Global sustainability and climate change mitigation, for instance, is a complex of interlocking behavioral contingencies that may be best addressed via policy change at the local, national, and international levels. This policy is likely to vary greatly across levels, too, given that policymakers are seeking to address concerns that are specific to their respective constituents. Local policy might focus on curbing excess water use for drought-prone locations, whereas national policy might set minimum standards for water quality or deliberate over shared nonrenewable resources (e.g., the Colorado River is shared by four US States' watersheds; see United States Department of the Interior, 2012).

Public policy serves as a critical outlet for elected and appointed officials to implement change with the potential for dramatic public health outcomes. A crucially important question, then, lies in how policymakers leverage sound science and reliable findings to guide their policy-making decisions. Ideally, new policy would be empirically derived, drawing on cutting-edge research findings and data-informed conceptualizations to produce maximally effective and equitable changes in behavior. Realistically, policymakers are expected to operate much like a skilled juggler, keeping multiple metaphorical "balls" in the air (as in the many concerns of their respective constituents, donor obligations, and reelection pressures). Policy changes at all levels can happen quickly, and particularly at the congressional level, policymakers seek to take decisive action to address constituent concerns. Easily accessible, digestible, and highly relevant research dissemination is key to garnering policymaker attention (Baron & Hoeksema, 2021). By understanding the unique pressures faced by policymakers, behavioral economic researchers can ensure their findings are optimally positioned for consideration as part of new empirical policy implementation.

On the importance of timing

Applied behavioral economic researchers should consider one important detail when postulating the extension of their findings to policy implementation: The timing of their outreach matters. Learning the schedule and process of policymaker decision making, and similarly considering the very lean scheduling allowance afforded to policy officials, may make the difference for a successful policy interface. Foremost, researchers should learn the budget renewal process for the offices governing their desired level of policy contact. Let us consider the US national policy change. The President of the United States submits a proposed budget to the US Congress, typically by the first Monday in February. Shortly thereafter, the congressional staffers that comprise Congress committees and subcommittees will begin to deliberate over how these monies might best be spent, paying particular attention to the constituents represented by committee leaders. During this deliberation period, researchers might strategically advocate for monetary allocation to support research interests or novel policy implementation. Similarly, closely tracking Congress' prioritization of a particular constituent concern may afford a strategic opportunity to establish a relationship with involved policymakers. The important point is to serve as a resource to those involved in policy making, ensuring a clear research implication that aligns with introduced legislation at a strategically timed moment (see Baron & Hoeksema, 2021).

Behavioral economic compatibility with empirical public policy

A significant advantage of the behavioral economic framework is the ease with which its conceptual interpretations and quantitative choice metrics lend to empirical public policy development (Reed, Strickland, et al., 2022). The conceptual interpretations and choice procedures characteristic of operant behavioral economics are based on decades of human laboratory and nonhuman conditioning science. As a science grounded firmly in a deterministic view of behavior, behavioral economics largely rejects the study of psychological constructs, focusing instead on observable instances of behavior that meaningfully correspond with the primary research question (see Strickland & Lacy, 2020).

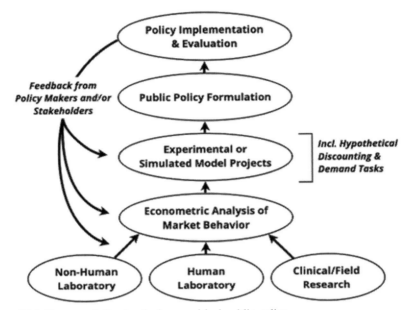

Figure 12.1 Framework for developing empirical public policy.
Note: Reprinted from Reed, D.D., Strickland, J.C., Gelino, B.W., Hursh, S.R., Jarmolowicz, D.P., Kaplan, B.A., & Amlung, M. (2022). Applied behavioral economics and public health policies: Historical precedence and translational promise. *Behavioural Processes 198*, 104640. 10.1016/j.beproc.2022.104640. Copyright 2024, with permission from Elsevier.

Beyond these rigorous foundations, the operant behavioral economic framework offers a powerful testbed for prospective policy outcomes. Fig. 12.1 presents a flow chart proposed by Reed, Strickland et al. (2022) that describes how empirical public policy might ideally be informed by operant behavioral economic research (based on Hursh, 1991). Pending the research context, preliminary basic laboratory and clinical research should initially inform understanding around the target concern, with data potentially guiding plausible intervention outcomes. For instance, xylazine adulteration of the illicit drug supply is a relatively new public health threat that has drawn a great deal of pharmacological and epidemiological research focus. Xylazine is a veterinary-grade sedative with notable human health risks that some illicit drug suppliers use to alter the pharmacokinetic effect of drugs cut with bulking agents (see review by Ball et al., 2022). As a starting place for empirical public policy design, it is important for researchers to have a general understanding of how xylazine adulterants impact acute decision making, alter drug pharmacological effects, and how these additives might interact with therapeutic interventions previously shown effective for use with unadulterated substances.

A strong empirical policy is based on a thorough basic understanding of the target public health concern. As initial questions are answered by laboratory studies, researchers can begin piecing together elements of an intervention that might affect meaningful policy-level change. Importantly, operant behavioral economic tasks can be used to experimentally evaluate how a novel policy intervention might translate to changes in human behavior. Research participants might be asked to "work" or make imagined purchases of a commodity in the presence of tightly controlled environmental manipulations, as informed by initial laboratory assessment. This econometric analysis of behavior facilitated by operant behavioral economic research serves as a fundamental scaling of prospective intervention effects—a low-cost, first-step pilot of policy outcomes outside the lab. Importantly, researchers get a chance to improve their understanding of the policy intervention before more expensive piloting in the community. One unique difficulty in addressing the public health risks of xylazine is testing—currently, there are few drug screens that can identify xylazine adulterants (Alexander et al., 2022). Therefore a potential policy option is to evaluate whether individuals who use drugs would allocate effort toward securing an unadulterated drug supply, an effect readily modeled through operant behavioral economic demand analysis.

Upon conducting a successful econometric demonstration of plausible intervention effects, interested parties should explore the development of experimental model projects enacted within the target community. These naturalistic demonstrations bring policy implications into the community by evaluating effects in samples behaving under natural contingencies absent the tight experimental control of laboratory simulation. Rigorous evaluation throughout this testing process ensures that variables or complexes of variables untested during behavioral economic simulation are appropriately considered before policy implementation.

Policy-relevant choice procedures

The goal for the applied behavioral economics researcher, therefore, is to develop research demonstrations that meaningfully model the behavior of interest in a context that closely resembles the expected decision-making environment. Fortunately, operant behavioral economics offers rich empirical frameworks through which researchers can model and subsequently predict policy-induced changes in behavior. This section briefly recaps the discounting and operant demand choice procedures, establishing these protocols against the specific goals of behavioral economic choice modeling as extended to public policy.

Discounting

Organisms generally prefer reinforcers that are immediate and guaranteed (Ainslie, 1974; Chung & Herrnstein, 1967). Discounting describes the unique sensitivity that individual organisms exhibit to temporal or probabilistic constraints (Odum et al., 2020). In discounting assessments, research participants conventionally make choices between immediately available or guaranteed outcomes and larger but delayed or less-than-guaranteed outcomes. Between each selection, some element of the choice presentation is manipulated (e.g., magnitude of the smaller outcome). Participants continue selecting their preferred outcome until they reach a point of indifference between the smaller and larger outcomes. These indifference points, thought to depict the value of the larger reward after imposed constraint in terms of the smaller reward, can be modeled to describe the extent to which participants are sensitive to delays to or odds against contacting the targeted outcome (Madden & Johnson, 2010).

In operant behavioral economics, the application of discount models yields the primary outputted metric, k, that corresponds to the rate of discounting or participant sensitivity to increasing outcome constraints. Research has shown discounting rate k to be both notably stable across repeat test completions up to periods of 2 years or more (see review by Gelino et al., 2024), yet sensitive to a wide variety of contextual manipulations (see review by Rung & Madden, 2018). This dual trait-state quality of discounting rate k (Odum, 2011a, 2011b) has drawn attention as a target for intervention, particularly as experts call for discounting to be considered a viable transdiagnostic process underlying behavioral health concerns (see review by Amlung et al., 2019).

Operant demand

Organisms generally prefer reinforcers that can be contacted at a low relative effort expenditure (Griffiths et al., 1979; Hursh, 1980; see also Bickel et al., 2000). Operant demand describes the unique price sensitivity that individual organisms exhibit when work is required to experience an outcome (Hursh & Silberberg, 2008; Reed et al., 2017). Price can be conceptualized as energy expenditure as in engaging with operant manipulanda (e.g., plunger pulls), monetary or time-based allocation, or some other metric of "work." In demand assessments, research participants first engage with a targeted commodity or outcome at "free price," after which subsequent commodity engagement is available only after emitting work to a predetermined threshold. The degree to which participants continue working to defend this baseline rate of consumption, sometimes depicted as units consumed at each price, can be modeled to describe the extent to which organisms and/or commodities are price sensitive.

Operant behavioral economic demand models describe several topographies of commodity interactions and can inform unique characteristics of the target commodity, responding organism, and their interaction. Demand metrics are notably sensitive to context as in the presence of low-cost substitutes (see review by Weinsztok et al., 2023) yet are sufficiently robust to demonstrate correspondence with clinically relevant behavior (see reviews by Strickland et al., 2019; Zvorsky et al., 2019). The distinct pattern of responding that organisms emit to maintain a baseline rate of contact with a given outcome serves as a proxy for the value, or reinforcing efficacy, of said outcome (Hursh, 1980). Conceptually, operant demand also provides a compelling framework through which to approach behavior change. The integration of microeconomic principles results in greater attention to the role of competing alternative reinforcers and the effect of effort or "price" manipulation on reinforcer valuation (e.g., Acuff et al., 2023).

Simulated and incentivized tasks

Historically, the described discounting and operant demand procedures were piloted and developed in nonhuman animal laboratories. Under these conditions, researchers were able to exact tight experimental control and examine changes in behavior as a function of directly experienced contingencies. As experimental questions and protocol advanced, these behavioral economic procedures were adapted for use in human laboratories (e.g., Johnson & Bickel, 2002; Green et al., 1997; Madden et al., 1997; see also Hursh & Roma, 2013). Conventional behavioral economic laboratory studies remain a gold standard for much of the behavioral health literature. Still, there may be contexts in which behavioral economic procedures are practically or ethically challenging to conduct with human participants. These tasks are often time consuming, requiring numerous lengthy research sessions from each participant over a relatively short time span. These participants also typically experience the contingencies in real time, a particular cost or time barrier to implementation in behavioral pharmacology research.

Publication of the first simulated operant behavioral economic tasks represented a significant milestone for the operant behavioral economic framework (Jacobs & Bickel, 1999; Petry & Bickel, 1998). This proved especially true for the extension of applied behavioral economic research to otherwise difficult-to-study topics (see Roma et al., 2016). Rather than requiring human participants to undergo lengthy laboratory trials, the simulated task instead relies on tightly controlled language manipulations and self-reported behavioral predictions to examine relative rates of discounting and demand. By removing the laboratory, researchers can employ operant behavioral economic procedures to answer a multitude of questions that would be near-impossible to adapt for laboratory study. Importantly, research has found strong say-do correspondence among simulated task respondents and suggests a noteworthy relation between laboratory-derived and simulated-task-derived behavioral economic indices (e.g., Amlung et al., 2011). Given this flexible yet sound scientific foundation, simulated tasks may offer a useful tool for expanding the policy impacts of operant behavioral economics (Roma et al., 2017; Reed, Gelino, & Strickland, 2022; see also Strickland et al., 2019; Zvorsky et al., 2019).

Policy targets for applied behavioral economists

As laid out in Hursh's (1991) framework for developing empirical public policy, a primary goal for the policy-driven behavior analyst is to generate meaningful econometric analyses of behavior (see Fig. 12.1). In short, behavioral economic procedures can be used to simulate how behavior might change as a function of environmental modifications proposed in the novel policy intervention. Researchers might program contingencies that replicate the market landscape, as in the effect of a novel competing alternative on commodity demand. These data can then be coupled with more naturalistic demonstrations to provide a comprehensive intervention of prospective intervention effects. Of course, econometric analyses and policy simulations more broadly will likely have a different function and topography depending on the specifics of the policy's intended effects. This section describes three categories of policy analysis that applied behavioral economists might conduct.

Describing molar patterns of behavior

Behavioral economics offers a conceptual interpretation of choice that can be invaluable for policy design. Operant behavioral economics differs from other behavioral economic or social scientific approaches to studying choice behavior in that the operant approach focuses on molar patterns of behavior (Critchfield & Reed, 2009). Data describe the likely distribution of responses across many momentary decisions, a pattern that offers useful foundational knowledge for gauging how a large sample of constituents might react to an anticipated change in the environment. Importantly, policy-relevant molar descriptions of behavior do not need to be complex experimental evaluations. Take, for example, the policymaker decision to mandate flood insurance for residents living in a floodplain. When individuals establish a residence near a river or other flood-prone body of water, they take a risk that heavy rains will bring floodwaters into their homes. Behavioral economic discounting insights would suggest that the probabilistic and delayed outcome that is home flooding is likely to be discounted by residents. That threat may not be salient enough to trigger sufficient demand for flood insurance. By leveraging such insights, policymakers can make a sound decision to incentivize or otherwise increase the likelihood that such individuals will be enrolled in protective insurance measures.

Data on how choice is likely to be allocated across concurrently available options might also be important for policy decisions. Operant demand describes price sensitivity when commodities are available on their own and as a function of a broader selection of competing alternatives. Conceptually, this can inform two lines of reasoning. First, foundational to operant behavioral economics is the idea that reinforcer valuation is relatively meaningless unless considered in the greater context of decision making. Extending consideration to the availability of environmental reinforcement has advanced connotations and framing around excessive commodity valuation, as might be observed in substance use treatment (Hursh, 1991). Existing findings that individuals reporting low substance-free alternative sources of reinforcement report consuming substances at higher rates, particularly when available at a low price, have shined light on the role of environmental enrichment as a promising route for emerging treatment lines (Acuff et al., 2023; Bickel et al., 2014). Continued study of this phenomenon should offer improved framing for pathologic commodity valuation beyond substance use.

Similarly, rapid changes in commodity prices may have an unexpected impact on human behavior. The alcohol happy hour task (Kaplan & Reed, 2018) described in the introduction to this chapter nicely exemplifies this data stream. Understanding how low-priced alcoholic beverage availability might differentially impact alcohol consumption across samples might be an important policy-level decision. Equally important is understanding the additive effects of other alternatives. For instance, how might a happy hour deal influence alcohol consumption in a community with low-priced recreationally available cannabis? Piecing together this landscape view of the commodity "market" can be a powerful source of information on which policymakers can rely.

Measuring reinforcer valuation

When a new product or service is being considered for mass availability, it may be important to consider the relative value of that commodity. How might the release of this product impact purchasing decisions? Could it result in excessive spending? In the case of novel licit and illicit psychoactive substances, products are likely to undergo rigorous testing to evaluate their relative abuse liability. The operant demand framework lends nicely to this type of data collection, offering a structured platform through which participants can document their likely behavioral allocation toward obtaining that commodity (Hursh, 1991; Hursh & Silberberg, 2008). Substances that retain greater levels of effort, particularly in the presence of competing alternatives, are those that might require greater regulatory guidelines via policymaker oversight or drug scheduling decisions (Koffarnus, 2023).

Importantly, the operant demand task advances upon previous methods for studying reinforcer valuation. The experimental analysis of behavior has historically employed the progressive ratio breakpoint, concurrent choice assessments, and peak responding measures to determine the relative reinforcing efficacy of a novel commodity. Research shows that these measures can be inconsistent in how they rank commodities, for instance, cigarettes and money, across participants and discrete evaluations (Johnson & Bickel, 2006). Reanalysis of these commodities using an operant demand curve measure accounted for these differences in reinforcing value, where previous measures of valuation parsimoniously correlated with these conventional reinforcer indices (e.g., operant demand maximum expenditure maps onto peak response output). Thus, the policy-driven behavioral economist can take advantage of this robust valuation analysis when describing the expected relative response allocation for a novel market commodity.

Evaluating intervention effects

Some policies may involve deliberate manipulations of the immediate choice context toward promoting or suppressing certain constituent behaviors (e.g., Strickland et al., 2024). Behavioral economic tasks may offer a useful framework for evaluating some of these proposed interventions (see review by Acuff et al., 2020). Task completers often behave as a function of contextual manipulations that have a detectable influence over allocated responding. Laboratory and simulated tasks have exhibited sufficient sensitivity to these manipulations to generate estimates on policy effects when scaled (e.g., Rung & Madden, 2018).

The advancement of simulated task designs has been fundamental to the ability of applied behavioral economists to offer insights on predicted intervention effects. Contextual modifications often require significant equipment, time, and/or resources to be simulated in laboratory space. In contrast, the flexibility afforded by a language-based vignette and self-reported choice predictions permits the study of a wide range of environmental changes. The assessment of proposed incentives and bans lends easily to this format. Choice architecture is a popular psychological and economic concept wherein aspects of the environment are manipulated to make certain choices more likely while still permitting constituents to freely make choices (Thaler & Sunstein, 2021; Johnson et al., 2012; see also review by Münscher et al., 2016). Examples might include increasing the response effort for less desirable options (e.g., positioning the escalator further from the entrance as compared to the stairs) and setting desirable options as defaults to force an opt-out response. Although it can be challenging to recreate the engrossing effects of a market dynamic within the lab space, researchers can readily manipulate the imagined scenarios and impose choice constraints that provide context for simulated tasks (see Roma et al., 2016).

Finding and filling the gap

As the policy-driven behavioral economist navigates this field of policymaker needs, it may prove difficult to arrive at an appropriate starting point. How is one to know which of these data streams is most crucial to address? Of course, the specifics of the research context might make that clear. Development of a new pharmaceutically available opioid should call for valuation data to inform abuse potential assessment at the forefront, with an evolving need for a broader landscape analysis as the global market takes shape. In other cases, research funding might be the driving force behind emergent research lines, where government entities and grant reviewers shape the landscape of prospective policy analysis. Grant funding, and notably government-sponsored grants, are likely to support research on an area of policy relevance. Researchers should be alert for funder-initiated requests for funding applications (e.g., the National Institutes of Health request for applications [RFA]; the National Science Foundation dear colleague letter) on topics of interest, as these calls generally indicate a concerted effort in generating policy-relevant data. Even if policymakers have not yet begun deliberating over possible interventions, providing a thorough foundational understanding as might be accomplished through behavioral econometric analyses can ensure that, when policymakers are looking for solutions, those data are readily available at their disposal.

Examples of policy-relevant choice data

Turning now to the published behavioral economic literature, there have been numerous research studies conducted to directly inform policy decisions or that proved relevant for policy development after the fact. What follows is an overview of some of these recent publications, the breadth of which offers a scoping take on the current state of behavioral economic policy analysis.

Nonhuman and human laboratory studies

The origins of the experimental analysis of behavior and operant behavioral economics are firmly rooted in nonhuman laboratory studies. This preclinical work set the precedent for policy relevance, offering key data to guide behavioral health policy around topics such as drug and food availability. And so, the nonhuman laboratory continues to generate such meaningful data today. For example, a recent study examined fentanyl demand and self-administration with and without concurrently administered xylazine or lofexidine (a medication FDA-approved for opioid withdrawal) in Long Evans rats (Sadek et al., 2024). This pharmacological comparison is an important benchmark in understanding the public health impact of xylazine adulteration in the opioid market. Although both substances are alpha-2 adrenergic agonists, lofexidine is a clinically supported medication to support opioid withdrawal whereas xylazine is a veterinary drug with relatively less research on its psychoactive effects in human participants given that it is not approved for human use. Differentiating (or demonstrating equivalence) of effects on drug intake can inform to what extent public health harms are attributable to pharmacological effects, contextual effects (e.g., legal or criminal justice implications of use), other adulterants, or some combination of these factors and the behavioral mechanisms underlying any effects observed. Results suggested that xylazine or lofexidine when combined with fentanyl suppressed demand for fentanyl across prices, particularly when doses were free (i.e., demand intensity). These data provide an example of how insights may be generated from rigorous preclinical research to evaluate behavioral mechanisms informing or guiding public policy for public health crises difficult or impossible to study in the human laboratory (also see discussion in Gipson & Strickland, 2024).

As might be expected with the change in respective ethical considerations and contextual sensitivity, policy analysis conducted in the human laboratory will often take a different form than nonhuman preclinical work. Given the experimental control and rich resource presence, human laboratory studies can provide data to guide decisions on some of society's most pressing public health concerns. And because human laboratories have access to on-site staff, it is often possible to examine substance self-administration directly.

The emergence of regulatory science, a discipline focused on navigating and mitigating the abuse liability of substances available on the global market, consists of study approaches including the laboratory analysis of human choice. In a recent demonstration of human laboratory regulatory science, participants responded in an operant demand framework for combustible cigarettes that varied by expected and actual nicotine content (Strickland et al., 2024). Reduced-nicotine cigarettes are posited as a potential policy-level intervention to curb some public health harm of cigarette smoking, with logic following a "threshold for addiction" pertaining to product nicotine content. It remains unclear if compensatory smoking or other unintended behavioral side effects would negate these prospective harm reduction benefits. Participants in that study did not differ in their demand for cigarettes regardless of nicotine content or nicotine expectation despite logical changes in physiological effects and nicotine expectations based on the experimental manipulations (e.g., increased heart rate in the nicotine compared to low nicotine conditions). These data demonstrate how behavioral economic methods may be used to evaluate public health factors and possible behavioral responses underlying the potential policy proposed.

Incentivized and simulated studies

With the introduction of the simulated and incentivized behavioral economic task came an increased flexibility to study decision making that might prove troublesome for laboratory simulation with direct consequences. For example, some work has examined substance use behavior in response to varying public health or regulatory contexts as in the influence of next-day responsibilities (e.g., Gentile et al., 2012; Miller et al., 2023, 2024) or transportation availability (e.g., Gelino et al., 2024). A recent line of work has modeled community-level decision making pertaining to natural hazard preparedness (e.g., Gelino & Reed, 2020). In that study, participants imagined a scenario in which they were at home during an extreme weather event when they received a National Weather Service tornado warning for their location. The sample was stratified based on the content of the considered emergency alert, where the language of some alerts described the expected impacts of the storm (i.e., impact-based warnings). Individuals who considered the more descriptive warnings also indicated that they would likely begin seeking shelter with more urgency—at longer lead times—relative to those who received the standard language alerts. Study outcomes support the effectiveness of impact-based warnings, now the standard protocol for all weather forecast offices in the US (National Weather Service, n.d.).

Next steps for continued policy success

Applied behavioral economics has contacted continued success in its ability to directly and retrospectively inform public policy. Many of the topics for which behavioral economics has offered policy-relevant data represent complex public health concerns. Yet as the scope of behavioral economic application expands, and as public health threats are exacerbated by global conditions (e.g., climate change, pandemic and endemic disease, and shifting illicit markets), applied behavioral economists might adopt new tactics to keep pace with emerging needs.

Advancing conceptual approaches

As novel research contexts continue to challenge behavioral economists' repertoires, conceptual advances may permit a wider array of methods with which to approach choice modeling. Some recent studies (e.g., Gelino et al., 2024; Hack et al., 2023) have described behavior as a function of delay using an operant demand framework. These studies employed conceptual advancements in demand, framing delay to commodity access uniquely as a "time cost" (see Schwartz & Hursh, 2022). The extension of operant demand procedures to study decision making as affected by delay is based on modifications to quantitative models (as of writing, specifically that put forth by Hursh & Silberberg, 2008). Similarly, the plausibility of a time-cost function is predicated on the idea that, under certain framings, organisms devalue delayed outcomes according to certain mathematical distributions (e.g., hyperbolic vs. exponential). Novel and updated theoretical interpretations should afford plenty of opportunities to fully explore the boundaries of this expansive research modality.

Incorporating new intervention frameworks

Bolstering behavioral economic methods with the insights offered by parallel frameworks may also lead to more meaningful insights. Packaging behavioral economic descriptions of choice with widely successful and highly flexible interventions, for instance, could offer a more rapid data stream that informs possible policy stances. Episodic future thinking is an intervention approach that may shorten participants' temporal horizons, increasing the salience of the downstream adverse effects of risky choice (Bickel et al., 2023; see also Koffarnus et al., 2013). Participants envision something about their future—an aged version of themselves, achieving goals and aspirations—and consider the impacts of present choices on these temporally distant outcomes (e.g., Athamneh et al., 2021; Kaplan et al., 2016; Naudé et al., 2021). Work in this area generally supports the implementation of episodic future thinking as a tactic to shift delay discounting in favor of more delay-oriented sustainable choice patterns (see Rung & Madden, 2018).

In a similar fashion, introducing contingency management approaches may also expand understanding of low-cost methods for encouraging desirable health-related choices. Briefly, contingency management is an implementation of arranged contingencies (e.g., vouchers exchanged for drug abstinence) that has been used to motivate responding in a diverse class of behavior (Petry, 2011; see reviews by Bolivar et al., 2021; Ellis et al., 2021). Concepts of contingency management could be evaluated as a prospective intervention to address new facets of public health concerns. Or, the underlying framework might offer an opportunity to further assess the strength of behavior maintained by a given outcome (e.g., "If you could receive a small voucher in exchange for your use of public transportation, how likely would you be to drive your personal vehicle at the following per gallon fuel costs?"). When merging behavioral economic tasks with sound science intervention approaches, the limits to meaningful data generation may well be bounded by the creativity of the researcher.

Establishing methodological consistency

More broadly, behavioral economic policy insights might be more plausibly realized as methodological approaches increasingly exhibit consistency across studies. Analytically, researchers have called for the use of modeling techniques that better handle atypical response formats and more adequately carry forward variance for use in inferential testing (e.g., Kaplan et al., 2021; Young, 2017). Such advances may simultaneously offer improved clarity on how to handle lingering arithmetic challenges, as in how to properly address nonsystematic or uncharacteristic response data (see Stein et al., 2015; Johnson & Bickel, 2008; see also Almog et al., 2023; Gilroy et al., 2022) or zero-response data (see Koffarnus et al., 2022). Related interpretational concerns have also generated discourse along the selection of ideal modeling techniques. The proposal of a hyperboloid discounting model, for instance, has forced consideration of the conceptual foundation for the novel s discounting rate parameter (McKerchar et al., 2009, 2010; a similar challenge for time-cost analysis; Schwartz & Hursh, 2022). Reconciliation of these potential inconsistencies should offer a stronger foundation from which applied behavioral economists can generate policy-relevant insights.

Conclusion

Applied behavioral economics offers a policy friendly framework, both to support the enaction of new legislation and to retroactively support past policy enactment. Behavioral economists can find many suitable pathways for generating policy-relevant data, for instance in procuring descriptions of behavior and potential intervention outcomes. This well-established body of literature features applications of behavioral economics to a wide array of public health concerns and should prove effective in addressing the next wave of emerging health threats. Through continued advancement and discourse around methodological improvement and consistency, behavioral economic research data can keep pace with the emerging interest from other disciplines, policymakers, and the public at large.

References

Acuff, S. F., Amlung, M., Dennhardt, A. A., MacKillop, J., & Murphy, J. G. (2020). Experimental manipulations of behavioral economic demand for addictive commodities: A meta-analysis. *Addiction, 115*(5), 817−831. https://doi.org/10.1111/add.14865

Acuff, S. F., MacKillop, J., & Murphy, J. G. (2023). A contextualized reinforcer pathology approach to addiction. *Nature Reviews Psychology, 2*, 309−323. https://doi.org/10.1038/s44159-023-00167-y

Ainslie, G. (1974). Impulse control in pigeons. *Journal of the Experimental Analysis of Behavior, 21*(3), 485−489. https://doi.org/10.1901/jeab.1974.21-485

Alexander, R. S., Canver, B. R., Sue, K. L., & Morford, K. L. (2022). Xylazine and overdoses: Trends, concerns, and recommendations. *American Journal of Public Health, 112*(8), 1212−1216. https://doi.org/10.2105/AJPH.2022.306881

Almog, S., Ferreiro, A. V., Berry, M. S., & Rung, J. M. (2023). Are the attention checks embedded in delay discounting tasks a valid marker for data quality? *Experimental and Clinical Psychopharmacology, 31*(5), 908−919.

Amlung, M. T., Acker, J., Stojek, M. K., Murphy, J. G., & MacKillop, J. (2011). Is talk "cheap"? An initial investigation of the equivalence of alcohol purchase task performance for hypothetical and actual rewards. *Alcoholism: Clinical and Experimental Research, 36*(4), 716−724. https://doi.org/10.1111/j.1530-0277.2011.01656.x

Amlung, M. T., Marsden, E., Holshausen, K., Morris, V., Patel, H., Vedelago, L., Naish, K. R., Reed, D. D., & McCabe, R. E. (2019). Delay discounting as a transdiagnostic process in psychiatric disorders: A meta-analysis. *JAMA Psychiatry, 76*(11), 1176−1186. https://doi.org/10.1001/jamapsychiatry.2019.2102

Athamneh, L. N., Stein, M. D., Lin, E. H., Stein, J. S., Mellis, A. M., Gatchalian, K. M., Epstein, L. H., & Bickel, W. K. (2021). Setting a goal could help you control: Comparing the effect of health goal versus general episodic future thinking on health behaviors among cigarette smokers and obese individuals. *Experimental and Clinical Psychopharmacology, 29*(1), 59−72. https://doi.org/10.1037/pha0000351

Ball, N. S., Knable, B. M., Relich, T. A., Smathers, A. N., Gionfriddo, M. R., Nemecek, B. D., Montepara, C. A., Guarascio, A. J., Covvey, J. R., & Zimmerman, D. E. (2022). Xylazine poisoning: A systematic review. *Clinical Toxicology, 60*(8), 892−901. https://doi.org/10.1080/15563650.2022.2063135

Baron, J., & Hoeksema, M. J. (2021). Science advocacy 101: Realizing the benefits, overcoming the challenges. *Behavior and Social Issues, 30*, 121−138. https://doi.org/10.1007/s42822-00069-9

Bickel, W. K., Freitas-Lemos, R., Myslowski, J., Quddos, F., Fontes, R. M., Barbosa-França, B., Faubion-Trejo, R., & LaConte, S. M. (2023). Episodic future thinking as a promising intervention for substance use disorders: A reinforcer pathology perspective. *Current Addiction Reports, 10*(3), 494−507. https://doi.org/10.1007/s40429-023-00498-z

Bickel, W. K., Johnson, M. W., Koffarnus, M. N., MacKillop, J., & Murphy, J. G. (2014). The behavioral economics of substance use disorders: Reinforcement pathologies and their repair. *Annual Review of Clinical Psychology, 10*(1), 641−677. https://doi.org/10.1146/annurev-clinpsy-032813-153724

Bickel, W. K., Marsch, L. A., & Carroll, M. E. (2000). Deconstructing relative reinforcing efficacy and situating the measures of pharmacological reinforcement with behavioral economics: A theoretical proposal. *Psychopharmacology, 153*(1), 44−56. https://doi.org/10.1007/s002130000589

Bolivar, H. A., Klemperer, E. M., Coleman, S. R. M., DeSarno, M., Skelly, J. M., & Higgins, S. T. (2021). Contingency management for patients receiving medication for opioid use disorder: A systematic review and meta-analysis. *JAMA Psychiatry, 78*(10), 1092−1102. https://doi.org/10.1002/jamapsychiatry.2021.1969

Chung, S., & Herrnstein, R. J. (1967). Choice and delay of reinforcement. *Journal of the Experimental Analysis of Behavior, 10*(1), 67−74. https://doi.org/10.1901/jeab.1967.10-67

Critchfield, T. S. (2024). A peek into the room where it happens: Quantifying ABA's influence on public policy discussions. *Journal of Applied Behavior Analysis, 57*(2), 288−303. https://doi.org/10.1002/jaba.1056

Critchfield, T. S., & Reed, D. D. (2009). What are we doing when we translate from quantitative models? *The Behavior Analyst, 32*(2), 339−362. https://doi.org/10.1007/BF03392197

Ellis, J. D., Struble, C. A., Fodor, M. C., Cairncross, M., Lundahl, L. H., & Ledgerwood, D. M. (2021). Contingency management for individuals with chronic health conditions: A systematic review and meta-analysis of randomized controlled trials. *Behaviour Research and Therapy, 136*, 103781. https://doi.org/10.1016/j.brat.2020.103781

Gelino, B. W., Graham, M. E., Strickland, J. C., Glatter, H. W., Hursh, S. R., & Reed, D. D. (2024). Using behavioral economics to optimize safer undergraduate late-night transportation. *Journal of Applied Behavior Analysis, 57*(1), 117−130. https://doi.org/10.1002/jaba1029

Gelino, B. W., & Reed, D. D. (2020). Temporal discounting of tornado shelter-seeking intentions amidst standard and impact-based weather alerts: A crowdsourced experiment. *Journal of Experimental Psychology: Applied, 26*(1), 16−25. https://doi.org/10.1037/xap0000246

Gelino, B. W., Schlitzer, R. D., Reed, D. D., & Strickland, J. C. (2024). A systematic review and meta-analysis of test-retest reliability and stability of delay and probability discounting. *Journal of the Experimental Analysis of Behavior, 121*(3), 358−372. https://doi.org/10.1002/jeab.910

Gentile, N. D., Librizzi, E. H., & Martinetti, M. P. (2012). Academic constraints on alcohol consumption in college students: A behavioral economic analysis. *Psychopharmacology, 20*(5), 390−399. https://doi.org/10.1037/a0029665

Gerston, L. N. (2014). *Public policy making: Process and principles.* Routledge.

Gilroy, S. P., Strickland, J. C., Naudé, G. P., Johnson, M. W., Amlung, M., & Reed, D. D. (2022). Beyond systematic and unsystematic responding: Latent class mixture models to characterize response patterns in discounting research. *Frontiers in Behavioral Neuroscience, 16*, 806944. https://doi.org/10.3389/fnbeh.2022.806944

Gipson, C. D., & Strickland, J. C. (2024). Integrating public health and translational basic science to address challenges of xylazine adulteration of fentanyl. *Neuropsychopharmacology, 49*(1), 319−320. https://doi.org/10.1038/s41386-023-01680-7

Green, L., Myerson, J., & McFadden, E. (1997). Rate of temporal discounting deceases with amount of reward. *Memory & Cognition, 25*(5), 715−723. https://doi.org/10.3758/BF03211314

Griffiths, R. R., Bradford, L. D., & Brady, J. V. (1979). Progressive ratio and fixed ratio schedule of cocaine-maintained responding in baboons. *Psychopharmacology, 65*(2), 125−136. https://doi.org/10.1007/BF00433038

Hack, G. O., DeLeon, I. G., Bonner, A. C., Weinsztok, S. C., Dallery, J., & Berry, M. S. (2023). Framing effects on hypothetical use of public transportation: A time cost demand analysis. *Behavior and Social Issues, 32*(2), 534−559. https://doi.org/10.1007/s42822-023-00142-5

Hursh, S. R. (1980). Economic concepts for the analysis of behavior. *Journal of the Experimental Analysis of Behavior, 34*(2), 219−238. https://doi.org/10.1901/jeab.1980.34-219

Hursh, S. R. (1991). Behavioral economics of drug self-administration and drug abuse policy. *Journal of the Experimental Analysis of Behavior, 56*(2), 377−393. https://doi.org/10.1901/jeab.1991.56-377

Hursh, S. R., & Roma, P. G. (2013). Behavioral economics and empirical public policy. *Journal of the Experimental Analysis of Behavior, 99*(2), 98−124.

Hursh, S. R., & Silberberg, A. (2008). Economic demand and essential value. *Psychological Review, 115*(1), 186−198. https://doi.org/10.1037/0033-295X.115.1.186

Jacobs, E. A., & Bickel, W. K. (1999). Modeling drug consumption in the clinic using simulation procedures: Demand for heroin and cigarettes in opioid-dependent outpatients. *Experimental and Clinical Psychopharmacology, 7*(4), 412−426. https://doi.org/10.1037/1064-1297.7.4.412

Johnson, M. W., & Bickel, W. K. (2002). Within-subject comparison of real and hypothetical money rewards in delay discounting. *Journal of the Experimental Analysis of Behavior, 77*(2), 129−146. https://doi.org/10.1901/jeab.2002.77-129

Johnson, M. W., & Bickel, W. K. (2006). Replacing relative reinforcing efficacy with behavioral economic demand curves. *Journal of the Experimental Analysis of Behavior, 85*(1), 73−93. https://doi.org/10.1901/jeab.2006.102-04

Johnson, M. W., & Bickel, W. K. (2008). An algorithm for identifying nonsystematic delay-discounting data. *Experimental and Clinical Psychopharmacology, 16*(3), 264−274. https://doi.org/10.1037/1064-1297.16.3.264

Johnson, E. J., Shu, S. B., Dellaert, B. G. C., Fox, C., Goldstein, D. G., Häubl, G., Larrick, R. P., Payne, J. W., Peters, E., Schkade, D., Wansink, B., & Weber, E. U. (2012). Beyond nudges: Tools of a choice architecture. *Marketing Letters, 23*(2), 487−504. https://doi.org/10.1007/s11002-012-9186-1

Kaplan, B. A., Franck, C. T., McKee, K., Gilroy, S. P., & Koffarnus, M. N. (2021). Applying mixed-effects modeling to behavioral economic demand: An introduction. *Perspectives on Behavior Science, 44*(2−3), 333−358. https://doi.org/10.1007/s40614-021-002299-7

Kaplan, B. A., & Reed, D. D. (2018). Happy hour drink specials in the alcohol purchase task. *Experimental and Clinical Psychopharmacology, 26*(2), 156−167. https://doi.org/10.1037/pha0000174

Kaplan, B. A., Reed, D. D., & Jarmolowicz, D. P. (2016). Effects of episodic future thinking on discounting: Personalized age-progressed pictures improve risky long-term health decisions. *Journal of Applied Behavior Analysis, 49*(1), 148−169. https://doi.org/10.1002/jaba.277

Koffarnus, M. N. (2023). Recommendations for the use of behavioral economic demand as an abuse liability assessment for drug scheduling. *Policy Insights from the Behavioral and Brain Sciences, 10*(1), 113−120. https://doi.org/10.1177/23727322221150197

Koffarnus, M. N., Jarmolowicz, D. P., Mueller, E. T., & Bickel, W. K. (2013). Changing delay discounting in the light of the competing neurobehavioral decision systems theory: A review. *Journal of the Experimental Analysis of Behavior, 99*(1), 32−57. https://doi.org/10.1002/jeab.2

Koffarnus, M. N., Kaplan, B. A., Franck, C. T., Rzeszutek, M. J., & Traxler, H. K. (2022). Behavioral economic demand modeling chronology, complexities, and considerations: Much ado about zeros. *Behavioural Processes, 199*, 104646. https://doi.org/10.1016/j.beproc.2022.104646

Münscher, R., Vetter, M., & Scheuerle, T. (2016). A review and taxonomy of choice architecture techniques. *Journal of Behavioral Decision Making, 29*, 511−524. https://doi.org/10.1002/bdm.1897

Madden, G. J., & Johnson, P. S. (2010). A delay-discounting primer. In G. J. Madden, & W. K. Bickel (Eds.), *Impulsivity: The behavioral and neurological science of discounting* (pp. 11−37). American Psychological Association. https://doi.org/10.1037/12069-001

Madden, G. J., Petry, N. M., Badger, G. J., & Bickel, W. K. (1997). Impulsive and self-control choices in opioid-dependent patients and non-drug-using control patients: Drug and monetary rewards. *Experimental and Clinical Psychopharmacology, 5*(3), 256−262. https://doi.org/10.1037/1064-1297.5.3.256

McKerchar, T. L., Green, L., & Myerson, J. (2010). On the scaling interpretation of exponents in hyperboloid models of delay and probability discounting. *Behavioural Processes, 84*(1), 440−444. https://doi.org/10.1016/j.beproc.2010.01.003

McKerchar, T. L., Green, L., Myerson, J., Pickford, T. S., Hill, J. C., & Stout, S. C. (2009). A comparison of four models of delay discounting in humans. *Behavioural Processes, 81*(2), 256−259. https://doi.org/10.1016/j.beproc.2008.12.017

Miller, B. P., Csölle, K., Chen, C., Lester, A., Weinsztok, S. C., Aston, E. R., & Amlung, M. (2024). Exploring the suitability of cannabis use with next-day responsibilities: A behavioral-economic and qualitative study. *Journal of Experimental Analysis of Behavior.* https://doi.org/10.1002/jab.4209

Miller, B. P., Murphy, J. G., MacKillop, J., & Amlung, M. (2023). Next-day responsibilities attenuate demand for alcohol among a crowdsourced sample of community adults. *Experimental and Clinical Psychopharmacology, 31*(3), 633−642. https://doi.org/10.1037/pha0000609

National Weather Service. (n.d.). Impact based warnings. National Weather Service. https://www.weather.gov/impacts/.

Naudé, G. P., Dolan, S. B., Strickland, J. C., Berry, M. S., Cox, D. J., & Johnson, M. W. (2021). The influence of episodic future thinking and graphic warning labels on delay discounting and cigarette demand. *International Journal of Environmental Research and Public Health, 18*(23), 12637. https://doi.org/10.3390/ijerph182312637

Odum, A. L. (2011a). Delay discounting: Trait variable? *Behavioural Processes, 87*(1), 1−9. https://doi.org/10.1016/j.beproc.2011.02.007

Odum, A. L. (2011b). Delay discounting: I'm a k, you're a k. *Journal of the Experimental Analysis of Behavior, 96*(3), 427−439. https://doi.org/10.1901/jeab.2011.96-423

Odum, A. L., Becker, R. J., Haynes, J. M., Galizio, A., Frye, C. C. J., Downey, H., Friedel, J. E., & Perez, D. M. (2020). Delay discounting of different outcomes: Review and theory. *Journal of the Experimental Analysis of Behavior, 113*(3), 657−679. https://doi.org/10.1002/jeab.589

Petry, N. M. (2011). Contingency management: What it is and why psychiatrists should want to use it. *The Psychiatrist, 35*, 161−163. https://doi.org/10.1192/pb.bp.110.031831

Petry, N. M., & Bickel, W. K. (1998). Polydrug abuse in heroin addicts: A behavioral economic analysis. *Addiction, 93*(3), 321−335. https://doi.org/10.1046/j.1360-0443.1998.9333212.x

Reed, D. D., Gelino, B. W., & Strickland, J. C. (2022). Behavioral economic demand: How simulated behavioral tasks can inform health policy. *Policy Insights from the Behavioral and Brain Sciences, 9*(2), 171−178. https://doi.org/10.1177/23727322221118668

Reed, D. D., Niileksela, C. R., & Kaplan, B. A. (2017). Behavioral economics: A tutorial for behavior analysts in practice. *Behavior Analysis in Practice, 6*(1), 34−54. https://doi.org/10.1007/BF03391790

Reed, D. D., Strickland, J. C., Gelino, B. W., Hursh, S. R., Jarmolowicz, D. P., Kaplan, B. A., & Amlung, M. (2022). Applied behavioral economics and public health policies: Historical precedence and translational promise. *Behavioural Processes, 198*, 104640. https://doi.org/10.1016/j.beproc.2022.104640

Roma, P. G., Hursh, S. R., & Hudja, S. (2016). Hypothetical purchase task questionnaires for behavioral economic assessments of value and motivation. *Managerial and Decision Economics, 37*(4−5), 306−323. https://doi.org/10.1002/mde.2718

Roma, P. G., Reed, D. D., DiGennaro Reed, F. D., & Hursh, S. R. (2017). Progress of and prospects for hypothetical purchase task questionnaires in consumer behavior analysis and public policy. *Behavior Analysis in Practice, 40*(2), 329−342. https://doi.org/10.1007/s40614-017-0100-2

Rung, J. M., & Madden, G. J. (2018). Experimental reductions of delay discounting and impulsive choice: A systematic review and meta-analysis. *Journal of Experimental Psychology: General, 147*(9), 1349−1381. https://doi.org/10.1037/xge0000462

Sadek, S. M., Khatri, S. N., Kipp, Z., Dunn, K. E., Beckmann, J. S., Stoops, W. W., Hinds, J.,T. D., & Gipson, C. D. (2024). Impacts of xylazine on fentanyl demand, body weight, and acute withdrawal in rats: A comparison to lofexidine. *Neuropharmacology, 245*(1), 109816. https://doi.org/10.1016/j.neuropharm.2023.109816

Schwartz, L. P., & Hursh, S. R. (2022). Time cost and demand: Implications for public policy. *Perspectives on Behavior Science, 46*(1), 51−66. https://doi.org/10.1007/s40614-022-00349-8

Stein, J. S., Koffarnus, M. N., Snider, S. E., Quisenberry, A. J., & Bickel, W. K. (2015). Identification and management of nonsystematic purchase task data: Toward best practice. *Experimental and Clinical Psychopharmacology, 23*(5), 377−386. https://doi.org/10.1037/pha0000020

Strickland, J. C., Campbell, E. M., Lile, J. A., & Stoops, W. W. (2019). Utilizing the commodity purchase task to evaluate behavioral economic demand for illicit substances: A review and meta-analysis. *Addiction, 115*(3), 393−406. https://doi.org/10.1111/add.14792

Strickland, J. C., Gelino, B. W., Naudé, G. P., Harbaugh, J. C., Schlitzer, R. D., Mercincavage, M., Strasser, A. A., & Johnson, M. W. (2024). Effect of nicotine expectancy and nicotine dose on cigarette demand, withdrawal alleviation, and puff topography. *Drug and Alcohol Dependence, 254*, 11042. https://doi.org/10.1016/j.drugalcdep.2023.111042

Strickland, J. C., & Lacy, R. T. (2020). Behavioral economic demand as a unifying language for addiction science: Promoting collaboration and integration of animal and human models. *Experimental and Clinical Psychopharmacology, 28*(4), 404−416. https://doi.org/10.1037/pha0000358

Thaler, R. H., & Sunstein, C. R. (2021). *Nudge: The final edition*. Yale University Press.

United States Department of the Interior. (2012). *Reclamation: Managing water in the west: Colorado river basin water supply and demand study*. https://www.usbr.gov/watersmart/bsp/docs/finalreport/ColoradoRiver/CRBS_Executive_Summary_FINAL.pdf.

Weinsztok, S. C., Reed, D. D., & Amlung, M. (2023). Substance-related cross-commodity purchase tasks: A systematic review. *Psychology of Addictive Behaviors, 37*(1), 72−86. https://doi.org/10.1037/adb0000851

World Health Organization. (2024). *The SAFER initiative: A world free from alcohol related harm*. https://www.who.int/initiatives/SAFER.

Young, M. E. (2017). Discounting: A practical guide to multilevel analysis of indifference data. *Journal of the Experimental Analysis of Behavior, 108*(1), 97−112. https://doi.org/10.1002/jeab.265

Zvorsky, I., Nighbor, T. D., Kurti, A. N., DeSarno, M., Naudé, G. P., Reed, D. D., & Higgins, S. T. (2019). Sensitivity of hypothetical purchase task indices when studying substance use: A systematic literature review. *Preventive Medicine, 128*, 105789. https://doi.org/10.1016/j.ypmed.2019.105789

Consumer behavior analysis as a foundation of operant behavioral economics*

Gordon R. Foxall[1,2], Jorge M. Oliveira-Castro[3] and Rafael Barreiros Porto[3]
[1]Cardiff University, Cardiff, United Kingdom; [2]Reykjavik University, Reykjavik, Iceland; [3]University of Brasilia, Brasilia, Brazil

Consumer behavior analysis applies operant psychology to the study of the socioeconomic basis of consumption. It comprises a multidisciplinary methodology that combines behavioral psychology, behavioral economics, and consumer research. This approach is based on the three-term contingency as it permits the prediction and possibly control of the behaviors that constitute purchasing and consuming economic goods in naturalistic settings. This behavioral paradigm is adapted to the analysis of buying and using products and services, broadly construed, and the contextual factors that shape these actions. It also provides a framework of conceptualization and analysis within which operant behavioral economics may be understood.

This chapter outlines the Behavioral Perspective Model (BPM), which is the device that has transformed the operant paradigm into a means of portraying and investigating consumer behavior, especially in modern marketing-oriented economies. It then reviews empirical evidence and links this with the development and progress of operant behavioral economics. Studies reviewed meet several criteria: They are based on empirical investigation, and they adopt concepts from the BPM as well as behavioral-economic concepts and methods. This also discusses the role of the marketing firm as a metacontingency, the output of which is the marketing mix that seeks to satisfy the requirements of consumers. Finally, it discusses how consumer behavior analysis is an essential foundation of operant behavioral economics.

Operant behavioral economics

Operant behavioral economics contributes positively to the objectives of various disciplines by bringing theoretical perspectives and novel methodologies to bear on each of its constituents. Although microeconomics permits the conceptualization of behavior as the allocation of scarce resources among competing ends, operant psychology (or behavior analysis, as it is more usually known) conceives behavior in terms of

---

*This chapter draws in part on Foxall, G.R. (2016). Operant behavioral economics. *Managerial and Decision Economics*, 37, 215-223.

the allocation of a number of responses that the individual can emit among alternative reinforcing outcomes (Staddon, 1980; Kagel et al., 1995; Foxall and Sigurdsson, 2013). The term "operant" denotes behaviors that operate on the environment to generate consequences, which are followed by changes in the rate at which the behaviors are performed. Those consequences that are followed by an increase in response rate are known as reinforcers and those followed by a reduction in rate, as punishers (Skinner, 1953).

The "three-term contingency" provides the basic explanatory device of operant behaviorism. This takes the form $S^D \rightarrow R \rightarrow S^r$, where a discriminative stimulus (S^D), is an element of the environment in the presence of which a response (R), has been rewarded by the appearance of another environmental element (S^r). The "strengthening" effect on the behavior resulting from the arrangement is known as reinforcement. When the occurrence of a response can be accurately predicted from the appearance of the discriminative stimulus, it is said to be under stimulus control, and this will be maintained as long as the response is followed from time to time by the reinforcer. For greater detail on the subtleties of operant psychology and its philosophical implications for the explanation of behavior, see inter alia, Baum (2006), Moore (2008), and Rachlin (2014).

As pointed out in Lea (1978), the essential components of microeconomics readily find referents in the operant analysis of choice. For instance, economic goods constitute reinforcers. As he points out, both are events, the contingent arrangement of which tends to maintain responding while price acts as a schedule parameter. Both indicate the amount of a limited resource that must be yielded in exchange for the commodity or reinforcer. Money equates to the number of responses upon which delivery of the reinforcer is contingent. Hence, the economist's demand curve, mapping as it does the quantity of a good that is bought onto its price corresponds to a function relating the magnitude of reinforcement obtained and the number of responses required to secure it.

While behavior analysis, encapsulated by the three-term contingency, and microeconomics are the constituents of "operant behavioral economics" (Foxall, 2016a), the addition of marketing science to form consumer behavior analysis, has generated abundant empirical evidence for an interdisciplinary social science of considerable scope and magnitude (Foxall, 2016b, 2017). Its contributions, not only to consumer psychology but also to behavioral economics and the theory of the firm are reviewed in part in this chapter. First, we describe the Behavioral Perspective Model of consumer choice (BPM), which has provided the conceptual base for much of this work. This is followed by a review of BPM-based studies which draw attention to empirical research featuring such familiar concerns as matching and maximization, price elasticity of demand, essential value, consumer's utility functions, and delay discounting. The extension of the thinking that underlies these interests to the sphere of organizational behavior has spurred the development of a concomitant theory of the marketing firm. The final section of our review is based on empirical work which has been inspired by, and which helps evaluate this endeavor.

The Generic Behavioral Perspective Model

Consumer situation

A visual of the Generic BPM is presented in Fig. 13.1. The generic BPM seeks to explain consumer choice by reference to the context in which it takes place. This context is the "consumer-situation," which comprises the stimuli that impinge on the consumer's behavior and her history of behaving in similar situations in the past. What the consumer does is assumed to be a function of this situation. The generic model proposes, therefore, simply that "consumer activity" is a function of "consumer situation" and that the situation in question is composed of the consumer's consumption history and the elements of her current setting that encourage purchasing and/or consumption. In other words, the consumer situation forms the immediate precursor of consumer activity. This consumer activity has consequences which, by modifying the consumer's learning history, shape her future consumer situations, and so influence whether she will repeat this behavior.

The consumer behavior setting is the complex combination of stimuli that make up the physical and social context in which one is purchasing or consuming (e.g., the store in which one is shopping and the people who are also present). These stimuli are assumed to be specifiable as observable entities whose (again, observable) effect on one's responses can be employed to predict and control further instances of this kind of activity. The accumulated behaviors of the consumer and the reinforcing and punishing outcomes thereof compose her "learning history", which can also be used to predict her future behaviors. In the aggregate, consumers' behaviors considered as part of a controlling context can often be rigorously observed in empirical research, whether within the laboratory or based on panel data (i.e., repeated measurements of purchases made by a sample of consumers over a period) subjected to statistical analysis.

The value of a product or service can accordingly be quantified in terms of the work (money) the consumer is willing to expend to acquire a reinforcement and avoid punishing consequences of consumption. Such work is objectively (or at least intersubjectively) apparent and has led to a considerable volume of findings that chart the sensitivity of consumers' choices to price and reinforcement contingencies.

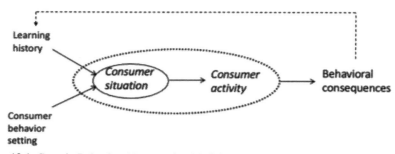

Figure 13.1 Generic Behavioral Perspective Model.

Scope of the consumer behavior setting

An important property of the consumer behavior setting as a contributor to the consumer situation is its *scope*. Scope refers to the number and variety of behavioral opportunities presented. A relatively closed consumer setting permits one, or at most a few, behavioral options. Take a bank, dental surgery, casino, or dining in a restaurant, for instance. In each case, the consumer is severely limited in terms of the range of behaviors she can perform, her opportunities to leave the situation, and the necessity to conform to a predetermined course of action while she is there.

A relatively open consumer behavior setting, however, allows a large number of behavioral options, which the consumer can adopt "at will." Examples include listening to the radio or viewing television in one's own home, alone, where one is free to switch stations as the mood takes one, or taking lunch in a self-service cafeteria. Between these are consumer behavior settings that are intermediate in scope such as supermarket shopping, traveling on a train or cruise ship, or wandering through an art gallery. These are partly structured and limited by physical and social encroachments, but they also provide a good deal of discretion in what one does and how one manages it.

Utilitarian and informational reinforcement

The outcomes of consumer activity are the ensuing reinforcers and punishers that influence the rate at which the consumer will repeat the behavior or action in similar contexts. The BPM bifurcates the idea of reinforcement into its functional and social components, which are termed utilitarian reinforcement and informational reinforcement, respectively. Utilitarian reinforcement refers to the consequences of behavior, which inhere in the functional benefits of owning and using a good, what it does practically for the consumer. The reinforcing consequences of owning and driving a car include the ease of travel, the convenience of visiting a large number of geographically separated places, of giving lifts to family members. In short, a car reinforces behavior by virtue of its capacity to assuage the problems of "getting from A to B." Almost any car in good working order provides these benefits, although they are not without costs. They are utilitarian (or functional) reinforcers.

However, some cars do more than provide transportation: For most people, a Rolls Royce or a Porsche also affords social status and a personally experienced sense of self-esteem. These are examples of informational (or social) reinforcement. The origin of the distinction is described by Wearden (1988) who reported on studies that showed that when participants in psychological experiments were required to perform simple tasks to attain rewards such as coins of little value, points, or small food samples, they often reacted by ostentatiously disposing of these items (e.g., by throwing them out of the window of the room in which the study was taking place). However, when the experimental tasks were undertaken by teams of participants, whose attainments were highlighted by charts showing their progress in amassing food items, currency, or points, their engagement increased noticeably and they participated with demonstrable involvement in the procedures.

The latter source of reinforcement referenced here was dubbed "informational" in contrast to the utilitarian reinforcement provided by the tangible remuneration they received. The distinction between utilitarian and informational sources of reinforcement has proved a valuable conceptual advance in the analysis of consumer behavior. This reflects not only the functional benefits accessed by owning and using products and services but also the social distinctions that many economic and social goods confer.

Reinforcement and reward

It is now possible to define the mechanism through which behavior and action are shaped and maintained in more detail. We often speak of the goods acquired and used in the course of consumption as "rewards." More technically, we may refer to them as "reinforcers." As Skinner (1953) took pains to point out, reinforcement is something that happens as a result of behavior, while a reward is something received by the individual who behaves. A reinforcer is something for which an organism will work (Rolls, 2018). More significantly, a reinforcer is something an organism will *continue* working for: its receipt increases the probability of the behavior that led to its delivery. By contrast, a punisher is something the organism will work to rid itself of. Its receipt leads to a reduction in the performance of the behavior that brought it about. In each case, it is the *behavior*, the behavioral response that the organism emits, that is reinforced or punished, not the person or animal. We shall return to the organism but for now, it is the probability of the response that is important. Such a response is described as operant because it operates on the environment to produce consequences, the reinforcers and punishers, goods (and, for that matter, "bads"), that influence the rate at which these and similar responses are performed in similar contexts.

Understanding a reinforcer as something the organism works for and a punisher as something it works to escape or avoid suggests that the former is an item it finds pleasing or *values* and that the latter is something it *dis*values, finds worthless, or is irksome. The good the consumer obtains is valued in terms of the amount of work she is willing to do to obtain it, usually understood as the amount of money she surrenders for it (which is after all usually a measure of the work she has done). Valued items can often be exchanged for other valued items in the marketplace, a practice that is enhanced by the appearance of a unit of exchange such as money. A monetary economy means that it is not necessary to find someone who coincidentally wants to exchange what I have to offer for something I want. Money provides a store of value that enables the consumer to postpone a purchase while taking advantage of the opportunity to raise funds for it by selling a commodity someone else wants. We can think of the buyer and seller in each case as having a personal or subjective value of the goods she wishes to trade. As a result of the market process, the subjective values of each party to a successful transaction result in intersubjective values, or prices, that are available to other potential consumers as indications of what an item is worth in a social situation.

Establishing a market value

The Expanded Behavioral Perspective Model

The specification of the BPM that has given rise to empirical research is firmly based on the "three-term contingency," the essential explanatory device of radical behaviorism which defines the "contingencies of reinforcement and punishment" from which behavioral responses are predictable, and in which behavior is a function of antecedent discriminative stimuli which set the occasion for reinforcement and punishment contingent on the performance of a particular response. An additional source of antecedent stimulation takes the form of motivating operations which enhance the relationship between the response and its consequences (Michael, 1983; see also Fagerstrøm et al., 2010). A basic motivating operation might be, for instance, an enhanced impulse to consume food if the consumer is in a particular state of deprivation ("hungry"). The discriminative stimuli and motivating operations comprise the consumer behavior setting which, primed by previous similar behavior and its consequences (i.e., learning history), form the consumer situation. The extended model is summarized in Fig. 13.2.

Generically, the consumer situation is the confluence of temporal and spatial influences on consumer choice, the immediate precursor of consumer action. In the BPM, the consumer situation is simply the interaction of the consumer's learning history and her current behavior setting. The synergistic effect of these influences, in which the learning history primes the stimulus field that composes the behavior setting so that its components become discriminative stimuli and motivating operations rather than neutral stimuli, is the immediate precursor and progenitor of consumer behavior. The primed stimulus field sets the occasion for the reinforcement of particular behaviors through the provision of utilitarian (functional) and informational (social) benefits. The consumer situation in this case is conceived entirely as an extensional entity, the elements of which can be objectively identified and measured. Similarly, the pattern of

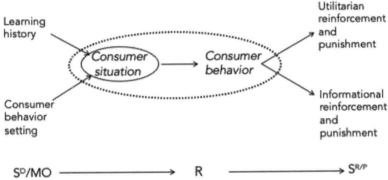

Figure 13.2 Extended Behavioral Perspective Model (see Foxall, 2023). R, response; S^D, discriminative stimulus; $S^{R/P}$, reinforcing and/or punishing stimulus.

reinforcement and punishment presented to the consumer as contingent upon her behavior is extensionally conceived and objectively specifiable.

The establishment of value at the superpersonal level

The exchange value of a commodity is established through the interlocking contingencies of the parties to a transaction that determines their bilateral (or multilateral) interactions, see Fig. 13.3. Before delineating the bilateral contingency that links the marketer and consumer, it is necessary to define the corporate behavior setting that characterizes the impetus the firm has for its behavior. This comprises, principally, its opportunities to earn sales revenue or profits in the marketplace (utilitarian reinforcement) and to enhance its reputation among current and potential consumers by displaying trustworthiness, innovativeness, and entrepreneurship (informational reinforcement). In return, the firm supplies utilitarian and informational reinforcement to the consumer in the form of better products and services (See Foxall, 2021, for a full treatment). These setting elements reflect the marketer's history of pursuing similar strategies, its competitive position, and its capacity to pursue its strategic ends.

The outcome of the reciprocal interaction of consumer and marketer in the situation defined by a particular bilateral contingency is the formulation of an intersubjective exchange value, V_I. This is value at the superpersonal level. Both buyer and seller concur in this evaluation, at least to the extent to which it reveals the price at which they were willing to exchange the good in question in an open competitive marketplace. V_I is a conceptualization of value as an intersubjective agreement based on the price at which an exchange has taken place. More formally, we may say that intersubjective value, established in the marketplace, is a socially constructed index based

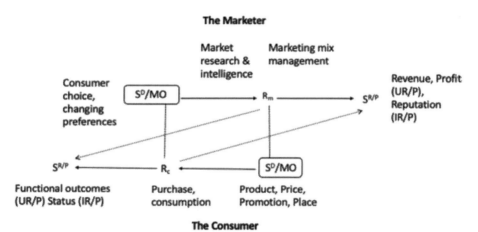

Figure 13.3 Bilateral contingency as reciprocal interaction of the three-term contingency. *IR/P*, informational reinforcement and/or punishment; *MO*, motivating operation; R_c, consumer response; R_m, marketer response; *SD*, discriminative stimulus; $S^{R/P}$, reinforcing and/or punishing stimulus; *UR/P*, utilitarian reinforcement and/or punishment.

on collective intentionality (Foxall, 2021). Said more simply, this reflects an understanding that the market is an institution that delineates the agreed worth of an item and that is reasonable for it to be exchanged for a given sum of money or another commodity. This level of valuation can be established intersubjectively and is the socially agreed worth of the item based on exchange value. Insofar as obtaining this level of value in an exchange relationship acts as an incentive to participate in a market exchange, goods or money of this value constitute a reinforcer for this behavior. This concept of value is a mainstay of most neoclassical economic analysis, including that provided by operant behavioral economics.

Empirical evidence

Matching and maximization

In most situations, consumers must choose among alternative products, brands, or stores differing with respect to price, quality, and other attributes. Hence, research and theories concerning choice behavior can be particularly informative to investigations of consumer behavior. Operant psychology has developed a large volume of experimental investigations of choice, many of which analyzed choices between two concurrently available alternatives offering different rates of reinforcement (e.g., differing average intervals between food availability). Results have shown that the distribution of responses between the two alternatives tends to be proportional to the distribution of reinforcement obtained in the two alternatives, which led to the formulation of the matching law (cf. Baum, 1974, 1979; Herrnstein, 1961, 1970). Eq. (13.1) below shows the generalized form of the matching law:

$$\frac{B_1}{B_2} = b \left(\frac{R_1}{R_2}\right)^s \tag{13.1}$$

Shown in Eq. (13.1), B and R represent responses and reinforcement, respectively, and subscripts indicate each of the two alternatives. Both b and s are parameters estimated from empirical data. When b and s are equal to 1, the distribution of responses perfectly matches the distribution of reinforcement between alternatives (cf. Herrnstein, 1961, 1970). Parameters b and s are interpreted, respectively, as measures of bias between alternatives (e.g., a constant preference for one of them due to uncontrolled factors) and of sensitivity to the distribution of reinforcement between alternatives, and have been used to investigate the variables that influence choice allocation (cf. Baum, 1974, 1979). A large body of research has shown that the distribution of responses between alternatives is proportional to the distribution of reinforcement they produce, both in laboratory settings (e.g., Baum, 1979; Davison & McCarthy, 1988; DeVilliers, 1977; Herrnstein, 1970) and in natural environments (e.g., Alferink et al., 2009; Billington & DiTommaso, 2003; Borrero et al., 2007; Conger & Killeen, 1974; Martens et al., 1990; Reed et al., 2006; Vollmer & Bourret, 2000).

The relevance of the matching law to marketing and consumer research was first highlighted by Foxall (1999), who analyzed the necessary conceptual and methodological adaptations for applying the model to interpret consumers' buying patterns. For instance, when consumers choose among different brands of routinely purchased products, the schedule of reinforcement is more akin to variable-ratio schedules, which define the amount of work (i.e., money) necessary to obtain a reinforcement (i.e., quantities of a product), than to variable-interval schedules typically adopted in experiments of choice. Moreover, since consumers do not always choose the cheapest brand available, as would be predicted in concurrent variable-ratio schedules, Foxall stresses the possible influence of brand differentiation on consumer choice, with emphasis on the possible effects of higher levels of informational reinforcement that might alter the values of parameters b and s in Eq. (13.1). In this context, the value of parameter s is particularly relevant for it has been interpreted as a measure of substitutability (or complementarity) between reinforcers (Rachlin et al., 1980), which could be extended to evaluate the level of substitutability between brands (cf. Foxall, 1999).

These insights gave impulse to a large body of empirical research that has investigated consumer choice of products, brands, and stores, inspired by the matching framework and related behavioral-economic concepts, such as analyses of demand and maximization (e.g., Curry et al., 2010; Foxall et al., 2004; Huynh & Foxall, 2016; Sigurdsson & Foxall, 2016; Wells & Foxall, 2013). In the case of brand choice, Eq. (13.1) is calculated based on the ratio of the amount paid (responding) for the preferred brand divided by the amount paid for the other brands as a function of the ratio of the amount bought (reinforcement) of the preferred brand divided by the amount bought of the other brands (cf. Foxall, 1999). In this type of research, the data can be obtained from consumer panels, formed by volunteers who record all their purchases within certain product categories during a certain period and provide the information to researchers or commercial firms. Adopting this methodology and using a small sample of consumers, Foxall and James (2001, 2003) demonstrated that the ratio of amount paid tended to match (i.e., s close to 1) the ratio of the amount bought when choice among substitutable brands was examined. When choosing among complementary or independent brands, the value of s was predominantly negative, corroborating existing predictions in the behavioral-economic literature (cf. Kagel et al., 1995).

Subsequent research, using larger sets of consumer panel data, replicated these main findings showing that: (1) consumers tend to match the ratio of amount paid to the ratio of amount bought, buying the cheapest brand among their consideration set of brands in each product category (e.g., Foxall & Schrezenmaier, 2003; Foxall et al., 2004; Wells & Foxall, 2013); and (2) matching analysis can be used to identify the level of complementarity and independence between product categories (e.g., Foxall, James, et al., 2010; Romero et al., 2006), subclasses of products (e.g., Foxall, Wells, et al., 2010), supermarket stores (e.g., Huynh & Foxall, 2016), and to examine consumer choice in simulated online environment (e.g., Fagerstrøm et al., 2011). The matching law has also been integrated with BPM variables of utilitarian and informational reinforcement as well as price, providing a framework to analyze the relevance of each variable on the amount consumers spend (cf., Oliveira-Castro et al., 2010).

Price elasticity of demand and essential value

Research in the marketing literature has reported that in routine grocery shopping the quantity consumers buy varies little across shopping occasions (cf. Driesener & Rungie, 2022; Ehrenberg, 1988). Even in the presence of promotions, the largest part of promotional sales peaks has been attributed to brand switching rather than changes in the quantity consumers buy (e.g., Bell et al., 1999; Gupta, 1988). Recent investigations, however, adopting concepts and measures from behavioral economics and the BPM, have indicated that the quantity consumers buy may include complex choice patterns (e.g., Foxall et al., 2013; Oliveira-Castro, Foxall, & James, 2008; Oliveira-Castro, Foxall, James. et al., 2008; Sigurdsson et al., 2013; Wells et al., 2010), which are described in what follows.

A demand curve, which expresses the relation between the quantity demanded and the price, is particularly suitable to examine the variables that influence the quantity consumers purchase. This perspective predicts, in typical circumstances, that the quantity demanded decreases with price increases. The amount of decrease in quantity as a function of price increases can be measured by price-elasticity coefficients, a frequently adopted measure in behavioral-economic investigations (cf. Hursh, 1980, 1984). Considering that consumer choice is not influenced solely by price, the BPM predicts that the quantity consumers buy is influenced by the amount of informational (i.e., socially mediated) and utilitarian (i.e., product mediated) reinforcement offered by different products or brands, relative to their prices. The integration of demand analysis and the BPM gave rise to a series of investigations that examined how consumers change the quantity they buy across shopping occasions as a function of the price they pay, the level of utilitarian reinforcement, and the level of informational reinforcement they obtain.

Initially, this line of research used data from a consumer panel containing information about purchases of 12 products routinely bought by 80 consumers during a period of 16 weeks. Results suggested that: (1) consumers tend to buy cheaper brands when buying larger quantities (intra-consumer elasticity) (cf. Oliveira-Castro et al., 2006); (2) consumers who buy, on average, cheaper brands tend to buy, on average, larger quantities (inter-consumer elasticity) (Oliveira-Castro et al., 2006); (3) consumers tend to buy larger quantities of a given brand when its price is lower (intra-brand or own-price elasticity) (Foxall et al., 2004; Oliveira-Castro et al., 2005); and (4) consumers tend to buy larger quantities when buying a less-differentiated brand (inter-brand elasticity; Foxall et al., 2004; Oliveira-Castro et al., 2005).

Considering that such results were based upon separate statistical analyses of the same, relatively small, data set, Foxall and colleagues replicated and expanded this research using data from a larger consumer panel, which included information concerning more than 1600 consumers purchasing four product categories for a period of 52 weeks. The main purposes were to test whether such complex patterns occur when the analyses are conducted simultaneously and to assess the relative contribution of each response pattern to overall quantity elasticity. The main results showed that: (a) the variance accounted for by intra-brand variables was larger than that accounted for by inter-brand variables; (b) the variance accounted for by intra-brand variables was inversely related to the number of brands in the category; (c) the variance accounted for by intra-consumer variables, compared to that accounted for by inter-consumer variables, increases with increases in the frequency of purchases in the category; (d) consumers buy larger quantities when paying lower prices, both within and across brands; (e) consumers who buy larger quantities tend to pay lower prices, both within and across brands; (f) purchase quantities tend to vary with the amount of informational and utilitarian benefits offered by the brands; and (g) intra-brand price variations, especially those associated with consumers switching across package sizes, account for the largest portion of changes in quantity bought across shopping occasions (cf. Oliveira-Castro, Foxall, & James, 2008).

Operant demand analyses, combined with the BPM, have also been applied to investigate caregivers' choices of behavioral treatments. Using hypothetical treatment purchase tasks, Gilroy and colleagues compared the price caregivers were willing to pay for treatments that differed with respect to the amount of evidence supporting them. The authors found that pseudoscientific alternatives function as a substitute for an established therapy (cf. Gilroy et al., 2022), that low-, moderate-, and high-evidence treatment choices all function as substitutes for a high-evidence behavior therapy (Gilroy & Feck, 2022), and that the level of evidence moderated their degree of substitution (Gilroy & Feck, 2022). When caregivers had to choose treatments differing in terms of utilitarian (i.e., the efficacy of treatment) and informational sources of reinforcement (i.e., community support for treatment), results showed that utilitarian and informational reinforcement jointly influenced treatment-related choices and that caregivers favored treatments with greater informational reinforcement over those with greater utilitarian reinforcement (cf. Gilroy & Picardo, 2022).

Analyses of price elasticity of demand have also been adopted in attempts to measure the essential value of reinforcers, that is, to develop a hedonic scale that would rank reinforcers (e.g., products and brands) based on how much consumers value them. The problem with this approach is that demand elasticity tends to increase as price increases to extreme values (e.g., Hursh & Winger, 1995) and is influenced by certain reinforcer dimensions, such as food amount (Hursh et al., 1988) and drug dosage (Winger et al., 2002). To overcome such difficulties, Hursh and Silberberg (2008) proposed an exponential model that measures demand elasticity relative to the point at which price is zero, a technique that allows for comparisons across reinforcers that differ in certain dimensions (e.g., drug dosage) and would generate elasticity coefficients that measure the essential value of reinforcers. In experimental tests, the model provided a good fit to the data and theoretically consistent results.

The expansion of the model to the analysis of consumer behavior occurred some years later (Oliveira-Castro et al., 2011; Yan, Foxall, & Doyle, 2012a, 2012b). The exponential demand model was applied to the measurement of the essential value of different brands, of routinely purchased products, bought in a natural environment. Data were obtained from consumer panels that recorded individual purchases during a period of 52 weeks. Results showed that the model fit the data moderately well and that its parameters were reliable across situations (Oliveira-Castro et al., 2011; Yan et al., 2012a, 2012b). Moreover, brands offering higher levels of utilitarian reinforcement showed larger essential value (Yan et al., 2012a, 2012b), brands offering higher levels of informational reinforcement showed larger essential value (Oliveira-Castro et al., 2011; Yan et al., 2012a, 2012b), and the essential value of brands varies inversely with the degree of openness of consumer settings (Yan et al., 2012a, 2012b). Such findings extend the application of the model beyond the essential value of primary, biologically important, reinforcers to the measurement of the essential value of secondary, socially defined, reinforcers, such as those associated with brand differentiation (cf. Oliveira-Castro et al., 2011).

Integration of the model and the BPM was also proposed with the incorporation of parameters to measure the elasticity of demand for levels of utilitarian and informational reinforcement, as well as price (Yan et al., 2012a, 2012b). Using data stemming from consumer panels, results showed that the integrated model fit the data better than the original exponential model (Hursh & Silberberg, 2008) and that parameters were reliable over time. Taken together, these results demonstrate the integration between behavioral economics and the BPM, corroborating the predictions that consumer behavior is influenced by utilitarian and informational reinforcement and punishment (e.g., price) and by variables in the consumer behavior setting, such as the scope of the setting.

Consumers' utility functions

According to the BPM, when consumers choose among products and brands, they are choosing among different combinations of utilitarian and informational reinforcement and their respective prices. If one assumes that consumers maximize utility, in the sense that they tend to obtain the largest amount of their preferred products at the lowest possible prices, it follows that consumers maximize their preferred combinations of utilitarian and informational reinforcement. To test such assumptions, Oliveira-Castro et al. (2015, 2016) employed the Cobb–Douglas utility function, on account of its analytical tractability, associated with simple well-behaved indifference curves and its frequent use in economics, to analyze brand choice of routinely purchased food items using consumer panel data. For the current context, the function was the following:

$$U_{(x,y)} = x^a y^b \tag{13.2}$$

In this expression, U represents utility, x is the quantity of utilitarian reinforcement consumed, y is the quantity of informational reinforcement consumed, and a and b are empirically determined parameters such that $a + b = 1$. Results indicated that the function fitted the data very well and that parameters a and b were specific to each product category and consistent for the same product across time periods, showing a always larger or always smaller than b (except for one out of 12 cases). Based upon these results it is possible to measure for each product category the relative importance, for consumers, of utilitarian and informational reinforcement.

This type of analysis also enables the calculation of the amount of utility obtained by each consumer buying each product category and the evaluation of the consistency of possible individual differences, concerning the total amount of utility, across time periods. Correlation coefficients, comparing the total amount of utility obtained by each consumer across periods, were all significant and positive, with all values above 0.80 for three products and above 0.60 for one product. Such results indicate that individuals differ with respect to the level of utility they obtain in each product category and that these individual differences are consistent and stable across time. Considering that brands and products that offer higher levels of utilitarian and informational reinforcement tend to be more expensive than those offering lower levels, it is reasonable to suppose that differences in utility are related to the level of income of consumers, higher incomes being associated with higher reinforcement levels. In a followed-up study, the authors discovered that, for supermarket food items, higher-income households obtained higher levels of utility than lower-income households by buying brands that offer more utilitarian and informational reinforcement per unit of product rather than by buying larger quantities of the product (Oliveira-Castro & Foxall, 2017).

Delay discounting

Delay discounting refers to the decrease in the subjective value of rewards as the delay in receiving them increases (Bickel & Marsch, 2001). Research, with human and nonhuman subjects, has shown that the rate of decrease in the subjective value of rewards with increased delay is not constant (hyperbolic function), which contradicted the assumption of a constant rate of decrease (exponential function) held by microeconomic theory (cf. Green & Myerson, 2004; Kagel et al., 1995) and, thus, increased the theoretical interest in investigations of delay discounting. Moreover, a growing volume of research has demonstrated that excessive discounting of delayed rewards is commonly associated with individuals with substance use disorders, obesity, and other risky behaviors (Bickel & Marsch, 2001; Green & Myerson, 2004; Rung & Madden, 2018). These findings have given support to a theory of reinforcer pathology, according to which addictive behavior is the result of an overvaluation of smaller immediate rewards relative to larger delayed rewards (delay discounting) and high drug reinforcing value (drug demand) (e.g., Acuff et al., 2023; Bickel & Athamneh, 2020).

Considering that substance use might be interpreted as one extreme form of consumer choice in a continuum that has routine consumer choice at the other extreme (cf. Foxall, 2016), measures of delay discounting and product demand can also be used to assess the effects of marketing variables on routine consumer choices. Knowing the effects of brand differentiation, particularly when related to informational (i.e., social) reinforcement, on consumer preference would be distinctly relevant for marketing activities, which revolve predominantly around the value of branding. It might be expected that consumers attribute higher reinforcing value (high demand) to more differentiated brands and that they show higher rates of delay discounting for more differentiated brands than for less-differentiated ones (i.e., it is harder to wait for more differentiated brands).

Pursuing this line of inquiry, Oliveira-Castro and Marques (2017) asked university students, engaged in a simulated purchase task, to state how much they were willing to pay to anticipate product delivery, which was free after 21 days. Two brands offering high or low levels of informational reinforcement of three product categories were used. Results indicated that brands associated with higher informational reinforcement showed higher temporal discounting rates, that is, participants would pay higher prices to anticipate their delivery. In another study, the investigation of search duration for three supermarket products in four stores revealed that search duration decreased with increases in brand informational level (Pohl & Oliveira-Castro, 2008), that is, the time taken to select products from the shelf was shorter when consumers purchased brands offering higher level of informational reinforcement. These results suggest that consumers show a higher rate of discounting (or more impulsivity) when purchasing more differentiated brands.

But do consumers also show a higher demand for more differentiated brands? An investigation of consumers purchasing across 15 supermarket products in two countries revealed that, for 12 products, increases in the level of informational reinforcement offered by brands increased significantly brand market share and revenue. For the other three products, however, informational reinforcement level associated with brands did not show statistically significant effects on brand market share, suggesting that they seem to behave as undifferentiated commodities (Oliveira-Castro, Foxall, James, et al., 2008). Overall, these results suggest that routine consumer choice does not necessarily differ qualitatively from addiction, for their differences seem to be quantitative, a matter of how much products are discounted and valued by consumers, as predicted by Foxall (2016).

The framework of delay discounting was also adopted to measure the monetary value of informational reinforcement obtained with the use of social media, another behavioral pattern that shares some features of addiction (cf. Robayo-Pinzon et al., 2023). In an experiment employing hypothetical scenarios, undergraduate students were asked to choose between a period of social media use or a monetary value, with manipulation of the duration of the period (5, 15, or 45 minutes) and the immediacy of the monetary reward (now or in 1 week) across conditions. Results showed that the relative informational reinforcement value of using social media increased when the duration of social media usage was larger and when the delivery of the monetary reinforcer was delayed.

The marketing firm

Robbins (1932) defined economics as the science of human behavior that studies the relationships between ends and scarce means that have alternative uses. In microeconomic relations, this behavior occurs between two agents, the producer, and the consumer, causing market relations. Thus, there is an offer for any demand that characterizes a market. The producing agents are called firms, the technical unit in which commodities are produced and delivered to consumers, extracting profit or bearing the loss (Henderson & Quandt, 1958). Brethower (2001) summarizes that producer organizations have two categories of value-adding outputs (the financial marketplace and the consumer service marketplace) and four specific categories of costly but necessary inputs (i.e., money, technology, materials, and labor). It is where the entrepreneur transforms inputs into outputs, trying to maximize profit or profit-constrained sales revenue (Foxall, 2021).

To achieve this output, marketing activities become central to the existence and permanence of firms in the market by focusing on pecuniary transactions (Foxall, 1984) or exchange relations of purchase and sale. These activities have been conceived as generating consequences for firms and consumers, making up a bilateral contingency (see Fig. 13.3). Research in this area has advanced empirically with Skinner's (1953) suggestions that economic studies could insert functional analyses of reinforcement contingencies. That is, consider the functional relationships between a class of operant responses in the economic environment and its consequences. According to Hyten (2009), behavior analysis should include an analysis of companies' business outcomes to make the investigation more applicable in the business realm. This is the path that investigations on this topic have followed.

Firm matching and maximization

At the individual level of analysis, investment choices in corporate stock funds using cash for monetary gains demonstrate that they are consistent with the matching law (Eq. 13.1), and the options are valued relatively, with the most chosen being those that offer the greatest magnitude of reinforcement (Hantula & Crowell, 2016). Research has progressed at the firm's analysis level using corporate financial and officially registered databases with inputs and outputs in companies' panel analysis. Porto and Foxall (2019), using the generalized matching law equation, demonstrate that every effort that characterizes a company's marketing response, measured through total marketing investments, encourages obtaining firms' utilitarian reinforcers, measured by monetary gains, such as profitable returns, market dominance by sales revenue, and market value on the stock exchange. These utilitarian financial reinforcements alter new marketing investment rates in an undermatching relationship. Thus dimensions of the marketing total marketing response class (frequency, magnitude, and immediacy) increase reinforcers, and these same reinforcer dimensions (frequencies, magnitude, and immediacy) also increase new rates of marketing investment (relative to other administrative activity investments) for several companies. Still, the latter influence is weaker than the former. It follows that marketing causes firms' utilitarian gains, which causes more reduced marketing activities. One implication is that the company needs to capitalize (or raise loans) to maintain or increase marketing rates for subsequent firms' utilitarian gains.

Results from Porto and Foxall (2020) complement previous findings, demonstrating that this total marketing response through marketing investments maximizes each firm's utilitarian gain depending on whether it was previously financially reinforced (vs. punished) and the macroeconomic context of growth (vs. recession) of the country. For gains in sales competitiveness, which are directly related to the macro behavior of consumer purchases, the context of economic growth and prior utilitarian reinforcement is critical to maximizing these gains from more marketing. As for the maximization of profitable returns and valuation of company shares in the capital market coming through marketing, the company also needs to have had a history of previous reinforcement, but in a recent context of recession (deprivation of commercial exchange). In this sense, doing more marketing outweighs the decrease in monetary earnings that the economic crisis would cause the company.

Going further, Porto and Foxall (2022) investigated the role of macroeconomic environments in the firm's contingency relationships in obtaining utilitarian financial reinforcers. Companies' sales competitiveness gains are maximized on a world scale when more marketing investments are allocated in conditions of economic growth. On the other hand, profitable returns and firms' value are maximized by the firm's total marketing response when there is an improvement in the income equality of a country's population. In this case, the increase in equality increases the marketing effort's efficiency, as it is easier to leverage sales to a population that previously did not have access (or sufficient income). Simultaneously, this improvement in distribution provokes a generalized sensation of optimism for the economic agents, and the company's prominence in the consumer market due to the increase in marketing makes investors look more closely and value the highlighted company's shares more.

Bilateral contingency and stimulus control in the marketplace

Much of what has been studied with consumers in the marketplace using the framework of the theory of the marketing firm is stimulus control effects, in which an antecedent marketing signaling operation controlled by a company's managers generates consumer responses and consequences back to the company (Vella & Foxall, 2011). Sigurdsson, Engilbertsson, and Foxall (2010) demonstrated that a point-of-purchase display is not enough to increase retail sales when the product offers utilitarian reinforcement as a lower-priced competing product. Ferreira and Oliveira-Castro (2011) show that the high quality of background music of a mall increases cash flow and decreases conversion rates. Porto and Walter (2022) conducted longitudinal research at a retailer. They demonstrated the immediate and short-term effects of the behavioral dimensions of promotions (presence, duration, simultaneity, and removal) on sales performance metrics (revenue, number of transactions, and average billing size). The results showed that nonmonetary and monetary promotions generate immediate and short-term positive effects on revenue and the number of transactions with a positive balance after their ending. Nevertheless, the monetary promotion harmed the average billing size after the promotional period.

In a study with hotel services, Porto (2016) showed that the seasonality of the greatest purchasing intensity exerts a more positive influence on revenues than the seasonality of demand characterized by heterogeneous reinforcements and that the effects of price discounts on sophisticated services produce higher revenues for firms during the low season, while those related to basic services produce greater revenue during the high season. On the other hand, Sigurdsson, Foxall, and Saevarsson (2010) demonstrated the existence of lower relative sales for the price reduction condition, suggesting that all the marketing mix factors, besides price, should be examined. In addition, Larsen et al. (2020) revealed more transaction costs for consumers' quick shopping trips than regular shopping trips, demonstrating friction between retail and consumer transaction costs.

Analyzing stimulus control in an online environment, Sigurdsson et al. (2020) investigated consumer-firm bilateral contingencies through consumer responses (engagements) in social media and the firm's social media strategy from a managerial perspective. They evidenced marketing research, segmentation, and targeted marketing activities carried out by managers. In an e-commerce study, Alemu et al. (2020) demonstrated the existence of interdependent managerial and consumer behavioral relationships, indicating the presence of bilateral contingencies and that cost-intensive activities are likely to be internalized within marketing firms. Fagerstrøm et al. (2020) studied the marketer and customer's co-creation process. Based on bilateral contingencies, utilitarian and informational reinforcing consequences from the marketer have a stronger impact on customers' co-creation behavior than informational reinforcing consequences from other customers. They suggested that the co-creation process increases the business companies' research and intelligence, strengthening their competitiveness.

Conclusion

This chapter has attempted to show how consumer behavior analysis might provide a conceptual and empirical basis for operant behavioral economics. It has, for reasons of space, limited its account to several of the main strands of the investigations to which the consumer behavior analysis framework has led, necessarily omitting some dimensions of the research and therefore mention of some of those who have contributed to the development of this interdisciplinary approach to economic psychology and behavioral economics. We believe, however, that the basis has been laid for an approach to the behavior analysis of economic choice, especially in the context of marketing (viewed as a fundamental human endeavor rather than as a corporate discipline), which has the potential to impact the social and behavioral sciences by highlighting a fruitful research program that is not only based on behavioral psychology and behavioral economics but also capable of unifying them.

References

Acuff, S. F., MacKillop, J., & Murphy, J. G. (2023). A contextualized reinforcer pathology approach to addiction. *Nature Reviews Psychology, 2*, 309−323. https://doi.org/10.1038/s44159-023-00167-y

Alemu, M. H., Sigurdsson, V., Fagerstrøm, A., & Foxall, G. R. (2020). Developing the e-commerce sector for the fishery industry: What business are we really in? *Managerial and Decision Economics, 41*(2), 274−290. https://doi.org/10.1002/mde.3089

Alferink, L. A., Critchfield, T. S., Hitt, J. L., & Higgins, W. J. (2009). Generality of the matching law as a descriptor of shot selection in basketball. *Journal of Applied Behavior Analysis, 42*(3), 595−608. https://doi.org/10.1901/jaba.2009.42-595

Baum, W. M. (1974). On two types of deviation from the matching law: Bias and undermatching. *Journal of the Experimental Analysis of Behavior, 22*(1), 231–242. https://doi.org/10.1901/jeab.1974.22-231

Baum, W. M. (1979). Matching, undermatching, and overmatching in studies of choice. *Journal of the Experimental Analysis of Behavior, 32*(2), 269–281. https://doi.org/10.1901/jeab.1979.32-269

Baum, W. M. (2006). *Understanding behaviorism: Behavior, culture, and evolution* (2nd ed.). Blackwell Publishing.

Bell, D. R., Chiang, J., & Padmanabhan, V. (1999). The decomposition of promotional response: An empirical generalization. *Marketing Science, 18*(4), 504–526. https://doi.org/10.1287/mksc.18.4.504

Bickel, W. K., & Athamneh, L. N. (2020). A reinforcer pathology perspective on relapse. *Journal of the Experimental Analysis of Behavior, 113*(1), 48–56. https://doi.org/10.1002/jeab.564

Bickel, W. K., & Marsch, L. A. (2001). Toward a behavioral economic understanding of drug dependence: Delay discounting processes. *Addiction, 96*(1), 73–86. https://doi.org/10.1046/j.1360-0443.2001.961736.x

Billington, E. J., & DiTommaso, N. M. (2003). Demonstrations and applications of the matching law in education. *Journal of Behavioral Education, 12*, 91–104. https://doi.org/10.1023/A:1023881502494

Borrero, J. C., Crisolo, S., Tu, Q., Rileand, W. A., Ross, N. A., Francisco, M. T., & Yamamoto, K. Y. (2007). An application of the matching law to social dynamics. *Journal of Applied Behavior Analysis, 40*(4), 589–601. https://doi.org/10.1901/jaba.2007.589-601

Brethower, D. M. (2001). A systemic view of enterprise: Adding value to performance. *Journal of Organizational Behavior Management, 20*(3–4), 165–190. https://doi.org/10.1300/J075v20n03_06

Conger, R., & Killeen, P. (1974). Use of concurrent operants in small group research-demonstration. *Pacific Sociological Review, 17*(4), 399–416. https://doi.org/10.2307/1388

Curry, B., Foxall, G. R., & Sigurdsson, V. (2010). On the tautology of the matching law in consumer behavior analysis. *Behavioural Processes, 84*(1), 390–399. https://doi.org/10.1016/j.beproc.2010.02.009

Davison, M., & McCarthy, D. (1988). *The matching law: A research review.* Erlbaum.

de Villiers, P. (1977). Choice in concurrent schedules and a quantitative formulation of the law of effect. In W. K. Honig, & J. E. R. Staddon (Eds.), *Handbook of operant behavior.* Englewood Cliffs, N. J.: Prentice-Hall.

Driesener, C., & Rungie, C. (2022). The Dirichlet model in marketing. *Journal of Consumer Behaviour, 21*(1), 7–18. https://doi.org/10.1002/cb.1975

Ehrenberg, A. S. C. (1988). *Repeat buying: Facts, theory and applications.* Charles Griffin & Company.

Fagerstrøm, A., Arntzen, E., & Foxall, G. R. (2011). A study of preferences in a simulated online shopping experiment. *Service Industries Journal, 31*(15), 2603–2615. https://doi.org/10.1080/02642069.2011.531121

Fagerstrøm, A., Bencheim, L. M., Sigurdsson, V., Pawar, S., & Foxall, G. R. (2020). The marketing firm and co-creation: An empirical study of marketer and customer's co-creation process. *Managerial and Decision Economics, 41*(2), 216–225. https://doi.org/10.1002/mde.3076

Fagerstrøm, A., Foxall, G. R., & Arntzen, E. (2010). Implications of motivating operations for the functional analysis of consumer choice. *Journal of Organizational Behavior Management, 30*, 110–126.

Ferreira, D. C. S., & Oliveira-Castro, J. M. (2011). Effects of background music on consumer behaviour: Behavioural account of the consumer setting. *Service Industries Journal, 31*(15), 2571−2585. https://doi.org/10.1080/02642069.2011.531125

Foxall, G. (1984). Marketing's domain. *European Journal of Marketing, 18*(1), 25−40. https://doi.org/10.1108/EUM0000000000581

Foxall, G. R. (1999). The marketing firm. *Journal of Economic Psychology, 20*, 207−234.

Foxall, G. R. (2016a). Operant behavioral economics. *Managerial and Decision Economics, 37*, 215−223.

Foxall, G. R. (Ed.). (2016b). *The routledge companion to consumer behavior analysis*. London and New York: Routledge.

Foxall, G. R. (2017). Behavioral economics in consumer behavior analysis. *The Behavior Analyst, 40*, 309−313. https://doi.org/10.1007/s40614-017-0127-4

Foxall, G. R. (2021). *The theory of the marketing firm*. Springer Nature International Publishing. https://doi.org/10.1007/978-3-030-86106-3_11

Foxall, G. R. (2023). *The continuum of consumer choice: A neurophysiological perspective*. London and New York: Routledge.

Foxall, G. R., & James, V. K. (2001). The behavioral basis of consumer choice: A preliminary analysis. *European Journal of Behavior Analysis, 2*(2), 209−220. https://doi.org/10.1080/15021149.2001.11434195

Foxall, G. R., & James, V. K. (2003). The behavioral ecology of brand choice: How and what do consumers maximize? *Psychology & Marketing, 20*(9), 811−836. https://doi.org/10.1002/mar.10098

Foxall, G. R., James, V. K., Oliveira-Castro, J. M., & Ribier, S. (2010). Product substitutability and the matching law. *Psychological Record, 60*, 185−216. https://doi.org/10.1007/BF03395703

Foxall, G. R., Oliveira-Castro, J. M., & Schrezenmaier, T. C. (2004). The behavioral economics of consumer brand choice: Patterns of reinforcement and utility maximization. *Behavioural Processes, 66*(3), 235−260. https://doi.org/10.1016/j.beproc.2004.03.007

Foxall, G. R., & Schrezenmaier, T. C. (2003). The behavioural economics of consumer brand choice: establishing a methodology. *Journal of Economic Psychology, 24*(5), 675−695. https://doi.org/10.1016/S0167-4870(03)00008-4

Foxall, G. R., Wells, V. K., Chang, J., & Oliveira-Castro, J. M. (2010). Substitutability and independence: Matching analyses of brands and products. *Journal of Organizational Behavior Management, 30*(2), 145−160. https://doi.org/10.1080/01608061003756414

Foxall, G. R., Yan, J., Oliveira-Castro, J. M., & Wells, V. K. (2013). Brand-related and situational influences on demand elasticity. *Journal of Business Research, 66*(1), 73−81. https://doi.org/10.1016/j.jbusres.2011.07.025

Gilroy, S. P., & Feck, C. C. (2022). Applications of operant demand to treatment selection II: Covariance of evidence strength and treatment consumption. *Journal of the Experimental Analysis of Behavior, 117*(2), 167−179. https://doi.org/10.1002/jeab.735

Gilroy, S. P., & Picardo, R. (2022). Applications of operant demand to treatment selection III: Consumer behavior analysis of treatment choice. *Journal of the Experimental Analysis of Behavior, 118*(1), 46−58. https://doi.org/10.1002/jeab.758

Gilroy, S. P., Waits, J. A., & Kaplan, B. A. (2022). Applications of operant demand to treatment selection I: Characterizing demand for evidence-based practices. *Journal of the Experimental Analysis of Behavior, 117*(1), 20−35. https://doi.org/10.1002/jeab.731

Green, L., & Myerson, J. (2004). A discounting framework for choice with delayed and probabilistic rewards. *Psychological Bulletin, 130*(5), 769−792. https://doi.org/10.1037/0033-2909.130.5.769

Gupta, S. (1988). The impact of sales promotions on when, what, and how much to buy. *Journal of Marketing Research, 25*(4), 342−355. https://doi.org/10.2307/3172945

Hantula, D. A., & Crowell, C. R. (2016). Matching and behavioral contrast in a two-option repeated investment simulation. *Managerial and Decision Economics, 37*(4−5), 294−305. https://doi.org/10.1002/mde.2717

Henderson, J. M., & Quandt, R. E. (1958). *Microeconomic theory: Investment theory of the firm*. McGraw Hill.

Herrnstein, R. J. (1961). Relative and absolute strength of response as a function of frequency of reinforcement. *Journal of the Experimental Analysis of Behavior, 4*(3), 267−272. https://doi.org/10.1901/jeab.1961.4-267

Herrnstein, R. J. (1970). On the law of effect. *Journal of the Experimental Analysis of Behavior, 13*(2), 243−266. https://doi.org/10.1901/jeab.1970.13-243

Hursh, S. R. (1980). Economic concepts for the analysis of behavior. *Journal of the Experimental Analysis of Behavior, 34*(2), 219−238. https://doi.org/10.1901/jeab.1980.34-219

Hursh, S. R. (1984). Behavioral economics. *Journal of the Experimental Analysis of Behavior, 42*(3), 435−452. https://doi.org/10.1901/jeab.1984.42-435

Hursh, S. R., Raslear, T. G., Shurtleff, D., Bauman, R., & Simmons, L. (1988). A cost-benefit analysis of demand for food. *Journal of the Experimental Analysis of Behavior, 50*(3), 419−440. https://doi.org/10.1901/jeab.1988.50-419

Hursh, S. R., & Silberberg, A. (2008). Economic demand and essential value. *Psychological Review, 115*(1), 186−198. https://doi.org/10.1037/0033-295X.115.1.186

Hursh, S. R., & Winger, G. (1995). Normalized demand for drugs and other reinforcers. *Journal of the Experimental Analysis of Behavior, 64*(3), 373−384. https://doi.org/10.1901/jeab.1995.64-373

Huynh, N. B., & Foxall, G. R. (2016). Consumer store choice: A matching analysis. In G. R. Foxall (Ed.), *The routledge companion to consumer behavior analysis* (pp. 96−120). Routledge.

Hyten, C. (2009). Strengthening the focus on business results: The need for systems approaches in organizational behavior management. *Journal of Organizational Behavior Management, 29*(2), 87−107. https://doi.org/10.1080/01608060902874526

Kagel, J. H., Battalio, R. C., & Green, L. (1995). *Economic choice theory: An experimental analysis of animal behavior*. Cambridge: Cambridge University Press.

Larsen, N. M., Sigurdsson, V., Breivik, J., Fagerstrøm, A., & Foxall, G. R. (2020). The marketing firm: Retailer and consumer contingencies. *Managerial and Decision Economics, 41*(2), 203−215. https://doi.org/10.1002/mde.3053

Lea, S. E. G. (1978). The psychology and economics of demand. *Psychological Bulletin, 85*(3), 441−466. https://doi.org/10.1037/0033-2909.85.3.441

Martens, B. K., Halperin, S., Rummel, J., & Kilpatrick, D. (1990). Matching theory applied to contingent teacher attention. *Behavioral Assessment, 12*(2), 139−155.

Michael, J. (1993). Establishing operations. *The Behavior Analyst, 16*, 191−206.

Moore, J. (2008). *Conceptual foundations of radical behaviorism*. Sloan.

Oliveira-Castro, J. M., Cavalcanti, P., & Foxall, G. R. (2015). What consumers maximize: Brand choice as a function of utilitarian and informational reinforcement. *Managerial and Decision Economics, 37*(4−5), 360−371. https://doi.org/10.1002/mde.2722

Oliveira-Castro, J. M., Cavalcanti, P., & Foxall, G. R. (2016). What consumers maximize? The analysis of utility functions in light of the behavioral perspective model. In G. R. Foxall (Ed.), *The routledge companion to consumer behavior analysis* (pp. 202−212). Routledge.

Oliveira-Castro, J. M., & Foxall, G. R. (2017). Consumer maximization of utilitarian and informational reinforcement: Comparing two utility measures with reference to social class. *The Behavior Analyst, 42*(2), 457−476. https://doi.org/10.1007/s40614-017-0122-9

Oliveira-Castro, J. M., Foxall, G. R., & James, V. K. (2008). Individual differences in price responsiveness within and across food brands. *Service Industries Journal, 28*(6), 733−753. https://doi.org/10.1080/02642060801988605

Oliveira-Castro, J. M., Foxall, G. R., & James, V. K. (2010). Consumer brand choice: Money allocation as a function of brand reinforcing attributes. *Journal of Organizational Behavior Management, 30*(2), 161−175. https://doi.org/10.1080/01608061003756455

Oliveira-Castro, J. M., Foxall, G. R., James, V. K., Pohl, R. H. B. F., Dias, M. B., & Chang, S. W. (2008). Consumer-based brand equity and brand performance. *Service Industries Journal, 28*(4), 445−461. https://doi.org/10.1080/02642060801917554

Oliveira-Castro, J. M., Foxall, G. R., & Schrezenmaier, T. C. (2005). Patterns of consumer response to retail price differentials. *Service Industries Journal, 25*(3), 309−327. https://doi.org/10.1080/02642060500050392

Oliveira-Castro, J. M., Foxall, G. R., & Schrezenmaier, T. C. (2006). Consumer brand choice: Individual and group analyses of demand elasticity. *Journal of the Experimental Analysis of Behavior, 85*(2), 147−166. https://doi.org/10.1901/jeab.2006.51-04

Oliveira-Castro, J. M., Foxall, G. R., Yan, J., & Wells, V. K. (2011). A behavioural-economic analysis of the essential value of brands. *Behavioural Processes, 87*(1), 106−114. https://doi.org/10.1016/j.beproc.2011.01.007

Oliveira-Castro, J. M., & Marques, R. S. (2017). Temporal discounting and marketing variables: Effects of product prices and brand informational reinforcement. *The Behavior Analyst, 40*(2), 475−492. https://doi.org/10.1007/s40614-017-0109-6

Pohl, R., & Oliveira-Castro, J. (2008). Efeitos do nível de benefício informativo das marcas sobre a duração do comportamento de procura. *Revista da Administração Contemporânea Eletrônica, 2*(3), 449−469.

Porto, R. B. (2016). The commercial cycle from the viewpoint of operant behavioral economics: Effects of price discounts on revenues received from services. *RAUSP Management Journal, 51*(3), 310−322. https://doi.org/10.1016/j.rausp.2016.06.005

Porto, R. B., & Foxall, G. R. (2019). The marketing firm as a metacontingency: Revealing the mutual relationships between marketing and finance. *Journal of Organizational Behavior Management, 39*(3−4), 115−144. https://doi.org/10.1080/01608061.2019.1666774

Porto, R. B., & Foxall, G. R. (2020). Marketing firm performance: When does marketing lead to financial gains? *Managerial and Decision Economics, 41*(2), 191−202. https://doi.org/10.1002/mde.3046

Porto, R. B., & Foxall, G. R. (2022). The marketing-finance interface and national well-being: An operant behavioral economics analysis. *Managerial and Decision Economics, 43*(7), 2941−2954. https://doi.org/10.1002/mde.3574

Porto, R. B., & Walter, M. C. (2022). Unpacking the behavioral dimensions of promotions and sales performance: Do real-life promotions drive more sales? In J. D. Santos (Ed.), *Sales management for improved organizational competitiveness and performance* (pp. 135−159). IGI Global. https://doi.org/10.4018/978-1-6684-3430-7.ch008

Rachlin, H. (2014). *The escape of the mind.* Oxford University Press.

Rachlin, H., Green, L., Kagel, J. H., & Battalio, R. C. (1980). Substitutability in time allocation. *Psychological Review, 87*(4), 355−374. https://doi.org/10.1037/0033-295X.87.4.355

Reed, D. D., Critchfield, T. S., & Martens, B. K. (2006). The generalized matching law in elite sport competition: Football play calling as operant choice. *Journal of Applied Behavior Analysis, 39*(3), 281−297. https://doi.org/10.1901/jaba.2006.146-05

Robayo-Pinzon, O., Rojas-Berrío, S., Paredes, M. R., & Foxall, G. R. (2023). Social media sites users' choice between utilitarian and informational reinforcers assessed using temporal discounting. *Frontiers in Public Health, 11*, 1−9. https://doi.org/10.3389/fpubh.2023.960321. Article 960321.

Robbins, L. (1932). The nature and significance of economic science. In D. M. Hausman (Ed.), *The philosophy of economics: An anthology* (pp. 73−99). Cambridge University Press.

Rolls, E. T. (2018). *The brain, emotion, and depression*. Oxford University Press.

Romero, S., Foxall, G. R., Schrezenmaier, T., Oliveira-Castro, J. M., & James, V. (2006). Deviations from matching in consumer choice. *European Journal of Behavior Analysis, 7*(1), 15−39. https://doi.org/10.1080/15021149.2006.11434261

Rung, J. M., & Madden, G. J. (2018). Experimental reductions of delay discounting and impulsive choice: A systematic review and meta-analysis. *Journal of Experimental Psychology: General, 147*(9), 1349−1381. https://doi.org/10.1037/xge0000462

Sigurdsson, V., Engilbertsson, H., & Foxall, G. (2010). The effects of a point-of-purchase display on relative sales: An in-store experimental evaluation. *Journal of Organizational Behavior Management, 30*(3), 222−233.

Sigurdsson, V., & Foxall, G. R. (2016). Experimental analyses of choice and matching: From the animal laboratory to the marketplace. In G. Foxall, R. (Ed.), *The routledge companion to consumer behavior analysis* (pp. 78−95). Routledge.

Sigurdsson, V., Foxall, G., & Saevarsson, H. (2010b). In-store experimental approach to pricing and consumer behavior. *Journal of Organizational Behavior Management, 30*(3), 234−246. https://doi.org/10.1080/01608061.2010.499029

Sigurdsson, V., Kahamseh, S., Gunnarsson, D., Larsen, N. M., & Foxall, G. R. (2013). An econometric examination of the Behavioral Perspective Model in the context of Norwegian retailing. *Psychological Record, 63*, 277−294. https://doi.org/10.11133/j.tpr.2013.63.2.004

Sigurdsson, V., Larsen, N. M., Sigfusdottir, A. D., Fagerstrøm, A., Alemu, M. H., Folwarczny, M., & Foxall, G. (2020). The relationship between the firm's social media strategy and the consumers' engagement behavior in aviation. *Managerial and Decision Economics, 41*(2), 234−249. https://doi.org/10.1002/mde.3052

Skinner, B. F. (1953). *Science and human behavior*. New York: Macmillan.

Staddon, J. E. R. (1980). *Limits to action: The allocation of individual behavior*. New York.

Vella, K. J., & Foxall, G. R. (2011). In *The marketing firm: Economic psychology of corporate behaviour*. Edward Elgar Publishing.

Vollmer, T. R., & Bourret, J. (2000). An application of the matching law to evaluate the allocation of two and three-point shots by college basketball players. *Journal of Applied Behavior Analysis, 33*(2), 137−150. https://doi.org/10.1901/jaba.2000.33-137

Wearden, J. H. (1988). Some neglected problems in the analysis of human operant behavior. In G. Davey, & C. Cullen (Eds.), *Human operant conditioning and behavior modification* (pp. 197−224). Chichester: John Wiley.

Wells, V. K., Chang, S. W., Oliveira-Castro, J. M., & Pallister, J. (2010). Market segmentation from a behavioral perspective. *Journal of Organizational Behavior Management, 30*(2), 176−198. https://doi.org/10.1080/01608061003756505

Wells, V. K., & Foxall, G. R. (2013). Matching, demand, maximization, and consumer choice. *The Psychological Record, 63*, 239−258. https://doi.org/10.11133/j.tpr.2013.63.2.002

Winger, G., Hursh, S. R., Casey, K. L., & Woods, J. H. (2002). Relative reinforcing strength of three N-methyl-d-aspartate antagonists with different onsets of action. *Journal of Pharmacology and Experimental Therapeutics*, 690−697. https://doi.org/10.1124/jpet.301.2.690

Yan, J., Foxall, G. R., & Doyle, J. R. (2012a). Patterns of reinforcement and the essential value of brands: II. Evaluation of a model of consumer choice. *Psychological Record, 62*(3), 377–394. https://doi.org/10.1007/BF03395809

Yan, J., Foxall, G. R., & Doyle, J. R. (2012b). Patterns of reinforcement and the essential values of brands: I. Incorporation of utilitarian and informational reinforcement into the estimation of demand. *Psychological Record, 62*(3), 361–376. https://doi.org/10.1007/BF03395808

Index

'*Note:* Page numbers followed by "f" indicate figures, "t" indicate tables and "b" indicate boxes.'

A
Abuse liability assessment, 15—16
Across-species research, 185—187
Adjusting-amount discounting procedure, 183—187
Adjusting-delay discounting procedure, 151—153, 182—183
Age box plots, 251
Akaike Information Criterion (AIC), 157
Applied behavior analysis, 132—133
Area under the discounting curve (AUC), 157—158, 241—243

B
Bayesian Information Criterion (BIC), 157
Bayesian methods, 239
Behavioral economics, 53, 93t
  applied behavior analysis, 132—133
  experimental microeconomics, 132
  macroeconomic methods and practices, 131
Behavior analysis, 262—263
Behavior analysts, 72
Bilateral contingency, 329—330, 329f, 338—339

C
Classical hypothesis test, 263
Closed economy, 4
Cognitive-behavioral economics, 23—24
Cognitive biases, 21
Cognitive interviewing, 83—84
Comprehensive R Archive Network (CRAN), 241—242
Concurrent chain procedure, 74, 190—191
Confidence intervals, 256
Consumer behavior analysis
  empirical evidence
    consumers' utility functions, 334—335
    delay discounting, 335—336
  matching and maximization, 330—331
  price elasticity of demand, 332—334
  generic behavioral perspective model, 325—327
  marketing firm, 336—339
  market value, 328—330
Consumer demand, 36
Contingency management approaches, 315
Continuous reinforcement (CR), 51—52
Convenience samples, 256
Correlation coefficient, 250—251
Corticotropin-releasing factor (CRF), 62—63
Cost-benefit ratio, 37—38
Cross-commodity demand curves, 42, 43f

D
Delay discounting, 2, 151
  behavioral pharmacological studies
    dopamine agonists, 193—194
    dopamine antagonists, 194
  diverse applications, 279—280
  human participants, 154—155
  human research methods, 205—206
  interventions, 167
  magnitude effect, 159—160
  neural substrates, 191—196
  nonhuman animals, 151—153
  nonhuman research
    across-species research, 185—187
    adjusting-amount discounting procedure, 183—187
    adjusting-delay discounting procedure, 182—183
    concurrent chains discounting, 190—191
    within-session adjusting-delay discounting, 188—189
  outcome effect, 161
  vs. probability discounting, 162—165

Delay discounting (*Continued*)
  state changes, 159
  strong test-retest reliability, 158
  transdiagnostic tool, 280–281
Delay-probability discounting (DPD) procedure, 163
Demand analysis
  data preparation and initial examination, 99–101
  metrics, 118–121
  model comparison and refinement, 118
  model fitting, 103–116
    fit-to-group approaches, 106–110
    k values handling, 103–105
    mixed-effects modeling, 115–116
    parameter estimation, 105
    two-stage approach, 111–114
  steps for, 98–99
  systematicity examination criteria, 101–103
  visual analysis and interpretation, 117–118
Demand approach
  and output curves, 38–41
  reinforcement constraints, 33
  unit price, 37–38
  validity, 41–44
Demand curves, 55, 55t, 121–123
Demand metrics, 308
Derived metrics, 119–121, 120t
Descriptive statistics, 254–257
Discounting
  delay discounting, 151
  effort discounting, 154
  human discounting, 150, 154–155
  indifference point, 155–157
  interventions, 167–168
  magnitude effect, 159–160
  nonhuman animal research, 149–153
  outcome effect, 161–162
  past discounting, 164–165
  practical applications
    delay discounting, 279–280
    environmentally relevant discounting, 286–291
    sexual discounting and implications, 281–284
  probability discounting, 151
  and public health, 166
  risky conditions, 165
  sign effect, 161
  social discounting, 163–164
  state variables, 158
  steep *vs.* shallow discounting, 157–158
  sustainability/environmental awareness, 165
  trait variables, 158
  treatment adherence, 166
Dopamine, delay discounting
  agonists, 193–194
  antagonists, 194
  obesity, 195–196

E

Economics and behavior analysis. *See also* Operant behavioral economics
  closed economy, 4
  concurrent variable-interval (VI) schedules, 3–4
  demand curve, 4–5
  experimental demand curves, 6–7
  fixed-ratio (FR) schedules, 2–3, 5–6
  linear elasticity model of demand, 9–10
  open and closed economies, 8–9
  price, 6
  two-commodity studies and reinforcer interactions, 7–8
  Walter Reed Army Institute of Research (WRAIR), 2–3
Effective delay 50 (ED50), 238
Effort-discounting tasks, 164, 206
Empirical public policy, 19–20
Environmentally relevant discounting applications
  environmental events, 288
  environmental research, 290
  individual behavior, 290–291
  monetary rewards, 287
  social discounting tasks, 287–288
  spatial discounting tasks, 287–288
  temporal and spatial discounting, 287–288
  zero discounting, 287
Episodic future thinking, 315
Essential value (EV), 12–17
Excessive delay discounting rates, 281
Expanded behavioral perspective model, 328–329, 328f
Experiential discounting task, 218

Index

Experimental analysis of behavior (EAB), 35
Experimental demand curves, 6—7
Exponential demand, 12—17
Exponential model of demand, 96
Exponentiated model of demand, 96

F

Fit-to-group approach, 94, 106—110
Fixed ascending/descending procedure, 210—212
Food Choice Questionnaire (FCQ), 284
Food discounting approach
    adjusting amount procedure for food (AA-F), 284
    decision-making tools, 286, 292
    healthy and clinical populations, 285
    intervention studies, 285—286

G

Generalized linear models, 92
Generalized reinforcers, 52—53
Generic Behavioral Perspective Model
    consumer behavior setting, 326
    consumer situation, 325
    informational reinforcement, 326
    reinforcement and reward, 327
    utilitarian reinforcement, 326
GraphPad Prism, 97—98

H

Haloperidol, delay discounting, 195—196
Histograms, 247
Human behavior, 71
Human demand studies, 18—19
Human research methods
    adjusting amount, 212—213
    adjusting delay, 214—215
    delay discounting, 205—206
    effort-discounting, 206
    experiential discounting, 218
    fixed ascending/descending procedure, 210—212
    indifference points, 210
    Kirby Monetary Choice Questionnaire, 215—216
    monetary versus nonmonetary commodities, 208
    multiple dimensions, 217—218
    multiple discounting process, 207
    neuroscience research, 219
    nonsystematic responding, 221
    probability discounting, 206
    real and hypothetical outcomes, 209—210
    single-question discount rates procedures, 216
    single-question indifference procedures, 215
    social discounting, 207
    task parameters and reward, 220—221
    three-choice discount rate, 216—217
Hursh and Silberberg equation, 55—56
Hyperbolic discounting function, 237
Hypothetical purchase tasks, 18—19, 75, 83—84, 84f, 209—210

I

Incentivized and simulated studies, 314
Increasing-delay procedure, 151—153
Indifference point, 156—157
Inelastic demand, 40
Inferential statistics, 254—257
Informational reinforcement, 326
Intermittent reinforcement (IR), 51—52
Interval reinforcement schedules, 52

J

Johnson & Bickel criteria, 236

K

Kirby Monetary Choice Questionnaire, 215—216

L

Law of Demand, 34, 71
Linear elasticity model of demand, 9—10, 96
Linear regression, 92
Logarithmic function, 235—236

M

Macroeconomic methods and practices, 131
Magnitude effect, discounting, 159—160
Marketing firm
    bilateral contingency and stimulus control, 338—339
    marketing activities, 337
    matching and maximization, 337—338
    value-adding outputs, 336—337

Market value
　expanded behavioral perspective model, 328–329
　superpersonal level, 329–330
Maximum likelihood estimation, 239
Mazur model, 236–237, 270
Microeconomics, 132, 323–324
Mindfulness, 167–168
Mixed-effects model approach, 115–116, 127f
Monetary Choice Questionnaire (MCQ), 154, 284
Mosaic plots, 251–252
Multiple discounting process, 207

N
Neurobiological mechanisms, 61–63
Neuroscience research, 219
nlmrt and nlme packages, 97–98
Nonhuman research methods/procedures
　delay discounting procedure
　　across-species research, 185–187
　　adjusting-amount discounting procedure, 183–187
　　adjusting-delay discounting procedure, 182–183
　　concurrent chains discounting, 190–191
　　within-session adjusting-delay discounting, 188–189
　preclinical reinforcement models. *See* Preclinical reinforcement models
　reinforcement schedules, 51–53
Nonlinear mixed effect modeling (NLME), 58–59
Nonlinear regression, 92
Normalized demand, 10–12
Normalized indifference points, 156–157

O
Observed metrics, 118–119, 119t
Open/closed economy, 44, 134
Operant behavioral economics. *See also* Economics and behavior analysis
　delay discounting, 2
　and empirical public policy, 19–20
　exponential demand and essential value, 12–17
　human demand studies, 18–19
　hypothetical purchase tasks, 18–19
　"laws" of behavior, 2
　microeconomics, 2
　normalized demand, 10–12
　retrospective and prospective views, 20–24
Operant Demand Framework, 34–36, 308
　neurobiological mechanisms, 61–63
　preference assessment
　　individual preference, 138
　　reinforcer preferences and schedule arrangements, 138–139
　　stimulus preference, 139
　quantitative models, 91–92
　reinforcement
　　elasticity of demand, 134–136
　　open or closed economy, 134
　　reinforcer complement/substitutes, 136–138
　reinforcer evaluations
　　demand elasticity and reinforcer durability, 142
　　demand intensity, 141
　　formal evaluations, 139–140
　　reinforcer magnitude, 141
　　token economies, 142–143
Operant psychology, 33
Ordinary regression problems model, 249

P
Pairs plot, 253–254
Past discounting, 164–165
Point estimation, 255–256
Policy implications
　behavioral economic compatibility, 305–307
　choice procedures, 307–309
　conceptual approaches, 315
　discounting, 307–308
　incentivized and simulated studies, 314
　intervention effects, 311–312
　intervention frameworks, 315
　methodological consistency, 316
　molar patterns of behavior, 310–311
　nonhuman and human laboratory studies, 313–314
　operant demand, 308
　public policy, 304–305
　reinforcer valuation, 311
　"SAFER" initiative, 303
　simulated and incentivized tasks, 309

Index 351

targets, applied behavioral economists, 309–310
timing, 305
Preclinical reinforcement models, 51
  drugs of dependence
    addiction-related behavior, 56–57
    environmental enrichment, 59
    intravenous nicotine threshold procedure, 57, 58f
    nicotine demand, 59–60
    nonlinear mixed effect modeling (NLME), 58–59
    synthetic contraceptive hormone treatments, 60
    timeout from avoidance (TOA), 59
    unit price, drug dose, 57, 58t
  natural reinforcers, 53–56
Price sequence methodology, 78
Probability-based purchase tasks, 121–122
Probability–delay discounting procedure (PDD), 163
Probability discounting, 151, 158–159, 245–246
  vs. delay discounting, 162–165
  human participants, 154–155
  human research, 206
  magnitude effect, 160
  nonhuman animals, 151–153
  outcome effect, 161–162
  outcomes, 157–158
  trait variables, 158–159
Probability discounting questionnaire (PDQ), 154
Progressive ratio (PR), 72–73
Purchase task methodology
  advantage, 75–76
  costs, 75
  hypothetical nature, 75
  progression, 76–79
  qualitative methods, 81–85
  sample vignette, 77b
  toolkit, 79–80, 79f, 80t
  verification and applications, 76–79

Q
Quantitative demand models, 95t
  contemporary statistical practice, 262–264
  data import
    comments, 232

  data frames, 233
  data location, 232
  data set, 232–233
  wide *versus* tall data format, 233
  descriptive statistics, 254–257
  estimated discounting rates, 246
  exploratory data analysis, 246
  exponential model, 96
  exponentiated model, 96
  function of age, 260–262
  inferential statistics, 254–257
  linear elasticity model, 96
  males and females, 257–259
  multivariate analyses, 249–252
  probabilities, 121–122
  quantitative, 95t
  R and RStudio, 230–232
  scientific investigation, 265–274
  simplified exponential with normalized decay, 96–97
  single participant's indifference point data
    area under the discounting curve (AUC), 241–243
    effective delay 50 (ED50), 238
    log-delay scale, 233
    for loop, 244–246
  smokers and nonsmokers, 259–264
  statistical training, 265–266
  tools and software, 97–98
  univariate analyses, 246–249

R
Randomization, 257
Random sample, 256
R and RStudio, 230–232
Ratio reinforcement schedules, 52
Regression, 260–262
  fit-to-group approach, 94
  linear *vs.* nonlinear regression, 92
  mixed-effects modeling, 94–95
  two-stage approach, 94
Reinforcement, 324
  elasticity of demand, 134–136
  open or closed economy, 134
  reinforcer complement/substitutes, 136–138
  schedule research, 35
Reinforcer, 327
Relative reinforcing efficacy (RRE), 72

Residual sum-of-squares (RSS), 239−240
Rewards, 327

S
SAFER initiative, 303−304
Scatter plot, 250−251
Sexual delay discounting task (SDDT)
   condom availability, 282−283
   educational programs, 283−284
   likelihood of condom use, 282
   monetary discounting tasks, 283−284
   various populations, 282−283
Sexual discounting and implications
   clinically relevant application, 281−282
   sexual delay discounting task (SDDT), 282−283
shinybeez application, 97−98
Simple linear regression, 260−261
Simple random sample, 256
Simulated and incentivized tasks, 309
Single-question indifference procedures, 215
Social discounting, 163−164
Statistical inference, 255

T
Three-choice discount rate, 216−217
Three-term contingency, 324
Timeout from avoidance (TOA), 59
Token economy, 142−143
Transdisease process, 280−281, 291
Two-stage approach, 111−114

U
Unit price, 37−38, 38f
Univariate analyses, 246−249
Utilitarian reinforcement, 326

V
Visual Analog Scale (VAS), 154−155

W
Walter Reed Army Institute of Research (WRAIR), 2−3
Within-session adjusting-delay discounting, 188−189

Printed in the United States
by Baker & Taylor Publisher Services